PROCEEDINGS OF THE
EIGHTH ECUMENICAL METHODIST CONFERENCE

PROCEEDINGS OF THE
EIGHTH
ECUMENICAL METHODIST
CONFERENCE

OXFORD

28th August—7th September
1951

LONDON : THE EPWORTH PRESS

PUBLISHED BY
THE EPWORTH PRESS
(FRANK H. CUMBERS)
25–35 CITY ROAD, LONDON, E.C.1.

*

New York . Toronto
Melbourne . Cape Town

*

SET IN MONOTYPE TIMES ROMAN, AND PRINTED
IN GREAT BRITAIN BY THE CAMELOT PRESS LTD.,
LONDON AND SOUTHAMPTON

CONTENTS

CONTENTS

LIST OF DELEGATES ELECTED TO ATTEND
THE CONFERENCE

SECTION 1

Methodist Church of South Africa

Mr R. Cingo, B.A., LL.B., Kroonstad, O.F.S.
Mr M. H. Eddy, M.B.E., Johannesburg.
Mrs M. H. Eddy, Johannesburg.
Rev. E. W. Grant, Healdtown, C.P.
Mrs E. W. Grant, Healdtown, C.P.
Mr W. H. Haley, Durban.
Mrs W. H. Haley, Durban.
Rev. L. A. Hewson, M.A., Grahamstown, C.P.
Miss Susie Kachelhoffer, M.A., B.D., Johannesburg.
Rev. Price S. Mbete, B.A., Sterkspruit, C.P.
Rev. J. B. Webb, M.A., D.D., Johannesburg.
Rev. H. T. P. Young, Durban.

SECTION 2

West Africa

His Excellency the President of Liberia (W. V. S. Tubman) and Mrs Tubman, Monrovia, Liberia.
Rev. G. R. Acquaah, Lagos, Nigeria.
Rev. M. O. Dada, Accra, Gold Coast.
Rev. T. F. Fenton, Dabou, Ivory Coast.
Rev. W. T. Harris, Segbwema, Sierra Leone.
Bishop Willis J. King, Monrovia, Liberia.
Mrs Willis J. King, Monrovia, Liberia.
Rev. R. Kirkpatrick, Uzuakoli, S. Nigeria.
Dr O. K. Ogan, London.

SECTION 3

Central and East Africa

Rev. Harry Buckley, Salisbury, Southern Rhodesia.
Bishop Newell S. Booth, B.P., Belgian Congo.
Mrs Newell S. Booth, Belgian Congo.
Rev. E. G. Nightingale, B.D., Lusaka, Northern Rhodesia.
Mr Pierre Shaumba, Atetela Tribe, Central Congo.
Miss B. Jones, Meru, Kenya, British East Africa.

SECTION 4

South Asia

Mrs J. R. Chitambar.
Mrs M. A. Hakim, Delhi Gate, Agra.
Mr Ee Soon Howe, Singapore.
Dr J. K. Mathews, New York.
Rev. J. K. Matthews, New York.
Rev. S. G. Mendis, Colombo.
Miss Daw Mi, Mandalay.
Bishop S. K. Mondol, Hyderabad, Deccan.
Rev. C. C. Pande, B.A., Raniganj, West Bengal.
Bishop J. Waskom Pickett, Delhi.
Rev. W. S. Reinoehl, B.D., M.A., Singapore.
Rev. J. T. Seamands, Belgaum, United Provinces.
Rev. G. A. F. Senaratne, Galle, Ceylon.
Mr Hero M. C. Singh, Lucknow.
Rev. Gabriel Sundaram, Domalaguda, Hyderabad.
Rev. T. Thangaraj, Rangoon.
Rev. U Po Tun, Mandalay.
Bishop J. L. Valencia, Ermita, Manila.
Mrs G. Garland, India.

SECTION 5

Eastern Asia

Mr Shiro Abe, Japan.
Mr John A. Moss, Shibuya-ke, Tokio.
Miss Oldridge.

Ex-Missionaries from China

Rev. J. J. Heady, Chessington, Surrey.
Rev. R. J. Hooper, London.
Rev. R. E. Kendall, London.
Miss Elsie Yen, China.

SECTION 6

South India (Methodist Missionaries)

Rev. W. Le Cato Edwards, B.A., Secunderabad, Deccan.
Rev. Donald H. Mason, B.D., Chikagalur, Mysore State.
Rev. J. Sankey, B.Sc., Negapatam, Tanjore District.
Miss O. M. Valentine, B.A., Nagari, Chittoor District.

1

SECTION 7

Methodist Church of Australia

Mr Peter Bailey, LL.M., Oxford.
Rev. Dr G. Calvert Barber, Carlton, Vic.
Mrs G. Calvert Barber, Carlton, Vic.
Mr H. W. Chancellor, Sydney, N.S.W.
Mr A. S. Egglestone, Ivanhoe, Vic.
Mr W. H. Frederick, M.A., Prahran, Melbourne.
Mr W. H. Green, Queensland.
Rev. G. R. Holland, New South Wales.
Rev. A. Norman Kemp, Geelong, Vic.
Rev. H. A. Lyth.
Mr Owen Parnaby, M.A., Oxford.
Rev. H. L. Perkins, LL.M., B.Com., B.D., Cambridge.
Rev. Gloster S. Udy, M.A., S.T.D. Mass., U.S.A.
Rev. J. W. Westerman, B.A., Edinburgh.
Rev. S. C. Wilcock.

SECTION 8

Methodist Church of New Zealand

Mr W. Charles Francis, Christchurch, N.Z.
Rev. I. D. Grocott, B.A., Wellington, N.Z.
Rev. E. W. Hames, M.A., Auckland, N.Z.
Mrs E. W. Hames, Auckland, N.Z.
Mr H. M. Patrick, M.V.O., J.P., Auckland, N.Z.
Sister Dorothy Pointon, Hokianga, N.Z.
Sister Rita Snowden, N.Z.

SECTION 9

Methodist Church of Great Britain

Rev. R. G. Ashman, M.A., Ph.D., Barry, Glamorgan.
Rev. Eric W. Baker, M.A., Ph.D., London.
Rev. Frank Baker, B.A., B.D., Cleethorpes, Lincs.
Rev. L. P. Barnett, B.A., B.D., London.
Rev. R. C. Bedford, B.A., St. Peter Port, Guernsey.
Mr H. G. Beer, Wembley, Middlesex.
Rev. N. A. Birtwhistle, M.A., B.Sc., London.
Ald. A. Wesley Blake, J.P., Peterborough.

Mr D. P. Blatherwick, O.B.E., Newark, Notts.
Mr Vernon Booth, Pinner, Middlesex.
Rev. S. K. Bridge, B.A., Leeds.
Mr F. H. Buss, Bournemouth.
Sister Megan Capon, London.
Rev. Leslie F. Church, B.A., Ph.D., Worthing, Sussex.
Mrs Leslie Church, Worthing, Sussex.
Rev. Basil Clutterbuck, London.
Mr Duncan Coomer, LL.D., Bournemouth.
Professor C. A. Coulson, London.
Rev. F. H. Cumbers, B.A., B.D., London.
Rev. R. E. Davies, M.A., B.D., Bristol.
Rev. Hugh A. Davison, Doncaster.
Ald. J. L. Dawson, M.A., Huddersfield.
Miss Barbara Dickinson, Gainsborough, Lincs.
Sir Arthur L. Dixon, C.B., C.B.E., Godalming, Surrey.
Rev. Maldwyn L. Edwards, M.A., Ph.D., Birmingham.
Mr L. A. Ellwood, M.A., LL.B., Guildford.
Mr Harold J. Emms, Colchester.
Rev. W. E. Farndale, D.D., Lincoln.
Sister Dorothy Farrar, B.A., Ph.D., Ilkley, Yorks.
Rev. P. J. Fisher, Woking, Surrey.
Rev. R. Newton Flew, M.A., D.D., Wesley House, Cambridge.
Mr J. M. Gibbs, M.A., Penarth, Glamorgan.
Dr Frank Gunstone, Glasgow.
Miss Elaine Hammerton, B.Sc., Harrow, Middlesex.
Mr A. H. Havelock, O.B.E., Ealing, London.
Mr Harold Hayward, Sheffield.
Mr Arthur R. Hill, F.R.C.S., Ipswich.
Mr A. B. Hillis, Ramsbottom, Lancs.
Rev. W. F. Howard, M.A., D.D., F.B.A., Cambridge.
Mr. Donald W. Hughes, M.A., Colwyn Bay, Denbighshire.
Mr Glyn T. Hughes, B.A., Ruthin, Denbighshire.
Mr H. Ibberson, Mapplewell, Near Barnsley.
Rev. R. Kissack, M.A., B.D., Oxford.
Mr W. H. Kneen, LL.B., Woking, Surrey.
Mrs David Lewis, Cannock, Staffs.
Rev. Greville P. Lewis, B.A., B.D., London.
Rev. A. Stanley Leyland, M.A., London.
Rev. A. Kingsley Lloyd, Enfield, Middlesex.
Rev. W. H. Hudspeth.

2

Mr A. C. Mares, Cardiff.
Rev. T. D. Meadley, B.A., B.D., Bristol.
Mr J. F. Mills, Bournemouth.
Mr Basil H. Mitchell, Liskeard, Cornwall.
Mr A. Victor Murray, M.A., B.D., Cambridge.
Mr David Foot Nash, Plymouth.
Mr C. T. Nightingale, Portobello, Midlothian.
Rev. W. J. Noble, Herne Bay, Kent.
Mr C. D. Parker, LL.D., Oxford.
Rev. J. Hamblin Parsons, Oxford.
Professor H. Cecil Pawson, Newcastle-on-Tyne.
Rev. E. Benson Perkins, M.A., Manchester.
Rev. W. J. Platt, London.
Rev. Colin A. Roberts, London.
Rev. Harold Roberts, M.A., Ph.D., Richmond, Surrey.
Rev. D. R. Rogers, M.A., Abergele, Denbighshire.
Rev. E. Rogers, M.A., B.D., London.
Rev. A. N. Rose, M.A., London.
Rev. E. Gordon Rupp, M.A., B.D., Richmond, Surrey.
Mr A. B. Sackett, M.C., M.A., Bath.
Rev. W. E. Sangster, M.A., Ph.D., London.
Rev. C. R. B. Shapland, M.A., B.D., Glasgow.
Rev. W. Russell Shearer, M.A., Birmingham.
Rev. R. V. Spivey, M.A., London.
Mr J. A. Stead, Retford, Notts.
Mrs Donald H. Stoate, Bristol.
Miss Helen M. Streat, Sheffield.
Rev. Wesley F. Swift, Leeds.
Sister Lilian Topping, London.
Mr C. W. Towlson, M.A., B.D., Pudsey, near Leeds.
Mr W. A. J. Tudor, London.
Rev E. C. Urwin, M.A., B.D., London.
Rev. Wilfred Wade, Harrow, Middlesex.
Miss Alice Walton, B.A., London.
Mr Arthur E. Warmsley, Middleton, Lancs.
Rev. H. Watkin-Jones, M.A., D.D., Headingley, Leeds.
Rev. P. S. Watson, M.A., Birmingham.
Rev. J. K. Whitehead, B.A., London.
Professor Basil Willey, Cambridge.

SECTION 10

Methodist Church in Ireland

Mr A. E. Anderson, Londonderry.
Major W. Devine, M.B.E., Enniskillen, Co. Fermanagh.

Rev. Albert Gamble, Monkstown, Dublin.
Rev. G. E. Good, B.A., Omagh, Co. Tyrone.
Mr W. Victor Hadden, Carlow, Eire.
Dr R. H. Harte, Bartra, Belfast.
Rev. J. B. Jameson, 2 Lorelei, Bangor, Co. Down.
Rev. R. E. Ker, M.A., Belfast.
Rev. W. L. Northridge, M.A., M.Th., Ph.D., Belfast.
Rev. C. W. Ransom, B. Litt., New York City.
Mr Norman Robb, Belfast.

SECTION 11

Wesleyan Reform Union

Rev. Wm. T. Burkitt, D.D., High Wycombe, Bucks.
Rev. Dr W. H. Jones, Sheffield.
Ald. L. F. Milner, O.B.E., J.P., Sheffield.
Coun. T. Roberts, Barnsley, Yorks.
Ald. T. Tomlinson, B.E.M., J.P., Elsecar, Near Barnsley.
Rev. A. Wortley, Bradford.

SECTION 12

Continental Europe

Germany
Superintendent Karl Dahn, Ansbach i. Mfr.
Superintendent Georg Haug, Stuttgart.
Dr Paul Huber, Frankfurt a.M.
Superintendent Ernst Scholz, Berlin.
Bishop Dr J. W. Ernst Sommer, Frankfurt a.M.
Rev. Paul Orlamunder, Frankfurt a.M.
Director Dr Friedrich Wunderlich, Frankfurt a.M.
Superintendent Walther Zeuner, Bremen.

Switzerland
Rev. Erwin Muller, Berne.
Rev. Dr Ferdinand Sigg, Zurich.

Belgium
Rev. Dr William G. Thonger, Brussels.

Poland
Professor Josephn Szezepkowski, Warsaw.

Czechoslovakia
Rev. Dr J. P. Bartak, Prague.

3

Austria
Rev. Ferdinand Mayr, Vienna.

Scandinavia
Bishop Theodor Arvidson, Stockholm, Sweden.
Rev. Sergei Dubrovin, Helsingfors, Finland.
Rev. G. Henriksson, Stockholm, Sweden.
Lector Harald Lindström, Boras, Sweden.
Tilsynsman Teol de Alf Lier, Oslo, Norway.
Rev. Niels Mann, Copenhagen, Denmark.
Rev. Lief Sevre, Norway.
Rev. Leo Vihersaari, Kuopio, Finland.
Mr Sigy Sorensen, Hamar, Norway.

Italy
Rev. G. A. Lardi, Rome.
Rev. E. Sbaffi, Rome.

Spain
Rev. G. Bell, Barcelona.

SECTION 13

The Methodist Church, U.S.A.

Dr Merrill Abbey, Madison, Wisconsin.
Mr Rufus Abernethy, Bel Air, Maryland.
Rev. D. Rhea Allison, Eagle Lake, Texas.
Rev. Fred A. Andrews, Detroit, Michigan.
Miss Ruth Aregood, Kearney, Nebraska.
Mrs Robert Armstrong, Cedar Rapids, Iowa.
Mrs Paul Arington, Jackson, Mississippi.
Dr C. Clifford Bacon, Des Moines, Iowa.
Rev. Donald E. Bailey, Fort Wayne, Indiana.
Mr Frank E. Baker, Philadelphia, Pennyslvania.
Bishop James Chamberlain Baker, Los Angeles, California.
Dr Milton H. Bank, Pontiac, Michigan.
Mr William N. Banks, Grantville, Georgia.
Dr R. E. L. Bearden, Jr., Forst Smith, Arkansas.
Mrs W. H. Beckham, Miami, Florida.
Dr Edwin Bohmfalk, Fort Worth, Texas.
Mr Phil Bosserman, Junction City, Kansas.
President J. P. Brawley, Atlanta, Georgia.

Mrs Frank G. Brooks, Mount Vernon, Iowa.
Rev. C. Maxwell Brown, Fargo, North Dakota.
Dr Earl R. Brown, New York.
Dr Ira A. Brumley Conway, Arkansas.
Dr Raoul C. Calkins, Des Moines, Iowa.
Dr William R. Cannon, Atlanta, Georgia.
Miss Marion Cattman, Philadelphia, Pennsylvania.
Dr Douglas Chandler, Westminster, Maryland.
Dr John R. Cheney, Toledo, Ohio.
Rev. Thomas F. Chilcote, Chattanooga, Tennessee.
Dr Matthew W. Clair, Jr., Chicago, Illinois.
Dr Elmer T. Clark, New York.
Rev. W. L. Clegg, Burlington, North Carolina.
Dr Herbert B. Cockerill, Manhattan, Kansas.
Mrs Stewart Colley, Grantville, Georgia,
Rev. T. E. Colley, Erie, Pennsylvania.
Rev. Pierce E. Cook, Rock Hill, South Carolina.
Dr Stanley Coors, Lansing, Michigan.
Bishop Fred P. Corson, Philadelphia, Pennsylvania.
Mrs Fred P. Corson, Philadelphia, Pennsylvania.
Dr Frank A. Court, Lincoln, Nebraska.
Dr Alva I. Cox, Akron, Ohio.
Rev. Harold H. Cramer, Needham Heights, Massachusetts.
Dr Weldon Crossland, Rochester, New York.
Rev. I. W. Curry, Florence, South Carolina.
Dr M. S. Davage, Nashville, Tennessee.
Dr Carl M. Davidson, Pueblo, Colorado.
Dr J. J. Davies, Fort Dodge, Iowa.
Dr Harry Denman, Nashville, Tennessee.
Rev. Phil Deschner, Clinton, Oklahoma.
Mrs James Dolbey, Cincinnati, Ohio.
Mr W. H. Dougherty, Freeport, Pennsylvania.
President Paul Douglas, Washington, District of Columbia.
Rev. E. Ezra Ellis, Minneapolis, Minnesota.
Dr J. A. Engle, New York.
Dr F. Gerald Ensley, Columbus, Ohio.
Rev. Harold Ewing, Nashville, Tennessee.
Rev. J. Ed. Fain, Columbus, Georgia.

4

President William C. Finch, Georgetown, Texas.
Rev. H. Ellis Finger, Jr., Oxford, Mississippi.
Dr Gaston Foote, Dayton, Ohio.
Dr George A. Fowler, Chicago, Illinois.
Dr Hamilton P. Fox, Wilmington, Delaware.
Rev. G. Stanley Frazer, Montgomery, Alabama.
Mr C. Cree Gable, Muncie, Indiana.
Dr Paul V. Galloway, Tulsa, Oklahoma.
Miss Henrietta Gibson, New York.
Dr Charles Ray Goff, Chicago, Illinois.
Mr Henry Gramling, Gramling, South Carolina.
Dr A Raymond Grant, Sacramento, California.
Mr Frank Greathouse, Rogers, New Mexico.
Dr John O. Gross, Nashville, Tennessee.
Dr A. Ray Grummon, Springfield, Illinois.
Dr Walter C. Gum, Richmond, Virginia.
Mr J. C. Haley, Tacoma, Washington.
Rev. John Hanger, Fort Lauderdale, Florida.
Dr I. M. Hargett, Louisville, Kentucky.
Dr Nolan B. Harmon, New York.
President M. L. Harris, Little Rock, Arkansas.
Rev. Winfield S. Haycock, West Duluth, Minnesota.
Dr Edmond Heinsohn, Austin, Texas.
Dr Waights G. Henry, Anniston, Alabama.
Mrs. Wayne Herrington, York, Nebraska.
Dr A. J. Hobbs, Rocky Mount, North Carolina.
Rev. I. C. Hoffman, Charleston, West Virginia.
Bishop Ivan Lee Holt, St. Louis, Missouri.
Dr Lynn Harold Hough, New York.
Rev. C. T. Howell, Jackson, Mississippi.
Dr Harold H. Hughes, Roanoak, Virginia.
Rev. Charles Harold Jack, Youngstown, Ohio.
Rev. Kelly L. Jackson, Baltimore, Maryland.
President Zach Johnson, Wilmore, Kentucky.
Dr Warren Johnston, Fort Worth, Texas.
President D. D. Jones, Greensboro, North Carolina.
Mr Edwin L. Jones, Charlotte, North Carolina.

Rev. T. Parry Jones, Sheboygan, Wisconsin.
Dr W. T. Jones, Bloomington, Indiana.
Rev. Francis E. Kearns, Wauwatosa, Wisconsin.
Rev. Charles S. Kendall, Phoenix, Arizona.
Bishop Gerald H. Kennedy, Portland, Oregon.
President Charles B. Ketcham, Alliance, Ohio.
Rev. Dow Kirkpatrick, Young Harris, Georgia.
Dr M. B. Kober, Cedar Rapids, Iowa.
Rev. D. Lawrence Landrum, Palestine, Texas.
Dr Edward G. Latch, Washington, District of Columbia.
Miss Elizabeth Lee, New York.
President Umphrey Lee, Dallas, Texas.
Mr DeWitt C. LeFevre, Beaver Falls, New York.
Rev. Noel Le Roque, Spokane, Washington.
Dr Franklin H. Littell, New York.
Mrs J. A. B. Lowry, Crewe, Virginia.
Dr C. E. Lundy, Cleveland, Tennessee.
Rev. Roswell W. Lyon, Kingston, Pennsylvania.
Mrs John O. Mabuse, Buffalo, New York.
Chancellor Daniel L. Marsh, Boston, Massachusetts.
Bishop Paul E. Martin, Little Rock, Arkansas.
Dr Thomas B. Mather, Kansas City, Missouri.
Mr James Matheson, Durham, North Carolina.
Dr Gerald O. McCulloh, Evanston, Illinois.
Rev. John R. McLaughlin, Englewood, New Jersey.
Dr N. C. McPherson, Memphis, Tennessee.
Rev. George Mecklenburg, Minneapolis, Minnesota.
Mrs Ruth Esther Meeker, New York.
Dr Ronald R. Meredith, Fresno, California.
President Joe J. Mickle, Shreveport, Louisiana.
Mr Bradshaw Mintener, Minneapolis, Minnesota.
Dr E. Harold Mohn, Chicago, Illinois.
Bishop Arthur J. Moore, Atlanta, Georgia.
Rev. George Morrell, Helena, Montana.
Dr Albert S. Morris, Philadelphia, Pennsylvania.

5

Dr John R. Mott, Orlando, Florida.
President Alvin W. Murray, Winfield, Kansas.
Dr T. Otto Nall, Chicago, Illinois.
Dr Fred B. Newell, New York.
Rev. Clifford H. Newham, Evanston, Illinois.
Dr G. S. Nichols, Ames, Iowa.
Mr Ray H. Nichols, Vernon, Texas.
Mr Alexander Nunn, Birmingham, Alabama.
Professor John Frederick Olson, Syracuse, New York.
Dr Oscar Thomas Olson, Cleveland, Ohio.
Mr Charles C. Parlin, Englewood, New Jersey.
Miss Camilla Parlin, Englewood, New Jersey.
Mr D. Stewart Patterson, Washington, District of Columbia.
Mr. Joseph J. Perkins, Wichita Falls, Texas.
Mr Ernest W. Peterson, Portland, Oregon.
Mr Andrew H. Phelps, Pittsburgh, Pennsylvania.
Mr Ellis L. Phillips, Plandome, New York.
Dr W. Kenneth Pope, Houston, Texas.
Dr J. Manning Potts, Nashville, Tennessee.
Rev. Emeral E. Price, St. John's, Michigan.
Dr Thomas H. Pryor, Kalamazoo, Michigan.
Dr William F. Quillian, Atlanta, Georgia.
Dr Karl Quimby, New York.
Mrs Franklin Reed, Westfield, New Jersey.
Mrs E. U. Robinson, Franklin, Tennessee.
Dr Lester Rumble, Atlanta, Georgia.
Dr W. B. Selah, Jackson, Mississippi.
Bishop Charles C. Selecman, Dallas, Texas.
Rev. Lester Schaff, Elmira, New York.
Dr W. S. Smeltzer, Duquesne, Pennsylvania.
Dr Alexander K. Smith, Ardmore, Pennsylvania.
Dr Eugene L. Smith, New York.
President Marion L. Smith, Jackson, Mississippi.
Dr Robert J. Smith, Enid, Oklahoma.
Dr Roy L. Smith, Chicago, Illinois.
Dr W. Stanley Smith, Columbus, Ohio.
Dr Ralph W. Sockman, New York.
Mr Edwin R. Spann, Dallas, Texas.

Dr J. Richard Spann, Nashville, Tennessee.
Rev. Laren M. Spear, Decatur, Illinois.
Rev. Frank B. Stanger, Haddon Heights, New Jersey.
Dr Ralph Stoody, New York.
Dr R. Marvin Stuart, Palo Alto, California.
Rev. Roy A. Sturm, New York.
Dr W. W. Sweet, Dallas, Texas.
Dr. B. C. Taylor, New Orleans, Louisiana.
Mr Pat Thompson, Bay City, Texas.
Rev. Fred B. Trotter, Alhambra California.
Mrs Charles A. Trowbridge, Pasadena, California.
Mr R. Carter Tucker, Kansas City, Missouri.
Mr Abbott Turner, Valdosta, Georgia.
Dr Joseph King Vivion, Nashville, Tennessee.
Rev. H. H. Waller, Tampa, Florida.
Dr Aubrey G. Walton, Little Rock, Arkansas.
Dr Dudley Ward, New York.
Rev. Wilson O. Weldon, Thomasville, North Carolina.
President L. A. Welliver, Westminster, Maryland.
Miss White (Laurice) Los Angeles, California.
Mrs R. M. White, Richmond, Virginia.
Rev. R. M. Williams, Washington, District of Columbia.
Dr Thomas A. Williams, Wichita, Kansas.
Dr Walter G. Williams, Denver, Colorado.
Rev. Walter R. Willis, Mesa El paso, Texas.
Rev. Alfred Wood, Taunton, Massachusetts.
Dr R. L. Woodward, Fayette, Missouri.
Mrs H. E. Woolever, New York.
Mr James Young, Delaware, Ohio.
Dr J. Otis Young, Cincinnati, Ohio.
Mr Henry Zimmerman, Fort Mitchell, Kentucky.

Reserve Delegates
Rev. Albert R. Ashley, Indianapolis, Indiana.
Rev. Lowell M. Atkinson, Hackensack, New Jersey.
Mr J. I. Ballengee, Trinidad, Colorado.
Mr Miles Barnard, Lincoln, 2, Nebraska.
Dr Carl A. Bergsten, Long Island, New York.

Rev. Carl C. Bosse, South Bend, Indiana.
Rev. John Branscomb, Orlando, Florida.
Rev. H. R. Brennan, Rockville Centre, New York.
Rev. Howard J. Brown, Cleveland, Ohio.
Rev. James T. Browning, Huntingdon, West Virginia.
Rev. Robert Justin Campbell, Chicago, Illinois.
Dr R. G. Carter, Toledo, Ohio.
Mr Rochelle Chandler, Washington, District of Columbia.
Dr B. G. Childs, Durham, North Carolina.
Rev. J. H. Chitwood, West, Birmingham, Alabama.
Professor Kenneth W. Clark, Durham, North Carolina.
Rev. Elbert Cole, Farmington, Missouri.
Rev. Ross Culpepper, Elkins, West Virginia.
Rev. G. M. Davenport, Birmingham, Alabama.
Rev. George Davies, Middletown, New York.
Rev. W. F. Dunkle, Wilmington, Delaware.
Dr B. L. Du Val, Springfield, Ohio.
President William W. Edel, Carlisle, Pennsylvania.
Rev. Samuel Emerick, Decatur, Indiana.
Miss Isabelle Fleming, Salt Lake City, Utah.
Mr Hollis C. Franklin, Marion, Kentucky.
Rev. E. D. Galloway, Hope, Arkansas.
Dr Ernest F. Harold, Everett, Washington.
Rev. Kenneth R. Hemphill, McAllen, Texas.
Rev. L. Lament Henninger, Altoona, Pennsylvania.
Dr Guy Hutcherson, Metter, Georgia.
Rev. James M. Hunter, Miles City, Montana.
Rev. Bryant Howard, Mishawaka, Indiana.
Dr Joseph S. Johnson, Norfolk, Virginia.
Mrs C. I. Jones, New Orleans, Louisana,
Rev. W. Arthur Kale, High Point, North Carolina.
Rev. M. L. Koch, Fayette, Missouri.
Rev. Russell Lambert, Glencoe, Illinois.
Dr Elmer C. Lewis, Rutherford, New Jersey.
Rev. Nat G. Long, Atlanta, Georgia.
Rev. I. B. Loud, Dallas, Texas.

Rev. Edward G. Mackay, Oxford, Georgia.
Mr S. E. McCreeles, San Antonio, Texas.
Rev. E. W. McMillan, Atlanta, Georgia.
Mr Holt McPherson, Shelby, North Carolina.
Mrs Olivia Cavanagh Maskiell, Bradenton, Florida.
Mrs J. W. Masland.
Rev. Virgil Morris, Alexandria, Louisiana.
Dr O. A. Murphy, Gainsville, Florida.
Mr W. D. Myers, Deemer, Mississippi.
Dr J. R. Nelson, Urbana, Illinois.
Rev. J. B. Nichols, Greenville, Alabama.
Dr Lawrence E. Nye, Portland, Oregon.
Rev. I. D. Piper, McKeesport, Pennsylvania.
Rev. B. V. Powell, St. Joseph, Missouri.
Dr E. J. Prendergass, Tampa, Florida.
Rev. Harry A. Price, Pittsburgh, Pennsylvania.
Dr Robert J. Rice, Minnepolis, Minnesota.
Mr Walter Richard, Atlanta, Georgia.
Rev. Ted Richardson, Austin, Texas.
Dr B. M. Ridpath, Kansas City, Missouri.
Dr Lloyd H. Rising, Pittsburgh, Kansas.
Rev. Leon Russell, Greenville, North Carolina.
Rev. W. L. Scranton, White Plains, New York.
Professor James Seehorn Seneker, Dallas, Texas.
Dr C. C. Sherrod, Johnson City, Tennessee.
Mr J. P. Stafford, Cary, Mississippi.
Rev. Roy P. Steen, Neenah, Wisconsin.
Rev. Dean Stroud, Nashville, Tennessee.
Rev. G. G. Thompson, Oxford, Georgia.
Rev. Burton F. Tarr, Kingston, New York.
Mr Van B. Taunton, Lanett, Alabama.
Rev. Wilson Tennant, Holt, Michigan.
Rev. Samuel J. Truscott, Scranton, Pennsylvania.
Mr Edmund Turnley, Nashville, Tennessee.
Rev. M. E. Van de Mark, Kalispell, Montana.
Captain Lee P. Van Sickle, Newburgh, New York.
Rev. W. L. Wallace, Jr., Holcomb, Mississippi.
Rev. George Watt, Jr., Maplewood, New Jersey.
Rev. Ewart G. Watts, El Paso, Texas.
Rev. Ewing T. Wayland, Little Rock, Arkansas.

Rev. Hiram Weld, Scranton, Pennsylvania.
Rev. Henry G. White, Indianapolis, Indiana.
Rev. E. E. Wiley, Jr., Kingsport, Tennessee.
Rev. A. C. Wischmeier, Kennewick, Washington.
Dr Paul D. Womeldorf, Oklahoma City, Oklahoma.
Dr Dempster Yinger, Dubuque, Iowa.

SECTION 14
United Church of Canada
Mr C. W. Burr, Belleville, Ont.
Mrs C. W. Burr, Belleville, Ont.
Rev. George Dorey, D.D., Toronto, Ont.
Rev. B. Eyre, B.A., B.D., Uxbridge, Ont.
Rev. Victor Fiddes, B.A., B.D., Orangeville, Ont.
Judge F. A. E. Hamilton, Winnipeg, Man.
Rev. Arthur Organ, B.A., B.D., Hamilton, Ont.
Rev. Gordon A. Sisco, D.D., Toronto, Ont.
Rev. S. B. Stokes, D.D., Niagara Falls, Ont.

SECTION 15
African Methodist Episcopal Church of America
Principals
Bishop A. J. Allen, Cleveland, Ohio.
Bishop George W. Baber, Detroit, Michigan.
Bishop John H. Clayborn, Little Rock, Arkansas.
Dr A. G. Gaston, Birmingham, Alabama.
Bishop S. L. Greene, Atlanta, Georgia.
Bishop John A. Gregg, Jacksonville, Florida.
Bishop Joseph Gomez, Waco, Texas.
Bishop L. H. Hemmingway, Washington, D.C.
Rev. Fred A. Hughes, Philadelphia, Pennsylvania.
Rev. Henderson R. Hughes, New York.
Dr A. S. Jackson, Washington, D.C.
Rev. Fred D. Jordan, Los Angeles, California.
Rev. Lutrelle G. Long, Montgomery, Alabama.
Mrs A. D. Lynen, Lexington, Kentucky.
Dr R. W. Mance, Columbia, South Carolina.
Bishop D. Ward Nichols, New York.

Rev. H. Thomas Primm, New Orleans, Louisiana.
Bishop Frank M. Reid, Columbia, South Carolina.
Dr O. N. Smith, Wilmington, Delaware.
Rev. Frank R. Veal, Charleston, South Carolina.
Rev. A. Wayman Ward, Chicago, Illinois.

Alternates
Rev. E. A. Adams, Columbia, South Carolina.
Rev. John A. Alexander, Detroit, Michigan.
Mrs Sadie T. M. Alexander, Philadelphia, Pennsylvania.
Rev. W. F. Ball, Miami, Florida.
Rev. G. W. Blakley, Little Rock, Arkansas.
Rev. Harrison J. Bryant, Baltimore, Maryland.
Hon. Herbert Dudley, Detroit, Michigan.
Bishop Carey A. Gibbs, Monrovia, Liberia, West Africa.
Rev. J. W. Hair, Jackson, Mississippi.
Rev. E. C. Hatcher, Nashville, Tennessee.
Rev. M. E. Jackson, Philadelphia, Pennsylvania.
Rev. A. L. Lynen, Lexington, Kentucky.
Rev. G. Dewey Robinson, Washington, D.C.
Rev. H. Bell Shaw.
Rev. V. M. Townsend, Little Rock, Arkansas.
Rev. Harvey E. Walden, Chicago, Illinois.
Dr A. W. West, Montgomery, Alabama.
Bishop W. R. Wilkes, Atlanta, Georgia.
Rev. A. O. Wilson, Macon, Georgia.
Rev. Wallace M. Wright, Dayton, Ohio.

SECTION 16
African M.E. Zion Church (U.S.A.)
Bishop Cameron C. Alleyne, Philadelphia, Pennsylvania.
Mrs Alleyne.
Rev. W. O. Carrington, Brooklyn, New York.
Dr R. E. Clement, Atlanta, Georgia.
Mr James W. Eichelberger, Chicago, Illinois.
Bishop Buford F. Gorden, Charlotte, North Carolina.
Bishop R. L. Jones, Salisbury, North Carolina.
Rev. W. R. Lovell, Charlotte, North Carolina.

8

Bishop J. W. Martin, Chicago, Illinois.
Mrs J. W. Martin.
Bishop Hampton T. Medeford, Washington, D.C.
Bishop W. W. Slade, Charlotte, North Carolina.
Bishop W. J. Walls, Chicago, Illinois.

Reserves

Bishop William C. Brown, Los Angeles, California.
Mr J. Carl Canty, New York.
Mr M. P. Fonville, Norfolk, Virginia.
Professor T. M. Patton, Greenville, Alabama.
Rev. D. C. Pope, Washington, D.C.
Rev. W. A. Stewart, Washington, D.C.
Bishop James Clair Taylor, Memphis, Tennessee.
Rev. J. S. Nathaniel Tross, Charlotte, North Carolina.
Bishop Edgar B. Waton, Greensboro, North Carolina.

SECTION 17
Coloured Methodist Episcopal Church (U.S.A.)

Dr W. R. Banks, LL.D., Prairie View, Texas.
Dr W. A. Bell, LL.D., Birmingham, Alabama.
Rev. M. L. Breedking, D.D., Cleveland, Ohio.
Rev. N. S. Curry, Ph.D., Los Angeles, California.
Bishop B. W. Doyle, Ph.D., D.D., Nashville, Tennessee.
Mr J. A. Hamlett, Jr., A.M., Kansas City, Kansas.
Mrs E. W. F. Harris, A.M., Greenville, Texas.
Professor F. T. Jeans, A.M., Jackson, Tennessee.
Rev. J. A. Johnson, A.M., D.D., Jackson, Tennessee.
Rev. J. M. Pettigrew, D.D., Saint Louis, Missouri.
Rev. L. H. Pitts, A.M., Cordele, Georgia.
Bishop A. W. Womac, A.M., D.D., Indianapolis, Indiana.

Alternates

Rev. H. H. Davis, D.D., Augusta, Georgia.
Mr H. W. Evans, A.M., D.D., Chicago, Illinois.
Rev. C. F. Odum, D.D., Jackson, Mississippi.

Rev. G. W. Washington, D.D., Nashville, Tennessee.
Rev. L. S. White, D.D., New York.

SECTION 18
Free Methodist Church (U.S.A.)

Mr George Fuller, Jr., Toronto, Ontario.
Bishop Leslie R. Marston, Greenville, Illinois.
Mr C. H. Snyder, M.D., Grand Rapids, Michigan.
Rev. O. S. Walter, M.D., McPherson, Kansas.
Mr Hugh White, Birmingham, Michigan.

SECTION 19
Primitive Methodist Church (U.S.A.)

Rev. Wesley Boyd, M.A., D.D., Shenandoah, Pennsylvania.
Mrs Wesley Boyd, Shenandoah, Pennsylvania.

SECTION 20
Wesleyan Methodist Church (U.S.A.)

Council Members were appointed but did not attend the Conference.

SECTION 21
Methodist Church in the West Indies

Council

Rev. W. H. Armstrong, Eleuthera, Bahamas.
Rev. T. S. Cannon, Watsonville, Jamaica.
Rev. K. E. Towers, B.A., B.D., Berbice, British Guiana.

Conference

Sister E. Bemand, St. Ann's Bay, Jamaica.
Miss K. La Trobe, Jamaica.

SECTION 22
Methodist Church in Brazil

Dr and Mrs Jalmar Bowden, Sao Paulo, Brazil.
Bishop Cesar da Corso.
Rev. Almir dos Santos, Sao Paulo, Brazil.
Exma, Sra, De Hordalia Kuhlmann, Rio de Janeiro.
Dr Rui Ramos, Rio grande do Sul, Brazil.
Rev. and Mrs Robert Whitfield Wisdom, Rio de Janeiro.

SECTION 23

Methodist Church in Mexico and Cuba

Professor Gonzalo Baez Camargo, Mexico City.
Dr Milton C. Davis, Mexico City.
Bishop Eleazar Guerra, Mexico City.
Mr Elias Hernandez, Mexcio.
Dr Adrian Acuna Still, Puebla.

SECTION 24

Methodist Church in Central and S. America

Sante Uberto Barbieri, Buenos Aires.
Rev. Carlos T. Gattinoni, Montevideo.

Rev. Legrand Smith, Cochabamba, Bolivia.
Dr B. F. Stockwell, Buenos Aires.

Fraternal Delegates

Church of South India
Rev. John P. Aaron, Dornakal.
Rev. J. S. M. Hooper, Stratford-on-Avon.

Independent Methodist Churches (England)
Mr E. J. Higham, Warrington, Lancs.
Mr D. Imeson, Portishead, Somerset.

OFFICIALS OF THE ECUMENICAL COUNCIL

Presidents:

Bishop Ivan Lee Holt, St. Louis, Minnesota.
Rev. Wilbert F. Howard, M.A., D.D., F.B.A., Birmingham.

Vice-Presidents:

Bishop Paul N. Garber, Geneva.
Professor A. Victor Murray, M.A., B.D., B.Litt., Cambridge.

Treasurers:

Mr Matthew S. Davage, LL.D., Nashville, Tennessee.
Mr Duncan Coomer, M.A., LL.D., Bournemouth.

Secretaries:

Rev. Oscar T. Olson, D.D., Cleveland, Ohio.
Rev. Harold Roberts, M.A., Ph.D., Richmond, Surrey.

OFFICIALS OF THE OXFORD CONFERENCE

President:
Rev. W. F. Howard, M.A., D.D., F.B.A.

Treasurers:
Mr W. A. J. Tudor, Mr L. A. Ellwood, M.A., LL.B.

Secretaries:
Rev. Harold Roberts, M.A., Ph.D.;
Mr Duncan Coomer, M.A., LL.D.

Assistant Secretaries:
Rev. Rupert E. Davies, M.A., B.D.;
Mr John F. Mills.

Meetings outside Oxford

Secretary:
Rev. A. S. Leyland, M.A.

Local Oxford Officials

Chairman; Rev. J. Hamblin Parsons.
Vice-Chairman and Supt. of the Oxford Circuit: Rev. Herbert D. Leigh.
Treasurer: Mr C. D. Parker, LL.D.
Secretary: Rev. R. Kissack, M.A., B.D.
Accommodation; Mr H. F. Wood.
Reception: Mr J. W. Clamp.
Steward: Mr Stanley Gillam, B.Litt.
Publicity: Mr S. Colegrove.
Choral: Mr V. Leach.
Excursions: Mr Cecil Mann.
Refreshments: Mrs Eldred.
Local Plan Arrangements: Rev. G. Frederick Hollinghurst, B.A., B.D.

DAILY PROGRAMME

Monday 27th August

7 p.m. **Demonstration in the Central Hall, Westminster.** (15)
Chairman:
. Rev. Howard Watkin-Jones, M.A., D.D., President of the British Conference.

Speakers:
Bishop J. Chamberlain Baker, Ex-Chairman of the Board of Bishops of the Methodist Church, U.S.A.(15)
Rev. G. R. Acquaah, Chairman of the Gold Coast District, West Africa. (18)

N.B.—Figures in parentheses indicate page numbers.

Speakers:

Bishop J. W. Ernst Sommer, of the Methodist Church of Germany. (20)

Rev. C. C. Pande, Chairman of the Bengal District, India. (22)

Rev. J. B. Webb, M.A., D.D., Ex-President of the Methodist Church of South Africa. (24)

Tuesday 28th August

8 p.m. Sheldonian Theatre, Oxford. Welcome Meeting. (27)

Chairman:

Rev. Wilbert F. Howard, M.A., D.D., F.B.A., of Handsworth College, Birmingham, Joint President of the Ecumenical Council. (27)

Speakers:

The Bishop of Manchester (The Right Rev. W. D. L. Greer, D.D.). (30)

Rev. A. D. Harcus, D.D., Moderator of the Free Church Federal Council of England and Wales. (31)

Rev. J. Hamblin Parsons, Chairman of the Oxford and Gloucester District. (31)

Response by:

Bishop Ivan Lee Holt, Joint President of the Ecumenical Council. (32)

Wednesday 29th August

9.15. Wesley Memorial Church. (33)

Morning Devotions:

Rev. Moses O. Dada, O.B.E., West Africa.

Address:

Bishop Paul Martin, Little Rock, Arkansas.

9.15-12.45. Methodist Traditions.

United Kingdom: Rev. Harold Roberts, M.A., Ph.D., of Richmond College, Surrey. (33)

United States: Bishop Arthur J. Moore, of Atlanta, Georgia. (38)

Australasia: Rev. G. Calvert Barber, D.D., President-General of the General Conference. (50)

South Africa: Rev. Leslie A. Hewson, M.A., of Rhodes University College. (54)

Younger Churches: Rev. S. G. Mendis, Chairman of Ceylon District. (59)

5.15-6.30. Examination Schools: Methodism in Relation to Catholic Tradition.

President Umphrey Lee, D.D., LL.D., Southern Methodist University, Dallas, Texas. (62)

Lecture followed by questions.

8.0. Wesley Memorial Church: Methodism in the Modern World. (72)

Chairman:

Sir Arthur L. Dixon, C.B., C.B.E.

The Message:

Rev. W. E. Sangster, M.A., Ph.D., Ex-President British Conference. (72)

Communicating of the Message:

Rev. Ralph W. Sockman, D.D., LL.D., Christ Church, New York City. (77)

Thursday 30th August

9.15. Wesley Memorial Church. (84)

Morning Devotions:

Bishop S. L. Greene of the African Methodist Episcopal Church, U.S.A.

Address:

Rev. J. F. Wünderlich, D.D., Germany.

9.50-10.45. Methodist Doctrines

Justification by Faith: Rev. W. R. Cannon, Ph.D., Emory University, Atlanta, Georgia. (84)

Perfect Love and the Divine Society: Rev. Harald Lindström, D.D., University of Uppsala, Sweden. (88)

11.15-12.45. Group Discussions.

3.30. Garden Party.

5.15-6.30. Examination Schools: Methodism in Relation to Protestant Tradition.

Rev. E. Gordon Rupp, M.A., B.D., Richmond College, Surrey. (93)

Lecture followed by questions.

8.0. Sheldonian Theatre: Hymn Festival. (106)

Chairman:

Mr C. W. Towlson, M.A., B.D., Ex-Vice-President British Conference.

Conductor:

Rev. F. B. Westbrook, B.A., D.Mus., Secretary Methodist Church Music Society and co-Editor of *The Choir and Musical Journal.*

Friday 31st August

9.15. Wesley Memorial Church: Morning Devotions. (108)

Rev. W. H. Jones, D.D., Wesleyan Reform Union.

Address:

Bishop J. A. Gregg, African M. E. Church.

9.50-10.45. The Methodist Way.

The Means of Grace: Rev. R. V. Spivey, M.A., Wesley's Chapel, London. (108)

The Life of Fellowship: Rev. F. Gerald Ensley, D.D., Columbus, Ohio. (113)

11.15-12.45. Group Discussions.

3.0. Ecumenical Council Meeting.

5.15-6.30. Christianity and Totalitarianism. (118)

Chancellor Daniel Marsh, Boston University.

8.0. Reception by the Vice-Chancellor.

Saturday 1st September

9.15. Wesley Memorial Church: Morning Devotions. (128)

Bishop Guerra, Mexico.

Address:

Rev. Gordon A. Sisco, D.D., United Church of Canada.

9.50-10.45. Methodism and other Churches.

What Methodism has to Offer: Rev. J. S. M. Hooper, M.A., Church of S. India. (128)

What Methodism can Learn from other Churches: Rev. Lynn Harold Hough, D.D., Sometime Dean, Drew Seminary, New York. (133)

11.15-12.45. Group Discussions.

5.15. Wesley Memorial Church: Plenary Session of the Conference.

8.0. Francis Asbury and the Advancement of Methodism in America.

Bishop Charles C. Selecman, Dallas, Texas. (139)

Chairman:

Rev. Leslie F. Church, B.A., Ph.D., London.

Lecture arranged by the International Methodist Historical Society. Bishop Paul N. Garber, *President*. Rev. Elmer T. Clark, D.D., New York, Rev. Frank Baker, B.A., B.D., Cleethorpes, England, *Secretaries*.

Sunday 2nd September

11 a.m. Wesley Memorial Church, Oxford: Holy Communion.

Rev. W. J. Noble.

Sermon:

Bishop Ivan Lee Holt. (147)

3 p.m. Women's Service

Mrs D. H. Stoate of Bristol.

Speakers:

Mrs Franklin Reed, New Jersey. (151)

Mrs Ladlay of the Mission House, London. (155)

6.30 p.m. Service of Worship.

Rev. Oscar T. Olson, D.D.,

Sermon:

Rev. H. Watkin-Jones, M.A., D.D., President of the British Conference. (158)

8.15 p.m. Whitley Hall, Reading: Youth Service.

Chairman:

Rev. L. P. Barnett, B.A., B.D., London.

Speakers:

Rev. Harold Ewing, Director, Youth Department, Methodist Church of America. (162)

Dr O. K. Ogan, West Africa. (170)

8.0 p.m. Central Hall, Swindon: Public Meeting. (173)

Chairman:

Mr David Foot Nash, Plymouth.

Speaker:

Bishop J. Waskom Pickett, Delhi, India. (173)

Monday 3rd September

9.15. Wesley Memorial Church: Morning Devotions. (180)

Rev. E. W. Hames, New Zealand.

Address:

Rev. Nolan B. Harmon, D.D., New York.

9.50-10.45. The Social Witness—I.

Marriage and the Family: Rev. Maldwyn Edwards, M.A., B.D., Birmingham (180)

12

Education: Mr Donald W. Hughes, M.A., Headmaster, Rydal School, Colwyn Bay. (184)

11.15-12.45. Group Discussions.

5.15-6.30. Examination Schools: Scientific Humanism.

Chairman:
Dr M. S. Davage, Nashville, Tennessee.

Professor C. A. Coulson of London University. (189)
Lecture followed by questions.

8.0. Wesley Memorial Church. Public Meeting. The Christian in the Changing Social Order.

Chairman:
Mr C. C. Parlin, New York.

Vocation: Rev. E. Benson Perkins, M.A., Manchester. (199)

Personal Relationships: Dorothy Farrar, B.A., Ph.D., Wesley Deaconess College, Ilkley. (206)

Tuesday 4th September

9.15. Wesley Memorial Church. Morning Devotions. (213)
Rev. H. D. Leigh of Oxford.

Address:
Bishop J. Waskom Pickett, Delhi.

9.50-10.45. The Social Witness—II.

The Economic Order: Rev. Edward Rogers, M.A., B.D., of London. (213)
Inter-Racial Relations: Rev. E. W. Grant, Healdtown, South Africa. (220)

11.15-12.45. Group Discussions.

3.30. Reception in the City Hall.

5.15-6.30. Examination Schools. The Impact of Biblical Criticism.

Rev. Norman H. Snaith, M.A., D.D., Wesley College, Headingley, Leeds. (225)
Lecture followed by questions.

8.0. St Mary's Church: Service in Commemoration of John and Charles Wesley.

Address:
Rev. J. Scott Lidgett, C.H., D.D., LL.D. (235)

Wednesday 5th September

9.15. Wesley Memorial Church: Morning Devotions. (238)
Bishop Theodor Arvidsen, Sweden.

Address:
Bishop B. W. Doyle, Coloured Episcopal Church, Nashville.

9.50-10.45. Personal Responsibility.

Within the Local Church: Mrs Frank G. Brooks, Iowa. President, Women's Society of Christian Service of the Methodist Church. (238)

Within the Community: Rev. E. Clifford Urwin, M.A., B.D., of the Department of Christian Citizenship, London. (245)

11.15-12.45. Group Discussions.

5.15-6.30. Examination Schools: Recent Theological Tendencies. (249)

Chairman:
Dr G. O. McCulloch, Evanston, Illinois.

Rev. A. Raymond George, M.A., Headingley College, Leeds. (250)
Lecture followed by questions.

8.0. Wesley Memorial Church: Methodism and the World Church. (259)

Chairman:
Rev. R. Newton Flew, M.A., D.D., Cambridge.

Speakers:
Bishop Fred P. Corson, Philadelphia. (260)

Rev. C. W. Ranson, B.Litt., Secretary of the International Missionary Council. (270)

Thursday 6th September

9.15. Wesley Memorial Church: Morning Devotions. (277)
Bishop Barbieri of the Argentine.

Address:
Rev. W. L. Northridge, M.A., M.Th., Ph.D., Belfast, Northern Ireland.

9.50-10.45. Evangelism.

Commending the Gospel: Professor H. C. Pawson, Durham University. (277)

The Missionary Motive: Rev. Eugene L. Smith, D.D., Secretary of American Board of Foreign Missions. (283)

11.15-12.45. Group Discussions.

5.15. Wesley Memorial Church: Ecumenical Council Meeting.

8.0. Plenary Session of the Conference. (289)

Friday 7th September

10.0. Wesley Memorial Church. Closing Devotional Session. (296)

Address:

Rev. Wilbert F. Howard, M.A, D.D., F.B.A.

14

EIGHTH
ECUMENICAL METHODIST CONFERENCE

Monday 27th August 1951

PRE-CONFERENCE MEETING AT WESTMINSTER CENTRAL HALL

A GREAT public meeting was held at the Central Hall, West-minster on 27th August 1951—the eve of the Ecumenical Conference beginning at Oxford on the following day. The Chairman was the Rev. Dr Howard Watkin-Jones, and the speakers, representing World Methodism, were Bishop James Chamberlain Baker, the Rev. Gaddiel R. Acquaah, Bishop J. W. Ernst Sommer, the Rev. Christa C. Pande, and Dr J. B. Webb.

The object of the gathering was to set the Ecumenical Conference in its proper perspective in relation to World Methodism, and to introduce some of the practical and theological problems which would be considered, in detail, at Oxford.

After Dr Watkin-Jones had welcomed the speakers, in the name of British Methodism, he stressed the need for modern Methodism to consolidate its position. There were two parallel movements in the Churches today—one in which the different Christian communities were rediscovering what they specifically stood for as branches of the Church Catholic, and the Ecumenical movement, which was, indeed, a movement of the Spirit of God during the past thirty-five years. In essence these movements were one. At Oxford they would look at the particular contribution of Methodism to the World Church. The whole question of evangelism would be examined and they would try to discover the ways in which it might operate in an age 'which sorely needs what our fathers called conversion'.

As Ex-Chairman of the Board of Bishops (Methodist Church of America), DR JAMES CHAMBERLAIN BAKER *said:*

I count myself happy in that I am privileged to bring greetings from The Methodist Church in America and to make some report of her stewardship in this time of troubles.

In late April of 1946 I heard Bishop Bergravv deliver the Burge Lecture at King's College in this city. I can never forget how, in the midst of his lecture, he stopped to ejaculate: 'And to think that we are again in England —the home of ancient freedoms, of great causes, of iron sacrifice of body, will and soul, on behalf of human decency and good.' The Bishop's words had the solemn background of the bitter experiences from which Norway had so recently emerged.

15

I too am moved by the same sense of history and heritage as I stand here tonight. At the very beginning I must acknowledge our profound and lasting indebtedness to Great Britain for what she has given to the world in the long years of her life—and especially for the way in which she stood in our stead, as well as her own, against the flooding tides of pagan totalitarianism. I recall Winston Churchill's words giving the theme to one of his recent volumes: 'How the British fought on with hardship their garment—until Soviet Russia and the United States were drawn into the great conflict.'

We may well hope and pray that one great thing which may come out of the Ecumenical Methodist Conference at Oxford will be a deepened realization that we are not two peoples, but one people, with a common destiny, rich and full in proportion to the friendship and co-operation manifest on each side of the Atlantic.

Surely today we hear '*the sound of running history*'.

The Methodists, for whom I speak, also would gladly acknowledge our indebtedness to British Methodism, not alone in the beginnings of our Church in the United States, but even up to this very hour. An emphasis upon a knowledge of our history in our present quadrennium is of far-reaching importance.

One of the most amazing evidences of the sweep of John Wesley's statesmanship was his change of attitude, after the fact of the separation of the American Colonies from England, which was such a profound grief to him. As Bishop McDowell once remarked: 'It must have cost Wesley more than we know to see the movement he had started and the men he had chosen getting beyond him, getting out of hand, so to speak.' Yet he did the creative deed—released his hold upon the new Methodist Episcopal Church, and gave it his blessing with the exhortation, 'that they stand fast in that liberty wherewith God has so strangely made them free.'

Let me add a word concerning our contemporary indebtedness to British Methodism; to your representatives to our General Conferences; to your scholars whose books enrich our thought; to your missionary leaders. I dare not attempt to name them, for in paying tribute I should surely miss some of great significance among the many.

American Methodists would wish me also to say how much we owe to Methodists in all parts of the world, and especially to those distinguished Methodist 'younger churchmen'—the products of the overseas work of Methodism who are the living evidences God has given us of the soundness of the missionary work in which we have been engaged.

I must hasten on to a brief word regarding the state of the Methodist Church in America, with some account of our stewardship.

The Methodist Church is 'the most evenly distributed Church' in the United States. A Methodist church is to be found in almost every county seat town, as well as in every considerable village and at innumerable country cross-roads.

Our last General Conference declared: 'We are a frontier church! we therefore summon The Methodist Church once more to take her position on a frontier' (*Discipline*, 1948, p. 603).

There are many frontiers today which challenge the Methodist Church to be true to its very genius. That of race has already been referred to. Labour is another; our great student bodies yet another; disintegrating family life another; and the geographical challenge is by no means past. The American people are moving westward by the hundreds of thousands. The greatest increase in population is on the Gulf Coast and on the West Coast.

16

The Methodist Church in America has had three special enterprises during the past thirty years: the Centenary inaugurated just before the close of World War I; 'The Crusade for Christ' following World War II in 1945; and now, in the present quadrennium, 'The Advance for Christ and His Church'. All three in their several ways have been churchwide movements for deepening and increasing the spiritual resources of the church, quickening its outreaching evangelization, and supplying the money for carrying on in strength its world-wide work. They give the answer to the question often asked, as to how the union of American Methodism prospers. In all our goals the endeavour has been remarkably successful. Large numbers of people have given their lives to Christ and joined the Church; the Sunday-school membership has been increased; the financial askings have been over-subscribed and paid. In the Centenary Movement, Methodism, North and South, raised $150,000,000. In the Crusade, the new united Church raised $27,000,000 for world rehabilitation and relief, and in addition $24,000,000 for World Service. The Advance for Christ and His Church is now in its fourth year. Figures have just been released for the first three years of the quadrennium. The grand total given by the whole Church for its general benevolence programme in that three-year period has amounted to $57,639,981. This figure is exclusive of Annual Conference benevolences.

Large as the amounts may seem, there is no room for boasting, for our *per capita* giving is far below that of many of the other denominations in the United States. We make the record simply to indicate that we are doing better than we have done previously.

Statistics, while true, do not by any means give an adequate picture. We dare to believe that the Methodist Church has been going deeper into the essential meanings and experience of Christ's redemptive grace. The Advance for Christ and His Church has not been primarily financial. It has involved 'a teaching and preaching endeavour in which Methodists may achieve a deeper understanding of and commitment to our Faith, our Church, our ministry, and our mission; a world-wide advance in which Methodists may share in carrying the Gospel of Christ to the peoples of the earth; a fellowship of suffering and service in which Methodists may participate in bringing relief to the hungry and destitute of war-ravaged lands'.

A word should be spoken concerning our ministry. Our young people are hearing the call of their Church, and most of our Annual Conferences are showing the largest entering classes on trial in our history. There is reason to believe that the shortages in our ministry will be made up. Our theological schools are crowded and our laity have new realization of their importance for training the leadership of our Church.

There is a mounting tide of evangelistic purpose and activity among us.

We face a sadly-divided, war-mad, disbelieving, morally lost world—a world in many particulars like the world of the first century which had lost its nerve and was overwhelmed with panic. Thoughtful men are sharply aware of the 'awful leakage of human value', with self-depreciation and frustration, uncertainty and despair of the possibility of goodness. In addition, there is 'the gathering gloom of modern determinism'. Even within the Church there is the renaissance of an old Calvinism, with the assertion that man is utterly impotent; that Satan is the successful rival of God; and that we must abandon hope for a world in which God's Kingdom cannot come.

We accept Canon Raven's statement that 'the greatest evangelist of our (*sic*) Church, John Wesley, was also the great opponent of determinism'.

17

To that we add these words of our Professor Harris Franklin Rall: 'John Wesley was a preacher and out of his preaching came the Methodist doctrine of man. A sinner? Yes. Wholly dependent on God? Yes. But by the grace of God a person, not a puppet; able to hear, to repent, to choose, to live in saving fellowship with God.'

I must say a brief concluding word regarding the relevance of American Methodism in this year 1951. We have been activists from the beginning and have gone forward on the assumption, solidly based on experience, that God and man must work together to build a decent world and a Christian society. At the first Methodist Conference, held in London, 25th June 1744, John Wesley asked: 'What may we reasonably believe to be God's design in raising up the preachers called Methodists?' On the fourth day those present recorded their answer: 'To reform the nation, more particularly the Church; to spread Scriptural holiness over the land.' Forty years later, at the Christmas Conference in Baltimore, at which the Methodist Episcopal Church was organized, the same question was asked and a like answer given: 'To reform the Continent and to spread Scriptural holiness over these lands.' Too often the first part of the answer is left unquoted, but there it stands as a call 'to serve the present age'—whatever that age may be.

The real peril of the Church today lies not in its doing a perilous thing, but in its drifting on in a kind of conformity to a world which has no peril in it. We must see that our faith is relevant to modern conditions.

Organized religion in the United States and throughout the world is on the spot in these days of unparalleled crisis. If the Church is to be relevant today, it must make it unmistakably clear that it desires to enlist all its members, and any others who will share in the task, in bringing to the judgement seat of Christ all our life—personal, social, economic, and political.

An address was then given by the REV. GADDIEL R. ACQUAAH, *Chairman of the Gold Coast District:*

Today we see fulfilled at this demonstration the dreams and visions of the Methodist Church leaders seventy years ago, that a day would come when the different Methodist Churches throughout the world would come together as one great family. As of old a concourse of people 'from every nation under heaven' gathered at the great Pentecost, even so are we assembled here today from all parts of both hemispheres to prepare for the Ecumenical Conference at Oxford, where we shall 'tarry and wonder' at the great things which, we feel sure, God is going to give to the world through the Methodist Church. Our Meeting here tonight on the eve of the Conference is a Divine challenge to put first things first; to sanctify ourselves in order to become worthy channels through which God the Holy Spirit may pour in abundance His blessings upon the Conference commencing its sittings tomorrow.

We look with gratitude to God 'unto the rock whence we were hewn, and to the hole of the pit whence we were digged'. We look backward and we look forward. We remember our black past and wonder at the great transformations which have taken place. We think of the power of God, who raised our Church both here in England and in other parts of the world practically out of nothing. We look backward to great things accomplished, and we look forward to still greater achievements which by God's grace our Church is destined to make in the Evangelical experience of assured forgiveness of sins, power over sin, and love to all mankind, with the world as the parish of every Methodist Christian.

18

Our world-wide Methodist Family, like a tree, insignificant at its beginning, has become mighty, stretching its branches to the remotest corners of the globe, giving life and light to over 12 million people. We in the Gold Coast pride ourselves upon being members of this world-wide Brotherhood. It is a Brotherhood in which are destroyed such social evils as polygamy with its degradation of African womanhood, intemperance which has played havoc in the national life of my people, gambling and racial discrimination; and the grave responsibility of the Church to the world is brought home to us more vividly than ever. It is a brotherhood in which the sacred and the secular are no longer treated as separate compartments in the life of our Christian community.

Methodism with its insistence on the cultivation of Scriptural Holiness accounts for the sanctified life which becomes the aim and purpose of the people called Methodists, who feel themselves 'called to be saints' here on earth. It is a saintly life in which our African Christians are brought up to draw no line of demarcation between the Ministry and the Laity.

Only yesterday, the Gold Coast with its coastline of 330 miles, its area of 91,000 square miles, about the size of Great Britain, and a population of over 4 million people, had the opprobrium of being called the 'White Man's Grave', owing to the very high death-rate amongst the early European missionaries.

During the past 116 years more than 100 Methodist missionaries have laid down their lives to make possible the spiritual, moral, social, mental well-being we enjoy today as a Church and a people. Both in Church and in State we have been granted a large measure of autonomy, with its implications; and this autonomy opens a new era of aggressive evangelism which is the greatest need of the Church of Christ today. Kumasi, the Capital of Ashanti, once the 'City of Blood' owing to its notoriety in making human sacrifices, is now become the 'Garden City' of West Africa through the transforming influence of the gospel of Christ; but its modern economic prosperity has attracted many from the villages who have lost their ancestral faith and have not yet been won to Christ. So throughout my country our Lord and Master Jesus Christ is called clearly for fervent, definite, and aggressive evangelism. The harvest truly is great and ripe to be garnered, but the reapers are lamentably few. Let us during this Conference pray to the Lord of the harvest to send us more ministers, catechists, teachers, evangelists, and devoted lay workers.

What is engaging the serious attention of all the Gold Coast Churches today through our Christian Council is the life and witness of the Christian community regarding aggressive evangelism, marriage and sex, Christian unity, the ministry, youth, and education. Christian leadership is a much-felt need in education and other departments of life, like the Legislative Assembly, this is become the chief concern of the Methodist people, who feel that any kind of progress without Christian principles as its mainstay spell disaster.

One outstanding problem facing the Gold African is the impact of Western civilization on the cultural heritage of the African Christians in their national customs, usages, and institutions. This calls for properly trained Church leaders capable of instructing newly converted members to understand God as revealed in Christ Jesus and to interpret Him in the light of the African's past and present.

The beauty and glory of this Ecumenical Conference is to see representatives of the older Churches like those of Europe and America sitting side by side with those of the younger Churches, singing together, praying together, talking together, worshipping together on a common platform without any trace of superiority or inferiority, brothers in Christ.

We pray therefore that the outcome of this Conference may be a closer fellowship between the older and younger Churches, so that every Methodist may feel himself a world Christian, and return to his respective Church rededicated to that evangelical calling in which he was first brought to the feet of our Lord and Saviour.

The representative of Methodism in Germany was BISHOP J. W. ERNST SOMMER, *who said:*

I count it a high privilege and an undeserved honour to have been asked to speak to you representatives of ecumenical Methodism here this evening. And yet perhaps I may with all due diffidence and modesty claim an historical justification—by grace, of course—for my standing here. When this great and noble edifice was to be erected, my father was minister at the German Mission in London, and so, as member of the then Wesleyan Methodist Church, with a great number of my German co-members, I also contributed my guinea to the Westminster Central Hall, and there was some talk of allocating one room in this building to the German Methodists in London. May I take my address this evening as a part fulfilment of that half-a-century old aspiration.

It is surely a testimony to God's Grace that this Ecumenical Methodist Conference meets at a time, when, in spite of all the divisive influences of the war and post-war situation, the flood tide of the ecumenical Methodist spirit is visibly rising in Continental European Methodism. Twice last year, in London and Zürich, under the sponsorship of the Relationship with European Churches Committee of the British Conference and the World Peace Commission of the General Conference, have representatives from most European Methodist Churches, including the three European Methodist Bishops, Paul Neff Garber of Geneva, Theodor Arvidson of Scandinavia, and your humble servant of Germany, met together, not indeed to discuss political problems, nor even matters of Church organization, but to exchange experiences and ideas about the work of God and the obligations imposed on the Church of Christ by her Master in the world of today. Our undisturbed harmony in the spirit of perfect love, our agreement in the conception of the central spiritual truths, and our unanimous desire for a closer fellowship were deeply gratifying and encouraging.

Perhaps I ought to add that we do not consider this ecumenical Methodist enterprise as a danger or impediment to the larger undertaking of the World Council of Churches, but rather as a necessary step for promoting this more effectually. How can we expect families successfully to work for the whole if they do not bring to it the uniting force of a warm and potent fellowship in themselves?

The Methodist fellowship has been an all-embracing ecumenical movement from the very beginning. No one can be a genuine follower of the man of the world 'parish' who desired an offensive and defensive alliance with every true Christian unless he too be earnestly striving for the unity of all who love the Lord Jesus Christ!

But here, in speaking of Methodist ecumenicity, I should be grossly neglecting my bounden duty if I did not gladly express the profound and abiding gratitude of the Methodist Church in Germany for all the material, moral, and spiritual help so lovingly rendered to her by the world-wide

20

Methodist Church in the day of her direst need and most glorious opportunity.

There is no doubt that the last five years have been the most richly blessed of all the 120 years during which Methodists have preached the gospel in Germany. Membership has increased by 30 per cent, Sunday-school enrolment by more than 50 per cent and the number of Sunday-school teachers by 70 per cent. The advance has been greatest in the Russian Zone, where membership has gone up by 41 per cent and there are a number of Sunday-schools with more than 1,000 children.

On the other hand, the value of church property destroyed by the war is estimated at $9 million. The currency reform has annihilated all savings, insurance receipts, reserve funds, and endowments. We are happy to say that industrial production has developed remarkably during the last two years. But as prices are going up and up and salaries and wages are keeping low, the majority of the German people are still poor. Nevertheless, we felt ourselves compelled to rebuild our churches when people were so eager to hear the gospel. In Stuttgart, for instance, where we have five churches and 1,500 members, the only preaching room left to us was a vestry into which we could hardly squeeze fifty people. German Methodists, out of their poverty, raised twice as much money as they received from Methodists abroad; even so, they have had to incur crippling debts and, as money is so scarce, are forced to pay ruinous rates of interest, up to 12 per cent.

But the meeting this evening is surely meant to be a Methodist love-feast, so I want to tell you three experiences of God's goodness, illustrating how He is using Methodists in Germany.

(1) The Methodist chaplains of the American and British occupation armies have performed a wonderful service of international reconciliation and proved genuine Christian brothers to us. One of them, an American probationer, had not been able to be received into full connexion into his conference for six years, because his military duties had prevented him from attending. I asked for his Bishop's cable-consent to transfer him into the South-west Germany Conference, and got it. So I transferred a Captain of the occupation Army into our Conference and had him admitted into full connexion by an unanimous standing vote, after he had answered the questions prescribed since Wesley's time, in the German language before a congregation of over 1,000 German Methodists. There was not a dissentient voice. Was he not a brother in Christ? All were delighted that the Methodist Church could thus overleap all national barriers and the effects of war.

(2) Three years ago a new movement arose among the State Churches, called the Evangelical Day of the Church. It conducts an annual week of mass meetings, bringing together about 200,000 Protestants. Its objective is to mobilize the laymen of the Churches and bring the influence of the Church to bear upon public life. The president is a layman, Dr v. Thadden, a product of the Student Christian Movement. This year the meetings took place in Berlin, and on Sunday, 15th July, a sermon was preached in every Protestant Church in Berlin on the same text: 'Romans 8[38, 39]. Nothing shall be able to separate us from the love of God.' The Bishop of the Methodist Church was asked to preach in the chief Lutheran church of Berlin, the Marienkirche, situated in the Russian Sector, the Church of Bishop Dibelius and Dean Grüber. In the vestry the young Lutheran clergyman who was to conduct the service suggested having a Communion service after the sermon. I looked at him in amazement. He smiled: 'I am a staunch Lutheran.' I replied: 'Then we are well

21

matched. I am a staunch Methodist.' So we had the Communion service, the Lutheran clergyman, the Methodist District Superintendent of Berlin, and the Methodist Bishop joining in administering the sacrament to about 600 people of all Protestant denominations.

(3) I freely and frequently cross the boundary from the Western to the Eastern Zone and back again. I preach the same sermons in East and West and make no concessions whatever. Last November, on my way out, the Communist policeman, suggesting that I might be a political agitator, went through all the papers in my attaché case. Finally, he picked out three typed sermons of mine and read them through with a care that probably has never been meted out to my sermons on any previous occasion. I sat delighted. It is not every minister who is privileged to preach three sermons at a time to a Communist policeman. When he had finished he was a changed man. Before gruff and harsh; now friendly and helpful.

Oh, that this Oxford Conference might bring us all closer together, in order that the world-wide Church may become a living reality and help us to unite without formal let or hindrance in preaching by word and deed that for which every human being consciously or unconsciously is hungry, in this poor world of ours so tortured by fear and hate, the gospel of the all-conquering love of Christ.

Speaking for India, the REV. CHRISTA C. PANDE, *Chairman of the Bengal District, said:*

I bring to you the greetings of the Church in India. We have assembled in this gathering to demonstrate to the world in ferment that in Jesus Christ alone lies the basis for the peace of the world and goodwill among nations. From different parts of the world we have gathered here in the name of our Redeeming Lord, united in the family of God, children with differing cultural heritage, language, race, and nationality. For nearly four months I have been richly blessed with my fellowship with the Methodist people in this country, and before I return, as an Indian, I have to say Methodism has something worth sharing.

The Christian Church in British India was sadly divided into different denominations, but with our independence the Christian community within the same denominations, with common culture and common language, were divided as Christians of two different autonomous sovereign states. The 9½ millions of Indian Christians were separated as 1 million Pakistani Christians and 8½ million Indian Christians. God has used the Church in these two sovereign states to remain loyal to the state to which they belong and yet to rejoice in the unity that the Church has in our Redeeming Lord. We stand to proclaim the Gospel of peace and love in our present independent countries, and to witness to the world also that in Christ alone is found universal brotherhood.

In British India the Christian Church was only a foreign religion. Both the Moslems and the Hindus suspected the Western missionaries as agents of the Western powers. The Indian Christians were suspected or were considered as the satellites of the foreign rulers because of our intimate connexion with the missionaries from the West. Today, both in Pakistan and in India, the Pakistani Christians and the Indian Christians are the children of the soil. The Christians are an influential minority community in the two sovereign states.

Pakistan is an Islamic state and, as such, the Christian Church will have the same freedom and opportunity as is granted to the Christians in

22

any Islamic states today. The door to evangelize the Moslem in an Islamic state is almost a closed door, though the State will in no way interfere with the preaching of the Gospel to non-Moslems.

India is a secular state; every religion has freedom of expression and equal opportunities subject to the law of the country. The Indian Government has Moslems, Christians, Sikhs, and Hindus in the State administration as equal partners and colleagues. The missionary activities are not suspected in any way, nor is there any restriction to our evangelistic work.

The Christian schools, colleges, and hospitals have a great opportunity in India to witness through service, the Christ's way of life, and the Church to draw men into the saving experience through our Lord. For over fifty years, the responsive group to the gospel message has been the depressed class, the untouchables of the Hindu communities, the primitive races with animistic religion.

Can the thinking Indians in my country build up a casteless and a classless society without Christ? The Church is the witness to the solution of our national problems today. The thinking Indians, the Hindus, and the Moslems in India are becoming gradually responsive to the gospel.

Both in India and Pakistan the Church of Christ is sadly divided in different denominations. The Gospel of Christ in India must be preached by one United Church to the heterogeneous communities of India. The divided Church has no message for the educated Indians and Pakistanis. The Christian Church in India must unite and there must not be any complacency in getting about it. It is a matter of necessity.

United Methodism alone is no reply to India's problems. In India you have a population nearly equal to the population of the whole of America and Africa. For this greater gain we must be prepared to make a greater sacrifice; to get together into one organic union all the major Christian denominations.

There is another problem—the ecumenical character of all the younger Churches. The relationship of the younger, the receiving Churches has grown intimate with the older Churches, particularly with the sending Churches, but the same intimacy and fellowship has not developed between the younger Churches themselves. India, Africa, Burma, and Ceylon should have an interchange of national missionaries. The Church must be ecumenical, and we should not lose this opportunity of having nationals from the younger Churches in active missionary work in the older Churches, nor should we miss the opportunity to send to India an African, a Burman, and a West Indian to work side by side other Western missionaries, and for Indians to go to the West Indies and Burma and Ceylon.

Finally, we have an economic problem. The Church has gathered millions of converts from different social and economic levels. Every convert has to pay a tremendous price to become a Christian. Every Christian Indian has to start life afresh from scratch. The majority of the converts are also from the lowest economic and social level, and many are illiterates. This makes fellowship within the Church very difficult. Within the Church we have a vast majority of Christians living on a most degraded economic level which Christ can never approve. The Church has to help to readjust the economic situation of the Church in Pakistan and India.

There is also the problem of the growing Communism in the country and also within the Church, especially among the young people. These young people have suffered, and they see the suffering of their brethren within the Church, due to the unfair distribution of the resources of God.

We shall gain everything for our Lord if we are prepared to share and build up the Church in India and Pakistan on a better and stronger economic, social, and spiritual level and experience.

We must evangelize. We must be out to help in the national reconstruction. We must bring the Gospel to the rich and also to the poor, to the educated and also to the uneducated. We must make the Church an example of Christian fellowship with a better economic and social condition for all within the Church.

The Pakistan and India of today is the gateway to the East and the Far East. We win India and Pakistan to win the Far East for our Lord also. May God help the deliberations of the Conference—and guide and bless you all.

The concluding speech was made by Dr J. B. Webb, *Ex-President of the South African Conference:*

Since the last Ecumenical Conference in Springfield, Massachusetts, at which I was privileged to speak on 'Sixteen Years of Methodism', great changes have taken place in the internal economy and structure of the Union of South Africa. Almost exactly a year ago we lost by death the last of the founding fathers of the Union, and in many respects the greatest of them—General Smuts. The party which he represented and for so many years led with dignity and distinction was thus deprived of a man whose shoes it was impossible to fill. His political lieutenant, and in some ways a man as brilliant as the General himself, had died a year or so previously. I refer to Jan Hofmeyr, one of the greatest and most literal sons of South Africa which the country has so far produced. The present leader of the United Party, now in opposition following the Parliamentary Elections of 1948, is, however, a man who has won his spurs, and together with him is a band of youngish, ardent politicians who are endeavouring to follow out the principles of a liberal Christian democratic tradition in circumstances of gathering difficulty. Meantime, the Nationalist Party, under the leadership of Dr D. F. Malan, with Mr N. C. Havenga as his deputy, has settled down firmly in the saddle of government, and in four successive Parliamentary sessions has given to the country an increasingly clearer conception of the content of its prime policy of *apartheid*, involving what is called the *baasskap* (the supremacy) of the European, and the preservation of white supremacy in the sub-continent of Africa, and the strict segregation of white and non-white in every sphere of the communal life—social, economic, and political. The form and content of this policy of *apartheid* have been made clear in the following measures which have been placed upon the Statute Book:

The Group Areas Act, which, when fully implemented, will have the effect of dividing the whole country into white, black, Coloured, and Indian areas. Into these areas no infiltration will be permitted by racial groups other than the one for which the area is zoned, save by permission of the authorities administering the Act.

The Representation of Non-Europeans Act, which provides for the representation in Parliament on a separate voters' roll of non-Europeans in the Cape and Natal Provinces. The main effect of this Act is to remove the Coloured voters of the Cape Province from the Common Voters' Roll.

The Immorality Amendment Act: which makes intermarriage between white and non-white illegal, and declares to be illegal such unions as have already been contracted between white and non-white.

24

Meantime, the laws already in existence which govern the movements of Africans from the rural to the urban areas are being much more strictly enforced than heretofore, and Africans from extra-Union areas are not being permitted to enter the Union except under the most closely circumscribed conditions.

To be fair, I must present one or two other facts. If the premises of the present Government's policy are accepted, then its actions are perfectly logical. The members of the Cabinet are without exception members of one or other branch of the three Dutch Reformed Churches, which are Calvanistic in broad theological outlook. This Church has declared that on Scriptural, ethnological, and historical grounds there can be no equality between white and black, and that there is Scriptural authority for the continuing and unchanging subservience of the latter, who are destined to be the hewers of wood and the drawers of water for ever. No limit, however, will be placed upon their development according to their ability to develop and within their own sphere. But there can never be any thought of their selling their labour, skill, or proficiency in the open market and in competition with the white man.

Further, it is contended that if *apartheid* works to the disadvantage of the non-European in some respects, and in some spheres, it works to his distinct advantage in others. It is designed, for example, to put a period to the exploitation by the white man of the black man in the latter's declared area of domicile and work. Moreover, the exponents of this doctrine of *apartheid* point out that although their detractors emphasize the essential inequity of the doctrine, and argue that it is oppressive in its application and working out, it remains a fact that, if they were permitted to do so, Africans from outside the Union would pour into it, and that, even under the present severe restrictions, there is a constant trickle of illegal infiltration on their part.

Meantime, the whole of the Union is undergoing an industrial revolution of the first magnitude. A whole new area of gold-mining has opened up, involving the expenditure of millions of money; base metals and minerals are being exploited on an unprecedented scale; raw materials urgently required in the interests of world strategy are being asked for and made available; and secondary industries are being established in many parts of the country which hitherto have been peacefully agricultural and pastoral. This revolution has involved great and swift movements of population, with the consequent problems of transport, housing, and the like. In short, the country has overgrown itself almost overnight, as it were, and the new clothes to fit it have not been manufactured quickly enough.

It is against this background that our Church, along with other denominations, has to do its work. The task is not easy, because, as you will readily understand, all that has happened and that is now taking place has created an atmosphere of suspicion and dull, brooding resentment against the white man which must sooner or later find expression. So far that expression has taken the form of sporadic outbursts of mass violence, following incidents which in themselves were not serious, but which proved to be the spark that touched off the explosion in a highly explosive situation. Another expression has taken shape in a developing African nationalism, which, within the orbit of the Church, has resulted in a multiplicity of Church denominations and sects which own allegiance to no European parent body. These separatist Churches are growing in numbers and rendering the work of the well-established churches very much more difficult, especially in that the ethical and moral standards of some of them are very low, and are little more than old heathenish practices

25

with a veneer of highly emotional and ecstatic religious fervour. The religious realm is the only one in which the African can really express himself without let or hindrance, and he takes full advantage of that fact.

It will be readily understood that in the circumstances our Church, the largest missionary Church in the country, with over 1 million members and adherents out of a total population of 12½ million, has a great responsibility, but I am happy to be able to state that within our own fellowship we have no serious trouble. Our people are loyal, and they trust us. The trust indeed is sometimes pathetic. They believe that we can do far more to assist in the general situation than in fact we can.

Added to this, in one field of our work at least we face difficulties of another order. In Portuguese East Africa we have an old work, going back some sixty to seventy years. Portuguese nationalism, however, closely linked as it is with the State religion of Roman Catholicism, has confronted us with many new problems. The present Cardinal of Mozambique has publicly stated that it is his avowed intention of closing down all Protestant missions in the territory within the next thirty years, and already conditions for the continuance of our day-schools have become so onerous that, unless help beyond our own resources is provided, we shall be compelled to close down.

Perplexed and discomfited at times, frustrated and uncertain at other times, we are not by any means defeatist. The Methodist Church has had far greater problems to solve and difficulties to face, and it has won through. History will repeat itself in this regard.

Do not condemn us or criticize from the standpoint of insufficient information. I hope that as a result of this Conference, some of you will be moved to come over and see us in our natural habitat. We should welcome visits from representative Methodism outside our own borders. Above all, go on praying for us.

26

EIGHTH
ECUMENICAL METHODIST CONFERENCE

OXFORD

FIRST DAY
Tuesday 28th August 1951

WELCOME MEETING

THE DELEGATES were welcomed in the Sheldonean Theatre, Oxford, on Tuesday evening, 28th August 1951, at 8 o'clock. The Rev. Dr W. F. Howard, F.B.A., Joint President of the Ecumenical Council, presided, and Bishop Ivan Lee Holt, of the Methodist Church of America, replied as Joint President to the greetings from British Methodism.

The Bishop of Manchester (Dr Greer), speaking for the Church of England, welcomed the Conference to Oxford. The Moderator of the Free Church Federal Council, Dr A. D. Harcus, brought the greetings of the Free Churches, and the Rev. J. Hamblin Parsons, Chairman of the Oxford District, represented Oxford Methodists.

This first official gathering of the Conference opened with the singing of the traditional hymn, 'O for a thousand tongues to sing', and then knelt in prayer, led by the Rev. Dr R. Newton Flew, Principal of Wesley House, Cambridge.

The Rev. Dr Harold Roberts, Secretary of this British Section of the Council, read His Majesty King George the Sixth's reply to the Loyal Address which had been sent on behalf of the Conference.

The Chairman, the REV. DR W. F. HOWARD, *F.B.A., Joint President of the Ecumenical Methodist Council, then delivered his address of welcome:*

Bishop Ivan Lee Holt, My Lord Bishop of Manchester, Moderator of the Federal Council of Free Churches, Methodists from every continent and islands of the seas, we bid you welcome to this opening session of the eighth decennial Conference of World Methodism. Greetings will be given on behalf of the Church of England, of the Free Churches of this country and of the Methodists of this city and district. My duty this evening is rather to remind you of the purpose for which we have come together from the ends of the earth, and to look forward to the programme

which awaits us in these addresses and discussions during the coming days.
For years before the outbreak of the recent war Oxford had been deter-
mined as the place of meeting in 1941. It was here that the 'People called
Methodists' received their nickname, even as the wits and wags of Antioch
coined another title for the followers of Jesus Christ in the first age of
Christianity. As I shall try to show in a few minutes, the first group of
Oxford Methodists prepared the way for that world-wide branch of the
Christian Church which we represent in this place tonight. There were no
doubt other reasons which turned the eyes of many across the seas to the
magic charm of the city of the dreaming spires. History and romance are
interwoven in the name of Oxford. The attraction proved irresistible. But
war intervened, and six years after the date which should have seen us here,
America came to our aid and invited us to meet four years ago at Springfield, Massachusetts, where we were welcomed with—I dare not say royal,
but with regally republican hospitality. Now once more the dream has
come to us, this time to be fulfilled.

You have come to this country on a holy pilgrimage. Before you return
to the lands from which you came, you will have visited many places of
historic interest to every well-instructed Methodist. Let me name a few,
taking each one as a symbol of one aspect of our religious inheritance and
responsibility. I must start with Epworth, that little old town in the Isle
of Axholme where Samuel and Susannah Wesley reared their large family.
You will, of course, want to see the churchyard and the place where the
famous Evangelist stood on his father's tombstone, because his father's
former curate and now his successor as Rector refused him the pulpit in
which he had preached so often in other years. But that is not the significant place to see at Epworth. This is rather the Rectory adjoining the
church. The home in which Wesley was born was burnt down, and everyone knows the story of the way in which the little boy of six was rescued
from the blazing bedroom, 'a brand plucked from the burning'. The
present Rectory is the home where that remarkable mother taught her
children to read and pray and study the Bible. There it was that they were
instructed in 'pure religion breathing household laws'. That Rectory
stands for the vital importance of family piety, and no study of Methodism
can ignore that factor in the providential training of John Wesley.

We must pass over the years spent at Charterhouse and come to
Oxford. It would be easy in this city to recall 'the last enchantments
of the Middle Ages which Oxford sheds around us', or, especially in view
of her rejection of John Wesley, to remember that she has been described
as 'the home of lost causes'. But we shall think of her as the birthplace of
the Holy Club, in which the regulated life of prayer and Bible study and of
works of mercy was practised 'as ever in the great Taskmaster's eyes'.
Let no one disparage those years of self-discipline in which the finely
tempered steel was fashioned into a sword for use in the battle of the Lord
against the powers of darkness. There are those who talk or write as
though Wesley's religious life began in the summer of 1738. It is true that
then a warmth of heart and an enlightenment of mind emancipated him
from many inhibitions. But without the stern training of those years of
preparation he would never have endured to the end the strain of fifty
years of incessant travel and toil. Long years after, in 1772, he wrote to
his brother Charles: 'I often cry out, Let me be again an Oxford Methodist!
I am often in doubt whether it would not be best for me to resume all my
Oxford rules, great and small. I did then walk closely with God and
redeem the time.' No one who looks into the private diaries of these
years, so skilfully deciphered by Nehemiah Curnock in the Standard

Edition of the *Journal*, can fail to trace the providential hand that guided the young zealot through this preparatory discipline. There was yet one more experience to pass through before the day of full liberation. Georgia, with its painful lessons of frustration and failure followed, and then we come to London.

It is disappointing for the pilgrim to find no relic of the epoch-making events of Whit-week, 1738. We cannot stand in the room in Aldersgate Street where, as one was reading from Luther's Preface to the Epistle to the Romans, Wesley's heart was strangely warmed. For us Aldersgate is a date rather than a place. It was there that 'the dungeon flamed with light', there that he could say.

> 'My chains fell off, my heart was free,
> I rose, went forth, and followed Thee.'

Later London was to become the headquarters of the Methodist Societies, first in the old Ordnance Foundery rebuilt to serve the needs of the Society; later in Wesley's Chapel in the City Road, which still stands as the Mecca of Methodism.

But Bristol, not London, was to see Wesley changed from an ecclesiastic into an evangelist. It will always baffle the psychologist to explain how it was that this austere and scholarly cleric, the very pink of propriety and a paragon of orthodoxy, achieved such instantaneous success when he preached to those drink-sodden and semi-barbarous colliers at Kingswood. We can only say that the mighty Spirit of God took his words and carried them right to the hearts of his hearers. Whitefield's example was at first a scandal to him. 'I could scarce reconcile myself at first to this strange way of preaching in the fields . . . having been all my life (till very lately) so tenacious of every point relating to decency and order, that I should have thought the saving of souls almost a sin if it had not been done in a church.' Yet two days later he writes in his *Journal*: 'At four in the afternoon I submitted to be more vile, and proclaimed in the highways the glad tidings of salvation, speaking from a little eminence in a ground adjoining to the city to about three thousand people.' That site was built over long ago, but Hannam Mount in Kingswood, where he preached to about 1,500 a few days later, has been set apart recently as a site of historic interest, with a suitable record of its religious significance. But the most important memorial of all is the New Room at Bristol, the first Methodist meeting room (afterwards chapel) in the world to be built. Thanks to the generosity of the late Mr Edmund Lamplough, this was secured and refurnished exactly as it was in Wesley's lifetime. No Methodist on pilgrimage in this country should omit this sacred shrine from his itinerary. Here he will see the rooms used by John and Charles Wesley, by Adam Clarke and other of Wesley's most trusted helpers. If Hannam Mount stands as the visible symbol of Wesley's aggressive evangelism, the New Room in the Horsefair stands for the constructive training that was given both to the members of the United Societies and to those heroic pioneers, the early Methodist Preachers. It has been customary to disparage these men as little more than illiterate. There could be no greater mistake. Some were sent by Wesley to receive education at the school which he founded at Kingswood; others went through a rigorous course of instruction at the New Room. There is no more apostolic career in the entire history of Methodism than that of Francis Asbury, born and bred within a few miles of Birmingham. Many years ago the late Dr John F. Goucher, of Baltimore, showed me in his library two well-thumbed books bound in stout leather. They were the Hebrew Bible which Asbury carried about with him in his saddle-bags. Where did that blacksmith's apprentice acquire that knowledge? It was almost certainly in the New Room at Bristol that Wesley started him in learning the elements of Hebrew grammar. (I wonder, my Lord Bishop, how many of Wesley's contemporaries on the episcopal bench could have read a sentence from those volumes!) Bristol, then, stands for evangelism; but intelligent evangelism. Those early Preachers were well grounded in the Bible, and the course of reading prescribed for them covers a very wide range of subjects. Of course, that curriculum would seem hopelessly out of date for our modern needs, but it represented a high standard of attainment in the eighteenth century. The Methodist Preacher was expected to love the Lord his God with all his heart, but also with all his mind.

We have time to think of only one more of these shrines. If you can travel so far north as Newcastle-upon-Tyne, visit the Orphan House. It was not only Wesley's resting-place when in those parts, but also a symbol of his zeal for the social application of the gospel. Wesley was not a Lutheran scholar, and many of his criticisms of the great reformer would be repudiated by those who have a wider knowledge of his writings. But we know that he was indignant with Luther for referring to the Epistle of James as 'a right strawy epistle'. No doubt one thing that endeared that Epistle to Wesley was the description it gives of pure religion and undefiled. Wesley was always eager 'to care for the widow and orphan in their affliction'. It would take far too long to give a list of the various activities in which the social conscience of early Methodism was expressed. No study of the Methodist tradition can leave that side of Wesley's work out of account.

Epworth, Oxford, London, Bristol, Newcastle—Family Religion, the Discipline of the Soul, Christian Assurance, Effective Evangelism, Social Christianity—all these belong to our tradition. Wesley was a man of his own age, even if sometimes in advance of it. It is worthwhile to remember the constant struggle between the conservative and the radical in his nature. He put all things to the proof that he might hold fast that which was good. At the same time, his life is one long story of the discarding of one prejudice after another. Someone once said: 'Mr Wesley, like a strong and skilful rower, looked one way while every stroke of his oar took him in the opposite direction.'

During the coming days we in this Conference shall be recalling the great things in the Methodist tradition, all that gave confidence and courage to our fathers in their faith and their discipleship, their witness and their worship, their service to God and to man. But ours must be no blind idolatry of the past. We wait for the impulse and the guidance of the Spirit of the living God, to follow where the Lord points the way.

Greetings from the Church of England

Greetings from the Archbishop of Canterbury were conveyed by Dr Greer, the Bishop of Manchester. After referring to the Archbishop's interest and initiative in Christian Reunion, Dr Greer spoke of the place occupied by the Church of England in the Reformation tradition. Anglicanism was a part of the Methodist tradition. 'You Methodists are our first cousins', said the Bishop. 'It was under our roof-tree that the father of Methodism died.'

Speaking about tradition, particularly in its relation to the reunion of the Churches he said that the very nature of the movement compelled them to concentrate on their several positions. The desire of so many people had been seen in Methodist Union, in the Church of Scotland, in South India, and in the establishment of the World Council of Churches. Linked up with the desire for unity was this natural concentration on their particular traditions, which tended to create a polemical attitude to ecclesiastical traditions that were alien to their own. They had been forced by events to become much more ecclesiastically self-conscious. This attitude might hold up reunion abroad, and lead eventually to a revolt among the younger Churches. As Christians, we are directed to preach the gospel—not Paul, Apollos, John Hooker, or John Wesley. 'Tradition', said Dr Greer, 'is like capital—useful in moderation, but in excess a burden that fetters free movement.' Today, the whole Christian Church must move quickly and decisively in a world torn by war and nationalism. Christians will never be able to bear the witness they would wish, unless they stand visibly together. Many recent reunion discussions had convinced him of three major facts: First, that the *faith* of the Church should take precedence over the *order* of the Church. Second, that the gap dividing historic Christian communions must be regarded as a schism within the family. In the third place, self-conscious denominationalism would never bring them closer together.

Message from the Free Churches

The Moderator of the Free Church Federal Council, Dr A. D. Harcus, spoke of the debt the whole country owed to Methodism. He felt that fellowship between the various Christian communions was of vital importance in furthering fellowship between the nations. Sincere friendly relationships in the Churches could form a solid rock of friendship in the world itself. Perhaps in years to come, when the inner history of the days in which we were living was written, it might be said that one of the forces which made for peace was this gathering in Oxford which had brought men and women from all over the world to renew their vows in Christ and to reconsecrate their brotherhood.

* * * * *

At this point in the meeting, the Rev. Frank H. Cumbers (Book Steward, London) presented the Bishop of Manchester and the Moderator with copies of Henry Carter's book, *The Methodist Heritage*.

Greetings from Oxford Methodists

The Chairman of the Oxford and Gloucester District, the Rev. J. Hamblin Parsons, in expressing the welcome of all Methodists in the area, said: 'You come with us to pool resources. Merely to crowd people together is not fellowship. But we are delighted to have you because you are not come to create an illusion of strength; but you are come to apply your minds to the root problems of today.'

* * * * *

31

After these addresses of welcome, the delegates received Dr John R. Mott, one of the great pioneers of the Ecumenical Movement. The applause which greeted him was witness, not only to his past achievement, but also to the place he has in the heart of the World Church.

Bishop Holt Replies

In thanking those who had given the addresses of welcome, Bishop Ivan Lee Holt referred to the heritage shared by Anglicans and Free Churchmen, and the prospects of a larger union. In paying tribute to the work of Dr Howard, he spoke of the effort to make the ecumenical Methodist movement something much more than an opportunity for fellowship and speech-making. The Conference was not merely an occasion for British and American Methodists to meet. Already they had divided the world into twenty-four areas and had begun the elimination of the distinction between Eastern and Western Methodism. He hoped that the Conference at Oxford would extend the work begun at Springfield in 1947. Certain things should now be done. Standing committees, with definite programmes, should be created. There should be a committee which could meet annually, and a permanent secretariat in London and New York. 'We must bring about a closer co-operation of all members of the Methodist family', he said. 'Thereby we can make a contribution to peace among the nations.'

．　　　．　　　．　　　．　　　．

Further messages of greeting were read by Dr Harold Roberts. They came from the World Council of Churches, the British Council of Churches, the Bishop of Oxford, who regretted that circumstances prevented his attending in person, and from the Bangor Youth Conference.

The meeting was almost over, but by no means the least impressive movement came when this company of Methodists of many races from all over the world rose to sing their closing hymn 'Captain of Israel's host, and Guide'. It was a committal of the Conference, and all whom it represented, to a pilgrimage and a crusade. The Bishop of Manchester pronounced the Benediction.

SECOND DAY

Wednesday August 29th 1951

FIRST DAILY SESSION

THE FIRST of the daily sessions opened with morning devotions conducted by the Rev. Moses O. Dada, O.B.E., the Chairman of the Western Nigeria District. An address was delivered by Bishop Paul Martin of Little Rock, Arkansas.

Taking as his subject 'Compelling Confidence', Bishop Martin analysed the paralysing fear which is a characteristic of the modern world. Pessimism and uncertainty can be overcome by Christian faith. Wrong conceptions of God and of the Christian life are fatal to such faith. When men identify themselves with an eternal purpose, they develop a sense of security and confidence. We need a faith great enough to look beyond our own relief and triumph to something bigger. 'This is the victory that overcometh the world, even our faith.'

* * * * * *

The morning session opened under the presidency of Bishop Ivan Lee Holt, who read further messages of greeting from the Lutheran World Federation, the World Convention of the Disciples of Christ, the Baptist World Alliance, and the World Presbyterian Alliance. Five addresses were then given by speakers representing Methodism in Britain, America, Australia, South Africa, and Ceylon. The subject was *Methodist Traditions* and the general purpose of the speeches was to reveal the underlying unity which exists in Methodism in every part of the world, and in all its diversity of expression.

METHODIST TRADITIONS

I. BRITISH METHODISM

An address delivered by the REV. DR HAROLD ROBERTS *of Richmond College, Surrey, England:*

The first fact about British Methodism that should be mentioned is its fundamental unity. Throughout its history, there has been evident a specific ethos fostered by its doctrines and discipline, but not to be equated with either or both. We miss our way if we identify the distinctive nature of Methodism with the doctrine of Assurance or Christian Perfection, or again with a particular system of Church government. Wesley had no serious quarrel with the contemporary theology of Protestantism, if we exclude the Calvinistic doctrine of election or with existing systems of Church government. In these matters, he was the friend of all and the enemy of none. What created and sustained Methodism was the rediscovery in personal and corporate experience of the Grace of God manifested in the person and work of Christ and liberated by the power of the

33

Holy Spirit. It is this fact that accounts for the unreserved rejection by Wesley of the Calvinistic doctrine of election. The reassessment of Calvinism, long overdue, should not lead us to underestimate the gravity of the issue which Calvinism, particularly in hardened form in which it appeared in the eighteenth century, presented to Wesley, or to follow the fashion affected by writers of dissertations for doctorates and argue that the controversy was due to misunderstanding on both sides. Wesley may not have been a technical theologian, but he perceived in the light of his own experience and his study of the New Testament that the beginning and end of any understanding of God and His dealings with man lie in the doctrine that God is Sovereign Love. This basic conviction gave to his theology a unity and a lucidity sadly lacking in more pretentious systems, ancient and modern. It provoked a concern for human needs and a sensitiveness to political and social issues affecting the physical and moral welfare of mankind. The passion for evangelism evinced by Methodists everywhere was born of the triumph of the Universal Gospel of Grace in personal experience, and found expression in missionary work at home and abroad. Methodism accepted almost from the outset a world-wide mission. When conditions in the Church at home cause discouragement, it is good to turn to what God has wrought overseas through the various branches of Methodism.

What kept the sections into which Methodism divided within the one family and made possible the healings of its divisions was the common emphasis on the grace of God available for all through the life and work of Christ and attested by the unceasing activity of the Holy Spirit. Of course, they all observed the sacraments of baptism and the Lord's Supper; they sang the same hymns and adopted in the main the same system of government. But their fundamental unity is to be traced to a common loyalty to the Gospel of the Grace of God. ' 'Tis love, 'tis love, Thou diedst for me.'

It was inevitable that certain issues affecting the constitution of Methodism should eventually demand attention. First, it was necessary to determine whether Methodism was to remain a society within the Church of England or fulfil the functions of a separate branch of the Catholic Church. Secondly, there was the question of the place of the laity in the worship and government of the Church. As members of the Fellowship of Grace, which is the Church, converts claimed the privilege of expressing their newly-found freedom in the administration of the society to which they belonged. Thirdly, when it became obvious that with the passage of time few Methodists would live and die as members of the Established Church, matters of organization came to the fore. There were those who had no wish to see Methodism settling down and becoming involved in the intricacies of a vast organization that might easily obscure the purpose for which its people had been raised.

Each of the divisions of British Methodism, however much they may have been affected by personal considerations and in some cases unbelievable folly, is to be attributed to one or more of these causes. Behind the agitations of Alexander Kilham and his party which led to the establishment of the Methodist New Connexion was the desire to build the Methodist societies on a more democratic basis. What came to be known as Primitive Methodism was an authentic expression of the Methodist witness to the subordination of Church Order to the supreme task of evangelization. Two other features are noteworthy in the contribution of Primitive Methodism. First, the place given to women as local preachers and for a time as itinerant preachers, and, secondly the leadership exercised in the working classes by local preachers. The Bible Christians, like the Primitive Methodists, were fearful of the bondage of a highly organized Church, and devoted themselves with apostolic zeal to the needs of the people of Devon and Cornwall. They also provided abundant opportunity for the service of women as an integral part of the life of the Church. The Society of Friends had numerous contacts with the Bible Christians, as with the Independent Methodists, who by their simple witness, sober behaviour, and repudiation of a separated salaried ministry attracted those Quakers who were recoiling from Quietism.

God is not the author of division, but He is able to make divisions the occasion for the advancing reign of Christ. This reflection is inescapable as we review the history of the branches to which we have referred. The causes of the great disruption of 1849 which led to the rise of the Methodist Free Church are another story. Even when we remember the political ferment of the time and the justice of the demand for greater lay administration in Conference and the circuits which incidentally Jabez Bunting initiated, there can be no excuse for the denial of the spirit of Christian charity on both sides illustrated by the *Fly Sheets*, and the methods no less defensible used by the Wesleyan Conference to discover the culprits. One hundred thousand members withdrew, and among them were men and women of unquestionable devotion and indomitable energy whose liberal and adventurous outlook was sorely needed to counteract the conservatism of the Wesleyan body. The reforms later introduced by Dr Rigg and Hugh Price Hughes into Wesleyan Methodism represent some of the lessons which disaster and division had taught.

Nevertheless, British Methodism never lost its essential unity. The recognition of that unity, combined with a growing penitence and for past betrayals and the pressure of events, created an appetite for the healing of divisions. The Bible Christians, the Methodist New Connexion, and the United Free Methodists led the way in 1907, and in 1932 the Wesleyan, Primitive, and United Methodists united in one body. To our regret, the Wesleyan Reform Union, which resolved to adhere to its own system of Church government, and the Independent Methodists felt unable to enter the Union.

The three bodies united in 1932 subscribed to a constitution which affirmed the inheritance of the Apostolic Faith, the fundamental principles of the historic creeds, and the Protestant Reformation. They resolved to commit themselves afresh to the spreading of Scriptural holiness throughout the land.

Within the framework of the agreed constitution, there is room for freedom of interpretation. It would be unreasonable to expect or desire now Methodist Union has been effected, that we should all sweetly think and speak the same. Each of the Uniting bodies brought to the Union a certain emphasis or approach that might well be described as a tradition. While all Methodists rejoice in the fellowship of the British Free Churches, the influence of the Free Church tradition is more marked upon some of us than upon others. Some Methodists distinguish sharply between the external and the internal in religion. They may find themselves in closer sympathy with the Society of Friends in regard to the Sacraments and the ministry than with many of their fellow Methodists or Free Churchmen. Episcopacy as a separate ministerial order they would repudiate not because they dislike bishops—indeed, they might show them far greater respect than the bishops receive from their own clergy—but because they believe that the introduction of episcopacy would make for legalism and that its acceptance involves the doctrine of apostolic succession in its

35

neat or hydrated form. There are, of course, other views represented among us which, as with those we have mentioned, reveal the influence of background and denominational history. None of us would equate faith with order or go further than St Thomas Aquinas, who denied that God is bound by His sacraments. Some would, however, regard order as sacramental, and although they would not attempt to grade the gifts of God, the sacraments for them are the unique expression and instruments of His grace. They cherish the sacrament of Holy Communion as the consummation of Christian worship, and hold that the gospel which it proclaims is the ground of our belief in the sacramental character of life as a whole. Further, the affection of the Wesleys for the Anglican Church, which not even arrogant and harsh treatment could destroy, still survives in Methodism, even though the ways and utterances of some sections of that Church are profoundly disturbing.

These differing approaches are found within the context of a common allegiance to the Gospel of Grace. Too often they have been isolated or unduly emphasized instead of being brought into a living synthesis creative of a distinctive approach to the Christian Faith. Let them grow together till the harvest, provided that the views of one party are not invariably branded as tares by the other. We need to bear in mind that the coming of Methodist Union does not mean that the participating Churches have jumped out of their historical skin and affected a rigid uniformity of belief and practice. It was Hugh Bourne who made the well-known words of Wesley one of the rules of his society: 'It is certain that opinion is not religion, not even right opinions.' Perhaps we all need to beware of identifying our own opinions and ways with the authentic tradition of Methodism.

As British Methodism faces the future, it is seeking to address itself to a number of tasks all of which arise out of its evangelistic mission. Some of the lessons of the past have been learnt, and the stage is free for the consideration of issues which in earlier years had not emerged or were left in abeyance.

We are summoned in the first place to re-examine and re-interpret our theological foundations in the light of the challenge of contemporary thought without and indeed within the Church of Christ. In the task of re-interpretation, the merits as well as the defects of what is known as the liberal movement in theology should be taken into account. The study of Biblical theology in which all the Churches share with its emphasis upon the primacy of revelation, the continuity of the Old Testament revelation with that of the New, the place of the Church as the covenanted people of God, and the significance of history should guard against the possibility of so exalting the Old Testament and the principle of continuity as to imperil the uniqueness of the divine revelation recorded in the New Testament. Those who have been nurtured in the grand simplicities of experimental religion which rest primarily upon what God has done in Christ have a special contribution to make in this connexion to ecumenical theology. I would also venture to hope that our theologians will have some regard for clarity of thought and expression. It may be a weakness in one's intellectual apparatus, but I find it difficult to appreciate a point unless I can see it. And if a little evidence could be thrown in for some of the positions which are so confidently maintained, speaking entirely for myself, my own progress in understanding would be considerably facilitated. When, for instance, a writer plasters the word 'eschatology' on every page without stopping to explain to a groping mind in what sense he is using the term and with what justification, I know that I have entered a tunnel

36

from which I shall not emerge until I lay the book down. Then our theology must catch fire—the fire of the Holy Spirit who leads us into all truth.

Secondly, we are called to consider afresh the meaning of Scriptural holiness. How can we build up our people, young and old, in their most Holy Faith and commend to them the discipline of Christian love? Love creates its own law and brings with it inexorable demands. How can we assist them to find the freedom and joy of corporate worship, to share in the fellowship of prayer, and to bear in daily life the fruits of the Spirit?

Thirdly, there is the call to evangelism. This involves the re-ordering of the life and thought of the Church with one end in view—the proclamation of the Gospel to men, women and children throughout the world. Our evangelism must be commensurate with the wider purposes of God disclosed in part by contemporary events. If it is to be effective, it calls for a revival of personal religion, a deepened and more enlightened concern for education within and without the Church, a social witness based upon the Christian doctrine of man, society, the home, and work, and a re-orientation of missionary policy in the light of cataclysmic changes in the political, economic, and religious scene. This is a task to be undertaken by the membership of the Church as a whole, ministerial and lay. We do not speak in Methodism of the apostolate of the laity. It is our claim that in apostolic labours we are all fellow pilgrims on the same road. That claim needs to be substantiated by action in the days that lie before us.

Finally, British Methodism, like other branches of world Methodism, looks beyond Methodism to the Church Universal of which it forms a part, and seeks closer fellowship with other communions. Church re-union with the Anglican Church or any other is not our main objective, nor do we take the view that the Church cannot hope to make an impact upon the world until it is re-united. We nevertheless believe that it is God's will that the Christian communions should become a fellowship of those who are united in worship and witness to one another through their common relationship to Christ. What is described as organic union is not a live issue in the United Kingdom. Nevertheless, Methodism is prepared to envisage the day when it no longer exists as a separate denomination, provided there is an assurance that its characteristic message and mission are not lost, but incorporated in a wider fellowship. It will welcome inter-communion with the Anglican Church when a way has been found to have fellowship at the Lord's table on a basis of reality as guests not of one another, but of our common Lord. But it cannot tolerate conditions of re-union which imply or seem to imply that our ministry and sacraments lack what is essential to their validity, even though the term 'validity' may be repudiated or left conveniently undefined. Further, no scheme of intercommunion or re-union can be contemplated which involves the impairment, let alone the severance, of existing relations with other branches of Methodism. There must be no rift in the Methodist family.

The magnitude of our task, the spiritual perils which beset us, and the hostile forces ranged against us would fill us with fears and misgivings but that our hope is not in ourselves but in God. There is no need for any of us to tremble for the Ark of God if the redeeming sovereign love of God, daily renewed in our experience, is the ground and inspiration of all that we undertake. Dr Begg, the arch-enemy of Robertson Smith, who was so unjustly removed from his chair at Aberdeen on account of what some held to be his subversive teaching about the Old Testament, ended his speech against Robertson Smith in the Assembly with the declaration that he trembled for the Ark of God. Robertson Smith in his reply said that he

37

knew only one character in Scripture who trembled for the Ark of God, and that was Eli, a worldly ecclesiastic who trembled because for him it had ceased to be a shrine of the living, revealing Word of God and had become a fetish. As he trembled, he fell and perished. But the Ark was safe because it was the Ark of God's revelation. No man, concluded Robertson Smith, need tremble for that. In that faith, we go forward in British Methodism—

> 'to serve the present age
> our calling to fulfil'.

II. THE METHODIST TRADITION IN THE UNITED STATES

An address delivered by BISHOP ARTHUR J. MOORE, *of Atlanta, Georgia:*

Did John Wesley intend to establish an independent Church in America when he sent Thomas Coke, Richard Whatcoat, Frances Asbury and others to represent him? is a question which has never been satisfactorily answered. There is considerable evidence that Mr Wesley did not intend the Methodists in America to become an entirely separate ecclesiastical body. However, in the New World the Wesleyan revival met environmental factors which necessitated changes in polity and practice if it was to be redemptively in contact with life and minister fully to the religious needs of these frontier people. The entire pattern of political, social, and cultural life was different from that left behind in England. In addition to the multiplicity and complexity of these problems, the results of the revival in the New World had to be conserved and guided into channels of service. Inevitably the new Church must have a name; strong and godly men must be put in places of administrative leadership; its ministers must be given status in which they could command legal recognition and public respect by being released from the crippling denial of the right to administer the ordinances. Mr Wesley recognized the importance of all these problems and gave his help in many ways to the organization of Methodism in America as a body distinct from the Anglican Church and differing in its essential features from British Methodism.

The minutes of the British Wesleyan Conference of 1770 lists 'Circuit Number 50—America' with a membership of 316. The first Annual Conference was convened in St George's Church, Philadelphia, 14th July 1773. In 1784 the Christmas Conference gave the Church a name, elevated Coke and Asbury to places of administrative leadership; and Methodism in America, despite its humble beginning, was alive and astir in these new surroundings with amazing speed and effectiveness.

The forty-fourth year in each of the last three centuries has played a decisive role in the history of American Methodism. In June of 1744 the first Methodist Conference convened in the Foundery in London. The Conference, held under the presidency of John Wesley, was composed of ten men. Six were clergymen, and four were lay preachers. This small group little dreamed that this meeting would become the germ of all subsequent Methodist Conferences. Of these ten obscure men Dr W. H. Fitchett wrote: 'They created unconsciously the most remarkable, and in some senses the most powerful, ecclesiastical council which is today the effective instrument of government for a Church of nearly thirty million people.'

Five years had passed since the first fires flamed in the hearts of the ten there assembled and their associates. Mighty tides of emotional life were

38

running high, but strange things were happening. False teachers had invaded that company of devout souls, affirming that 'the means of grace' were not necessary to those who had been awakened. Such teaching was repugnant to all John Wesley believed as a loyal churchman and to all that had come to him in his heart-warming experience. Then it was that the Conference was called to conserve the awakened enthusiasm filling the hearts of these eager people, to discipline this new life and direct it into creative and redemptive channels. This purpose in part explains the questions that formed the basis of the discussions of that first Conference. They were: What shall we teach? How shall we teach? What shall we do? During the intervening two centuries many changes have been made, but these inspired leaders planted that day 'the seed which has grown to a towering, far-spreading tree sheltering millions of Methodists'.

The General Conference of 1844 in America met in the already gathering storm-clouds of a national tragedy. When the delegates assembled, there was every reason to believe that ways of meeting the perplexing problems would be discovered. The Episcopal Address pointed toward peace and goodwill and called for the extension of the Kingdom of God. But sectional and political differences arose which could not be reconciled, resulting in the disunion of American Methodism. When the delegates felt there was no honourable way to reconcile the differing viewpoints, in the magnanimity of their souls they said: 'Let there be no strife between us, for we are brethren. Let us part in peace, let us divide our common inheritance, adjust our common obligations, and preserve as a sacred treasure our common principles.' Thus our fathers passed through the storm of the 'sixties, somewhat apart, but never out of hailing distance in time of trouble.

Today as one people we are at home in the house of our fathers, as heirs and trustees of a great heritage, accepting the full responsibility of our history and all to which our great ideals conscript us.

Every experience since the consummation of union has clearly demonstrated the wisdom of that action. The influence and power of Methodism has been immeasurably increased by union. The baffling difficulties and grave dangers which today surround us clearly reveal that only united and co-operative planning and action are sufficient. The great Head of the Church prayed for the union of His disciples, not as an end in itself, but in order to insure one great objective—namely, 'that the world may believe'.

In the Church we now have a fine blend of the very best Methodism has produced across these two centuries. Here are the devotion and democracy of the Methodist Protestant Church; here are the churchmanship, the efficiency, and the aggressiveness of the Methodist Episcopal Church; here is the warmheartedness of the Methodist Episcopal Church, South, with its genius for Christian education and evangelism. We were all the children of John Wesley. We traced our history to a common origin. We had affinities of tradition and outlook and ideal. We stood for the same things. We cherished the same spirit of a vitalizing experience. Separately, we laboured with hearts filled with love for men, believing that Christ could redeem humanity, transform the world, and change the course of human history. Each brought its distinctive contribution into union, not to be swallowed up, but to find wider expression, resulting in an enlarged fellowship and an enriched experience. What we did well apart, we now do better together. The unwise and unnecessary duplication of effort which attended our divisions is gone, and we are together not as competitors, but as comrades. For us has been answered the prayer of

39

St Augustine: 'A whole Christ for my salvation; a whole Bible for my staff; a whole Church for my fellowship; a whole world for my parish.'

Methodism in America, as it is now, is an ecclesiastical organization capable of mobilizing the entire resources of its membership for the promotion of righteousness in a developing world in an era characterized by change.

We are now a Church of many millions representing differing geographical sections, many racial groups and varying social strata. It would be impossible and also unwise to reduce these varieties to a common uniformity and to make Methodists everywhere a copy of an approved type employing an identical theological emphasis, using an identical form of liturgy, revering the same religious terminology and employing the same methods of promotion. This plan, were it possible, would do violence to individual temperaments and tastes. Some of our people prefer elaborate organization with the aid of full ritual while others are at home in the freer life of a more informal service. We must seek to avoid rigidity of form and expression and to give to every man the right to worship and witness in the way that is best suited to him. Likewise, there are diversities of methods and traditions in the several geographical areas of the nation. We have not attempted to change the individual capacities and gifts, or to deny to them the form of work and worship in which they can best express their religious experience.

When we survey the record of American Methodism across more than 200 years, we have every reason to rejoice and be grateful. In order to transmit to a distraught world and to coming generations the gospel which has seen such splendid triumphs, we have sought to keep faith with our fathers; keep faith with our children; above all, to keep faith with Christ. We sought to preach the Gospel with confidence and with passion. We have told men that while they inherit the infirmities and sins of the race, they also inherit the salvation which Christ offers all mankind; that they live not in a lost world, but in a redeemed world, and that when man accepts his true relation to Christ, he lives under a new heaven and on a new earth.

In order fully to appreciate our spiritual heritage, we go again and again to the story of the remarkable experience through which John Wesley passed on the evening of the 24th May 1738. It has been the fashion among some modern biographers of Wesley to depreciate more or less the significance of that experience and to assign little importance to it in the creation of the Wesleyan movement. It remains true, however, that the astounding and speedy triumphs of Methodism cannot be explained on any other basis.

Mr Wesley never failed either in preaching or writing to refer to his transforming experience and to give his testimony concerning what the Lord had done for him. We need not here debate the name which properly describes the experience nor discuss whether it was gradual or instantaneous. Instead, let us remember only that it was the culmination of the long search of a hungry-hearted man for an experience of the saving grace of the Lord Jesus Christ, and that the experience manifested itself in such joyous witness and victorious power that the formal priest of Oxford became the prophet of Methodism, taking his place as the most forceful and efficient Evangelical of modern times.

When Wesley began his work he knew that he had received from God the direct assurance of the forgiveness of his sins and of his adoption into the Divine Family. He refused to believe that this privilege was inaccessible to other men. What he had received, he contended, every man might

40

receive through faith in Christ; the glorious blessings which God had given to him were intended to be the common inheritance of all believers. Out of that transforming experience came Methodism, bringing life and vigour to the Church of that day. Those early Methodists believed something more was possible to a believer than a faltering hope; hence their insistence that man should never rest until he knew for himself that Christ had delivered him from sin. In this assurance they found the source of strength, the secret of unity and the certainty of triumph, and it produced a host of witnesses with exulting songs giving their testimony to the power of Christ to restore man to God.

The methods by which a living Church discharges its duty must of necessity vary from age to age. Nevertheless, wise men do not disregard tradition, for tradition is the cumulative heritage of actual experience. It was the faith of the last generation which under God helped create the faith of the present; likewise, the faith of the present generation must under God help create the faith of the next generation.

In the realm of traditions, Methodism is both weak and strong. It sprang out of another Church, and its founders desired to keep as close thereto as possible. Strong and definite traditions of its own were, in consequence, inhibited. The early Methodists did not stress the things out of which traditions grow. On the other hand, Methodism is strong because its very lack of tradition has enabled it to avoid rigid and dogmatic conservation. In spite of more or less vexing innovations which have from time to time arisen, the main current of thought and attitude has been kept fluid, responsive to changing conditions, open to new truth, and always ready to make adaptations in methods and attitudes.

Theoretically, the Methodist tradition may be summarized. It is the evangelical tradition of the Protestant reformers. At times Mr Wesley appeared to place little stress upon theology. Yet even a slight acquaintance with his teaching shows that such was not his real attitude. He criticized the theological opinions of great men freely, but the very fact of his doing so indicates the importance he attached to careful and accurate theological thinking.

The Methodist insistence has not been so much upon opinion as upon life. Its distinguishing mark is not so much what men believe as what they are, what they experience, how they act. The unique traditions of Methodism are, therefore, to be sought in patterns of action rather than systems of dogma.

American Methodism proudly offers the following credentials as proof of its love for and loyalty to the original meaning and mission of the Wesley revival. We have always stood for a rich inner experience of Christ's redeeming grace; a world view of the Church, an evangelistic passion, and a corporate conscience acutely sensitive to social needs. We have insisted upon the infinite worth and dignity of every man and urged that life is intended, not for a short struggle for bread, but as a glorious adventure as the child of God and the comrade of Christ. We have spoken clearly and positively about the world-wide Kingdom of God. We have sought to bring men into a saving knowledge of the grace of God and train them for unselfish service. Over against the insanities of hatred, ignorance, and oppression we have insistently proclaimed our conviction that the hope of the world is not in some dictator produced by a turbulent era of the world's life, nor in some teacher, however great, bound by the limitations of his age, but in the Divine Saviour who alone is big enough, brave enough, and divine enough to give us a safe, friendly, redeemed world.

41

For more than 200 years we have encouraged evangelistic and missionary aggressiveness. We have sought to follow Him to whom all continents, tongues, and races belong. In the face of war and international unrest we have sought to keep aloft the banner of love and righteousness, freedom and service in a world of sin and selfishness. We are justly proud of a long procession of heroes and heroines whose eyes were on far horizons bent. No range of mountains was high enough to stay their progress, no rivers deep enough and broad enough to daunt them, no forest dark and dense enough to withstand their advance. They have pressed onward from continent to continent, frontier to frontier, offering the Christian faith to the sceptical, scornful, and sinful. The song of the pioneer has been in our hearts and on our lips, and that accounts for the fact that the flag of our branch of the Church floats proudly this morning over more than a half-hundred of the nations of the earth, and more than nine million souls are enrolled in our membership.

I. A Wise and Winsome Evangelism

The one fact that sent Methodists early to the open fields and eventually to the ends of the earth with infectious joy was that God in Christ had come to the rescue of sinning humanity. They witnessed everywhere because they had found Christ as the Saviour from sin, the Creator of new character and the Guarantor of everlasting life. Their main emphasis was upon the fact that God had heard the cry of broken humanity and had sent in the person of His Son a divine Saviour to deliver mankind. They never overlooked the implications of that fact. They never dismissed it, nor obscured it by any naturalistic interpretation. They declared it in creed, experienced it in life, and expressed it in a glad and intense evangelism. With warm hearts and eager spirits, they went everywhere to bring men into a saving knowledge of the truth as it is in Christ Jesus. They felt that a special responsibility rested upon them for the redemption of mankind.

From then until now the normal mood of Methodism has been the evangelistic mood. The stirring story of our advance across the American continent and of the establishment of younger Churches around the world is the story of a resistless evangelism. God raised us up to be Christianity in earnest, and no Church can forget its original mission and have bright prospects. Methodism set out two centuries ago to win men from the kingdom of darkness and evil and to organize them into a Church which would help save the world. It was not necessary to acquire or develop a spirit of evangelism; we were by nature evangelistic. From the very beginning we went everywhere proclaiming the story of the transforming Cross, the empty Tomb, and the risen and glorified Lord. We are the trustees of a complete gospel which holds hope for society and offers men release from sin.

What is more needed today? One could hardly claim that we are in the midst of a revival at the present time, but undoubtedly we are witnessing a general turning of the masses to an interest in the things of the spirit. Soldiers, statesmen, and writers are confessing their faith, sometimes in language the Church has not employed. The facts of spiritual life have come into the common speech of man. Writers no longer hesitate to discuss religion. In fact, one of the great gains out of the stress and anxiety of the war is the recovery of the consciousness of God and a sense of responsibility to Him. The time seems ripe for the Church to interpret Christ to the inquiring mind and seeking heart of our time. We must be diligent lest this new search for God by-pass the organized Church. The

42

business of the twentieth-century Church, as was true of the early Church, is to help men find God. In order to lead them to Him, we must have an unquenchable faith in the reality of the gospel we proclaim and a keen awareness of the infinite importance of the things that make for righteousness. Only thus can the Church become what it was meant to be, 'the place where those who march with God can find their point of rallying'.

The urgency of soul which characterized our fathers must possess us. Surely by this time we have discovered that soft sayings about virtue, the evolution of the race, and the inherent goodness of mankind will not produce the evangelism the world sorely needs. We must speak again of the ghastly reality of sin, of the atonement of Christ, of justification by faith, of the eternal profit of goodness, and of the everlasting loss to those who will not have Christ. We should be particularly careful to deal adequately with the intellectual difficulties and the moral and spiritual problems of these exciting days. Our gospel must be suited to the anguish of our time. But we will not help groping humanity to find the way by underestimating the need of man for redemption or failing to declare that the Cross of Christ with all its typifies is something more than an example of how a good man should bear pain. This generation, like all others, must come to see that sin is the gulf which separates man from God, and must learn that Christ by dying on the Cross did something for man which he could not do for himself.

We marched into the eighteenth century singing, 'no foot of land do we possess, no cottage in this wilderness'. We lacked numbers, social standing, and stately cathedrals. The mighty and learned of the earth were not numbered in our membership, but with its message of a divine Saviour we brought salvation to the sinning, comfort to the sorrowing, rest to the weary, security and confidence to the dying, and to men everywhere a spiritual and intellectual awakening. What a tragedy if twentieth-century Methodism should lose this power! With its vast membership, its trained ministers, and its up-to-date methods, it must steadfastly continue to exercise its power to transform the individual and regenerate society.

In all generations it has been the voice of the inspired prophet that has aroused a slumbering Church and quickened a dying world. The great need of this generation is a succession of such prophets to stand in our pulpits with an interpretation of the Christian gospel which will enlighten the intellect, quicken the imagination, stir the conscience, and reinforce the will. There are always new truths to be discerned, and unless God's ministers discover them for themselves and preach them with power, the world will not be brought to the certainty and confidence of a vital faith. The truth as we have it in Christ is sufficient for the individual, for society, and for the world. It cannot be given up without darkening the hope of the world.

Methodism with its modern message and methods will prove to be only so much cumbersome machinery except as it is a channel through which the grace of God is poured upon the world.

Originally Methodism in America was in a peculiar sense the Church of the people. It went everywhere the people were. Upon every advancing frontier of American life the pioneers were accompanied by the Methodist minister, and in every new township there was erected a Methodist chapel. In 1801, one in seventy-two Americans was a Methodist; in 1941 the number had increased to one in nineteen. In 1861, one in every three Protestant Church members was a Methodist. Between 1800 and 1830 Methodism increased sevenfold. This startling growth was the direct result of the Church following the people and identifying itself with their hopes, aspirations, and problems.

We are now faced with the danger of becoming a fixed Church. The tendency is toward training our young ministers to go to established pulpits, there to put on a church programme and a service of worship. We sometimes assume that the people, having been invited, will come, but if they fail to do so we have no other plan to secure their attention and attendance.

The future with us lies in the hands of the masses. All great social and religious movements rise from the bottom, and there is now a world-wide stirring of the common people. In their hands lies the destiny of tomorrow socially, economically, and in every other area of life. We must be careful lest we become a fixed type, a solid, respectable, middle-class people. We are honoured to have as a part of our fellowship many educated and cultured people, but a Church that neglects the great toiling masses will not dominate the tomorrows. It is highly important that we minister to people of education and culture. We would not in the least minimize this part of our mission; nor would we lower our standards for the ministry and ignore the necessity of carrying on the programme of a fixed church. But to discharge our full obligation, we must minister to those in every sphere of life. We must have the technique for every different demand made upon us. We must not depend upon one stereotyped form of ministry alone. There must be a definite rural approach that will give us a fixed leadership in the country and a definite urban programme that will enable us to cope with the demands of the city.

The future of Methodism is bound up with its ability to adapt its policies and programmes to the age in which it lives. The early Methodists went forth with an initiative and mobility which resulted in a spiritual advance almost without parallel in Christian history. When churches were closed, they went out on the streets; when ordained ministers were insufficient, they laid the burdens upon Christian laymen, who achieved admirable results. Ministers and laymen alike felt that when there was work to be done they were under obligation to find the most effective way of doing it.

II. An Insistence on the World Mission of the Church

Christianity was intended to be, and of necessity is, a missionary religion. To take away its world view, to steal away its missionary passion, is to rob it of its character and leave it something other than its true self. Christianity is not a religion of averages, and it never flourishes by maintaining the *status quo*. It lives and expands only when world vision is constantly before its eyes and when its ministers and people are heroic adventurers and brave pioneers, ready to follow their Leader in the dangerous way of the Cross.

The world mission of the Church is the one thing that can save it from the corroding influences of a secular civilization. Perusal of the history of the Church across the centuries discloses that its golden pages have been written when the missionary passion was strongest. Its power and influence in the homeland are inseparably linked with its passion for the ends of the earth. Either it takes all men into its love or it forfeits the right to claim God as the supreme ruler of the world and Jesus Christ as the Universal Saviour. Christ's gospel was intended for all men, and the Church must, therefore, have a field as broad as the whole wide world if it is truly to represent Him.

One of Methodism's missionary leaders described this vital activity of

44

the Church in these words: 'The missionary enterprise is the supreme adventure of history. It is the challenge of hope and courage in a world of paralysing fears and demoralizing futility. It is the sole claimant as a moral substitute for war. It is the only accredited messenger of good news to a bewildered world and the lone champion of love and goodwill in a world of hate and war. Any lowering of its standards or lessening of its power or cheapening of its motive is the betrayal of the race, and a yielding of the only fortress that flies the flag of brotherhood.'

It follows that the missionary work of the Church at home and abroad is not to be kept going because of our love for or loyalty to our fathers. It is an attempt on the part of the Church to carry out the dearest wish of the heart of Christ. When we are drawn into union with Him, the fires of love for all mankind burn in our hearts. This is the passion which constrains us to give our sons and daughters and substance for the salvation of mankind.

A formal, fainthearted, self-indulgent, dress-parade Christianity will not suffice for a crisis such as is now upon us. Our love for Christ and men must be able to stand foul odours and loathsome sights, and to go down to the gates of Hell to save a lost soul. Such Christ-like devotion will love iniquity into goodness, hostility into brotherhood, a lost world into a redeemed world. From all over the earth comes the same urgent message, which must be pressed home with all the earnestness at our command. There must be no faltering in the face of present-day difficulties, but rather a recognition that the black forces that threaten to overwhelm mankind constitute a call from God to His Church for aggressive action.

The responsibility of the Church in the United States is not overlooked. At this time the home base brings a new challenge, and we are devoting ever-increasing thought and effort to it. We have provided spiritual oversight for our soldiers and sailors through the ministry of devoted and highly efficient chaplains. New communities have sprung up, many of which will be permanent. Here is a new mission field, and we must evangelize for the sake of the future.

We speak of war as global. Our attitudes must be global also. It was once said that this nation could not endure half slave and half free. Now we know that the world cannot be half good and half bad, half Christian and half pagan. If Christ is to be supreme anywhere, He must be supreme everywhere. America must be Christianized, not only for its own sake, but for the sake of its influence in the future. Here is destined to be one of the main bases of both Christian missions and political democracy and freedom, probably for a century to come. We must, therefore, make a more determined effort to Christianize the homeland in order to insure that our country comes with clean hands into the council of nations as the exponent of peace and justice. The task at home looms larger and more imperative than ever before. An urgent demand is a re-study of the whole home mission policy and the evaluation of the new factors that have emerged as a result of war.

Not only have familiar problems been accentuated and new emergencies created in the areas where we have long worked, in cities, towns, and country, among the minority groups, but new developments have brought forward entirely new home mission fields. According to recent statistics relating to population, we have experienced in our country one of the greatest migrations of history. Our population has shifted. Cities have increased, and rural areas have decreased. We do not know what will transpire, but we do know that Methodists find themselves face to face with a mission situation at home that requires better methods and more money than we have customarily applied to the problem of Christianizing the home base.

The deep conviction of Methodists that the Atonement is universal carries over into an attitude that makes Methodism essentially a missionary movement. Wesley's famous statement, 'I look upon all the world as my parish', was not made with reference to missions in the sense of sending the gospel to the whole world. Nevertheless, the fact that it has nearly always been given that interpretation involves no real distortion of Wesley's meaning, since no man could have made such a statement in any connexion except one who possessed the mind of missions. And that mind Wesley certainly possessed, not only in the sense of extending the Christian message to those who sat in darkness, but also and especially in his attitude toward the under-privileged and the outcasts of his day. The social ministry which he carried on at the Foundery and elsewhere, his natural assumption that along with the British Isles the New World was included in his evangelizing endeavours, his missionary trip to America, his impatience with the duties there that kept him from preaching to the Indians, and his treatment of such social problems as slavery, poverty, war, and intemperance furnish eloquent proof that he shared the Master's compassion for the low, the lost, and the last.

We must not take Mr Wesley out of his time and judge him in the light of what was then unknown. The recent idea that missions include the Christianization of areas of social life as well as the geographical extension of the Gospel came into existence after his time. But here, as in so many other fields, subsequent study shows that Wesley's work and teachings anticipated modern developments in a remarkable way.

As a matter of fact, Methodism itself was a missionary movement in a very real sense. John Wesley and his fellow workers differed from the men who today bear the title of missionary in no distinguishable quality. 'The need they faced was a missionary need, their gospel a missionary manifesto.' The date commonly accepted for the inauguration of the period of modern missions is 1792. Dr Cannon of Duke University declared: 'The new spirit of enthusiasm among the Nonconformist Churches of England, and the Established Church as well, which found expression in modern missions is traceable almost directly to the response of these bodies to the influence of the Wesleyans during the preceding half-century. John Wesley was in his grave when William Carey sailed for India, but Wesley made Carey possible.' Still another writer has pointed out that 'amongst the larger Protestant Churches the Methodist Communion is that which alone, from the outset and distinctly, adopted a world-wide aim'.

It would be a work of supererogation to mention the missionary labours of Bishop Coke, 'the foreign minister of Methodism', who drew up a plan for a missionary society and actually planted Methodism in foreign places long before Carey began his work. The Wesleyans were raising funds for their work among the destitute as early as 1756, and in 1769 Wesley sent two missionary volunteers to America. The same Conference which organized the Methodist Church also appointed missionaries to Nova Scotia. A multitude of similar facts crowd the early record, indicating the process by which the missionary attitude entered the Methodist tradition. It has persisted and has become more intense as the years have lengthened. Though it has never enlisted the active co-operation of all the membership, it has always dominated the councils of the Church. No anti-missionary movement has ever swept through its ranks.

46

III. An Unyielding Conviction that Learning and Piety go Together

It has been a boast that 'Methodism was born in the university', but there is certainly truth in the retort that 'if nothing had happened to Wesley except what happened in the university, there would never have been a Methodist Church'. However that may be, it is of considerable significance that the eighteenth-century revival, though almost exclusively concerned with the poor and the ignorant, was led by highly trained men who always laid heavy emphasis upon the culture of the intellect. The nature of that emphasis is well known. Though Wesley's helpers were nearly all un-lettered men, the reading and study he demanded of them was such as might have been recommended to ripe students. The Methodist converts, as well as the preachers, were expected to improve their minds. Wesley wrote, translated, published, and circulated books by the hundreds, and in his *Journal* and *Letters* he insisted a thousand times over that training of the mind is an essential part of the Christian life. The first Methodist institution was not a church nor a chapel for preaching, but a school. Not one of the early American circuit-riders was a college graduate, but when they came up to their first General Conference they already had cash in hand for the building of a college.

This is one tradition which American Methodism has neither outgrown nor drastically modified. It has always been educationally minded. It has filled the world with its institutions of learning of every grade. Today in the U.S.A. alone the Methodist Church operates 125 schools, colleges, and universities, with 6,000 teachers, an enrolment of 117,000 students, and an annual budget of $42,000,000.

In those first years of Methodism the stress was not exclusively, nor was it even mainly, upon formal or institutional education. Nowhere are the essential sanity and breadth of view of early Methodism more apparent than in its natural integration of religious education and evangelism—an integration that is somewhat remarkable in view of the prevalent attitude of the day and the powerful zeal of the early preachers for the salvation of souls. It is a profitless proceeding to search the writings of eighteenth-century authors for philosophies and principles which were not then in existence. Nevertheless, Wesley in a very real sense anticipated the modern idea of the place of religious education. Not only did his Methodists operate Sunday-schools long before Robert Raikes began his famous experiment, but they realized with a considerable degree of clarity that culture has its place in the whole Christianizing process. Men have spoken and written as if the early Methodist preachers aroused emotion, secured cataclysmic conversions, and then passed on, having little regard for either religious education or social morality. Their mistake is great and inexcusable. The mere fact that the converts, instead of falling away, multiplied into the present millions refutes the idea.

'Will you diligently instruct the children in every place?' has been asked of every Methodist preacher since the Methodist Church was organized in 1784. When the circuit-riders won converts, they were under instructions to 'build them up in that holiness without which they cannot see the Lord'. They made an interesting use of their Class Meetings. In these small and private gatherings inquiry was made into the experience and conduct of the converts, and their famous testimony meetings were based upon a fundamental psychology. The early Methodists were ignorant of modern techniques and wholly without the materials and equipment now deemed essential, but their sanity, hard common sense, and knowledge gained through experience stood them in good stead. They made religious education a tradition in the movement they projected.

47

Secularism, which is but another name for what our fathers called worldliness, has taken its toll of spiritual life. Whatever its material excellencies, and they are many, our modern civilization is largely the product of secular forces which are either non-Christian or anti-Christian. It does not subscribe to the principle that man lives not by bread alone; nor does it pursue a spiritual ideal. In fact, in many ways it gives practical denial to these convictions. Some would pass the problem by lightly with the reflection that we are only witnessing a change in our spiritual taste. With that view we cannot agree. Something more dangerous is taking place. There are trends and tendencies active in modern life which endanger the perpetuity of our Christian civilization and the life and witness of the Church. We are compelled to a fearless study of the underlying causes.

Life to-day, for adults and youth alike, is surrounded by conditions and forces which have sprung up so swiftly as to take them unawares. The tempo of modern life has been so accelerated that it has become difficult to give attention to those things which make for faith and knowledge. The development of the religious sense of our children is hindered by adverse forces, which tend to weaken and sometimes almost extinguish it. For several years we have been passing through a period in which such forces have been particularly numerous and active. Life has become so highly secularized that faith and devotion have been made difficult. The cheap and ofttimes unwholesome pleasures that have multiplied tend to crowd out religious study and observance. In many homes the family altar has disappeared. To these obviously destructive influences must be added a subtle effect of defective religious teaching. In the so-called emancipation from the religion of authority, many swung to an imaginary freedom, in which the great truths of the Christian message were questioned. We are, therefore, in the midst of a transitional period of uncertainty in which many ignore religion. Our foolish affectations, our deceptions, our poor ideals, our chaotic readings of God's purpose have all followed the loss of that overmastering sense of God which was the possession of another generation. Religion gave to our fathers and mothers the certainty and consolation of God's presence and power, in which they found a guide for this life as well as a hope for a future life.

If the principles of the Christian faith are applicable to the needs of our age, perplexed as it is with intellectual difficulties which affect belief and moral difficulties which affect conduct, there must be more widespread and effective instruction in religion. Christian education must not only continue to resist, but aggressively combat the secularizing tendencies of our times by an insistence upon the eternal verities. The faculties of our youth must be put to school on their spiritual side. They must be taught to bow in reverent humility before the eternal wisdom and to live according to the immortal truths which came from the lips of the Teacher of Galilee.

IV. The Assertion of the Christian Conscience

The challenge of evil never ceases. In every age the Church is called upon to define and defend those standards which undergird the moral life of the community and guarantee the ethical and spiritual health of mankind. Its business is to redeem human character and purify human society.

As Methodists we envisage the Christian social order as one in which every human being has full opportunity to live the abundant life physically, intellectually, and spiritually. A social order is good in so far as it enriches personalities and it is bad in so far as it stunts or impoverishes them.

If the Church is a living society inspired by the spirit of the living

48

Christ, then we must think not only of its origin and ordinances, but of the goal toward which it is moving and the purpose it was organized to serve. Its best credential is that it follows Christ on His redemptive pilgrimage. The question at present centres, not on what the Church has been, but on its present status. What is it now? For what is it intended in this crucial epoch? What is it doing today to fulfil its mission? It was the Head of the Church, Jesus Himself, who prayed to the Father: 'As Thou hast sent me into the world, even so have I also sent them into the world.' Certainly He means that men are to be redeemed one by one and brought into conformity with the divine purpose, but He also means that the saved of the community will in turn save the community. The Church must be the body of Christ in the world, the society through which God is revealed to men and His will is made operative in the social order. One of the true tasks and functions of the Church as an organized society is the redemption of the social order.

It would be a mistake to conclude that the religious life is complete in experience alone, as vitally important as that element is. It was Paul who said: 'God was in Christ, reconciling the world unto Himself.' Reconciliation with the Father surely means experiencing the forgiveness of sins and the restoration to the favour and family of God, but it also includes enlistment in the Christian purpose to make all the areas of life conformable to the will of God. Thus the Church, engaged as it is in preparing men for the life hereafter, must also give attention to life here and now. It must look upon all men in the light of their eternal destiny. In so doing, with moral courage and realism it must resist every tendency of society to becloud the sacredness of human life and resist every effort to deny to men the inalienable rights which belong to the children of God. Christ's purpose must be above all human and earthly considerations.

In the great task of transforming men and movements, the Church must follow its Leaders. In Christ one discovers God caring for this sinning, suffering world and setting out to rescue it. Beyond any question, there is spiritual value to the soul in quiet withdrawal from the noisy whirl of a distraught world for meditation and fellowship, but a spirituality which reaches this hands-folded, reposeful state and there stops, complacently hesitant, will not produce a Church redemptively in touch with life. A Church so motivated will shrink from venturing abroad on dark nights to rescue lost sheep and perishing sinners. Unwilling to fight the forces of evil, it will therefore have no scars. It may remain beautiful in ceremonies, devout in temper, and perhaps clean in habit, but it will surely fail to put forth the effort essential to the making of a better world. The people of God must develop a militant faith which will keep them alive in every fibre of their being and imbue them with an impulse to action that will make them implacable foes of injustice and iniquity and enthusiastic champions of whatever promises to hasten the coming of the kingdom of God on earth.

V. A Confident March into a Greater Age

To nations and to Churches, as to individual persons, there come great moments, spring tides of the soul, when mysterious and awesome forces make themselves felt. Surely, even now a great moment is impending! The world picture in the present crucial hour, as seen by the mind's eye, looms dark indeed and perplexing; yet there is in the hearts of those who have discovered the eternal and inexhaustible resources of faith an ineradicable conviction that we are about to witness another striking and arresting manifestation of Christ's power. God in Christ is behind human

49

life and within it. He will not allow human nature to lie idle, to waste itself on trifles, or to be content with low ideals. There is something He would do with humanity, and He means to carry out His eternal purpose. He will not allow the tyrannies of men to prevail for ever, for He has not abdicated His throne nor abandoned His plan of redemption. God is not bound by human movements, nor is He dependent on the obvious human resources. Always He has reserved an absolute freedom for the sending of His spirit into the wilderness of men's lives and earthly confusions. All about is a world tremulous with change. In millions of yearning hearts there are unutterable longings for another spiritual awakening, a new thrust forward toward the realization of the Kingdom of God on earth.

It is indeed essential that the Church shall no longer evade the challenge of the world in which it lives. Too long it has been enamoured of the safe and easy way; too long it has been held by a comfortable and complacent interpretation of discipleship; too long it has had an armistice with fear and doubt. This is not the way to victory. The whole inheritance of our spiritual past is a witness to our God. He has been everywhere with His people. He will be everywhere with them now. ·Before this generation passes, His Church may see a new world take shape before its eyes.

It may be true that for the moment the general life of the world, amid the many confusions of the hour, does not realize that only Christ can furnish the creative and directing spiritual energy it so sorely needs. This only makes it the more imperative that Christians everywhere make a fresh discovery of those abiding realities which cannot perish because they have their alliance with God. The great need of our day is a deeper understanding of the majestic purpose of God, a nearer vision of the face of Christ. We are in a bigger world than our fathers knew; our interests are wider; our knowledge in many fields is more extensive and exact. We lack only that consecration which sent them forth with surprising gladness to obey the commands of their Lord.

Christ is the deathless Leader of His Church, and no cause is forlorn with Him at its head. He has illimitable resources at His command, and that guarantees the ultimate supremacy of righteousness in the world. Shall we not then take our appointed way with Him, evading no peril, seeking no discharge, but in confidence follow Him as He goes forth on His redemptive pilgrimage.

Arise, Methodism! The light that falls upon your pathway is not the light of the setting sun. It is the light of the morning. Before you is the gateway to a greater age and a more Christ-like world.

III. THE METHODIST TRADITION IN AUSTRALASIA

An address given by the REV. PROFESSOR G. CALVERT BARBER, *President General of the General Conference:*

We in Australia stand in the British tradition, and what has been said concerning Methodist tradition in Britain is in the main true also of Australia. Ours is a country two-thirds as big as the whole of Europe, and twenty-five times the size of Great Britain and Northern Ireland. We have a population, at the census of two years ago, of 7½ million, of whom just on 12 per cent are Methodists. Australia began its settled history as a colony established by Great Britain in 1788 when a penal settlement was set up there. In 1794, at the instance of William Wilberforce, the Rev. Samuel Marsden was appointed chaplain. He was the son of Methodist parents living at Horsforth, near Leeds. Before he left

England he had been acquainted with a Mr James Butterworth, who was Treasurer of the Wesleyan Methodist Missionary Society. Marsden appealed to him for help in choosing a schoolmaster for the settlement, and Thomas Bowden, a Class Leader, came out in 1812. On 6th March 1812 he and another Methodist schoolmaster held the first class meeting in Australia. Seven years later there were nineteen meeting regularly in class. Then the population of the country was about 15,000, of whom 100 were Methodists. Fifty years later there were 372 places of Methodist worship, with accommodation for 33,562. What had happened? Gold was discovered in 1851, and a wild rush set in. From then on, the *story of Methodism is that of the devoted and fearless ministry of local preachers and class-leaders.* Amongst the great stream of migrants were many Cornish miners and Irish Methodists, whose hearts were aflame with the evangelistic zeal of Methodism. Class meetings were held in tents, and services in the open. These Methodists were evangelists who, with a new country before them, went everywhere preaching the gospel and establishing societies. Here lies the secret of the fact that today we are the second largest Protestant denomination in the country. While others were waiting for priests and ministers, Methodists, true to their tradition and equipped by their previous training, were equal to the situation.

Australasia was constituted a separate Conference in 1855, and there were forty ministers present at the first meeting of Conference. That was less than 100 years ago. Now we have six independent annual Conferences under the General Conference, and seven mission districts through the islands of the Pacific and India, with a membership of more than 200,000, with 1,189 ministers, 133 Probationers, and 10,749 local preachers. We have had Methodist Union since 1902, a year after the establishment of the commonwealth, when the separated branches of the Methodist family closed their ranks. This has been a magnificent achievement, and we give God thanks that under the guidance of the Holy Spirit and by his grace this has been brought about. I am happy to be able to report that all traces of the old separation have disappeared. We are a completely homogeneous body. I hope that our experience will be an encouragement to others who more recently have taken the road of Methodist Union.

Australia, of course, has grown steadily in population. The first census was taken nine years after Union, and the population was then 4½ millions. At the last census of 1949, it was 7¼ millions. During the period between this Census and the previous one the general population increase was 14·3 per cent but the Methodist increase was 27·4 per cent, just on double the rate of general increase. Ours was easily the largest Protestant increase, and we moved up into the second strongest Protestant Church numerically. The reason for Methodism's advance in Australia was succinctly put by one of our state presidents, and serves to indicate some points at which the authentic Methodist tradition is very much alive amongst us. 'The Methodist Church', he wrote, 'has maintained her pioneering spirit. Centres have been established wherever possible, often at first in the homes of the people. Larger churches also propagate themselves by throwing off new churches in nearby districts as population spreads. Another cause is the great stress we place on Sunday-school and youth work. On social issues, Methodism has always made a distinctive contribution to the welfare of the people. Then too the democratic nature of Methodism makes a great appeal. Finally, the Connexional system by which the strong churches can help the weak is most suitable for a "frontier" situation which we still face in Australia.'

But while this is so, there is a darker side to this picture. True nearly

51

900,000 people named themselves Methodist, but we have only 146,000 adult members in the area of the Census, and we have a known community of about 500,000. *Where are these almost half a million nominal Methodists?* This question soon drove out the feeling of joy which our high proportional rate of increase had engendered. Where is this legion? This situation stabbed the Church broad awake to the necessity of recovering our evangelistic zeal and pastoral concern. It is true that before this we had felt the world-wide stirring of evangelistic concern which is so marked a feature of the universal Church in these dislocated days. The General Conference of 1948, in a memorable session, launched a 'Crusade for Christ', to be undertaken for a period of three years. The stimulus, as to technique, in this came from the fine Crusade which had been carried out by our brethren in America. As we read of what had happened there, and as we faced the mounting challenge in our own land our hearts were stirred, and the authentic flames of Methodist evangelism began to burn again amongst us. Here again the Connexional spirit, which is the very genius of Methodism, enabled us to pool our resources both of money and of manpower. Directors of Evangelism were appointed in each state, and a Federal Director by the General Conference. The immediate strategy was *a return to the original Methodist tradition*—every member an evangelist, with the local church as the basic unit of advance. Here, we have to confess, our hopes have not been fully realized. We started further back than we had imagined, and the initial work was a 'dead lift'. But of this we are sure: the Church is on the move in its most essential work. Particularly is this so amongst our young people. There is a serious spirit of inquiry amongst them, a courageous readiness to dedicate their lives to Christ and the Church, and an infectious enthusiasm which is working like yeast in the churches. Already the flow of candidates for the ministry has been increased, and amongst them candidates of such a quality as to stir the pulses of those of us who are ageing. Ours *is* an ageing ministry. Indeed, that is a characteristic of the country, young though we are as a people. The Dead Sea fruits of the years of depression are now being eaten, and they are sour to the taste. But the tide is turning, and our young people are responding. And this can be said: they are not fired primarily with a vision of the gospel as a social panacea and the Church as simply a cultural centre of community life. No; the gospel which they have heard and to which they are responding is that of salvation from sin and into Christian wholeness of life. Once again the authentic gospel of God's redeeming love declared in Christ, and in His redemptive deed in history, is winning greater numbers of our young people, and firing them with a determination to 'commend my Saviour to you'. We have discovered again that our main task is *to proclaim* and *not to exhort*, and that the Methodist emphases on the central truths of personal salvation are the trusty weapons of our warfare.

There is amongst us *an increasing awareness of the place of the Church* in the purpose of God. It is not being regarded simply as a place of humanly created fellowship, but is known to be part of the Gospel itself. It is a gift of God—a fellowship created by the Holy Spirit. There is an increasing and joyous discovery that the very *esse* of the Church is love—a love not to be professed only by word, but manifested in deed. We have come to see that the Gospel needs not only the presentation to the world of the 'man healed', but of the group reconciled. Consequently there is amongst us *a real longing for the manifestation of the essential unity of the Church*, and our Conference is ever holding out hands of brotherhood to our sister communions.

This is the stage which the 'Crusade for Christ' is in at the present time. 'Methodist weeks' have been held in all the capital cities, and in many of the larger provincial centres. Here the message of Methodism to the nation has been sounded, not only from pulpits, but in ways quite similar to those used in the 'Commando campaigns' here in Britain. We have gone to factories, to mines, to wharves, to Rotary clubs and chambers of commerce. We are endeavouring to close the gap which separates the Church and the industrial and commercial life of the community, particularly as it is organized in trades unions. We have recalled that that movement was virtually cradled in Methodism, and have been filled with grief that we have become 'settled on our lees'—too long content to be the Church of the comfortable, and very often the complaisant.

At the recent General Conference two things were clear: First, that though it was essential to begin with a renewal of the inner life of the Church, it was a mistake to plan for yearly stages in a Crusade as if they followed chronologically. It is all an ongoing work, a constant work of inner commitment and growth into the likeness of Christ, and an outer work of witness both to individuals and to the nation. The Crusade is to go on—indeed, must never cease. We are greatly anticipating the visit of Dr Donald Soper, who will spend the last three months of the year with us, and we plan and pray that his work on the frontiers will be owned of God.

Methodism in Australia, even in the period when her evangelistic zeal was cool, never lost *her missionary enthusiasm*. In the past fifty years we have raised nearly £4,000,000 for overseas missions. When the first Conference was established in Australasia, one of the provisions laid down was that the new Conference should take over the management of the mission in New Zealand, the Friendly Islands, and Fiji, and it was stated that the 'Australasian Conference is expected to follow the model furnished by the Missionary Society in England'. How well that has been done is seen in the fact that the Friendly Islands, now known as Tonga, is a separate and self-supporting Conference which sends both money and men to other fields. Fiji is approaching the time when it will be a separate Conference, and with this significant approach. Indentured labour was imported from India into Fiji years ago, and has multiplied so rapidly that there is now an Indian community numerically stronger than the indigenous Fijian population, and organized on a strictly national basis. But when the Conference is formed, it is to be a united Conference in which *nationals of each group will have equal standing—and this by their own decision*. Surely this is a work of grace, and in the true Methodist tradition. New Guinea was opened in 1875, and Papua in 1891. Both missions suffered severe war damage at the hands of the Japanese. Many of our native ministers and teachers were beheaded rather than betray the faith. And such was the gentle and self-sacrificing character of these native Christians that our troops came to call them 'Fuzzy-wuzzy Angels'— the adjective referring to their hair, and the noun to their hearts. These are the children of head-hunting cannibals of a few years ago. When European missionaries were withdrawn, or were captured or killed—we lost thirteen white missionaries by death—these men of God carried on their work with unabated zeal, so that, though buildings were razed, the Church still stood. A major task of rehabilitation is now being carried through.

The evangelistic zeal of these members of our mission Churches is something for which we are grateful to God. A Tongan Methodist went with the original party to Fiji, a hostile land. Since then a long line have gone to all fields. The triumphs of God's grace have made them also leaders amongst their own folk. The Queen of Tonga is a devout Methodist, and the Crown Prince, trained in Law at Sydney University, is a local preacher. One of our young Tongan probationers is the most highly qualified medical practitioner in that land.

Now the last General Conference, which met in May of this year, has entered a new field in the highland plateaux area of New Guinea-Papua, where it is estimated there are 1 million people whose existence was never even suspected, and who are quite untouched by any civilizing influences let alone by the Gospel. A survey party went in last year for four hazardous months, plotting out the field. The bulk of the members of this party were native Methodists from the adjoining mission districts. A fine tribute was made to the quality of our work when this year, in Western Australia, the Government of that state, impressed by our success in other fields, and after the dismal failure of its own purely secular approach in dealing with the aboriginal problem there, requested us, before all other Churches, to take over the Moore River station, and we have accepted that responsibility and entered a new field. We have other missions in the north to the aborigines and the half-caste population.

And so the story goes on. In every field, homes for the aged, hostels and hospitals, organizations for the under-privileged and the wayward—these are scattered all over the Commonwealth. In 1938, when Dr J. Alexander Findlay was in Brisbane, he saw the Garden Settlement for the Aged, and exclaimed: 'This is the most beautiful thing I have seen in Methodism.' In crowded cities our missions are using every modern technique, and are meeting with encouraging success. One superintendent said recently: 'Ninety per cent of the young people in my Church have come from non-Christian homes.' In community centres a new field of service has been pioneered, and fresh routes to the people are being explored.

With deep thankfulness to God, one can report that all over Australia and in the islands of the Pacific Methodism is beginning to march again proclaiming the all-sufficient grace of God for every man and in every situation. The Church is back once again upon her true foundations, a Church committed to prayer, to the cultivation of scriptural holiness in fellowship and by study of the Scriptures, and by the power of the Spirit to an active witness that the multitudes may be lead out of the darkness into the marvellous light of the Kingdom, and that the life of the nation may be reformed.

IV. THE METHODIST TRADITION IN SOUTH AFRICA

An address delivered by the REV. LESLIE A. HEWSON, *of Rhodes University College:*

What is to come out of the South African crucible? The *ingredients* of the crucible are human beings: black, white, coloured, and brown. Though South Africa is not unique in having these ingredients in its national life, it is unique in that here alone on earth a dominant white minority is living among a black majority in a land which both now regard as the homeland of themselves and their children's children.

The *temperature* of the crucible is rising. Of the situation in 1940, Dr Kenneth S. Latourette wrote: 'The whites were determined to remain in control, politically, economically, and socially. The result was discrimination and acute and chronic interracial tensions which, next to the anti-Semitism of the Third German Reich, were the most serious on the planet.'

Forty years ago, the builders of the Union of South Africa chose as the national motto, 'Union is strength', or, in Afrikaans, '*Eendrag maak mag*'. Since Dr Latourette wrote the comment quoted above, a new Government has come into power with a policy which tacitly alters our national motto to read, '*Apartheid* (total separation) is strength'. The friction between policies of *eendrag* and *apartheid* is one significant factor in the mounting temperature of South African affairs. The whites are divided in their attitude to this burning question; even English-speaking people are not all of one mind; and the Christian Church in South Africa is not united in its attitude, but the leaders of the Methodist Church have made quite clear where they stand.

Methodism, then, is an important element in the crucible. In the century and a half of its history, its northward advance toward the heart of Africa has been spectacular. Between the Southern Ocean and Central Africa five great rivers separate five vast territories. In the first half-century we had crossed the Orange, and were planning to cross the Vaal. In the second half-century, we crossed the Vaal, the Limpopo, and (in our Primitive Methodist Mission) the Zambezi, and were advancing towards the Congo. At this stage we joined hands with our American Methodist comrades at work in Africa.

In numbers, Methodism stands first in African membership south of the Limpopo, for 88 per cent of our membership is black. We stand second in total membership, third in European membership, and fourth in Coloured membership.

What marks does the authentic Methodist tradition bear, and how far are they represented in South African Methodism?

> Witness
> Evangelism
> Sacrament
> Literature
> Edification
> Youth Work

1. *Witness*. In so far as Methodism is 'Scriptural Christianity', we should expect it to have both *kerygma* and *didache*—that is, a given word of witness and a way of life that springs from that message, a testimony, and a teaching.

Part of our purpose here at Oxford is to possess our great possessions in this witness and this way of life: the proclamation of what God has done in the holy Birth, the wonderful words, the mighty deeds, the atoning death, and the glorious Resurrection of Jesus Christ, and in the coming of the Holy Spirit, the Lord and Giver of the life of God in the soul of man, and in the community of mankind.

Here we gratefully acknowledge our vast and incalculable debt to the Methodism of Great Britain, this mother of so many and such great modern Christian missions. From these islands (and I use the plural, for we have our Irish Methodists in South Africa too), from these islands we have received the missionaries, men and women who proclaimed not only with their lips but with their lives the Methodist testimony and the Methodist teaching. To these islands we still turn for guidance in matters of faith and practice.

Is that witness borne today? Listen to the voice of Methodism on the air, or listen to our African Methodists sing in the great congregation

'*Kosi yam ubunditanda*' ('Love divine, all loves excelling'), and ponder on all that must have happened to make this thing possible, and you will know that the Methodist witness has found its authentic interpretation, and its inspired reinterpretation in South Africa.

2. *Evangelism.* The word of witness needs a preacher; the rock upon which Christ builds His Church is the faith incarnated in confessing Peter and his spiritual children.

Our history in South Africa shows that evangelism has been of prime importance in the remarkable growth of Methodism. The first Methodists to set foot in South Africa were soldiers of the British Army of occupation right at the end of Wesley's century. They brought with them a Christian faith and a Methodist fervour that were highly contagious. The first missionaries were all zealous evangelists: Barnabas Shaw the pioneer, William Threlfall the romantic and martyr, and William Shaw the wise master-builder.

But no evangelistic mission has affected South African Methodism more profoundly than the Taylor mission of 1866. Not only did it reap the harvest of the pioneers, but it had vast and continuing effects in its impetus to the creation of an indigenous African ministry, and to the birth of *Nzondelelo*, the 'fervent desire' of Africans for the conversion of their kinsmen according to the flesh. It is strange that, owing so great a debt to American Methodism, we should not have developed a closer association. Perhaps part of the answer is that even American Methodism cannot produce a Taylor in every decade to lease or lend!

Two results follow from the evangelism of South African Methodism: one calculable, the other incalculable. The calculable result is the fact that since the establishment of the South African Methodist Conference in 1883, the Church has multiplied its membership fifteen times, and has been increasing at an average rate of 10,000 new members a year for so long that this mass movement in steady motion has ceased to be an abnormal feature of the Church.

The incalculable result follows from the fact that the great army of our African preachers have kept Christ and Him crucified central in their preaching at a time when 1,000 ephemeral sects have sprouted up in response to the preaching of racialism and Bantu nationalism. If all our African preachers were to become prophets of Bantu nationalism, the result would be a catastrophe of unpredictable magnitude.

3. *Sacrament and Liturgy.* Both the hymns of Charles and the practice of John Wesley throughout his apostolic life convince us that sacramental worship is an authentic mark of the Methodist tradition. Further, Wesley abridged the Book of Common Prayer for use by American and British Methodists because he was convinced that 'the Scriptural primitive religion of love, which is now reviving throughout the three kingdoms, is to be found in [the] Morning and Evening Service, and in [the] daily, as well as occasional, prayers; and the whole of it is beautifully summed up in that one comprehensive petition: "Cleanse the thoughts of our hearts by the inspiration of Thy Holy Spirit, that we may perfectly love Thee, and worthily magnify Thy holy name." '

Methodist historians have noted a wasting of the sacramental heritage in the post-Wesley period. This same deficiency disease appeared later in South African Methodism. Among its symptoms are the tendency to regard an Evangelical flavour in a service as an adequate substitute for worship, to make the most sacred rite of our holy religion merely an appendage to the 'real' service, and to be sour and suspicious about liturgical worship.

56

Let two comments suffice here. First, our African Church has never given up the liturgical inheritance bequeathed by the early missionaries, though there are signs that familiarity may breed a slick facility, if not contempt. Nevertheless, this liturgical tradition, together with the hymns of Charles Wesley, must have a quite inestimable effect in fulfilling Pollock's prayer for the Church: 'Keep her life and doctrine pure.' Second, there are welcome signs that the whole Church in South Africa is coming to see that Evangelical fruits need sacramental and liturgical roots.

So far as the other of the dominical sacraments is concerned, we note that comment of Henry Carter, 'It cannot be said that an adequate account of Christian baptism is a part of the heritage bequeathed by John Wesley.' The subject is assuming a growing importance in South Africa, and we are following with the keenest interest the contemporary debate within and beyond British Methodism.

4. *Literature.* The first appeal for literature to reach England from South Africa came in a letter dated 1808 from a soldier at the Cape: 'We would thank you to send us some Hymn Books, Bibles and Mr Wesley's Works.' The order is suggestive. Is it characteristic of Methodists to sing more than to read the Bible, and to read the Bible more than Mr Wesley's works?

'A little body of experimental and practical divinity' John called the hymn book of 1779. The theology of the Methodist Revival caught fire in the hymns of Charles Wesley, and they have kindled fire wherever the Revival has spread. If poetry was made the handmaid of piety, printing became the maid of all work.

English, however, is not the language medium through which most of our mission work is done. Our pioneers have to begin right at the beginning. They had to learn the new language, then to give it a written form, and then to provide it with a Methodist literature. Methodism in South Africa has made an outstanding contribution here, with W. B. Boyce, the Bantu grammarian, J. W. Appleyard, the philologist and translator of the Xhosa Bible, and H. H. Dugmore, the hymn-writer, as the representative names.

All these were Europeans, but the time has now happily come when African Methodists—musicians, poets, and writers—are composing and translating in eleven Bantu languages and dialects.

Europeans and educated Africans are amply supplied with Methodist literature from Great Britain and America, but our own Publishing House faces perplexing and intricate problems in the dissemination of vernacular literature: there is the dead weight of illiteracy, the conflicting orthographies which wake echoes of Babel in the ears of the Book Steward, and the dire poverty of African converts at a time when printing costs are mounting steeply. Yet our Book Room and missionary executives are keenly aware of these problems and are facing them with enterprise and determination.

5. *Edification.* In one of his best-known hymns, Charles Wesley links the saving of a never-dying soul and fitting it for the sky with the service of the present age. Let edification in its fullest meaning of building up stand for this mark of the Methodist tradition.

(a) *Fellowship.* The Class Meeting in its historic form barely survives in our European congregations, but it is still vigorous in the Coloured and African societies. There have been various attempts to supply this lack of fellowship by Wesley Guilds, Preparation Classes for Church Membership, Weekly Devotional Meetings, and the Men's League. We envy what we have heard and read of the American Sunday-school system, but as motor cars have become more common in our sunny land, we have had to transfer most of our Sunday-schools to the morning in order to keep the children.

Of all the more recent forms of fellowship meeting, none has attained the success of the Women's Auxiliary in our European work, with its devotional, missionary, and practical aims. Its counterpart in the African Church is the Women's Manyano or prayer union, with the striking uniform of black skirt, red blouse, and white collar and hat. These signify the blackness of sin, the blood of Christ, and the purity of a life truly cleansed.

(b) *Education*. In African education, the Methodist Church has a place of unchallenged primacy, shouldering great responsibilities in primary, high, secondary, and training or industrial schools, while our great missionary institutions, by their very names, furnish a stirring commentary upon Methodist missionary history. Further, we have three European colleges, and one Coloured training institution of which we are justly proud.

(c) *Medical missions* have taken their place side by side with evangelism and education as our service to the present age. At three missionary hospitals and numerous clinics we are seeking the total answer to our Lord's question, 'Wilt thou be made whole?' for we believe that the Church, like her Lord, must be concerned with the whole man, body, mind, and soul.

(d) Primarily, edification refers to the building up of the body of Christ; and Methodism has been well and worthily represented in every significant movement for *Christian co-operation*. We hold a peerless record in service to the Christian Council of South Africa, the greatest association of Christian Churches and missions in the sub-continent; and we are the major partner in two great ventures of faith in joint theological training— the training of African and Coloured probationers at the South African Native College at Fort Hare, and of Europeans at Rhodes University, Grahamstown.

6. Finally, *youth work*. The first Sunday-school in South Africa was established by the Methodists of the 1820 Settlers within a year of their arrival upon that savage and precarious frontier. One hundred and thirty years later, Methodism is still making pioneer ventures in youth work. A Department of Religious Education has recently been established, and has met with encouraging success. Perhaps the finest thing that has come out of our Post-war Development Commission has been to capture the South African passion for camping out and use it for the direct presentation of the gospel to modern young people at the youth camps now regularly organized in most districts.

Let these swift glimpses suggest the outline of the Methodist Church now facing a significant hour of its destiny in the South African crucible. As never before, we need you—you in this dear land where so many of us found birth and the second birth; you of the New World, to whom God has given at this time matchless powers and immeasurable opportunities; you of the mission fields of Africa and Asia, whose opportunities are inseparably the same as ours, and yet significantly different; you in Australasia, through whom God has wrought greatly beneath the same Cross and the same Southern Cross that we know.

We need you. But you need us. Methodism has no voice in our land but our voice; no hand but our hands. Trust us then. Believe in us. But evermore pray for us, that our faith fail not, that we fail not in our witness to the Faith of the Lord Jesus Christ.

V. THE METHODIST TRADITIONS IN THE YOUNGER CHURCHES

An address given by the REV. S. G. MENDIS, *Chairman of the Ceylon District:*

When the steamer that brought us to England was entering the Mediterranean Sea, I was reminded of the incident nearly 1,900 years ago, when the Church at Antioch, led by the Holy Spirit, set apart Barnabas and Paul, prayed and laid hands on them, and sent them to preach the Gospel, as a result of which churches were founded in Asia Minor and later in Europe. In the same way Dr Thomas Coke set out in the early days of Methodism to preach the Gospel in the West, and later in his life, after much prayer and pleading with the Conference set out to the East with a small band of followers. This band without their leader arrived in Ceylon in the year 1814. And today we find Methodist Churches in all parts of Asia and South-east Asia. The Churches known as the younger Churches are the result of missionary work in all parts of the world. The small mission stations established by pioneer missionaries in prayer and faith have grown and are still growing, and many of them are today strong Churches which are being used by God to bring many more countries and peoples to a knowledge of Himself and His Son Jesus Christ.

What I am going to say on this subject is mainly based on my own knowledge of the Methodist Church in Ceylon, the first of the Asian Methodist Churches to be established, and to a great extent of India and Burma, and on conversations I have had with the representatives of the African Churches whom I met in this country after my arrival here.

Dealing with the subject of Methodist traditions in the younger Churches, I may begin by saying that in organization and administration the Methodist Church in Britain has reproduced itself in the younger Churches, and they have emphasized the importance of the distinctive Methodist doctrines and have given prominence to them in preaching and teaching.

The friendliness and fellowship so characteristic of Methodism have expressed themselves in no less a degree in the younger Churches. And these outward manifestations have been influenced often by the national traditions and cultures of the peoples.

These Churches have faithfully followed the organization and observed the law and discipline of the older Churches. The younger Churches have not lost by closely following the rules and usages of the mother Churches, but this may be said that if the younger Churches in the early stages of their development but had had the freedom to develop on indigenous lines more suited to their respective countries their growth and development might have been faster and more natural.

Worship. The forms of worship and orders of service in the younger Churches are more or less identical with those of the older Churches. In their growth the younger Churches have kept in touch with all that is best in the world-wide Methodist Church and other Free Churches, and in recent years the Churches have tried to develop their worship on indigenous lines and to use hymns and lyrics set to local tunes, so that the people of the country may feel more at home in it, and that it may be more easily understood by the non-Christian. The majority of the hymns used are translations from our own English Methodist Hymn-books sung to Western tunes. However, hymns written by nationals and set to Eastern music are more and more used. Churches and other buildings for worship are also being built in the architecture of the country.

It is gratifying to note that the younger Churches are beginning to lay more and more emphasis on the Communion service, the central act of our worship. Services of Holy Communion are being conducted where possible more than once a month in each place of Worship, and early morning Communions, both on the Lord's day and on week-days, are beginning to be appreciated. The worship life of the younger Churches can be said to be more liturgical than in most churches in England.

The major festivals of the Christian year are observed with great care, and domestic festivals of the people, such as birthdays and wedding anniversaries, are linked up with the life of the Church. Special thank-offerings are a common feature on such occasions.

The Itinerant Ministry. The period for which a minister should serve in a circuit had been prescribed by Wesley himself, and had been rigidly observed by his followers. However, the period both in the older and younger Churches has been increased from three to five years, and more in special cases. But this practice or regulation has gradually fallen into disuse and the period of a minister's stay in a circuit or institution is governed by other circumstances which are more important to the progress of the work. Very often the Churches have lost and not gained by the frequent transfer of their ministers and other workers. Especially in the evangelistic areas, men and women who have had long years of continuous service in a given place have been able to do more effective work and their labours have resulted in bringing larger numbers to the Church.

The Place of Lay Men and Women in the Church. Lay men and women have come forward and filled the places allotted to them in the younger as in the older Churches. We thank God for the great army of lay workers who, not only by the services they render to the Church, but also by their life and work, are a living testimony to the saving power of the gospel of Jesus Christ. Lay people in larger numbers are coming forward to take their full share in the work of the Church in the local societies, in the circuits and in the districts. Today we have not only men but women who, particularly in the urban areas, are serving the Church as stewards—circuit, chapel, and poor—as local preachers and Sunday-school teachers, and also take responsibility for Women's Fellowships and work amongst women and children.

The presence of lay men and women who have been sent as lay mission-aries by the missionary societies to do educational, medical, and evangel-istic work in the mission fields has given an impetus to the laity of these lands. Their life and self-sacrificing spirit and devotion to duty have been an inspiration and an example to all.

An order for women similar to that of the lay women missionary has been organized in Ceylon. The candidates are accepted by Synod and undergo a preliminary course of study and a further training in the special work they are expected to do, and are received by Synod and, after a probationary period of two years, are ordained as sisters of the Order of Lay Women Workers. It is hoped that it will be possible to create a similar order for men who will take the place of lay men missionaries.

The *Ashram* movement in the Churches in India and Ceylon has passed its experimental stage and has come to stay, and will prove a blessing to the life and work of the Church in deepening the Spiritual life of its people and as a mode of evangelism.

Education. The great contribution made through the younger Churches to their own countries with the help rendered by the missionary societies by the establishment of educational institutions has been readily acknowledged both by the governments and the peoples. The rapid progress made by many a country in its development is largely due to the Christian educational institutions in that land. The Prime Minister of Ceylon, who is himself a Buddhist, speaking at a public function, said that Ceylon would not have had independence so soon but for the work of the missionary educational institutions. Though education and medical work is now becoming more and more the responsibility of the State, the Churches must continue to carry out in the future the same policy with regard to educational, medical, and social work as they have done in the past. There is a great work to be done for the advancement and progress of the countries in which we live, and as long as the doors are open it is our duty to carry on and play our part in hastening the day of the coming of God's Kingdom on earth.

If we are to train Christian leaders who can take their place in the life of the Church, it is essential that we carry on our educational and training institutions. One drawback at the present time is the dearth of leaders, both ordained and lay, and this problem can only be solved if we are able to give our Christian boys and girls the necessary training in our own institutions.

Social Concern and Wide Interest in Public Affairs. The younger Churches are showing the same concern as the older Churches for the social betterment of the people, and are taking a wide interest in public affairs. The Churches often work in co-operation with public institutions for the social and general welfare of the people, and have been able to emphasize the truth that Christianity stands for the salvation of the *whole person* by being engaged in educational, medical, and social work. While in the countries of the West such work is largely the responsibility of the government. In many parts of the East the Churches had to give the lead, and the work done in this way has been a great credit to the Church in the eyes of the non-Christian population. The Churches have very often been the pioneers in the national and social development of the people.

Home and Foreign Missions. The younger Churches are not only concerned with the evangelization of their own countrymen, but in many cases are doing what they can to help foreign missionary work by contributing money to outside fields and in some cases in sending both men and money.

The older Churches should help the younger Churches to send their men and women as missionaries to neighbouring lands by supporting them, instead of all the time sending out missionaries from the West. The work of evangelization could then be carried out more efficiently and effectively and with less expense. Many Churches show a very keen interest in the missionary enterprise, and young men and women who may feel called to go out to foreign parts can be used in this way, until the time comes when these Churches will be able to support their own missionaries.

Co-operation with Other Churches. The Churches in the mission fields have always been ready to stretch out the hand of fellowship to other Churches. Methodism has played a unique part in bringing the Churches together and in acting as a link between the episcopal and Free Churches. There is very much more co-operation between Churches in the mission field than in the sending countries.

A recent feature in our Church in Ceylon has been the Bible schools and theological conferences of an interdenominational character. These are helping to bring together the leaders of the Churches, both ministerial and lay.

The time also has come when the Churches of Africa and the West Indies on one side and the Churches in Asia on the other should come together to consider the common problems with which they are faced, and find strength and courage in each other's fellowship.

Church Union. The attempts to bring about a union amongst the Churches in the mission field have borne fruit, and we know of the negotiations that are taking place in many parts of the world to bring together the Anglican, Lutheran, Methodist, Congregational, Baptist, and Presbyterian Churches. These attempts are being successfully carried out under the guidance of the Holy Spirit, and we are confidently looking forward to the day when the Churches will unite, because we know and believe that it is God's Will that we all should be one.

One effect of the Church union negotiations has been to make the younger Methodist Churches turn their eyes to the Churches round about them, and not so much to the Churches of the West from which they have sprung. It has also helped them not only to make a worthy contribution from their heritage, but also to understand and value the contributions that can be made by other Churches to a united Church. The younger Churches, looking only at their own mother Churches and not at the Churches of other denominations in their own area, have overlooked the great value of closer co-operation with each other. The South-east Asian Christian Conference at Bangkok revealed to those who had come together what large and powerful Churches were close at hand facing the same problems and doing the same task.

The younger Churches in all parts of the world today are confronting the problems presented by the non-Christian religions and the economic and political conditions of their respective countries as they have never done before. Therefore there are two very important and vital things (as far as I can see) that need our attention, thought, and prayer. The first is that the younger Churches can no longer be divided and separated by denominational differences. They must stand together as one body in order to confront and overcome the problems that are facing them. Secondly, the time has not come, as some imagine, for the sending Churches to withdraw from older mission fields or reduce the support given to them, but to stand by them at this critical stage of their life when their countries, with their newly won independence, have vast national and economic problems to face and help the Churches to make an all-out effort to win their fellow men to Christ and to show that Christ, and Christ alone, is the answer to all world problems.

AFTERNOON LECTURE

THE AFTERNOON session was held in the Examination Schools. Prayer was offered by Bishop Raymond L. Jones of North Carolina, and Bishop C. C. Alleyne of Philadelphia presided over the lecture which followed.

METHODISM AND THE CATHOLIC TRADITION

A Lecture delivered by PRESIDENT DR UMPHREY LEE, *of Southern Methodist University, Dallas, Texas:*

To discuss intelligently the subject, 'Methodism and the Catholic Tradition', one should know what Methodism is and what is the Catholic tradition. As to the Methodists, it is not easy to define a movement which has spread almost throughout the earth and has taken on different forms in different nations. I have been told that the British Methodists do not always agree on every point, and I have seen British visitors attempting to conceal their surprise—if not consternation—at some aspects of American Methodism. A student from Pakistan recently asked a colleague of mine, 'What is the difference between Methodists and Christians?' To discuss adequately the subject of this paper, I should have to consider the differences between Methodists and Methodists.

Although arguments still continue as to what John and Charles Wesley believed, it would seem better to discuss today the Catholic tradition and John Wesley. Here there will be difficulty enough, since, as everyone knows, competent scholars have disagreed as to what Wesley believed and intended: Father Piette thinks that Wesley inaugurated a reaction against Protestantism, and the late Dr Cell believed that Wesley re-declared the pure faith of the Reformers.

Nor is it easy to define the Catholic tradition. There are too many claimants to the inheritance. It is true that some Anglo-Catholics write and speak as if there were a body of Doctrine and a practice which are accepted equally by the so-called Catholic branches, the Greek Orthodox, the Roman Catholics, and the Anglo-Catholics. But as that excellent little book, *The Catholicity of Protestantism*, has pointed out, the Orthodox Eastern Churches hold that the Orthodox Church is 'the whole and only Catholic Church' and the Roman Catholic Church holds that it is dangerous error 'to think that one can adhere to Christ, the Head of the Church, and refuse allegiance to his Vicar on earth'. The hospitality of the Anglo-Catholics in acknowledging the Catholicity of the Orthodox and of the Romans is not returned. There are times when one feels that the Free Churches are unduly sensitive to the claims of the so-called Catholic groups, but one can not escape the feeling also that the writings of the Anglo-Catholics show an uneasy awareness of the uplifted eyebrows of Rome.

Professor Clement C. J. Webb once referred to the Difficulty of recovering the theology of the Oxford Movement because of changes in thought since the middle of the nineteenth century, particularly those changes brought about by the doctrine of evolution and by Biblical criticism. It is sometimes difficult to recover the theology of earlier Anglicanism because of the Anglo-Catholic controversies. When we ask what Wesley believed, we are likely to begin arguing about what, in the light of nineteenth-century controversies between Protestants and Catholics, we think Wesley should have believed. Instead of attempting to fit the discussion of Wesleyanism to the Procrustean bed of nineteenth-century disputes, it is better to attempt at least to see the problems of the eighteenth century in the light of that century.

It is admitted by all that Wesley grew up a High Churchman in the home of a High Churchman. His parents were themselves converts to High Churchmanship, and therefore, as converts frequently do, held the more tenaciously to their views. In later years John Wesley described his childhood training:

'From a child I was taught to love and reverence the Scripture, the oracles of God; and next to these, to esteem the primitive Fathers, the writers of the three first centuries. Next after the primitive Church, I esteemed our own, the Church of England, as the most scriptural national Church in the world. I therefore not only assented to all the doctrines, but observed all the rubrics in the Liturgy; and that with all possible exactness even at the peril of my life.'

As everyone knows, this description does not cover all of Wesley's

High Churchmanship. It is interesting to compare his beliefs and practice with those which the Tory firebrand of Queen Anne's age, Sacheverell, declared to be the marks of a High Churchman.

'A High Churchman', said Sacheverell, 'is High for the divine right of Episcopacy, High for the uninterrupted Succession, High for the Liturgies against extempory prayers, High for the primitive doctrine and discipline of the Ancient Church. . . . He believes separation from the Church of England to be a damning Schism, and the Dissenters to be in a very dangerous state, notwithstanding the toleration. . . . He is so High as to observe the traditional customs as well as the written laws of the Church, and he always bowed very low before the Altar and at the name of Jesus' (quoted by G. M. Trevelyan, *England Under Queen Anne, Blenheim*, p. 52).

When one compares Wesley's views in his earlier years with this statement of Sacheverell, it is obvious that there is much agreement. Wesley regarded the threefold order of the ministry as authorized by Scripture, and believed that none should administer baptism or the Lord's Supper unless ordained by bishops in the uninterrupted succession. This view he held until 1746. In 1745 he thought it providential that he had not persisted in the impetuosity of his High Church zeal. If he had done so, 'neither should we have been willing to converse with Dissenters, nor they to receive any good at our hands'. In that same year he was defining schism as a causeless breach, rupture, or division within the Church, a definition which enabled him to avoid discussion of the sin of schism as separation from the Church.

Whether Wesley practised some of the acts mentioned by Sacheverell I do not know, although I suspect that he did. Certainly he did follow so closely the rubrics of the liturgy as to cause great offence to less zealous Churchmen.

The dates mentioned, 1745 and 1746, indicate that the older theory that Wesley discarded his High Church views at the time of his conversion in 1738 cannot be maintained. It is unnecessary to stress this, since modern historians, especially Dr J. E. Rattenbury, have proven the point beyond any necessity of argument. It seems wise, however, to consider briefly the manner in which Wesley's changes of opinion came about.

It has been often taken for granted, I believe, that Wesley moved almost carelessly from his inherited opinions, often making radical changes after reading a single book. The two instances cited most frequently as examples of this deplorable lack of intellectual earnestness are Wesley's denial of his High Church views of the ministry after reading Lord King's book on the early Church, and his change of attitude toward the Americans after reading Dr Johnson's pamphlet, *Taxation no Tyranny*.

Elsewhere I have discussed in some detail the latter of these instances. It is enough to say here that there is good evidence for the view that Wesley did not change his mind about the Americans except as to their intentions. He had pleaded for a consideration of the American position on the grounds of justice and of common sense, but at no time did he advocate their independence. It can be shown that at the time he was reading Johnson's pamphlet he most probably received the official account of the Battle of Lexington, with the King's statement that the Americans must be either colonists or independent. There is no doubt that Johnson's pamphlet influenced Wesley, but there seems to me no doubt also that the King's statement and the account of the Battle of Lexington convinced him that the Americans aimed at independence, as they did. This Wesley, both as a Tory and as an admirer of George III, could not condone. To

Wesley the English Government's actions were unwise, but they did not justify rebellion.

It seems to me that a similar explanation must hold for the year 1746, when Wesley read Lord King's book on Church government. He had a little while before declared himself convinced of the necessity of episcopal ordination by one in the uninterrupted succession for the valid administration of the sacraments, yet when he read Lord King's book Wesley noted in his *Journal*: 'In spite of the vehement prejudice of my education, I was ready to believe that this was a fair and impartial draught; but, if so, it would follow that bishops and presbyters are (essentially) of one order. . . .' And in later years he said that Lord King's book convinced him that bishops and presbyters are of the same order and have the same right to ordain.

To understand why Wesley was ready to accept evidence that seemed to prove views so opposed to 'the vehement prejudice' of his education, it is necessary to notice how Wesley had been modifying his High Church opinions. Many years later he wrote to the printer of the *Dublin Chronicle*:

'In my youth I was not only a member of the Church of England, but a bigot to it, believing none but the members of it to be in a state of salvation. I began to abate of this violence in 1729. . . . When I was abroad, I observed every rule of the Church, even at the peril of my life. . . . I was exactly of the same sentiment when I returned from America.'

But Wesley had abated some of his High Church violence (as he called it) while in America. In the self-analysis entered in his *Journal* under date of 24th January 1738—that is, while Wesley was on shipboard returning to England—there are some paragraphs in the *Standard Journal* which were added from a manuscript in the possession of Henry Moore. The entries are revealing:

'For many years', wrote Wesley, 'I have been tossed by various winds of doctrine. I asked long ago, "What must I do to be saved?" The Scripture answered: "Keep the Commandments, believe, hope, love; follow after these tempers till thou hast fully attained, that is till death; by all those outward works and means which God hath appointed, by walking as Christ walked." '

Wesley felt that he had avoided leaning too much either to dependence on outward works or on faith without works. But he had not found a great deal of help in some places.

'But before God's time was come, I fell among some Lutheran and Calvinist authors, whose confused and indigested accounts magnified faith to such an amazing size that it quite hid all the rest of the Commandments. I did not then see that this was the natural effect of their overgrown fear of Popery; being so terrified with the cry of merit and good works, that they plunged at once into the other extreme. In this labyrinth I was utterly lost; not being able to find out what the error was, nor yet to reconcile this uncouth hypothesis either with Scripture or common sense.

'The English writers, such as Bishop Beveridge, Bishop Taylor, and Mr Nelson, a little relieved me from these well-meaning, wrong-headed Germans. Their accounts of Christianity I could easily see to be, in the main, consistent both with reason and Scripture. Only when they interpreted Scripture in different ways, I was often much at a loss. And again, there was one thing much insisted on in Scripture—the unity of the Church—which none of them, I thought, clearly explained or strongly inculcated.'

Wesley found what he thought was a sure rule of interpreting Scripture in the Vincentian Canon, the consensus of the ancients as to what was everywhere and always believed; but he had gone too far here:

'Nor was it long before I bent the bow too far the other way: 1. By making antiquity a co-ordinate rather than subordinate rule with Scripture. 2. By admitting several doubtful writings as undoubted evidences of antiquity. 3. By extending antiquity too far, even to the middle or end of the fourth century. 4. By believing more practices to have been universal in the ancient Church than ever were so. 5. By not considering that the Decrees of one Provincial Senate could bind only those provinces whose representatives met therein. 6. By not considering that the most of those decrees were adapted to particular times and occasions; and consequently, when those occasions ceased, must cease to bind even those provinces.'

At the time that Wesley was revaluing his views about salvation and the early Church, he had become acquainted with Christians or other communions, particularly with the Moravians, whose orders he apparently considered valid. After the centre of his religious interests shifted to present salvation, peace, joy, love, brought into the heart through faith, Wesley was thrown with some who did not hold communion with any episcopal Church. Were all these lost? Is a Church with an episcopally ordained ministry, with the uninterrupted succession necessary? In this frame of mind Wesley, student of the early Church for so many years, was, as he put it, 'ready to believe' that Lord King's book was a 'fair and impartial draught', even though accepting the conclusions was distasteful.

This somewhat lengthy consideration of Wesley's change of mind about the divine right of episcopacy and the identity of episcopal and presbyterial orders has been for a double purpose. In the first place, it is not correct, I think, to suppose that Wesley simply read some book and immediately adopted its views. His changes of opinion on important matters came at the end of a train of thought and of circumstances and were often crystallized by the arguments of a skilful proponent. In the second place, this particular change of mind was fateful for Wesley and for Methodism. It cut him off forever from those to whom episcopacy is a matter of Doctrine —the majority of Christians today, according to Dr Sparrow Simpson. Although this argument from numbers seems somewhat American, yet it is true that the Orthodox Church, the Roman Catholic Church, and the Anglo-Catholics believe their own Episcopacy to be a matter of Doctrine. The Methodists, following John Wesley, do not.

This change of opinion about episcopacy did not cause Wesley to abandon his view of the Church, a fact which his contemporaries would have understood better than our contemporaries, who must needs think in terms become rigid from much controversy. Three years after he had declared that he did not believe in the uninterrupted succession or that bishops form a distinct order of ministry, Wesley wrote to a Roman Catholic: 'I believe that Christ by His Apostles gathered unto Himself a Church, to which He has continually added such as shall be saved; that this catholic (that is, universal) Church, extending to all nations and to all ages, is holy in all its members, who have fellowship with the holy angels, who constantly minister to these heirs of salvation; and with all living members of Christ on earth, as well as all who are departed in His faith and fear.' If this is taken seriously it must be recognized as a catholic definition of the Church.

Nor did Wesley's change of mind about episcopacy cause him to alter his views about the Lord's Supper. What Wesley believed about this sacrament when he was a High Churchman in Oxford he continued to believe all his life. This Dr J. E. Rattenbury has brought out admirably in his most recent book, *The Eucharistic Hymns of John and Charles Wesley*, and, therefore, needs the less notice here. The Lord's Supper is a memorial, but not a mere memorial. It is a sign of present graces, a means of grace, a pledge of future glory, a commemorative sacrifice, a sacrifice of ourselves and of our goods. To be sure, the emphasis is placed upon the disposition of the communicant—there is nothing of the magical in Wesley's theory—but a pragmatic age may find it difficult to realize that when Wesley spoke of the means of grace he meant just exactly that. Wesley was particularly insistent that the sacrament of the Lord's Supper is a converting ordinance: 'What surer way have we of procuring pardon from Him, than the showing forth of the Lord's death; and beseeching Him for the sake of His Son's sufferings, to blot out all our sins?'

Wesley seems not to have been deeply interested in the question of baptism, possibly because most of the converts of Methodism were those who had already been baptized. It is true that in 1756 Wesley reprinted his father's tract on baptism, and that tract does speak of baptism as conferring benefits among which are 'the washing away the guilt of original sin, by the application of the merits of Christ's death'. It speaks, too, of baptismal regeneration. Wesley made no comment upon this tract to indicate that he did not agree with it, but he did make some changes in the office of baptism in the *Sunday Service* which he prepared for the American Church. In the minister's closing exhortation to thankful prayer after the baptism of an infant he is to say, 'Seeing now, dearly beloved brethren, that this child is grafted into the body of Christ's Church,' whereas in the Prayer Book he said: 'that this child is regenerate and grafted into the body of Christ's Church'. Later in the Thanksgiving Prayer the minister is to say, 'that it hath pleased Thee to receive this infant for Thine own child by adoption', instead of 'it hath pleased Thee to regenerate this infant with Thy Holy Spirit, to receive him for Thine own child by adoption'. But Wesley still retained the prayer 'to sanctify water to the mystical washing away of sin', and 'that he may receive remission of his sins by spiritual regeneration'.

The truth seems to be that Wesley did not have any consistent doctrine of baptism. It has always seemed to me that, if Wesley had tried to be consistent in his theory of baptism, particularly of infant baptism, he would have retained Confirmation in the Church.

In his Preface to the First Collected Edition of his *Works*, Wesley declared that here in this corrected edition were his 'last and maturest thoughts, agreeable, I hope, to Scripture, Reason, and Christian Antiquity'. These authorities, so familiar to those acquainted with seventeenth-century Anglicanism, were always acknowledged by Wesley.

It is unnecessary here to go into detail as to what Wesley meant by reason. He was not only of the eighteenth century, but he was a man devoted to logic, a former moderator of university disputations. Wesley believed that religion is reasonable. We must have revelation, as we cannot by reasoning find out God, but the God who is revealed to us and His works in this world, including Scripture, are not irrational.

As to Christian antiquity, Wesley believed that the writings of the Apostolic Fathers are 'not of equal authority with the Holy Scriptures. . . . Yet as worthy of a much greater respect than any composures which have been made since' (Preface to the *Epistles of the Apostolical Fathers*). These Fathers Wesley believed 'were not mistaken in their interpretation of the gospel of Christ; but that in all the necessary parts of it, they were so assisted by the Holy Ghost, as to be scarce capable of mistaking'. Wesley admitted that some of the primitive Fathers did not have 'strong natural sense', few of them had much learning, and none 'the assistance which our age enjoys in some respects above all that went before'. The ante-Nicene

Fathers Wesley thought to be 'the most authentic commentators on Scripture, as being both nearest the Fountain, and eminently endued with the Spirit by which all Scripture was given'. It should be remarked that the last statement was written eighteen years after Wesley had recorded in his *Journal* that he had bent the bow too far in his regard for the ancient Fathers.

What about the authority of experience? 'The conjunction of belief in the authority of an organic Church with insistence upon the value and reality of individual experience as the final test', wrote Dr H. B. Workman, 'gives to Methodism its special position in the catholic Church.' But is experience an authority in the same sense as the Bible? Mr Stanley B. Frost, in a German thesis written several years ago, thinks that Wesley in practice tried to bring the Bible and experience together as the grand authority, and he quotes what John Wesley wrote to Charles concerning the doctrine of instantaneous sanctification: 'For if there be no living witness of what we have preached for twenty years, I cannot, I dare not preach it any longer.'

Whether the authority of experience was more than that pragmatism which Paul Elmer More thought to be part of the spirit of seventeenth-century Anglicanism I am not sure. The Methodist, like More's Anglican, 'May come to know by effects which leave for him no doubt of their cause that the Christ in whom he trusts is not dead but living, and that faith has brought him into touch with fact.' There is a mystical certainty which is 'authority' in one sense.

Wesley was unquestionably pragmatic, unquestionably experimental. He did believe that experience is the test of religion, and while he advocated and discarded a good many theories about how the Christian should behave, in the end he still believed in experience. But I am not convinced that experience would have been acknowledged by him as authority in the sense in which the Bible is the Christian's authority. When it was objected to the doctrine of the witness of the Spirit that 'experience is not sufficient to prove a doctrine which is not founded on Scripture', Wesley replied: 'This is undoubtedly true, and it is an important truth.'

It seems to me that experience takes its place for Wesley alongside reason and the primitive Fathers. Neither could take precedence of the Bible. Of course, practically, Wesley was sure that he found in the Bible whatever he thought his reason or other people's experience proved to be true.

When Wesley modified his views about the early Church, he was convinced by Anglican authorities, particularly Bishop Beveridge. When he changed his mind about episcopacy and the uninterrupted succession, he thought that he was bowing to the authority of the early Church. When he worked out his doctrine of salvation so that it had the neat, ordered form which he liked, he adopted a synthesis advocated by another Caroline divine, Bishop Bull. But in this case Wesley felt that he was achieving the union of elements which were separated in the teachings of Protestants and Catholics.

That Wesley believed and taught the doctrine of justification by faith is beyond dispute. He even used the word 'alone'. 'Who has wrote more ably than Martin Luther on justification by faith alone?' he asked. But Wesley never fully appreciated either Luther or Calvin. Although it was a reading from the Preface to Luther's *The Epistle to the Romans* which was the catalyst in Wesley's Aldersgate experience, he was very critical of Luther's commentary on Galatians. The German touched him at two of his most sensitive points: his estimate of the place of reason and his ethical concern.

Wesley thought that Luther decried reason and spoke blasphemously of good works and of the law.

Whether Wesley understood Luther or not is here unimportant. Mainly, Wesley was reacting against what he conceived to be the mistakes of the Moravians. Wesley thought his own doctrine of justification by faith to be the doctrine of the Church of England as taught in the Articles and Homilies. After quoting Dr Trapp to the effect that Law was responsible for Methodism, and Bishop Warburton, that the new movement was a child of Count Zinzendorf, Wesley wrote:

'The book which, next to the Holy Scripture, was of the greatest use to them, in settling their judgment as to the grand point of justification by faith, was the *Book of Homilies*. They were never clearly convinced that we are justified by faith alone, till they carefully considered them, and compared them with the sacred writings, particularly St Paul's Epistle to the Romans.'

For Wesley and most of his Anglican predecessors saw that the problem was not whether man could be saved without good works provided he had the opportunity for them, but whether he could earn his salvation by good works. On that there could be no hesitation so far as Wesley was concerned; no man could do enough to earn his eternal salvation. As Bishop Beveridge, who died when Wesley was a small boy, said: a man who thinks he can merit eternal glories by temporal duties 'must either have very high thoughts of his own merit, or very low ones of God's presence'. And the Bishop added: 'For my own part it is a greater happiness I expect when dead than I am able to deserve when I am alive.'

Because Wesley would not speak blasphemously of the Law as he thought Luther did, and yet would not deny justification by faith, there were times when the great Methodist's explanations of his position were confusing. There could be no good works properly so-called before justification. On the other hand, Wesley insisted that a man must repent and certainly he must believe; but these were 'conditions' and not good works. In 1770 the Conference adopted certain so-called 'Doctrinal Minutes', in which some statements were made which seemed to some to deny justification by faith. The incident has long since been forgotten save by those interested in Methodist history, and therefore must be given in a little more detail here. The offending sections of the Minutes said in part:

'We have received it as a maxim, that "a man is to do nothing in order to justification". Nothing can be more false. Whoever desires to find favour with God should "cease from evil and learn to do well". . . . Whoever repents should "do works meet for repentance." And if this is not in order to find favour, what does he do them for?

'Once more review the whole affair:

'(1) Who of us is now accepted of God?
  'He that now believes in Christ with a loving, obedient heart.
'(2) But who among those that never heard of Christ?
  'He that, according to the light he has, "feareth God and worketh righteousness".
'(3) Is this the same with "he that is sincere"?
  'Nearly, if not quite.
'(4) Is not this salvation by works?
  'Not by the merit of works, but by works as a condition.
'(5) What have we then been disputing about for these thirty years?
  'I am afraid about words, namely, in some of the foregoing instances.

69

'(6) As to merit itself, of which we have been so dreadfully afraid: We are rewarded according to our works, yea, because of our works. How does this differ from "for the sake of our works"? And how differs this from *secundum merita operum*? which is no more than "as our works deserve". Can you split this hair? I doubt I cannot.'

When the storm about these Minutes broke (a storm which it is hard for us to understand today), Wesley and some of his followers signed a statement denying that they had declared for salvation by works. They had, so they wrote, no confidence in anything but the merits of Christ 'for Justification or Salvation, either in life, death, or the day of judgment'. Our works cannot have any part in meriting or purchasing our salvation; but they added: 'though no one is a real Christian believer (and consequently cannot be saved) who doth not good works.'

Good works do not earn salvation, but you cannot be saved without them. Some formula to reconcile the theological difficulties was needed. Wesley thought that he had it.

In writing to several preachers and friends concerning these Doctrinal Minutes of 1770, Wesley said: ' 'Tis true thirty years ago I was very angry with Bishop Bull, that great light of the Christian Church, because in his *Harmonica Apostolica* he distinguishes our first from our final justification, and affirms both inward and outward good works to be the condition of the latter though not the former.'

To see precisely what it was that Wesley had repudiated earlier, let me quote from Bishop Bull.

'What we have said concerning the absolute necessity of good works is most certain; nevertheless, even here there is need of some caution, that the Christian reader may accurately distinguish between the first and second justification, and so between the good works which are necessary to each. And here it must be understood, that only the internal works of faith, repentance, hope, charity, etc., are absolutely necessary to the first justification; but the other external works, which appear in outward actions, or in the exercise of the above-named virtues, are only the signs and fruit of internal piety, being subsequent to justification, and to be performed provided opportunity be given.'

In 1741 Wesley had resented Bishop Bull's distinction between a first and a second justification, but Wesley had accepted it in the early part of 1745, for at that time he published *A Farther Appeal to Men of Reason and Religion*, and on 2nd February 1945 he wrote to the Rev. THOMAS CHURCH, quoting at length from the *Farther Appeal*. In this he explains that justification 'sometimes means our acquittal at the Last Day. But this is altogether out of the present question; that justification whereof our Articles and Homilies speak, meaning present forgiveness, pardon of sins, and, consequently, acceptance with God. . . .'

The Doctrine of the Church of England as Wesley understood it from her Liturgy, Articles, and Homilies, could be summed up as follows:

'1. That no good work, properly so-called, can go before justification. 2. That no degree of true sanctification can be previous to it. 3. That as the meritorious cause of justification is the life and death of Christ, so the condition of it is faith, faith alone. And, 4. That both inward and outward holiness are consequent on this faith and are the ordinary, stated condition of final justification.'

And he added later: 'I not only allow, but vehemently contend, that none shall ever enter into glory who is not holy on earth, as well in heart, as "in all manner of conversation".'

Thus Wesley went on emphasizing the two sides of salvation as he saw them: 'Who of us is now accepted of God? He that now believes in Christ with a loving, obedient heart.' Without holiness, no man shall see the Lord. Perhaps God gives holiness in the moment of death, but in one way or another a man must be holy before he can be finally justified. To help along this road, therefore, those who associated themselves with the Wesleys must cease to do evil; they must do good to one another; they must attend upon the ordinances of the Church.

There were times when Wesley, believing that he had brought together St Paul and St James, as Bishop Bull had done in his *Apostolic Harmony*, grew weary of theological argument. The whole thing was a strife about words; there were times when he did not care whether you said that man is saved by faith or saved by works. The main thing was not to lose either faith or works.

'It is, then, a great blessing given to this people, that as they do not think or speak of justification so as to supersede sanctification, so neither do they think or speak of sanctification so as to supersede justification. They take care to keep each in its own place, laying equal stress on one and the other. . . . Therefore they maintain with equal zeal and diligence, the Doctrine of free, full, present justification, on the one hand, and of entire sanctification, both of heart and life, on the other; being as tenacious of inward holiness as any mystic, and of outward, as any Pharisee.'

Those who know the early history of Methodism know that the description of the Wesleys as romantics who encouraged a religion of individualism and emotionalism is far from all the truth. Whatever some Methodists may have done, the Wesleys did not deserve the gibe of Washington Irving, that the Methodists are always pulling up their souls by the roots to see if they are growing. According to the Wesleys, we are not saved by faith in faith, but by faith in God. Our salvation has been bought by the life and death of Christ, and we are dependent upon His grace. The means of grace are not only the preached word, but the sacraments, and the Church is not a voluntary band of converted people met together for mutual comfort and good works, but one Church, militant and triumphant, founded by Christ by his Apostles to which he has added those who were to be saved. The visible Church is distinguished by doctrine and sacraments. The form of government is not essential, but only ministers set apart by ordination can administer the sacraments.

This part of Wesley's teaching was, of course, overshadowed for his contemporaries by the preaching of heart religion and by the more spectacular aspects of Methodism. To modern eyes, this part of Wesley's teaching, his doctrine of the Church and of the sacraments, of justification and of sanctification, of religious authority, seem a compound of Protestant and Catholic views. To Wesley's contemporaries when they were aware of this side at all, the teachings seemed Catholic enough. As one critic, more astute than the rest, once said: 'You halt between Protestant and Catholic.'

In other years, when the present controversies have faded into the past, it may be that the aspect of Wesleyanism which shall seem most authentically Catholic, agreeing most fully with the early Church and the New Testament, will not be a matter of Church Order or of Apostolic Succession, but of the nature of the Christian religion. As many have noticed, there is much of Easter in Methodism. The Cross is important, but the atmosphere of early Methodism was not that of those who go mourning all their days, but of those who rejoice in the Risen Lord. And the essence of religion is not fear, but love.

This religion of love Wesley stated best in his *Appeals*, especially the

71

First Appeal, written in 1743. In this he was appealing to those intelligent men who were not theologians. The religion that Wesley recommended was 'a religion worthy of God that gave it, and this we conceive to be no other than love; the love of God and of all mankind; the loving God with all our heart, and soul, and strength, as having first loved us, as the fountain of all the good we have received, and of all we hope to enjoy; and the loving every soul which God hath made, every man on earth, as our own soul. . . .

'This religion we long to see established in the world, a religion of love, and joy, and peace, having its seat in the inmost soul, but ever showing itself by its fruits, continually springing forth, not only in all innocence (for love worketh no ill to his neighbour), but likewise in every kind of beneficence, spreading virtue and happiness all around it.'

I would not myself argue as to whether Wesley is in harmony with modern conceptions of the Catholic tradition, but I am quite sure that there is a very considerable Catholic tradition in which Wesley does stand, and that is the tradition of those who interpret religion as primarily the love of God in the heart of man. Wesley is one who took St Paul seriously, the Paul of First Corinthians as well as the Paul of Romans. 'And now abideth faith, hope, love, these three; but the greatest of these is love.' So said St Paul; and Wesley believed him.

PUBLIC MEETING

METHODISM IN THE MODERN WORLD

THE first of the public meetings was held in Wesley Memorial Church at 8 p.m. on Wednesday. The Chairman was Sir Arthur L. Dixon, C.B., C.B.E., who said that in this critical hour in world history it was significant that the Methodist message should be examined afresh by Methodists in Conference, and proclaimed to all the world in the strength of its own worth and timelessness. The two speakers at this memorable meeting were the Rev. Dr W. E. Sangster, Ex-President of the British Conference, and the Rev. Dr Ralph W. Sockman, of Christ Church, New York City.

I. THE MESSAGE

An address delivered by DR W. E. SANGSTER:

Methodism was not called into being by any novelty of doctrine. John Wesley never claimed to bring a new revelation, as Joseph Smith of the Mormons did, or Mrs. Eddy, or Pastor Russell. His message was 'the faith once delivered to the saints': the *old* gospel: the *Bible* gospel: the central message to which the Church, with all her failings, had witnessed through 1,800 years. No one familiar with the mind of John Wesley can doubt that if he had been convinced that any part of what he taught was not founded in the Scriptures, he would have abandoned it immediately. If there were, and are, certain doctrines on which the Methodists put a special emphasis, they are in no sense exclusively theirs. Wesley would

72

have said: 'These are in the Scriptures. They seem novel only because they have been overlooked.'

In the light of this, it may seem strange to some people how Methodism came into being at all, until they remember the somnolent and, indeed, in some areas, the decadent state of religion in this country in the eighteenth century. To multitudes the Faith was unknown. To others—including many of the clergy—it was a formality, a dead, powerless thing, the very revival of which was to be avoided lest it open the door to that great bogy of the eighteenth century, enthusiasm.

And that, in the strictest etymological sense of the word, was what happened. John Wesley, a typical son of this University and this nation, always regarded it as 'good form' to be restrained in the expression of feeling Meiosis, and not exaggeration, was the bias of his nature. Yet this was the man who became 'enthused'. Ἐν Θεός—God-possessed indeed! And he began to carry through this land, not a *new* gospel, but the *old* gospel, alight, arresting, offensively challenging; and pressed it upon the people with such persistence and urgency that the people stoned him and wrecked the first buildings he was led to put up.

But his message was nothing new. 'Methodism,' said another discerning son of this University years afterwards, 'Methodism is not a new religion, but the old religion *in earnest*.' It is still that. When it is most itself, it is still that. It is religion in earnest. Those who seek something new in doctrine: those who dread enthusiasm: those who don't want a religion which sings, must all avoid this faith. It is still—at its best—the gospel once delivered to the saints, but alive, and alight, and on the march.

Alive, and alight, and on the march? Is that true? In all the important senses, a Methodist in the modern world says precisely the same things that Wesley and his helpers said 200 years ago, but are they really alive, and alight, and on the march?

Five universals were said to summarize all early Methodist preaching:

All men need to be saved.
All men can be saved.
All men can know that they are saved.
All men must witness to their salvation.
All men must press on to perfection.

Are those truths alive today? Are they made to seem relevant? Are they pressed home on the people and shown to answer all the unbelief of our age?

When our Ecumenical Conference meets every ten years, it does not meet to discover in what ways our central message has changed, because we hold that the message is unchanging, but only to inquire how we may the more apply that eternal message to the changing resistance and unbelief of men.

Let us apply ourselves to that task at this Conference of 1951. Can it honestly be said that our message is alive, and alight, and on the march? Is it not rather true that we are halted in many places, irresolute in others, actually in retreat in some areas, and gone underground in still more?

Nor are these setbacks to be easily and lightly and entirely ascribed to the sin of others. There is need to examine our own hearts. Have we been loyal to our central message? Have we applied it faithfully and fearlessly in the modern world? Would any honest observer say of our Methodism in the year 1951: 'It is religion in earnest'?

1. First, then, have we failed in the proclamation of the faith? Do we still believe that all men need to be saved, or has the secularism of the world

73

so seeped into our churches that it is tacitly accepted among us that to be a decent fellow is all that we can reasonably ask of men?

Most of us know by now that one of the words Americans and Britishers do not use in precisely the same sense is the word 'humanism'. In many religious circles in England, it is almost synonymous with paganism. In religious circles in America, I find it commonly employed as though it were *Christian* humanism. It doesn't matter, of course, just so long as we know what each means, and just so long as we never part from the first of our universals, that all men are sinners and need to be saved.

It is not just stupidity from which a man needs to be saved. It is sin.

Man is utterly incapable of saving himself—now or at any conceivable time in the future; alone or in the mass.

We have many differences with our chief opponents in the world today, but they all centre in this. They deny the existence of God and believe that man can save himself. We assert the existence of God and deny that unaided man can ever find peace in his own soul, or peace in the world.

It is no part of our purpose to disparage the achievements of modern science and technology. We are not of those who deride the machine, or deny the operations of the Holy Spirit outside the organized Church. We bless God for all that the research student has found for the blessing of mankind, and yet we still assert that all men are sinners and need to be saved.

God forgive us if, failing to emphasize that, we have encouraged men to think that redemption is by human effort alone, and that there is no great loss to those who do not bow the knee 'unto the Father from whom every family in heaven and on earth is named'.

2. Secondly, have we failed in the application of our principles?

We assert that all men can be saved and, theoretically no doubt, we mean it. In Christ, we have been taught that there cannot be Greek and Jew, circumcision and uncircumcision, barbarian, Scythian, bondman, freeman, but Christ is all, and in all.

And now take a glance at that modern world we are considering, and at the activities of those who fight our faith.

On 12th August, in East Berlin, the Communists had a youth rally. It would be easy to ignore that piece of news, and easy to deny any significance to it, but then you would be blindly refusing to look at the modern world, and that is part of our purpose tonight. A million and a half youth were there. They were there from almost every country of the globe. They marched. They marched for eight hours. 'It was like a rally of the Hitler Youth', you say. Yes! but with this difference. It was an *international* rally. In Lenin, they say, there cannot be Greek and Jew, circumcision and uncircumcision, barbarian, Scythian, bondman, freeman, but Lenin is all, and in all.

And look, they were there from South Africa too—the most racially divided land in the world: a land where a Christian Church (on Calvinist and Old Testament principles) can disenfranchise the people to whom the land originally belonged and work for eternal separateness.

But there was no *apartheid* in the Communist delegation from South Africa to Berlin. White and black, they marched together. 'We really *are* one in Lenin, they say. 'The Christians say it also, but it is all humbug when they say it. When they welcome their coloured friends into the family of Christ, they really mean that they welcome them to a nice seat on the doorstep. They can't even worship in the same church.'

People wonder sometimes how the Communists get such a grip on youth. One of the reasons may be here.

74

Have we failed with the application of our own principles? When we said, '*All* men may be saved', did we mean it—and mean it fully—mean to work it out?

3. In the third place, have we failed to impart assurance to the people? We have said, 'All men can *know* that they are saved', but have we failed as Methodists so to live that other people know, without telling, that we are in some glorious open secret?

Assurance—and consequently joy—were among the marks of the early Methodists. They sang and they *meant*:

'My God! I know, I feel Thee mine.'

That was the secret of their infectious rapture. The assurance did not desert them in the hour of death. When Thomas Carlyle read in the papers of an amazing act of heroism in a Cornish mine, and of how one miner had thrust his friend to safety at the sacrifice of himself and gladly opened his own arms to death, he was so moved by the story that he made inquiries, first, as to the facts, and then as to the explanation. The facts he fully confirmed. The explanation I give in Carlyle's own words. He says of the miner that he was 'an honest, ignorant, good man, entirely given up to Methodism . . . perfect in the faith of assurance'.

We live in a world made grey by the atomic bomb. Is there anything that would more, and better, publicize the faith than life lived with joy and assurance—the gay abandonment of those who live to better all things but who know, at the same time, that if the worse comes to the worst they need not fear those who kill the body and afterwards have no more that they can do? The world is hungry for that kind of assurance. What a pity that we seem not able to pass it on.

I was in Sils-Maria in the Upper Engadine the week before last. I noticed the house near the Post Office where Nietzsche lived for seven years and wrote his chief works. I remembered the time when he felt the appeal of our faith, and set himself to study it in the lives of some Christians he knew, and I remembered also the acuteness of his disappointment in their joyless natures, and how he said: 'These Christians will have to look more redeemed before I can believe in them.'

Do we look redeemed? Is joy characteristic of Methodism still? Does our appearance suggest that we know that we are saved?

The American members of this Conference will hear without surprise, I imagine, that the wealth of America is sometimes a cause of envy in other lands: abundance of food; big, fat, shiny motor-cars; smart clothes . . . and 82 million of your people Church members. What a land!

But we have been surprised to learn also, from the reports of your publishers, that the best-sellers are books on how to be happy. The titles vary, of course: *Peace of Mind, How to Stop Worrying and Start Living, Look Younger, Live Longer, A Guide to Confident Living, The Way to Power and Poise.* . . . Food, cars, clothes, money . . . *and how to be happy*!

Is that, then, what people really want? And can they even hope to get it from a columnist in a newspaper, or some specialist in human uplift? Don't they plainly need Christ and the assurance of His salvation? And have we not been specially commissioned to meet that need?

4. In the fourth place, are we failing this age as Methodists in not bringing that passion to religion which it surely requires?

We began by asserting that we offer the world nothing new in doctrine. We glory in that. Ours is the *old* faith: 'the faith once delivered to the saints'.

Our *raison d'être* wasn't in a novelty of doctrine, but in the conviction and passion we brought to its proclamation. *Religion in earnest!* What has happened to that awful earnestness which fired Wesley and Asbury; John Nelson and Caleb Pedicord; Peter Jaco and Freeborn Garrettson; Alexander Mather and Jesse Lee? ... On and on they went. They seemed to live in the saddle. If Asbury had a slogan, it was this: 'I must ride or I will die.' Do you remember the day when they thought he *was* dying, and called a doctor to that mighty man? He was struggling to rise when the doctor came. One glance at him and the doctor said, 'If you ride, you will die,' and even in his pain and utter weakness, the St Francis of the Western world replied: 'No, Doctor. You have it wrong. If I do *not* ride, I will die.'

What drove our pioneers on? What fed the ceaseless stream of their zeal?

Think again of that youth rally two weeks ago in Berlin. A million and a half, and all young. From almost every country in the world. . . .

Oh yes! there was an International Boy Scouts' Rally at the same time in Australia. By no means so large. Hardly as meaningful. What has happened to our Christian youth organizations? Do we keep our young people young too long? Would a million and a half youth make a long journey anywhere to march for the United Nations? How is it that that God-denying creed can beget a devotion greater than that of those who pursue the Christ Himself?

A passionate pursuit of the evil—or half-evil—can only be matched by a passionate pursuit of the good.

Here is scope for the God-possession the Methodists claim to enjoy! All our Sister communions stand in need of it, too! Not a 5 per cent extra effort dragged out of people already working beyond their conviction, but a glorious abandonment to the purposes of God in this age and a thrilling readiness to undertake whatever He will command.

5. Finally, I must ask you whether we are failing our age in not holding before the people the ideal of Christian perfection. 'All men', said our fathers, 'must press on to perfection.'

There is a suspicion among people—and who among us will say that it is groundless?—that, whatever men undertake, self-interest is really the driving motive. In king or commissar. In president or bishop. In minister or layman. Get down to the base of things, they suspect, and it is always self.

Inevitably, this has spread a certain cynicism through the community. The ache which all normal men and women feel for the highest is mocked by doubts as to the purity of motive in those who lead.

It is hard to believe that our pioneers suffered that suspicion. Their poverty, their sufferings, their toil, their virtual homelessness, the scorn with which they were so often treated, the absence of material rewards, must have had its slow part in convincing people of the sincerity of their motives, and that they were, indeed, moved by 'the pure flame of love'.

But what of us and our contemporaries? Modern psychology, in taking the lid off the subsconscious, has made us to realize more than ever what shabby creatures we are, but it has said nothing to disprove the power of grace in the soul and a good deal to convince us that we have greater need than ever to say:

> 'O to grace how great a debtor
> Daily I'm constrained to be!'

But the grace is there.

We can face this disillusioned age and offer them perfection in Christ. The sheer audacity of it will startle them, if nothing else does.

'All men must press on to perfection.'

'He wills that I should holy be;
That holiness I long to feel.'

I grow more sure that if we want power with the people—and with youth especially—this is the way to it. God forbid that we should despise learning, but, at the last, it is not great learning which subdues men but great goodness. The saints are the men of real power in all ages. The time will come when historians will cease to label their periods with the names of crude conquerors and label them with the names of outstanding saints.

And—by grace—sanctity is a gift we may all aspire to. A body of believers, living right at the Christ-centre of things in this evil world, would be the grandest contribution we could make as Methodists to this present age. Holiness—being of the very life of God—is so powerful that even a little bit is mighty. We know the way to it. It is part of our spiritual heritage. Daily waiting on God. Rigorous self-examination. Merciless-ness with all discovered sin. A ceaseless yearning after the highest. . . .

So—unaware of it ourselves—we shall grow like Him and, in so doing, render our greatest service as Methodists in the modern world.

II. COMMUNICATING THE MESSAGE

An address delivered by DR RALPH W. SOCKMAN:

The word 'witness' is commonly used in two different senses. For instance, if we were to visit a courtroom in which a trial was being conducted, we might take our place in the spectators' gallery. Thereby we would become witnesses of the trial. But up near the judge's bench and the jury box is a chair reserved for those who are to give testimony. The persons who take that seat become witnesses at the trial.

In his closing discourse, as recorded by St Luke, our Lord said to His disciples: 'Ye are witnesses of these things.' Moffatt and others make clear that Christ's words implied testimony rather than mere spectatorship. Up to the time of Jesus' death, His disciples had played the role of observers. They had watched him in His work and Passion. But some-thing happened after His Crucifixion and Resurrection which transformed the timid company of onlookers into courageous radiant heralds of the Risen Christ. They left the spectators' gallery for the witness chair to give bold and convincing testimony concerning what they had seen and heard.

The trial of the living Christ is still on. Today His principles are being tested with unprecedented scope and intensity. The cause of Christ is now warring, not merely against flesh and blood, but against principalities and powers, against ideologies entrenched in titanic economic and nationalistic systems.

And if we think of this contest between Christ and the world after the pattern of a courtroom, what is the situation? Certainly it could be said that the spectators' gallery is well filled. The Christian Church, in its large official actions, in its pronouncements on political and social questions, makes the headlines. People who may never go to church are interested to know where the Church is going. What attitude will the Church take about Communism, about race relations in South Africa or the United States, about birth-control and divorce, about war in Korea and arms in Germany? Such questions enter into dinner conversations and public discussions. To the formation of the World Council of Churches at Amsterdam in 1948 more than a mile of newspaper column space was devoted in the secular Press of America. And the trial of

Cardinal Mindzenty was the most-publicized single event of the year 1949 in America's newspapers.

· · · · ·

But while the observers' gallery is thus crowded, the counsel table is inadequately manned. Every Protestant communion of which I happen to know is short of properly trained preachers. The Methodist Church in America has some 25,000 ministers, of whom one-fourth are supply pastors—that is, men not fully qualified to be members of annual conferences. To be sure, one hopeful sign is that our theological seminaries are now generally crowded. But my observation as a visitor to several seminaries and as a teacher in one is that parish preaching is being overshadowed in appeal by other ecclesiastical functions. So many theological students seem to assume that the best minds go into teaching or administrative work. Hence, if we are to vitalize the communication of the Christian message, we must exalt the preaching office.

The word 'preach' is not a popular term. It savours somewhat of moral smugness. It carries a connotation of condescension, as of a speaker handing down unrequested advise to listeners whom he feels to be in need of his counsel. 'Do not preach to me' is an expression often heard as people begin adjusting their defence mechanisms against the invasion of unsolicited piety. If a minister wishes to test the popular attitude toward preaching, let him stand up and say: 'I am not going to preach to you this morning. I just want to talk as man to man.' Instantly there is a quickening expectancy of something real. The preaching function needs to be freshened in manner as well as refurbished in content.

The increasing competition to which the pulpit is subjected demands its improvement. Once the parish minister was almost the sole public voice of the community and his words lingered in the minds of his listeners throughout the ensuing week. Now the air is filled with voices and the morning sermon very easily drowned in a deluge of messages before the Sabbath day is ended. In the simpler day, our grandfathers going to church was an exciting break in the monotony of the week. Now secular living has become so filled with so-called attractions that going to church is poularly regarded as a monotonous break in the excitement of the week.

Nevertheless, the apostolic statement still stands, that 'it pleased God by the foolishness of preaching to save them that believe'. And if we preachers have the apostolic stuff in us, the growing difficulties of our task will serve as a challenge of our utmost for the sake of the highest.

Preaching holds a unique place among the multitudinous voices of our time for a threefold reason: its origin is in Biblical aims, its place is a part of worship and it essays to be a revelation of the will of God. If the pulpit keeps its eye on these three facts, its voice will have a sustained appeal.

The preacher is more than a public speaker. The secular orator may be moved to inspiration and sway his audiences with a gratifying sense of power. But the preacher comes with a revelation, plus or even minus an inspiration. The man who stands up in the pulpit can scarcely claim to be inspired every Sunday morning at eleven o'clock. The late Heywood Brown, one of our American columnists, is reported to have said that he might go to church if the ministers would be honest enough to keep silent when they had no divine inspiration, if, for example, they would be sufficiently frank to get up on some Sunday mornings and say: 'Perhaps next Sunday, but not today.'

But the point which Brown missed is that the pulpit is not solely dependent on the preacher's personal inspiration. He is the bearer of a revelation.

78

And when the preacher carries the Bible, he finds the Bible carrying him. It keeps fresh the sources of his inspiration when secular topics run dry. True preaching transcends oratory as a mountain spring surpasses a hydrant.

Furthermore, the preacher is more than an actor. It often might seem that the stage has more appeal than the pulpit, and some are saying that in future we must count more on religious drama than on preaching for the communication of the Christian message. But there is a fundamental difference between acting and preaching. The actor seeks to interpret a character or situation. He is shut off from the audience by footlights. The test of his work is how well he enters into the personality of the character he is portraying. The preacher, on the other hand, is concerned not only with the interpretation of his message, but also with the helping and saving of the people before him. No footlights shut him off from his congregation so that he can be confined to the drama he is enacting.

LeGrand Cammon, in his book, *A Mighty Fortress*, makes a seasoned evangelist say to a young preacher fresh from seminary: 'Forget about yourself. What you want to do is to think about those people. Then maybe you can make them forget about themselves. That's what they've come for. When you can give it to 'em, you'll be a preacher.' A good actor lives his part. A good preacher lives both in his part and in his people. A good actor with a good play as a vehicle can keep running on Broadway or in Piccadilly for perhaps two or three seasons. But a preacher perhaps possessed of far less ability, by putting himself into the drama of salvation and the hearts of his people, can keep running in the same pulpit for decades.

Much attention is now being given to another channel of conveying the Christian message. I refer to counselling and psychiatry. The good minister of Jesus Christ is a practitioner in the tradition of the Great Physician. And yet he must be more than a physician, just as Jesus was more than a healer. Nothing in the minister's work is more worth while than to give the healing touch and guiding word to the distraught individuals who come to him for counsel. But the pastor, though a physician of the spirit, must watch the proportion of time given to private practice in counselling and the time given to public service through preaching and participating in social causes. Ministry to the abnormal must not overshadow ministry to the normal. Wisdom must be used lest so much time be consumed by those who come to the pastor's study that he has too little time for the service of those who must be sought out. Christ's ministers are called to challenge as well as to comfort, to alert people by asking the right questions as well as to quiet them by giving the right answers. When Jesus said, 'Come unto me all ye that labour and are heavy laden', He added: 'Take My yoke upon you and learn of me.' The preacher must be leader and prophet as well as physician.

Furthermore, the preacher must be more than the prophet. It would be presumptuous to say what difference would have been made in the messages of the great Hebrew prophets if they had been the pastors of settled congregations. Their clarion voices might have been muted by a pastoral consciousness. Sometimes it happens that our shepherding care in tempering the mind to the shorn lambs also is tempted to adjust the heat to the fur coats! Nevertheless, the preacher of today has the task of preaching the will of God and also of preparing the people to hear it.

In the fortieth chapter of Isaiah the command is given: 'Prepare ye the way of the Lord.' In the sixty-second chapter the injunction is: 'Prepare ye the way of the people.' Put the two commands together and you have the double duty of the preacher. He is the guide in a twofold search. On the one side is God, longing for His wandering children, seeking to reconcile them unto Himself. On the other side are men feverishly searching for the secret of wholeness and restless till their souls find rest in God. As guide in this twofold search, the preacher is a prophet interpreting the voice of God to men and also a priest introducing men to God. Therefore the parish preacher, moving among his people as a man of God, incarnating his message in his own life, is still our basic hope in conveying the Christian message, and he will not be dislodged from his primary by radio preaching or televized religious drama.

Now, if the preacher is to fulfil his high calling, he must, as Fenelon said, be able to prove, picture and move.

When King Zedekiah shut Jeremiah in prison, he asked the prophet: 'Wherefore dost thou prophesy and say, Thus saith the Lord?' Our generation is still more sceptical. The public demands proof of the person who presumes to speak in God's name. And the pulpit must demonstrate an authority convincing to free minds.

Some years ago the magazine *Fortune* published an oft-quoted editorial containing this plea: 'There is only one way out of the spiral of confusion. The way out is the sound of a voice—not our voice, but a voice coming from something not ourselves, in the existence of which we cannot disbelieve. It is the earthly task of the pastors to hear this voice, to cause us to hear it, and to tell us what it says.'

Such a call from the pew demands more Biblical preaching from the pulpit. An agonizing generation is groping for faith. The preacher must do more than flog the wills with moral urging. He must feed the minds and hearts. Life is a quest as well as a conquest. It is not enough to say: 'Have faith.' We must be able to say, 'Have a faith', and then give men a reason for the faith that is in them. Our time calls for a teaching ministry.

Let us catch men's interest at the points where they are living and then lead them into the uplands of the soul, where flow the springs of living water. And these are found so variously and invariably in the Bible. Let us rise from thin ethical homilies and little psychological 'pep' talks to the Word of God. When we open the Bible, we turn on voices other than our own—voices which haunt us and the ages before us with their heavenly appeal. Through the opened Bible we hear the palmists whose noble songs make us feel that they were thinking God's thoughts after Him. We hear prophets who uttered truths so far ahead of their time that they cannot be explained as echoes of the crowd, but must have been inspired of God. And above all we hear words of a Galilean who spoke as One having authority and then lived out the truths that He voiced in such matchless fashion that, like the centurian at the Cross, we too cry: 'Surely this was the Son of God.'

In a world so full of words, let us preach the Word with such cogency and consistency that men will hear the Voice above our voices.

If the pulpit is to communicate the Christian message, it must picture as well as prove. Colourless abstractions cannot hold the contemporary mind, inured to the movies, the tabloid Press, and television. The true preacher is an artist painting pictures in the mind. 'He is the best speaker who can turn an ear into an eye.'

Jesus possessed this genius in supreme degree. 'The words I speak unto you', He said, 'they are spirit and they are life.' Our Lord did not lull people to sleep by using vague, general terms such as 'humanity' and 'society'. He spoke in sparkling parables, leaving unforgettable portraits of a prodigal boy picking himself up from among the swineherds of a sinful country and of a Good Samaritan lifting a wounded man on the Jericho road.

In cultivating the art of making truth sufficiently picturesque to impress the modern mind, we should study the use of imagination. Psychologists tell us that imagination is more powerful than the will. When the two are in conflict, the imagination wins. It is the picture which hangs in our mind rather than the purpose on which we grit our teeth that will eventually shape our action.

And if our broken world is to be made brotherly, it would seem to need imagination even more than information. Mere increase of factual data about other races and nations does not guarantee better understanding. Cold facts seem to make cold wars. Only as we sensitize our imaginations by practising the art of putting ourselves in other people's places do we come to feel how life looks to those of different colour, creed, and culture. Both pulpit and pew must develop the power to picturize the Gospel of God's love and the personalities of God's children whom we are to love.

And, to follow Fenelon's formula still further, preaching must not only prove and picture, but also move. 'Study without action is futile. Action without study is fatal.' President Mackay of Princeton Seminary expresses the truth: 'There can be no true knowledge of ultimate things—that is to say, of God and man, of duty and destiny—that is not born in a concern and perfected in a commitment.'

The preacher is a transmitter of spiritual power, but only when he is linked both to God and to his fellow men. A moving sermon must do more than stir the emotions. It must so channel them that they start the dynamo of the will and generate power for living. If contemporary preaching is to be possessed of moving power, it should not copy the spurious and superficial methods of certain flamboyant evangelists, but seek the deep, central themes of our Christian faith. John Wesley's preaching possessed genuine emotion and moving power, though filled with solid scholarship.

The late Evelyn Underhill's criticism should cause us to resurvey the area of our pulpit message. She remarked that the great defect of present-day religion is that it spends its time running around the arc and takes the centre for granted.

We shall not lack genuine emotion if we keep to the centre of our gospel. The centre of our global gospel, like the centre of our globe, is hot. The burning love of God revealed in the passion of our Lord Jesus Christ is the heart of our eternal message. In a time when our whole civilization faces life and death issues, in a world so full of suffering that the prayers of all thoughtful, sensitive persons look up to God like wounded animals with great, large, round eyes of pain, our message will have moving power if we preach Christ crucified, the power of God, and the wisdom of God.

. . . . . .

Returning now to our figure of the courtroom, after discussing the counsel table, let us look at the witness chair. The most imperative need of the Christian Church today is not for improved preaching, but for more and better lay witnessing. The task of communicating Christ's message is too great for the pulpit alone.

Some of us have just returned from the Central Committee of the World Council of Churches. There we were thrilled to hear of the *Kirchen* observed this summer in Berlin. Some 400,000 churchmen from the eastern and western sectors of Germany came together in a mighty witness for Christ. That defeated land is realizing the need of enlisting the laymen if religion is to be revitalized.

81

Such lay witnessing restores the apostolic secret of vitality. In the earliest Christian Churches there were no ordained preachers. Those first Churches were merely companies of Jesus's friends telling what they knew of their crucified and risen Lord. What began as a living movement was transformed into an institution. And the conventional Church of today has deteriorated all too much into a professional propaganda financed by silent spectators. We hire preachers to preach our sermons for us. In many of our parishes we engage singers to voice our emotions. Frequently we pay evangelists to recruit our members. The laity merely sit back and pay the bills—and some just sit back! Very much of the listlessness and lustrelessness of conventional religion is due to the lack of lay participation.

John Wesley recaptured the apostolic principle of lay witnessing. And British Methodism, with its wide use of local preachers, is preserving the practice far better than are we in America. We have seen how a movement like Christian Science can grow by utilizing lay testimony. Also the movement called 'Moral Rearmament' has had a measure of success through its practice of sharing experiences.

We might well take a leaf from the guide-book of Communism on this point. If the Marxists can spread so rapidly by using the 'cell' principle, why cannot the followers of Christ have their 'cells'. We know how one devout Christian in a family can change the atmosphere of a household even when the other members are pagan. We know, too, that a half-dozen consecrated Christians can stir a lethargic parish. Let us create 'cells' of consecration within our churches. Where two or three are gathered together in thorough commitment, there is God in the midst of them, and only God knows the possibilities of such a programme.

A revival of religion could be started in any community if those who know Christ would talk about their relations with Him in the same simple, straightforward, matter-of-fact language in which they discuss their secular business. The World Council of Churches is seeking to stir Christian laymen to the study of Christ's relation to their vocations: what is involved in being a Christian doctor, a Christian lawyer, a Christian business-man. Some of us have seen how such discussions can arouse interest in local parishes. When the Christian witness is thus made relevant to our ordinary everyday activities, these activities cease to be ordinary.

A revival of lay witness would also restore the apostolic emphasis. The early Christians told others what God in Christ had done for them. This is a note which needs to be revived, for all too much of our current preaching emphasis is concerned with what men may do to us rather than with what God has done for us. To be sure, we are surrounded by real dangers from Communistic and other anti-Christian forces. And Christianity is our best defence against these evils. But a message of mere defence and security is not the original gospel of Christ. 'They shall call His name Jesus because He shall save His people from their sins.' Christ came primarily to save us from our own sins rather than to protect us from the evils others may inflict upon us. Only as we revive the original gospel of salvation shall we show that the Cross has something the Kremlin cannot rival or destroy.

Moreover, when laymen take the witness stand for Christ, they recover the apostolic confidence. Ours is a time of deep pessimism. It has been called 'The Great Age of Fear'. When I listen to long and continuous forums on world problems, I find myself falling into despair. The issues seem so complicated that they baffle solution. But when I go around my parish and see what a Boy's Club is doing for a wayward lad or what Alcoholics Anonymous is achieving in reforming drunkards, I find the batteries of my faith being recharged. As Thomas Carlyle said, when we do the duty nearest to us and then the duty next to that, we find light beginning to break on the ultimate duty.

Dr Washington Gladden, one of the formative preachers of the last generation, was ever holding before his people the great social problems, such as world peace, racial brotherhood, and industrial harmony. But he could not always see his way through. So he wrote these words:

'I know that right is right,
        That it is not good to lie,
    That love is better than spite
        And a neighbour than a spy.'

'In the darkest night of the year,
        When the light is all gone out,
    That love is better than fear
        And faith is truer than doubt.'

(From W. Gladden, *Ultima Veritus*.)

If laymen will come into the councils and work of the Church, bearing their witness in relevant terms, learning from within what the Church is doing, they will not be misled by demagogic attacks on our ecclesiastical programme nor run off into eccentric cults. I am pleading for a cultivation of true churchmanship, sufficiently informed to be efficient and sufficiently active to be enthusiastic.

And I believe that such lay witness will eventually win the confidence of those vast groups now indifferent and hostile to the Church just as John Wesley's impassioned approach melted the hearts of the Bristol miners two centuries ago. No curtain between nations or classes can ultimately keep out the Light of the World.

If I remember correctly, John Masefield, in his *Trial of Jesus*, has a scene in which Pilate's wife holds conversation with the Roman centurion who kept watch at the Cross. She asks the Roman officer: 'What think you of this man Jesus?'

'Lady,' he replied, 'when a man believes a thing enough to die for it, He will get others to believe in it too.'

Then she asked: 'Do you think Jesus is dead?'

'No,' he answered.

'Where, then, do you think He is?'

'Let loose in the world where neither Roman nor Jew can stop Him.'

The Christ is going on. The question is: 'Are we going with Him?'

83

THIRD DAY

Thursday 30th August 1951

MORNING devotions were conducted by Bishop S. L. Greene of the African Methodist Episcopal Church, U.S.A. After reading Romans 8¹⁴⁻¹⁷, the Rev. Dr J. F. Wunderlich of Germany stressed the words: 'You have received the spirit of adoption.' In one sense, he felt, they remind us of our Methodist heritage, for they describe the change in the life of John Wesley in 1738, when the slave or servant suddenly realized his sonship. In the midst of this world of sin 'being justified by faith we have peace with God through our Lord Jesus Christ'. Fear passes, because the minds of the children of God are set on the Spirit. A unique gift is entrusted to us by our Father. We shall never be slaves again: we are sons. This is our witness—a witness the whole world needs today.

. . . .

At the morning session Dr Howard paid tribute to the late Dr H. B. Workman, who had played so considerable a part in earlier Conferences and, indeed, in the whole ecumenical movement. The delegates, standing in silence, gave thanks to God for the life of this faithful soldier of Christ.

The topic for the session was *Methodist Doctrines*. One address on *Justification by Faith* was given by the Rev. Dr W. R. Cannon of Emory University, Atlanta, and another on *Perfect Love and the Divine Society* by Dr Harald Lindström of Uppsala University, Sweden.

METHODIST DOCTRINES

I. JUSTIFICATION BY FAITH

An address delivered by the REV. DR WILLIAM R. CANNON, *Professor of Church History and Historical Theology, Emory University, Atlanta, Georgia:*

'In my heart reigns this one article: faith in my dear Lord Christ, the beginning, middle, and end of whatever spiritual and divine thoughts I may have, whether by day or by night.' So wrote the great reformer, Martin Luther, in the introduction to his commentary on Paul's Epistle to the Galatians in 1538; and thereby announced to the world the Protestant manifesto.

Just as the Magna Charta is the cornerstone of constitutional liberty throughout the British Empire, the Declaration of Independence is the political beginning of the United States as a nation of free and equal men, each enjoying the right of life, liberty, and the pursuit of happiness, and *Das Kapital* is the foundation of contemporary Communism, the assertion that the means of production should be owned and controlled, not by individuals, but by the State, even so Justification by Faith is the cardinal

84

principle of Protestant Christianity, at once the basis of unity and sympathetic understanding among the many and diverse denominations which have arisen since the Reformation and the single cause both of the original and continuing separation of the Protestant Churches from Rome, the absolute and, I fear, irrevocable distinction between the heritage of the Reformation and that of Catholicism in either its Eastern or its Western form.

Martin Luther defined the doctrine in this manner: 'The true way of Salvation is this. First, a person must realize he is a sinner, the kind of sinner who is congenitally unable to do any good thing. Those who seek to earn the grace of God by their own efforts are trying to please God with sins. They mock God and provoke His anger. The first step on the way to Salvation is to repent.

'The second point is this. God sent His only begotten Son into the world that we may live through His merit. He was crucified and killed for us. By sacrificing His Son for us, God revealed Himself to us as a merciful Father who donates remission of sins, righteousness, and life everlasting for Christ's sake. God hands out His gifts freely unto all men. . . .'

Then comes the final phase: 'We say, faith apprehends Jesus Christ. Christian faith is not an inactive quality in the heart. If it is true faith, it will surely take Christ for its object. Christ, apprehended by faith and dwelling in the heart, constitutes Christian righteousness, for which God gives eternal life.'

So much for Luther's definition. It would be difficult to find outside the Bible itself a clearer and more adequate expression of this or any other religious truth throughout the entire range of doctrinal history. The reformer begins his theology at precisely the same point where psychologically religion itself begins in the consciousness of every religious man— namely, at the point of his recognition of *need*. Human self-satisfaction is incompatible with redemption. There can not be a Saviour unless first there are sinners who are in need of being saved. Jesus came into the world but for one reason: to save sinners from their sins. Therefore, the single aim of all religion is salvation, and according to Protestant teaching salvation is not a human achievement, but a divine gift—God's generous bequest to His children which is received without labour as a son inherits an estate from his father. To be sure, there is one condition imposed: the gift must be claimed. But the act of making the claim is itself a denial of any human right or earning. It is itself an expression both of gratitude to, and confidence in, the Divine Benefactor. In this instance the Reformer employs faith only in the sense of trust. Like a little child taking a gift of his parents, man receives what God gives in loving confidence that it will do for him what he could never do for himself and will work altogether for his good.

The Protestant doctrine of Justification by Faith, therefore, includes both a negation and an affirmation; it is at once a confession and a declaration; despondency and triumphant joy are alike its elements; it judges, condemns, and destroys only to forgive, to comfort, and to restore. By it man is made to abhor himself and to despise all his works, but at the same time he is led to know, to appreciate, and to love God, and in that divine experience to find himself again, a new and better creature, more perfectly reflecting the image of the Creator, and consequently to take satisfaction in his works, too, for he realizes that they are inspired of God and the Heavenly Father has given him the power for their fulfilment. Jesus's words, 'Ask and ye shall receive, seek and ye shall find, knock and it shall be opened unto you', are for him of faith translated from admonition into accomplished fact. For he has already asked and received, sought and found, knocked and had the door opened before him. In confidence, he can pray Augustine's prayer, 'Command what Thou wilt', for, like Augustine, he knows by experience that God always grants what He commands. He does what he ought, not because he feels he ought to do it, but rather because he wants to do it, since his inner disposition is now in harmony with God's external law. The doctrine of Justification by Faith, in a sentence, means this: We know God for Christ's sake has forgiven and will continue to forgive us for all our sins, and we trust Him daily to grant unto us the moral and spiritual power to be what we ought to be and to do what we ought to do according to His own divine standard and not according to any standard of our own.

Thus in Protestantism this doctrine of Justification by Faith governs every phrase and aspect of theology. It acknowledges no other religious principle or concept as master; but, like the love of God and the love of man in the ethics of Jesus, it in the realm of dogma summarizes and fulfils all the Law and the Prophets. Like the syllogism in formal logic, if it stands, its subsidiary principles stand with it; but once it is taken away, the entire dogmatic structure collapses. 'Whoever gives up this article of justification', wrote Martin Luther, 'does not know the true God. It is one and the same thing whether a person reverts to the Law or to the worship of idols. When the article of justification is lost, nothing remains except error, hypocrisy, godlessness, and idolatry.' What the Reformer meant is that a man's consciousness of God's favour determines his entire outlook on life, so that he sees the world and all that constitutes it from the Heavenly Father's point of view.

The weight of this consideration becomes apparent when we examine the other major doctrines of Protestant Christianity. We are taught, for example, that the sole basis of authority in religion is the Bible, but the Bible is a book which must be read and interpreted, and this can be properly and effectively done only by the man of faith who has the Holy Spirit Himself as his teacher. Each man is declared to be his own priest, but then his ordination is his baptism, and baptism itself is but the initial act of faith. All life is sacred, and every vocation is theoretically on a parity with every other vocation. Each job is potentially an act of worship. But it does not become worshipful until the worker himself is consciously a worshipper, and this is brought about solely by his faith in God. Even Christian perfection, so dear to the heart of every loyal Methodist, is itself but a continuation or prolongation of justification, for the same faith which forgives sinners in the beginning produces and sustains righteousness and brings it to perfect holiness in the end. The saints were never aware of their saintliness; they did not style themselves experts in the art of holiness; but the good works they performed they performed by the grace of God alone, and that which men admired in them was but an occasion to glorify their Father in Heaven. As one of your British theologians has put it: 'Any sinlessness of ours is the adoration of His.'

Not only is the doctrine of Justification by Faith the summary of the theology of the Reformation; it is still the basic dogmatic principle of contemporary Protestantism—the ideational driving force behind every action we perform in the world. If we believe it as our fathers did, then the power of that same conviction which enabled them to subdue kingdoms, to bring about righteousness, and to obtain promises will still bring to successful issue the enterprises of their sons; for, though our society is vastly different from theirs and our problems are not the same as the problems they faced, God Himself is not altered; He has not modified His

86

manner of dealing with His children; His love is as sensitive to our cries as it was to the cry of Abraham at the dawn of history, and His heart is as responsive to our needs as it was to the needs of the Children of Israel throughout their desert wanderings in the adolescence of their national life. For this doctrine of Justification by Faith is not an aberration of the Gospel, but rather the true statement of its essence, a picture as it were of its very soul. Consequently, it did not begin with the Reformation; it is as old as the Bible itself; St Paul was its most vigorous exponent; the sixteenth-century Reformers did not create something new; they discovered the primitive Christianity which the Middle Ages had lost. The glory of Protestantism is in the confession that man is saved and the world remade through trust in our Divine Saviour and in Him alone.

The strength of this doctrine is apparent when we apply it to our own life situation and observe its effect upon religion and morals whenever it is seriously believed. To begin with, it fashions a religion that is entirely theocentric and saves us, on the one hand, from the triviality of ethical humanitarianism and psychological self-adjustment, and, on the other hand, from the barbarity of a mechanical Statism which denies God and likewise the inalienable right of the human individual to the fruits of his own mental and physical toil. In the United States, for example, along with the multitudinous mechanical gadgets which add to our conveniences, such as dry-cleaning establishments which clean and press a suit of clothes in one hour, drive-in garages which wash and dry an automobile, and polish it, too, in three minutes, and dictating machines which spare the preacher the ordeal of writing his sermons, there has arisen a popular and widespread cult of self-help where men are taught to overcome worry by reading rules on a card every morning on the bus as they go to work, to inspire faith in themselves by telling themselves aloud that they are an admirable people, and to destroy the ill-effects of a guilty conscience by enumerating their past faults to a counsellor and then promptly forgetting them. But only God can forgive sins. Before we build up self-confidence, we ought to assure ourselves that we are persons in whom our confidence can be imposed. The man who is free from worry is not always the good man. Often he is trivial and inconsequential. Worry at times is legitimate. The sinner, if he is not worried, ought to be. Repentance is hardly to be described as peace of mind. Worry is ultimately healthful if it leads the worrier to self-abnegation and genuine faith in God. The person who deserves to be free from worry is not he who has faith in himself, but rather he who has faith in God.

Likewise, mere humanitarianism can be inimical to the best interests of humanity as a whole. Oftentimes we engage in practices to secure the welfare of our fellows when we do not know in what that welfare really consists. A full stomach does not mean character, and self-reliance through honest toil is, from the Christian point of view, as essential to the best interests of the individual and of humanity as freedom from financial insecurity and physical want. Any social order is less than what it ought to be when the Kingdom of God is not its pattern. Only those who seek constantly to know and to do the will of God can bring about real and abiding good to humanity.

The doctrine of Justification by Faith turns our minds and hearts away from an introspective and selfish gaze upon ourselves toward God and the things of God. It gives us our purpose for life and likewise the power to do and to achieve. By it we realize we are not our own; we have been bought with a price, the precious blood of the Divine Saviour which was shed for the remission of our sins. We are no longer free to do as we please, but we have been translated from the slavery of self-liberty into the real freedom of citizens of the Kingdom of God, those whose delight is in the law of the Lord upon which they meditate day and night. Legal standards have all broken down, for what good are requirements when the things demanded have already been met and the statutes on the tables of the law are now expressed as abiding desires of the human heart. We love Him and the things He loves because we have assurance that He first loved us. 'For by grace are ye saved through faith, and that not of yourselves; it is the gift of God.'

II. PERFECT LOVE AND THE DIVINE SOCIETY

An address delivered by DR HARALD LINDSTRÖM, *University of Uppsala, Sweden:*

Is the Methodist doctrine of perfect love a doctrine that exclusively refers to the individual, or does it also imply a corporate idea? Does the idea of Christian perfection or perfect love include not only a divine change in man, but also a divine change in society?

Before dealing with the doctrine of entire sanctification from this angle of the individual or society we must, however, emphasize the importance of the doctrine for the whole theological outlook of John Wesley.

The theology of John Wesley aims to do justice to Biblical realism. This is evident in his idea of the nature of man as well as in his view of salvation. In marked opposition to the shallow rationalizing of Deism, Wesley underlined the real situation of man, as this situation could be seen in the light of Scripture and experience. Thus, the natural man was considered totally corrupt and dead to God. But this man, Wesley preached, must be saved and could be saved by the grace of God. His view of salvation was just as realistic as his conception of sin. Salvation must include not only the work of Christ *for* man, but also the work of Christ *in* man. Salvation must mean not only the justification of man, his liberation from the guilt of sin, but also sanctification, the liberation from the power and the root of sin. Thus, faith, by which salvation is given to man, can never be isolated from its fruits. It must be active in love, and it appears as real only in so far as it is thus active.

This realistic attitude in the doctrine of salvation is shown particularly in the idea of sanctification, where the fruits of faith in the Christian life are most strongly emphasized. In the love of the heart and holiness of life religion reveals its truth and reality. Therefore, it is said about the original Methodists that they 'met together in order to help each other to be real Christians', and that they pursued only 'one point, real religion; the love of God and man ruling all their tempers, and words, and actions'. Accordingly, the doctrines of repentance and of faith were called the porch and the door of religion, while holiness was considered religion itself.

This ethical renewal of man, that became the end of salvation, not only includes that love which was shed abroad in man's heart in the new birth, but also the ensuing process of sanctification which aims at perfect love. This love was a pure love expressing itself in a pure intention and a will totally in accordance with the Will of God. This love was the fulfilment of the commandment of Christ to love God and one's neighbour with all one's heart.

It is evident that this doctrine of perfect love is an integral part in the view of salvation. Christian perfection is organically connected with the whole process of salvation and is the end of that development. Thus

88

Wesley preached that 'without holiness no man shall see the Lord'. Therefore Wesley, when he wrote his tract, *The Character of a Methodist*, at the beginning of the great revival, described an entirely sanctified Christian, thus emphasizing the end of the Christian life. And the year before his death he called this doctrine of Christian perfection 'the grand depositum which God has lodged with the people called Methodists'. And he adds: 'And for the sake of propagating this chiefly He appeared to have raised us up'.

The fact that Wesley thus emphasized the doctrine of perfect love must not, however, be misunderstood. It did not mean that he stressed one part of salvation, neglecting and overlooking others. But it meant that he preached a richer, a far more complete Christian message than had been preached for many centuries. It meant that he did justice to all sides of the Biblical view of salvation. He did not overlook the doctrine of God the Creator, nor of Christ the Redeemer. On the contrary, he emphasized them both. The whole process of salvation had its source in the Atonement. But in his message he also included the third article in the Apostolic Creed, the work of the Holy Spirit. It was now a question not only of the acts of God in time past, in the creation and the atonement, but in the present time. It was a question of God's actions here and now through His Spirit. Regarding the Christian life in this light, Wesley emphasized the new possibilities of this life through the Spirit. Therefore it must be considered under a new and wider perspective, comprising not only the beginning of this life, but also its growth and perfection in love.

Thus the apostolic message of victory, the message of God's ability to change a man entirely, appears in Wesley. This doctrine of perfect love was the consequence of the same realistic attitude that characterized his whole religious outlook. If the Christian life is to be real, it must be a life in love, inspired by the love of God. In its highest reality, it must be a living in perfect love. This doctrine of entire sanctification, then, completed his view of salvation. It showed the realism of salvation in its full scope.

But then we ask: Did this idea of sanctification, which thus enlarged the vision for the Christian life, mean a limitation in another respect? Was this doctrine restricted to the life of the individual or did it also include a message for the fellowship of men and for society?

Apparently sanctification must refer to the individual. Sanctification belongs to the experience of the individual. Only the individual can be sure of God's love and the forgiveness of sins. And man's assurance of God's love kindles man's love to God. Sanctification as well as salvation as a whole is therefore summed up by Wesley in the words of St John: 'We love God, because He first loved us.'

This individual character of sanctification is particularly evident when regarded as a path to perfection which man has to travel in order to reach his ultimate goal in eternity. The Christian is a pilgrim on earth, and must reach his goal in order to be definitely saved at the final justification.

However, this individualism does not exclude a collective view. On the contrary, they are knit together. That love, which is the essence of sanctification, is a love to God. But, just because of that, it is also a love to man. Neighbourly love is a necessary fruit of love to God. Therefore the fellowship of man must be a consequence of the fellowship of God. Further, since love to one's fellow man and works arising from that love are necessary for one's continuance in the faith, a right relation to man is involved in a right relation to God.

Thus, sanctification never isolates the Christian from his neighbour.

It does not put him alone, creating for him a private religion without any influence on his fellow men and society, because sanctification not only includes a new mind, but also a new action. Accordingly, Wesley writes: 'The gospel of Christ knows of no religion but social religion; no holiness but social holiness.' It means, he explains further, not only that Christianity 'cannot subsist so well, but that it cannot subsist at all, without society— without living and conversing with other men'. Against quietism and passive mysticism, Wesley emphasizes the active character of perfection. 'Faith working by love,' he writes, 'is the length and breadth and depth and height of Christian perfection.' To grow in holiness does not only mean to be worthier for entrance into the eternal world. It also means to be 'fit for farther and more eminent service'. Perfection, therefore, has a social purport.

But this social purport of sanctification goes far wider and deeper. The neighbourly love of the Christian does not imply benevolence, goodwill, and responsibility for all men in general. It does not mean a fellowship with men in general. It means such a fellowship, such a relation to ones fellow men, as is in harmony with the law of God, since love is the fulfilment of that law.

Thus, love appears as obedience to the will of God. While sin is disobedience to God and separates man from man, love unites. The obedience to God's law, where His will is expressed, has, however, a wider scope. Sin separates man from man as it separates man from God; but the disintegration goes deeper and wider. Sin corrupted the whole original order of creation. It brought about disorder. It corrupted and still corrupts the moral world order of God, which involves the right relations between the Creator and the creatures and between man and man. Thus sin spoils God's design for His world. Therefore, obedience to God aims at the restoration of God's corrupted world order and at the realization of His plan. As love is the means to that end it not only works a moral change in the individual, but also in the whole society. Perfect love is, using the words of John Wesley, 'the great medicine of life; the never-failing remedy for all the evils of a disordered world; for all the miseries and vices of men'.

The law of love, revealed in Christ, must harmonize with that law, which rests already on the nature of things. This law appears as an immutable rule of right and wrong and is also an expression of God's will. As God is righteous, this law is a law of righteousness. As God is just, this law is a law of justice rendering to all their due. And further, as God is the eternal reason, this law must be, in a true sense, reasonable.

It is evident that social requirements are involved in this law. These requirements are requirements of justice. Thus, the relations between individuals must be considered in the light of that divine unchangeable law of justice. Social, economical or political questions have to be dealt with and have to be solved from time to time according to this fundamental principle. Thus the idea of love also involves the idea of social justice. Being obedient to God's law of justice the Christian, therefore, is taking part in rebuilding a society ruled by this law.

Love, however, does not only fulfil these requirements of justice. Love also fulfils the requirements of mercy. As God is not only just, but also merciful obedience to Him also means mercy. It means compassion and sympathy, benevolence and goodness. It shows itself in the deepest solidarity with men, and creates a society where men feel their joint responsibility. Thus, the idea of love involves an idea of a society, where, according to St Paul, men bear one another's burdens. Therefore

90

obedience to God not only appears as social justice, but also as social mercy.

As we have seen, the idea of love does not set aside or overrule the idea of justice. They unite in the idea of obedience to God, where love completes justice. Accordingly, the idea of love implies the idea of a society, built on the unshakable rock of justice and righteousness, but also inspired by that mercy, which is revealed in Christ. And this vision of a divine society is particularly emphasized in the doctrine of perfect love, as this love implies the perfect fulfilment of the law of love. This is a perfection as far as purity of intention is concerned. The aim of this perfection is that the will of God may be done on earth as it is done in Heaven.

Thus the doctrine of perfect love rejects such an individualism as overlooks the social import of sanctification. In this view the idea of the society is involved. But, on the other hand, this doctrine also rejects such a collectivism as disintegrates the personality of the individual and makes him a will-less tool of the mass. Instead, this doctrine includes the idea of the personality of man. This idea is not opposed to the Christian view of society. On the contrary, the former is a prerequisite of the latter, because this society forms a fellowship of free personalities.

This does not mean, however, that man is regarded in a false way as independent before God. Being totally corrupted by sin, man is totally dependent on God for his salvation. This is true of justification, but also of sanctification. The development of man in sanctification means a development in the dependence of God at the same time. Nobody is so aware of his total dependence on God as the entirely sanctified man.

But the fellowship of the Christian with God does not exclude human responsibility, because God gives all men through His prevenient grace the possibility of a free choice. Thus man becomes responsible for his relation to God. Man therefore never becomes an impersonal tool, which God uses for His purposes. Man is a person who has his own will and is responsible for his actions. And by that grace that God further confers on him, he co-operates with God in the sanctification. The Calvinistic doctrine of an unconditional election, therefore, must be rejected. The consequence of that doctrine is that man loses his moral responsibility and his personality, and that therefore his fellowship with God loses its personal character, as does the fellowship between man and man in society.

Founded on the grace of God, the fellowship of the Christian with God thus includes both man's dependence on God and his own responsibility. Man's continuance in the faith can therefore be described, not only as the fruit of God's work, but at the same time as the fruit of man's own work. And in the same way, entire sanctification can be considered as the gift of God and at the same time as the entire commitment of man to God.

This view of man implies, as we have seen, a view of the society including the idea of a personal fellowship, a fellowship between men acting under personal responsibility. This is true of a human society, based on prevenient grace; it is no less true of a divine society based on justifying or sanctifying grace. Thus, the society involved in the idea of perfect love must be a society where the personality of man, the responsibility of the individual, is preserved. Since man's love is a personal love to a personal God and to his fellow man, all fellowship formed by that love must be personal.

Most clearly the idea of personal fellowship appears in the idea of the Christian brotherhood or the Church formed not by neighbourly love in general, but by love between Christian brothers.

The relation between the Church and salvation is most intimate.

Salvation is a life of the individual, but as such a part of the life in the Church. The Church is a fellowship of salvation. Thus the Church is not only a fellowship of the forgiveness of sins, but also a fellowship of sanctification, as the former cannot be isolated from the latter. The Church is a fellowship of faith, but if so it must at the same time be a fellowship of love, as faith reveals its reality in love, the essence of sanctification.

In opposition to conceptions of the Church characterized by an unreal formalism, the Methodist idea of the Church emphasizes the reality of a holy Church. Confessing our belief in 'the holy catholic Church, the communion of saints', we mean precisely what we say. The realism in the idea of salvation corresponds to the realism in the view of the Church. 'The Church is called *holy*,' Wesley declares, 'because it *is* holy: because every member thereof is holy; though in different degrees; as he that called them is holy.'

It is evident that this holiness of the Church is not a holiness isolated from Christ, who is the Head of the Church. Its sanctity must be rooted in the sanctity of Christ. The Church is the body of Christ; it is the work of the Spirit. But this body is a living body, a living fellowship. To be incorporated with this fellowship of the Spirit means, then, to share in its spiritual life. It means fellowship with that Spirit who sanctifies man. And therefore it also means that those who have communion with this Spirit and are formed by it have fellowship between each other. As the fruit of the Spirit is love, this love must create fellowship in accordance with the nature of love to unite men.

The Church being a fellowship of life, thus is it a fellowship in sanctification. This is shown both in its depth and in its breadth. It is a deep fellowship born of that love that comes from above. And in proportion as man's love reflects the love of God, being a pure love with the only intention to do the will of God, this communion becomes pure and deep. The fruit of a development in sanctification will be a development in fellowship. Accordingly, the perfect fellowship is the consequence of the perfect love.

Just because of its depth, this fellowship is shown in its breadth, too. As members in the body of Christ, Christians are one. They belong to the universal Church consisting of all believers throughout the world. This unity is the consequence of their unity in Christ. But it becomes real as a unity in that life that comes from Christ. Thus the unity is a unity of life, a unity in and through love. While sanctification promotes unity, lack of sanctification impedes it. Perfection in love, therefore, must result in perfection in unity between all Christians, too.

This unity of love means also a unity of faith, as this fellowship of life is a fellowship in the life of faith. It must, however, be emphasized that this unity above all is a unity in love, as faith is the means and love the end. If faith is real, it must be active in love.

This does not mean, however, that the intellectual side of faith can be overlooked. The fellowship in the Church is a fellowship in the doctrine too. The Christian unity is also founded on the fundamental truths of faith. Considering the relation between the unity of life and the unity of doctrine, we have to stress two things. The same Holy Spirit who creates the life and the fellowship of Christians will influence their thinking too, because the thinking is a part of life. Thus, as far as the fellowship grows in sanctification so far it will also grow in the fellowship of doctrine. Further, as faith is the means and love the end, the purity of doctrine is subordinated to the purity of life. Life is superior to doctrine. 'I believe', Wesley says, 'the merciful God regards the lives and tempers of men more than their

92

ideas.' And he continues: 'Without holiness, I own, no man shall see the Lord; but I dare not add, or clear ideas' (*S.*, II, 485).

Defining the Church as the body of Christ and as the creation of the Spirit, we will not overlook another side of the Church either, the institutional side. The Church is not only the living fellowship of the Spirit. It is also an organized society. The form of the Church, however, has to be subordinated to the life of the Church. As the Church above all is an organism, not an organization, its form of organization must be subordinated to the living organism and its needs.

We find this principle in Wesley when forming the classes, bands, and select bands of the Methodists. In fellowship they should help each other to work out their salvation. The principle of organization was the need of life. They aimed at the life of salvation in its full scope, in its beginning, growth, and perfection, and the form of organization was accommodated to this purpose.

The Church thus is a fellowship of life. As such it must also be a fellowship of activity—an activity within itself and without itself. This activity is the activity of love, by which the Church shares in the work of Christ, in His work of salvation. Sharing in this work, the Church takes responsibility for itself as well as for the world. The more love grows to a perfect or a pure love, the more the work of the Church will be identified with the work of Christ.

After the two addresses had been delivered the Conference divided into six groups, which met in the Examination Schools, in Wesley Memorial Church, and in Regent's Park College to discuss the morning topic. (A summary of the findings of all group discussions will be found on p. 289 in the Report presented to the Plenary Session by the Rev. Walter J. Noble.)

. . . . .

On the afternoon of 30th August a Garden Party was held in the grounds of St John's College. The hosts were the Oxford Branch of the English-Speaking Union and the City of Oxford Publicity Board. Guests were received by Mrs Burrell, representing the English-Speaking Union, and by Mr E. J. Haylor, Chairman of the Publicity Board.

AFTERNOON LECTURE

THE afternoon session was held in the Examination Schools. The Chairman was Professor A. Victor Murray, Joint Vice-President of the Ecumenical Council, and the lecture on *Methodism in Relation to Protestant Tradition* was delivered by the Rev. E. Gordon Rupp.

METHODISM IN RELATION TO
PROTESTANT TRADITION

A lecture delivered by the REV. E. GORDON RUPP, *Lecturer in Church History, Richmond College, University of London:*

It is now more than forty years since the famous *New History of Methodism* was written: in order, as its editors said, 'to utilize the results of recent study upon the origins of the Methodist Churches, manifest the sense of

93

their oneness which all increasingly feel, and set forth World-Wide Methodism as branch of the Church Catholic with its own notes, and an essential Unity underlying its several forms in many lands'. Those volumes began with a chapter on 'The Place of Methodism in the Life and Thought of the Christian Church' written by the Editor, Dr H. B. Workman, who this very day was laid to rest, a great son and servant of Methodism, and a scholar who must rank as one of the really great Protestant Church historians. Dr Workman began that classic essay with the clause in the Creed, 'I believe in the Holy Ghost, the Holy Catholic Church, the Communion of Saints', and in it he wrote: 'Every Communion of thinkers, every phase of faith, has its place in and its relation to the great whole, and plays some part . . . in the progress and development of the Holy Catholic Church.'

Much has been learned in the last forty years: an impressive band of Methodist scholars have brought new facts to light, new insights to bear upon the problems of our origins and our development. Perhaps one fitting memorial of this Conference might be the inauguration of another such 'History of Methodism'—this time more centred in theology than in descriptive history?—and reassessing our tradition in the light of Biblical theology, the ecumenical conversation, and the new, pressing intellectual problems of our time. But it, too, would need to begin, where the scholars of the last generation began, with the fundamental fact that there is one holy Catholic Church, because there is one lamb of God, who takes away the sins of the world.

This is that ultimate human solidarity of which all societies are broken intimations, that City of God which is seated partly in the course of these declining times, and partly in that solid estate of eternity. This is the Mystical Body in which Christ lives and rules His faithful people. (And if you think 'Mystical Body' has a Popish ring, turn to the loveliest of all our pastoral addresses, and see how aptly the Conference of 1793 employed it, fifty years before it was re-discovered by the Church of England!)

But Christ is Head of the Church according to His humanity. (And if that also sounds papistical, you will find an exposition of it in Luther's great hymn about the Church, '*Sie ist mir lieb, die werte Magd*'.) As, in the days of His flesh, He really and truly became man, that is, He belonged to history; so at His Ascension He raised that human nature to the Right Hand of God, and henceforth history belongs to Him and He rules it, in a double revelation: first, as Lord of the Church, and, second, as Saviour of the World, for, as Charles Wesley sings—

'Head of Whole Mankind art Thou.'

Tradition matters, because of this intervention of God in history, because 'under Pontius Pilate' the Divine Revelation was pin-pointed once upon a time as precisely as the Battle of Hastings or of Valley Forge, and removed from the timeless realm of myth and legend. And here an important distinction is to be observed about all history; between history as it really happened, and history as we know it. History as it really happened took place, once for all: nothing can un-happen the fact that King Alfred burned the cakes, that the Old Guard lost the last charge at Waterloo, and that Judas earned his thirty pieces of silver. But history, as witnessed and recorded and remembered, may change the total pattern and so the ultimate significance of a series of events. And when that remembrance takes place within a single community, it becomes the creative force we call tradition.

The classic example is Magna Carta, which originally was a feudal document wrested from King John by the Barons in 1215, but which became the 'palladium of Liberty' for the great Parliamentary lawyers of the seventeenth century, and a creative element in political change. Thus within the historical continuity of national life, the past can be evoked with striking power: the words of Queen Elizabeth at Tilbury in 1588 brought inspiration to many Englishmen in the similar invasion hours of 1940.

These things apply to all history, and to all societies. But tradition in this sense, this flow of life from one generation to another, has special significance for Christians. For it is the vehicle of the communion of saints, by which the past and present are joined in the one living, worshipping communion of the people of God.

The problem arises of poison in the bloodstream. Tradition in itself provides no criteria between history and myth. The pondering of ideas by devout minds, over many centuries, as the Passover recalled the mighty action of the Exodus for the Jews, and the Eucharist the mightier Passion of the Saviour, has meant a continual enrichment of the life of the Israel of God. But the pondering by millions of devout minds, over many centuries, of ideas may equally produce the impious obscurantism of the dogma of the Assumption of the Virgin Mary. It is here that the problem of the relation of Scripture to tradition intervenes, so fundamental in the Catholic-Protestant dilemma.

By affirming the primacy of Scripture over the holy tradition, Protestantism seeks, not the repudiation but the safeguarding of tradition. That safeguard is the witness of the Apostles and the Prophets recorded in Holy Scripture: and here is the strength of the appeal to the 'old Fathers' and to the Primitive Church. The great Reformers charged their opponents with innovation.

'These many years passed, this godly and decent order of the ancient Fathers hath been altered, broken and neglected', says Thomas Cranmer in the Preface to the Prayer Book. We are the old, true Church, says Martin Luther in his *Wider Hans Worst* (1540). 'The former old Church shines forth again now, as the sun out of the clouds, behind which that same sun was shining all the time, but not clearly.' And in that enormous and learned compendium with which the seventeenth-century Anglicans demonstrated the catholicity of Protestantism—or, as they put it, 'The Preservative against Popery'—they retorted to the taunt: 'Where was your Church before Luther?'

'Our religion was long before the times of Luther, and believed and settled in many kingdoms and nations of this world, and hath neither novelty and singularity in it. It is an old religion. I am sure it is of age, and can speak for itself. It hath lasted now these 1,600 years and more: founded at first by Christ and His Apostles, handed down to us through many sufferings and persecutions and here it is preserved. It contracted indeed in the coming down a great deal of rust by the falseness and carelessness of its keepers, particularly by the Church of Rome: we scoured off the rust and kept the metal: that is the Romish religion, this is the English. They added false doctrines to the Christian faith: we left the one and kept to the other: this is ancient, and those are new.'

Church history does not begin for Methodists in 1738, or in 1517, or with John Huss or John Wycliffe or Peter Waldo, but with Abraham, and indeed, in a precisely Arminian sense, with Adam. We need to beware that sectarian interpretation of history which would dissolve its pedigree into certain isolated pockets of so-called 'purely spiritual religion' and picks its ancestry a little too choosily among those 'Reformers before the

Reformation' who can be made to fit their version of Reformation principles.

That is why I shall not attempt to relate Methodism to a set of so-called 'Protestant principles' or this or that norm of Protestant orthodoxy. Such a direct confrontation between John Wesley and Calvin was attempted by Dr Croft Cell, or between Wesley and Luther, as has been recently outlined by Dr Franz Hildebrandt, may be fruitful and illuminating. We must be after bigger game. We have to try to look at Methodism in its home, its life setting (*Sitz im Leben*) within the Western Church, and especially that pure and reformed part of it disestablished in this Kingdom. That is not to be taken in hand lightly or unadvisedly. A great community —nation, culture, or Church—is a spiritual complexity the texture of which is intricate as that of any human body. To examine Methodism within the setting of the Protestant tradition is an operation as delicate as that with which the surgeon's knife must cut between the bone, sinew, nerve, and tissue. It is too high for me. I cannot undertake that operation here, though before I have done many of you may feel I have administered the anaesthetic. All I can do is scrawl a few blackboard comments on the nature of the job, and sketch where as I think the incisions need to be made.

You will please discount what I say in three regards. First, Church history is made, and, more than we can know, conditioned not by the great leaders and documents and movements and institutions, but by the quiet witness or the silent apostasy of many millions of ordinary men and women. Second, an intellectual investigation is almost bound to exaggerate one element, the thinking, in the life of the Church. Third, I am what Ruskin calls 'Protestant Cavalier rather than Protestant Roundhead,' and may do less than justice to some important elements in our many-sided tradition.

I have already hinted that our main clues lie, not in Continental Protestantism, but within the English Protestant tradition—that pattern of life, thought, and devotion which has sprung from within the Church of England and the historic Free Churches, and from the tension, always fruitful, always tragic, between them, and which has deeply influenced, and in turn been influenced, by the changing life of the English peoples. In the making of that tradition, under God, men and movements have counted for much. Six university movements in particular: the five great Cambridge Movements—the Cambridge Reformers of the sixteenth century and the Cambridge Puritans who followed them, the Cambridge Platonists of the seventeenth century, and the Cambridge Evangelicals of the nineteenth; and last, the influence of that group of friends, Charles Kingsley, F. D. Maurice, and Julius Hare, whose circle of influence includes the famous scholarly trio, Westcott, Lightfoot, and Hort. All these influences, directly and indirectly, influenced Methodism. The sixth movement, Methodism, itself began here at Oxford.

The English Protestant Tradition in the Sixteenth Century

The Reformation in England began with a group of Cambridge scholars, students and Dons, who met together for study and prayer, who ministered to the outcast and to those in prison, and who were noted for their frequent communion. Their leader, Thomas Bilney, was, like John Wesley, 'a little single body, but of a good upright countenance' whose evangelical zeal led to the conversion of his friends (including noble Hugh Latimer), and who got into trouble for preaching in the open fields. But, unlike John Wesley, Bilney was burned at the stake, and, unlike the members of

96

the Holy Club, his friends were thrown into prison or driven into exile. One of them, Robert Barnes went to Wittenberg and sat at the table of Luther. He wrote the earliest English exposition of Justification by Faith and of the Bondage of the Will, and John Wesley reprinted this rare document in 1739.

These men and their friends gave us the English Bible. They defied that fugitive and cloistered virtue which feared to put the Word of God into the hands of Christian men. 'When they ask us,' cried William Tyndale, 'how we know it is the Scripture of God, ask them how John the Baptist knew, and other prophets which God stirred up, in all times when the Scripture was in captivity . . . who taught the eagles to spy out their prey? Even so, the children of God spy out their Father: and Christ's elect spy out their Lord, and trace the paths of His feet and follow: yea, though He go upon the plain and liquid water which will receive no step, and yet there they find his feet. His elect know him.' I need not emphasize what the English Bible meant to the Wesleys. Charles's hymns notoriously are a patchwork quilt of Scriptural quotation, and that is hardly less true of the prose of John, for the *Sermons* and the *Journal* are steeped in the rhythm and the vocabulary of the tongue which Tyndale spake.

All but one of the makers of the English Prayer Book were Cambridge reformers. You remember how John Wesley gave its liturgy as a kind of christening present to American Methodism, and said: 'I believe there is no liturgy in the world, either in ancient or in modern language, which breathes more of a solid, Scriptural, rational piety than the Common Prayer of the Church of England.' And how our beloved Adam Clarke declared: 'This book I reverence next to the Bible . . . next to the Bible it has been the depository of the pure religion of Christ . . . had it not been, under God for this blessed book, the liturgy of the British Church, I verily believe Methodism had never existed.' They would have had little sympathy with the radical Puritanism which dismissed those prayers as 'old written, rotten stuff', or its antiphons as 'like the tossing to and fro of tennis balls'. Cranmer's Liturgy was one of the great creative works of the Protestant Reformation. It blended clergy and people together in a form of worship understanded by the people. The significance of the Communion Service can be best seen by reading it side by side with that Homily of Salvation which we owe to the same great genius, and which, as Article XI says, expounds the doctrine 'very wholesome and full of comfort' that we are saved by 'only faith'. For when the Reformers attacked Popery, they attacked the intrusion into the holy place of ecclesiastical man, who has bedevilled European history more grievously than political or economic man. By proclaiming Justification by Faith and by a drastic operation on the canon of the Mass, the Reformers tried to make sure, once for all, that the centre of the life of the Church should be, not ecclesiastical man, but the God Man and His one oblation of Himself once offered. To these important principles, wrote Thomas Jackson, John Wesley's attention was 'forcibly directed by the Moravian Brethren . . . but he was more specially led to the practical adoption of them by a careful study of the Church's Homilies.' Bible, Prayer Book, Homilies—theology, devotion, preaching. To these we must add the witness of life and of death. The place where the greatest Cambridge Reformers were burned is said to be one of the sights of Oxford. There were many others. The third great normative document in the making of the English Protestant tradition next to the English Bible and the Prayer Book, is Foxe's *Book of Martyrs*. Among the first volumes of Wesley's 'Christian Library' are three volumes of extracts from that book, which was read in innumerable homes right up to the end of the nineteenth century. This book helped to make and confirm the sturdy Protestantism of the Elizabethan Age. It was read to the crew by Sir Francis Drake as his ship nosed into the Pacific: and it was read aloud in the quiet peace of Nicholas Ferrar's High Church gathering at Little Gidding. These men and their witness made England safe for the rich, swelling glories of the Elizabethan Age, whose praises have recently been so nobly sung by Mr A. L. Rowse. And the Great Queen and the little ships of 1588 were part of the same preservative against Popery.

The English Puritan Tradition

That was the age of the pioneers: the sailors, the astronomers, the Reformers. They were followed by the age of the map-makers, who plotted and charted those discoveries, framed them and giving them a habitation and a name made it possible for wayfaring men to follow and not err therein. Such were the Puritans.

Here a new interpretation has been made necessary by the distinguished works of a number of American historians, Perry Miller, William Haller, Knappen, Wright, and others. It is clear that, as we had suspected, Macaulay's Puritan is a Victorian Evangelical in fancy dress. These historians do not fear to speak (Tell it not in All Souls: whisper it not to Mr Trevor Roper) of a Puritan humanism. 'If we wish to take Puritan culture as a whole', says Perry Miller, 'we shall find that about 90 per cent of the intellectual life, scientific knowledge, morality, manners and customs, notions and prejudices, was that of all Englishmen. The other 10 per cent made all the difference.'

The Cambridge Puritans provided a trained and educated intelligentsia which responded to the new lay intelligentsia of the lawyers of the Inns of Court. Their love of learning left an imprint on two generations. 'In contrast to all other pioneers', says Perry Miller of their American successors, 'they made no concession to the forest, but in the midst of frontier conditions, in the very throes of clearing the land and erecting shelters, they maintained schools and a college, a standard of scholarship and of competent writing, a class of men devoted entirely to the life of the mind and soul.'

William Haller has drawn attention to those Cambridge Puritans who from within the Church of England provided a combination of scholar, preacher, and pastor. Out of dozens, we mention Richard Greenham, who left his Fellowship at Pembroke to labour for twenty years in the poor parish of Dry Drayton, and who gathered young men around him in a 'kind of school, the members of which devoted themselves to the searching of the Scripture and of one another's hearts.' There was John Dod, never out of the pulpit, who, like Wesley, laboured for simplicity so that 'poor simple persons that never knew what religion meant . . . could not choose but speak of his sermon. It mightily affected poor creatures to hear the mysteries of God . . . brought down to their language and dialect.'

Above all, they attended to the care of souls. The two great figures of George Herbert and of Richard Baxter remind us of the diversity of the English Protestant ideal of pastoral care; and Wesley was indebted to both. Their writings, like *The Pilgrim's Progress*—the fourth founding document of the tradition—are all that have survived of a once vast literature of Puritan moral and devotional literature. Some of it was of ephemeral worth: much of it was taken up into the later casuistries of Jeremy Taylor's *Ductor Dubitantium* and Baxter's *Christian Directory*. But some perished because of the head-on collision of political and ecclesiastical revolution. This moral and devotional theology is important. In one way, Puritanism and High Church Laudianism were the continuation of medieval asceticism by other means. It is a key to the age 1555-1660 that to the dimensions of Word and Sacrament had been added a disputed third —Word and Sacrament, and the 'Discipline of Christ'. Two of these Puritans gained European fame for their skill in practical counselling troubled souls: William Ames, and the even greater William Perkins. We read that before his conversion he was known as 'Drunken Perkins', but that after he had become something of an expert in problems of social ethics, games of chance and the like he was known as 'Painful Perkins' (in the seventeenth-century usage of painstaking, of course!) The word 'damn' uttered by him from the pulpit made men tremble for their sins. Out of the fifty-two volumes of the Christian Library, the greater number of selections are from the Puritan tradition. We owe Wesley's *Journal* and the rich Methodist biographical literature to the Puritan initiation of the spiritual diary. If we remember that there is a lot of Calvinism left when you take away predestination and Church polity, we can say that through these men Calvinism affected the whole temper of the English people and gave us a quality which foreigners recognize more clearly than we do, especially in the incurable moralism of our foreign policy—'*perfide Albion*'.

I have not spoken of the Puritan left. There is something to be said for their version of the four freedoms: freedom from Popery, freedom from bishops, freedom from persecution, and freedom from Presbyterians. For in seventeenth-century England it became clear that the evil of ecclesiastical man was not confined to Popery: that whether bishop or presbyter are the same or different in origin does not matter in the end if they involve an arrogant clericalism which knows no other way with truth than the threefold engine which Christian men bestowed on modern Europe— the closed shop, the Iron Curtain, and the 'party line'.

Looking back, we can see with Professor Jordan that this age saw 'one of the most momentous changes in the history of English thought'. Then it took a Milton to conceive that the intellectual ferment which produced more than 22,000 pamphlets between 1640 and 1660 could be a work of God—for the reform of Reformation itself, a portent more significant than all the Parliamentary armament. Our world, our Christian world, is not yet abreast of Milton's *Areopagitica*: it has not yet learned that neither rack nor thumbscrew, branding iron or bullet, cavalry charge or push of pike—nor yet jet fighters and atom bombs—can kill a lie or advance truth one jot or tittle. But Milton's sublimities had been anticipated in those little fustian bands of men and women, badgered from pillar to post, from East Anglia to Holland, and at last to a new world. True, they were, as has been said, a little too inclined to equate the Holy Catholic Church with a back parlour on the first floor in Amsterdam—but it was partly because they remembered how once the whole of catholicity descended on such a back room in Jerusalem, upon what was after all a very petty bourgeois company. It matters that the case for toleration and liberty of thought was not left to go by default to the *Politiques* and cynics, but claimed in the name of that Word of God which, as Roger Williams said, 'is only in soul matters able to conquer'. Englishmen owe much to the Christian cussedness of the Puritan left, to the men who removed their hats in the presence of God but before no other dignities, and who doggedly refused to be pushed around by Pope or prelate, king or committee, or even by a People's Government. And the Quakers put a question mark, which must ever and again be put, against all institutional religion, and against all ecclesiastical frills and furbelows. They hovered on the edge of an even greater truth which St Paul expounded, that every believer may become ecclesiastical man, and that among other things, the priesthood of all believers implies that dread and fiery judgement awaits when an individual man may claim to be the Pope of his own soul.

Puritanism won its war, and lost its peace. A fine thesis by an Australian Methodist scholar, Dr Harold Wood, has shown how real was the possibility of a comprehensive Church settlement in 1662—on paper: how close together were the Church politics of Bishop Usher's *Reduction of Episcopacy* and Baxter's presbyterial supplement to that 'old diocesan framework' which he abhorred. But civil wars leave an exceptional momentum of fear and bitterness. The Nonconformists went out into centuries of political and social disabilities, and among them Bartholomew and John Westley (i.e. John Wesley's grandfather) and Dr Samuel Annesley. Within a generation came the crisis of 1688 and the secession of the Non-Jurors. I have said nothing of that fine Caroline High Church tradition which rejoiced to be both Catholic and Protestant, of its patristic learning and its great divines. But these men, and the Non-Jurors with their liturgical experiments, are another element in the Wesley heritage, and the greatest of them are represented in his publications and abridgements, many of them in the Christian Library.

The Cambridge Platonists were a little withdrawn from that ardent, heroic world of the Church struggle. But their prodigious learning, their deep devotion matched the new learning, the mathematics, the Cartesian philosophy, the science of the Royal Society, and, in Professor Raven's phrase, made 'a religion fit for scientists'. Through the Scottish mystics, Scougal and Leighton, they prepared the way for the tolerant, practical moralism of the Latitudinarian divines. There was always more of the Latitudinarian about John Wesley than in these days of neo-orthodoxy, we always care to discern. But it was Stillingfleet's *Eirenicon* which, with Lord King's book, brought John Wesley to his catastrophic conclusion that he might, in a recent phrase, try out episcopacy, by taking it into his system: there was quite a bit already there! But he blended them all, Cambridge Platonists and Latitudinarians, into the Christian Library, and he made his preachers read them long and hard. Thus all the richest elements in the English religious life of two centuries were woven into the mind of John Wesley. He spent fifty years giving the people called Methodists a piece of his mind, and the extent to which he succeeded is the measure by which Methodism will not fit into any compendium history of Christian 'enthusiasm'.

The Methodist Tradition in the Eighteenth Century

Samuel and Susannah Wesley were what Bernard Manning calls 'lapsed Dissenters', though the Dissent from which they turned away was not the heroic 'Church under the Cross', but second-generation religion, the *epigoni* of the 'Calves' Head Clubs' with their sour rebellious gossip, of the Nonconformist Academies with their truculent inferiority sense, and the landslide into Unitarianism, though it was, the Dissent of Henry and Isaac Watts. At any rate, John and Charles Wesley were bred up in the High Church tradition, and from the Holy Club to Savannah moved within this framework. Not without uneasiness, for Wesley's nickname among his lady friends, 'Little Primitive Christianity', shows that he was seeking Evangelical perfection in the apostolic age and practice. But the English Protestant tradition badly needed a blood transfusion. Wesley found that new element in Continental Protestantism, in the great Lutheran hymns, in the example and precept of the Moravians, and in the Biblical philanthropy of Pietism. But he was never more firmly Anglican than when he most openly admired the Moravians.

There are, it seems to me, two fallacies at this point. One to play down the reality of the Evangelical conversion of the brothers Wesley. Dr Elmer Clarke has dealt very faithfully with that. The other is to play down the permanent significance of Wesley's life and work before 1738. Yet how much of Methodism existed by then. The first *Hymn Book*, some of the sermons, the beginning of the Christian Library, 'the society, the class meeting, the leaders and lay assistants, the beginning of an itinerancy, extempore preaching and prayer, even the building of a meeting house'— all this, says Nehemiah Curnock, 'came to Wesley in Georgia'. And when his angry parishioners expostulated, when they demanded of John Wesley what this new religion was, which was not any Protestantism they knew, which was neither Anglican fish, nor Presbyterian fowl, nor Moravian good red herring, neither he nor they could know that there, before their eyes, growing from embryo to flesh, was that which one day millions of us across the world would call 'our beloved Methodism'.

I shall not talk of 'our doctrines' in terms of Protestant theology. That is being done by a number of Methodist scholars, in themselves a kind of ecumenical movement: Dr Lindström, David Lerch, Stanley Frost, Percy Scott, William Cannon. But I offer two comments about that 'Evangelical Arminianism'. One of the deadly features of seventeenth-century Protestantism and Catholicism was a one-sided Augustinianism, what M. Rondet has called 'a Pessimism of Grace'—the notion that God is only concerned to snatch a tiny handful from the mass of doomed humanity. In contrast was the optimism of Nature of the Rationalist enlightenment. The Arminianism of Wesley had little to do with the academic writings of Arminius. You will find the heart of it in Wesley's hymns and in the continual refrain—'For All'.

> 'Thy undistinguishing regard
> Was cast on Adam's fallen race:
> For all thou hast in Christ prepared
> Sufficient, sovereign, saving Grace.'

It maintained the Biblical, Protestant diagnosis of the depth of our human tragedy, which we only realize when we confront the Righteousness of God. But it set 'total grace' over and against 'total sinfulness'; it breathed an optimism of Grace which changed the whole mood and temper of English Christianity and nerved it for the battle against the giant evils of the coming industrial age. Above all, the words 'For All' unloosed a missionary passion which spilled across England into other lands and continents, and which brought, in its favourite phrase, of 'myriads' of converts:

> 'And lo, in thee
> We myriads see
> Of Justified Believers.'

It is the mood of those noble instructions to missionaries written by great Jabez Bunting after a 100 years of revival. 'We unite in tens of thousands in fervent prayer to God for you. May he open to you a great door and effectual, and make you immediately or remotely the instrument of the salvation of myriads.'

Second, Evangelical Arminianism stands for a combination of doctrines, a shape of the gospel which makes Methodism an autonomous doctrinal form and not simply a mongrel blend of Protestantism and Catholicism.

The doctrines of Justification by Faith and of Perfect Love affirm that height and depth of the Christian gospel which opens again the great New Testament horizons. The doctrine of the Spirit relates this to present Christian experience. Here is a new note unknown to Jeremy Taylor—read his miserable sermon on death-bed repentance—or to the doleful piety of Dr Pusey. Dr Pusey complained that Methodists are taught to look for 'a present salvation', i.e. a sensible assurance of salvation 'such as is vouchsafed often to God's servants on their dying beds, but rarely until the close of their lives, still less at their first conversion'. But the doctrine of the spirit safeguarded the truths of Christian experience against sentimentalism, by guarding them within the objective Divine action.

Third, and much less often remarked, is Wesley's use of the law in relation to Believers. Wesley explains that this is law in inverted commas, so to speak. It is not mere command, but it is a branch of the glorious liberty of the Children of God. By defining the law as 'the commands of Christ briefly comprised in the Sermon on the Mount' rather than the Decalogue, Wesley goes beyond the third use of the law in Protestant orthodoxy, and gives his ethical teaching another orientation than that of Luther or of Calvin. This doctrine safeguarded Justification against Antinomianism, and Perfect Love against a fanatical perfectionism. But those doctrines prevented it from relapsing into the rigid moralism of later Puritanism and modern Nonconformist pietism. And this was more than teaching, or even preaching. This shape of the gospel rests on the great four-fold Methodist economy. 'Our Doctrines'—the *Sermons*. 'Our Discipline'—the ordinances of Word and Sacrament, the society and class, the watchnights vigils and fasts. 'Our Hymns'—those hymns of Watts and of Charles Wesley which James Rigg called 'our Prayer and Hymn Book, our Liturgy, our theological standard . . . our unique blessing, advantage, possession, birthright'. And 'Our Literature'—the Bible, the Christian Library, the tracts, the great literature which Wesley created or adapted that he might bring up his enormous brood of children in the nature and admonition of the Lord.

The Methodist Tradition in the Nineteenth Century

It was something of a miracle that Methodism survived the strains and stresses of the revolutionary age and of the Industrial Revolution. It owed much to its flexibility and freedom from the doctrinaire. 'Methodism came down from heaven as it was wanted', cried one of the preachers in 1836, 'piece by piece'. A little exuberant, perhaps, but it is true that, like Topsy, Methodist polity 'just growed', and that some of our characteristic institutions were originally inspired improvisations. Methodism was 'the Body' with its own self-contained world curiously athwart the social and political structure of the age. Our beloved and honoured Henry Carter said to me a few months ago that in one sense the Methodist societies never separated from the Church of England because they had never been a part of it. There is an important truth here which Thomas Jackson expressed strikingly in 1842. The first Methodist preachers went, he wrote, 'to the masses of London, the colliers of Kingswood and Staffordshire, the keelmen of Newcastle, the manufacturers of Yorkshire and Lancashire and the peasantry in the farming districts. . . . Was the conversion of these outcasts an act of schism?' As for the present Methodist societies, 'with very few exceptions, they consist of the descendants of the early Methodists who walk in the way of their fathers, and such other persons who were previously unacquainted with religion in its life and power'.

We can say this as long as we remind ourselves that not only the occasion, but the results of separation have to be considered. When we have defended the sincerity of John Wesley and when we have repudiated the discussion in Anglo-Catholic terms, we have still to face the question whether there has not been in consequence, a moving away from deep elements in historical Christian continuity, which gave original Methodism a depth and a stability not always evident in later days.

Like an escalator, the sociological stratum in which Methodism lived, moved slowly upwards. Thrift, sobriety, confidence counted in that rough age of self-help. In that thrilling book, J. T. Quinlan's *Victorian Prelude*, you may read how Methodism and Evangelicalism made literate a whole population of millions and then captured this vast audience for its own literature of tracts, devotional books, and moral stories. I suppose one of them, Legh Richmond's *Dairyman's Daughter*, might rank with *The Pilgrim's Progress* and *Paradise Lost* among the great normative documents of Protestantism. It was an all-time best-seller, and even the French prisoners of war clamoured in their thousands for *La Fille du Laitier*. This great educational work affected the whole temper, the moral earnestness of the great Victorian Age.

Methodism continued to grow rapidly. But it could not keep pace with the swift increase of population—swiftest where it was most concerned, in the industrial North. 'Go to your history', cried Disraeli. 'What are your invasions of the barbarian nations, your Goths and Visigoths, your Lombards and Huns, to our population returns?' It was the great age of chapel-building, and inevitably with each new building one of the most flexible instruments of evangelism in history became pegged down, so that Wesleyan Methodism suffered a new rigidity which in part reflected the stiffened class distinctions of the time.

We are not to think of the Primitive Methodists and other nineteenth-century bodies as though their prime objective was to apply modern principles of a social gospel. It was their standing glory to preach Christ, and to go not only to those who wanted them, but those who wanted them most, in the genuine primitive Methodist way. They did not take a leaf out of the politicians' notebooks. As far as I know, only Jabez Bunting was accused of doing that. The politicians copied them. Dr Wearmouth, in those fine studies of his, has shown how the radical movements and the new trades unions copied the very polity of Methodism, the class meeting and the like—as sign that, as the Dominican and Franciscan polity responded to changing sociological patterns in the thirteenth century, so Methodism touched a new level of society through a congenial pattern. But the social and political repercussions of these movements were far-reaching. They brought Christian compassion and Christian responsibility in the place of doctrinaire ideology, into movements which enjoyed a reproach as fierce and couched in the same language as our antagonism to atheistic Communism—I had almost said the 'pink fringe' today.

The Oxford Movement changed the relation between Methodism and the Church of England and provoked the great Nonconformist alliance which was so powerful in the last part of the nineteenth century. The change of mood can be detected by comparing the writings of Thomas Jackson in 1834-42 with those of James Rigg twenty-years after. Like the great Methodists of his age, Adam Clarke, Richard Watson—even like James Everett—Jackson was steeped in the great Anglican divines. 'Some of the best hours in my life have been spent', he said, 'in the use of her truly sublime and evangelical liturgy. The sanctified scholarship of her sons has produced the richest theological literature in the world.'

The note of affection has gone from Dr Rigg. 'Cherishing no hostility or ill will against the Church of England, the Wesleyan Methodists decline without thanks all overtures whatsoever for re-union (or, what is the same thing, for absorption).' Indeed (a happy thought for those engaged in conversations with Anglicans and Episcopalians in these days), since Methodism as a world communion outnumbers Anglicanism, and is 'as a world power more potent in its operation and influence', he concludes, 'it is just as likely that Methodism should absorb Anglican episcopacy as that it should absorb Methodism!'

In another direction, Dr Rigg is significant. The old Methodist frame was breaking up and in some ways Victorian Nonconformity had narrower horizons than the old Arminian catholicity. Jabez Bunting's lucid sermons are the last great exposition of Justification by Faith: thereafter the preaching of the Cross is split into an abstract doctrine of Atonement on the one hand and an emotional crisis of conversion on the other. William Arthur's *Tongue of Fire* apart, it seems that the doctrines of the Spirit and of Perfect Love were left to those who, under the influence of new revival movements, would equate Scriptural holiness with fundamentalist pietism. Thomas Jackson could counter Dr Pusey with Bishop Pearson and the Puritan divines; Rigg brandishes the lesser talismans of Magee and Dr Pye Smith in the face of his opponents.

Most significant of all is Rigg's *Modern Anglican Theology*. This is a formidable all-out attack upon the new theology of Frederick Denison Maurice and his friends. Rigg represents the reaction of Evangelical Augustinianism against Maurice's revival of the great Alexandrian and Athanasian tradition, and not a few of the insights of Luther. Yet it was Maurice who had recaptured that trumpet-note of original Evangelical Arminianism, the affirmation that all men have been created and all men redeemed in Christ: the one theology capable of meeting the revolutionary ferment of science, Biblical criticism, and political revolution. Two of the young rebels saw something of this, John Scott Lidgett and Hugh Price Hughes, in their writings and in their deeds, have left us clues to which we might profitably return in a time when it is possible to correct the defects of Maurice in the light of Biblical and ecumenical theology.

The last part of the century provided what Dr Townsend has called the 'Golden Age of Nonconformity'. It was the time of new revivals, of great preachers, of crowded churches, of the solid sanctities of home and Sunday. It was an awakening of the sense of responsibility towards the dark places of great cities, and the need to maintain standards in public life. Hugh Price Hughes, champion of a hundred battles, was the mouthpiece of the Nonconformist conscience in those incredible days when the ruling classes trembled before a Nonconformist meeting, and when Cabinet Ministers lay awake at nights wondering what the *Methodist Times* would say of them next morning. But one sentence of Hughes was ominous:

'We must not allow our Churches to be identified with party politics, and in the twentieth century party politics will not be Whig or Tory, Liberal or Conservative, but collectivist and individualistic . . . woe to the Church which commits itself to either side. . . . Our Churches must be as impartial and comprehensive as the Bible, or they will be involved . . . in disaster.'

Soon the political power and moral influence of Nonconformity seemed to have gone with the wind, or with the Liberal Party. In two great centuries, the Elizabethan and Victorian ages, Protestantism came very close indeed to the conscience of the nation. But it is no accident that 'in all time of our wealth' precedes in the Litany 'in all time of our tribulation'. Here is something which our American friends might care to ponder as we enter the great American century, and where their great Church life flows with the promise of spring—or it might be an Indian summer. We all need to remember Dean Inge's saying that the Church which marries the spirit of the age will be left a widow in the next generation.

Now it is apparent that no Church can meet or even survive the coming age which is confined to one social class, least of all the middle classes, or which succumbs before the barrier of race, or which thinks in terms of one nation or continent. Our intellectual and spiritual problems cannot be met, cannot even be formulated in denominational terms.

Now we need all our past. To ponder the story of the English Protestant tradition is to believe that these things were written for our example, on whom the ends of the world have come: God has planted clues all along our providential way. We need to remember the courage of the pioneers, the great Reformers and their creative works. If our gospel is to come home to an estranged humanity, we shall need to do their works anew: new vehicles of Christian proclamation, teaching and worship, new institutions of piety and discipline. It may well be that in our time new forms of Christian existence must arise as different from those we have known as our modern Church life differs from that of the Middle Ages.

We need not only this 'Parrhesia', this holy boldness of faith, but that other great stay and comfort of Martin Luther—the communion of saints, the holy tradition. In a famous essay, Sir Arthur Quiller Couch quoted Sir Joshua Reynolds and his celebrated lectures on the art of painting:
'And then, he proceeds to preach the Old Masters: but how, why and to what end? . . . Does he commend his old masters for copying, for mere imitation? Not a bit of it. . . . Then for what? Listen. . . . The more extensive your acquaintance with the work of those who have excelled the more extensive will be your powers of invention . . . and what may appear still more like a paradox—the more original will be your conceptions.'
We need to remember the old masters in our craft. And then we need the map-makers as well as the pioneers. We need those enormous moral platitudes, those godly customs which are the foundation of good living and lasting culture. We must attend the breaches in our fourfold framework—'Our Doctrines', 'Our Discipline', 'Our Hymns' (I believe, were I an American Methodist, I would be more concerned about Charles Wesley's hymns than about the vexed problem of the divided chancel), and 'Our Literature'—in these days, when religious publishing houses have made profitable friendship with the mammon of unrighteousness, we shall need to support quite firmly our Book Stewards in their fight against the infiltration of unholy custom against the good tradition of our fathers, since the prime object of Methodist publishing is to teach and to evangelize.

The Church lost grip of two traditions in the sixteenth century: one, a tradition of truth, in letters, in science and philosophy, which we can roughly call 'humanism'. The other, of social justice, underlying the revolutionary dynamism of the last four centuries. The Church must be able to meet those traditions with inward and reconciling sympathy, and even in their most twisted, arrogant, anti-clerical, atheistic form it cannot win them with truculent reproach. Protestantism ought to be fitter for this than Catholicism. It is its strength and weakness that it has always been more apprehensive of new things, closer and more sensitive to the currents of the age and culture through which it moves. That is its strength; but our time affords ugly examples of the weakness whereby a Church

105

succumbs and becomes adjectival to the spirit of the nation, class, or culture.

But when we have read our Paul Blanshard and our Professor Binchy, when we have said all we must about the underhand methods, the log-rolling, and obscurantism of modern Popery, let us remember that there has always been much more to the Catholic Church than Popery. And I have sometimes wondered whether the Roman Church is not in these days a praying Church, as large areas of Protestantism have ceased to be! I don't know about a religion fit for scientists, but perhaps a good Protestant religion fit for Hell-deserving sinners, which is all I want to know, might do for scientists, and make them fit for religion, if it were purged of the funk and fudge and fear of truth which again and again has been the poison in our Protestant bloodstream. And we shall need the courage of com-passion not to abate one jot or tittle of our social witness. I heard some-thing in America about a 'pink fringe': and it would I think be a mistake to treat Christian left-wing intellectuals as seriously as they take themselves, but do let us remember that the one deadly group in Church history has been the 'yellow fringe' of those who just sit on the fence.

Above all, we need one another. We need that moving confidence of great American Methodism, the forward look, the knowledge that the Church militant here on earth is not the 'Church under the weather', but the Church under the Lamb who is Lord and Leader. We need the reminder of the Methodists of Europe and of China—that the Church is the Church 'under the Cross', and that our finest hours have been the times of tribulation. We need the eager impatience of the younger Churches, the conviction—and I would not have spoken so far did I not believe this —that this Bountiful God is a God who showers gift upon gift on His Church and is waiting to do for us exceeding abundantly above all the rich traditions of the past. Separately, there are still some evident signs of sectarianism upon each one of us: together we may stride the limitations of class and race and nation. Together we may speak that optimism of Grace which is mighty to the overthrow of strongholds. And when once again we dare to go, not only to those who want us, but to those who want us most, in the dark places of cruelty and the habitations of violence, where we sit in the seat of the scornful and stand in the way of sinners, we shall meet the Lord of the Church already there, standing where He has never ceased to stand in the midst of His broken world bearing its sins, perfectly, sufficiently, and offering the greatest of all His gifts to His chosen people, that they may share of the travail of His soul, and may be satisfied.

METHODIST HYMN FESTIVAL

IN the evening of 30th August the delegates to the Conference, with Methodists from the Oxford and Gloucester District, joined in a hymn festival held in the Sheldonian Theatre. The choir was comprised of representatives from many Methodist choirs in the district, and the Conductor was the Rev. Dr Francis B. Westbrook, Ministerial Secretary of the Methodist Church Music Society. The organist was Mr H. Stanley Mountford of the Central Hall, Birm-ingham. The Chairman was Mr Clifford W. Towlson, ex-Vice-President of the British Methodist Conference, Chairman of the Methodist Church Music Society, and at one time a chorister of St Margaret's Church, Oxford. In his introductory remarks, Mr

Towlson said: 'Methodism has always been able to sing its creed, and this festival sets out to show how this can be done.'

All the hymns chosen for the festival were written by Charles Wesley, with the exception of John Wesley's translation of Johann Rothe's 'Now I have found the ground wherein.' The *Te Deum* was sung to Sir Charles Stanford's setting in B flat and the anthem, 'Thou wilt keep him in perfect peace', was composed by Samuel Sebastian Wesley.

FOURTH DAY

Friday 31st August

THE opening devotions were conducted by the Rev. Dr W. H. Jones of the Wesleyan Reform Union. An address was delivered by Bishop J. A. Gregg of the African Methodist Episcopal Church.

Expounding the first eight verses of the fifteenth chapter of St John's Gospel, Bishop Gregg stressed the need for pruning and purifying by the discerning husbandman, the close relationship of the branches to the Vine, and the danger of modern attempts to graft wild branches which are proclaimed as substitutes for Christianity. Only Christ, the True Vine and God the Keeper of the vineyard can bring unity and peace through salvation from sin, and such salvation comes through faith in the atoning blood of Jesus Christ.

The morning session, under the presidency of Bishop Ivan Lee Holt, was concerned with a consideration of *The Methodist Way*: This involved an examination of the relevance of the sacraments and the importance of fellowship, especially the Class-Meeting, in the Methodist Church today. An address on *The Means of Grace* was given by the Rev. Ronald V. Spivey, of Wesley's Chapel, London, and another on *The Life of Fellowship* by the Rev. Dr F. Gerald Ensley of Columbus, Ohio.

These addresses were followed by group discussions, a summary of which appears on p. 289.

THE MEANS OF GRACE

An address delivered by the REV. RONALD V. SPIVEY, *of Wesley's Chapel, London:*

Within the apse of Wesley's Chapel, City Road, London, is a famous marble tablet erected to commemorate John Wesley. The inscription was written by Dr John Whitehead, who had been a travelling preacher for seven years before he retired to practise medicine in Finsbury Square. He became John Wesley's friend, physician, and executor, and was invited to preach his funeral sermon. In the noble words of the inscription, Dr Whitehead paid tribute to—

A man in Learning and sincere Piety scarcely inferior to any
In Zeal, Ministerial Labours and extensive usefulness Superior (perhaps)
to all
Since the days of St Paul.

Nevertheless, I am sorry that there is no record of the artist who carved this memorial tablet, for of all the many characterizations of John Wesley and his work none surpasses the insight of a sermon in stone which is carved on its pediment. In the centre of the carving is the globe, for the world was John Wesley's parish. It is appropriate that the portion of the globe which confronts the eye is the Atlantic Ocean with its many shores.

108

Protruding from behind the globe are the two Biblical symbols of a winged trumpet and a shepherd's crook, for Wesley's labours combined equally the work of preacher and pastor. It is important, however, to notice that in this carving the world is held in its place by two books: one is the Bible and the other is the Liturgy of the Church of England. This signifies that for a proper understanding of Methodism in history and in the world today it is essential to remember that the Evangelical Revival was also a revival of that private prayer and corporate worship upon which the souls of many generations of Christians had been fed. The revival resulting from the proclamation of the gospel of grace was sustained and kept alive by the provision of the means of grace.

It is one of the strange ironies and misfortunes of history that there have been times and places when Methodism has been represented as an opponent of the very things for which John Wesley so stoutly contended. To see but part of our Founder's greatness and to exaggerate it by ignoring another part is but to caricature him. There has, alas! been evidence in our history for those who, like Reinhold Niebuhr, have dubbed Methodism a 'belated, pietistic, evangelistic sect of the eighteenth century', but that is a caricature which is not substantiated by a knowledge of our historical source documents. As a matter of fact, it was precisely because of Wesley's inflexible opposition to the pietistic sects of the eighteenth century that Methodism became a separate organization and developed its own ethos. Indeed, Wesley's uncompromising affirmation of catholic doctrine and the traditional means of grace so distinguished him from the rest of the evangelical movements of the eighteenth century that he was more frequently suspected as a Papist than a Pietist! Much as one may admire Niebuhr's thought in many fields, one cannot but conclude that here he has not considered all the facts.

The struggle with the Pietists began immediately after Wesley's Aldersgate Street experience. At that time both John and Charles were members of the religious society which met in Fetter Lane. This group, remember, was a society within the Church of England and, although it was greatly influenced by Moravian teaching, all its members professed allegiance to the doctrines and disciplines of the Established Church. After two years Wesley quarrelled with them precisely because he did not approve of their Pietistic and sectarian tendencies. The Moravian doctrine of 'stillness' disparaged, if it did not altogether dispense with, the need for private devotion and public worship, and it was for that very reason that, dressed in his cassock, gown, and bands, John Wesley read a paper to the Fetter Lane Society on Sunday evening, 20th July 1740, condemning the tenets of the Pietists. Immediately after the paper was read, he and eighteen other members withdrew their persons and their membership from Fetter Lane to the Foundery in order that they might the better maintain the orthodox faith and practice of the Church of England!

It was about this very time that John Wesley wrote and published his famous sermon on *The Means of Grace*, which was then, and still is, definitive of Methodist doctrine. He writes:

'By "Means of Grace" I understand outward signs, words, or actions, ordained of God, and appointed for this end, to be the ordinary channels whereby He might convey to men, preventing, justifying or sanctifying grace.

'I use this expression "Means of Grace", because I know of none better; and because it has been generally used in the Christian Church for many ages—in particular by our own Church, which directs us to bless God both for the means of grace and the hope of glory, and teaches us that a sacrament is "an outward sign of inward grace, and a means whereby we receive the same".

'The chief of these means are prayer, whether in secret or with the great congregation; searching the Scriptures (which implies reading, hearing, and meditating thereon) and receiving the Lord's Supper, eating bread and drinking wine in remembrance of Him; and these we believe to be ordained of God, as the ordinary channels of conveying His grace to the souls of men.'

We may, therefore, clarify our thought by saying that in the Methodist tradition, the essential means of grace are prayer, whether secret or with the great congregation, searching the Scriptures (reading, hearing and meditating), and partaking of the Lord's Supper.

Although this sermon was written in such a definite historical context, the fact that it was chosen to be one of the forty-four *Standard Sermons* for Methodist doctrine shows that this was one of the many points of orthodoxy on which Wesley never wavered. The same is borne out by Sermon 101 on *The Duty of Constant Communion*, which has a most significant Preface which reads:

'The following Discourse was written above five and fifty years ago, for the use of my pupils at Oxford. I have added very little, but retrenched much; as I then used more words than I do now. But, I thank God, I have not yet seen cause to alter my sentiments in any point which is therein delivered. J. W. 1788.'

In this sermon, which epitomizes the teaching of a lifetime, Wesley adduces as reasons for proclaiming the duty of constant Communion, first, that it is the plain command of Christ; secondly, that the benefits are so great. He concludes:

'Whoever, therefore, does not receive, but goes from the Holy Table, when all things are prepared, either does not understand his duty, or does not care for the dying command of his Saviour, the forgiveness of his sins, the strengthening of his soul, and the refreshing it with the hope of glory.'

As in most doctrinal points, Charles Wesley supports his brother here in song.

> Suffice for me, that Thou, my Lord
>   Hast bid me fast and pray:
> Thy will be done, thy name adored;
>   'Tis only mine to obey.
>
> 'Thou bidd'st me search the Sacred Leaves,
>   And taste the hallow'd Bread.
> Thy kind command my soul receives,
>   And longs on Thee to feed.
>
> 'Still for Thy lovingkindness, Lord,
>   I in Thy temple wait;
> I look to find Thee in Thy word,
>   Or at Thy table meet.
>
> 'Here, *in Thine own appointed ways*,
>   I wait to learn Thy will:
> Silent I stand before Thy face,
>   And hear Thee say "Be Still!"
>
> 'I wait my vigour to renew,
>   Thine image to retrieve,
> The veil of outward things pass through,
>   And gasp in Thee to live.'
>   (C. W., The Means of Grace.
>   From *Collected Works*, I, 233.)

Nor should we forget that in early Methodism a revival of the use of the Means of Grace accompanied the preaching of the gospel of grace. It is not unfitting to remember here that during a generation in which the Bishop of Oxford was recommending his clergy to add a fourth celebration of Holy Communion to the three customarily observed at Christmas, Easter, and Whitsuntide, Wesley himself was communicating on the average about twice a week throughout his ministry. Throughout the Methodist Revival, the preaching of the Word was accompanied by the regular use and advocacy of the Means of Grace. In 1743 Wesley acquired the use of the West Street Chapel in London, and of the services there on 29th May he wrote: 'I preached ... and administered the Lord's Supper to some hundreds of communicants.' Thirty years later we read of similar impressive services: 650 communicants were at a service at Bristol in 1771, 700 at Leeds in 1779, and in May 1783 Wesley wrote: 'Such a sight I believe was never seen at Manchester before. It was supposed there were thirteen or fourteen hundred communicants, among whom there was such a spirit as I have seldom found, and their whole behaviour was such as adorned the Gospel.' One of his preachers wrote in 1763: 'I had now an opportunity to receive the Holy Sacrament among the children of God. And to see the large and deeply serious congregations that attended the Chapels, the uncommon number of communicants, their devout behaviour and the order with which the whole Service was conducted, was highly pleasing to me. O how divinely pleasant and how truly profitable is it to wait upon God in His holy ordinances.'

These great services depended on the presence of the band of ordained ministers who were part of the Methodist Movement, but they indicate a sometimes forgotten aspect of the Evangelical Revival. In the *Journal* for 25th December 1774 we read:

'During the twelve festival days we had the Lord's Supper daily; a little emblem of the Primitive Church. May we be the followers of them in all things as they were of Christ.'

Nor should we forget that the reason why the final breach with the Church of England was precipitated was because Wesley set apart some of his preachers by ordination for the administration of the sacraments, and that in the first instance this was done at the request of Methodists in America, that they might receive the sacraments from regularly ordained ministers.

·   ·   ·   ·   ·

Anyone whose knowledge of Methodism was limited to certain chapels in this century might be forgiven for thinking we were but the descendants of a Pietistic sect, in which private prayer, and that only when we felt the right mood, was the only requisite devotional exercise of a Christian. So our task in the world today would seem to include the revival of that fuller devotional life which characterized our forefathers in their private lives and their public worship. The words of Isaiah are still pertinent to modern Methodism:

'Hearken to me, ye that follow after righteousness, ye that seek the Lord: look unto the rock whence ye were hewn, and to the hole of the pit whence ye were digged.'

(Isaiah 51[1])

Visitors to John Wesley's house in City Road, London, are always moved when they enter the bedroom in which he died and have pointed out to

111

them that famous Prayer Room of his. In this little room he could follow literally his Lord's injunction and enter: 'But thou, when thou prayest, enter into thine inner chamber, and having shut thy door, pray to thy Father which is in secret, and thy Father which seeth in secret shall recompense thee' (Matthew 6[6]). In the preface to his diary begun on 2nd December 1782 he wrote a shortened form of the resolutions which guided his private devotions which includes the line: 'I resolve to dedicate an hour, morning and evening; no excuse, reason, or pretence.'

I take courage at the fact that even this great man of prayer had to be on his guard against making excuses, even at the age of seventy! A proper consideration of our subject would really demand a devout inquiry into the practice of our forefathers' private prayers and devotional study of the Bible, for I conceive our first task to be the re-discovery of that tradition of ordered and regular devotion in private prayer and public worship which was the source of the power of the Revival 200 years ago.

As I have no time to consider adequately the whole field, I would urge that deep and lasting revival needs a background of a worshipping community, and though it may not be necessary to insist on the actual Prayer Book John Wesley used, Methodism has not yet found an adequate alternative. Ordered and regular corporate prayer is complementary to private prayer, and even if we do not follow John Wesley's example exactly, we must seek to develop a corporate worship which is as God-centred, Biblical, comprehensive, and succinct as the Book of Common Prayer which he used. I would further urge that one of our main tasks in the worship of the Church is to restore the sacrament of Holy Communion to the central position it should have in Christian worship, and to refuse any longer to regard it as a kind of afterthought of the Sunday evening service. It was after a service of Holy Communion which had been conducted according to the rite John Wesley used, and enriched with Charles Wesley's hymns, that a one-time Anglo-Catholic said: 'This is the very thing I left Methodism to try and find twenty years ago.' Were we true to our traditional worship, there would be little in that of any other denomination which would have the power to seduce our thoughtful and devout members.

Bernard Lord Manning's *Hymns of Wesley and Watts* has already quickened the interest of discerning students in that mine of sound theology and rich devotion in the hymns of Charles Wesley. Indeed, in the realm of prayer, Bible study, and public worship we still have much to learn from the pit from which we were digged and the rock from which we were hewn. Methodism would be well served by the reprinting and wide dissemination of all our important source documents of history, theology, and devotion.

Furthermore, great advantages would come from a better knowledge of Methodist publications in countries other than one's own. We need a cross-fertilization of the thought of world Methodism.

Such a re-discovery of our sources would do much to assist us in the second main task I would suggest. We must deny in our thought and worship that dichotomy which some profess to see between Wesley the evangelist and Wesley the churchman. There never were two John Wesleys separated distinctly by any particular date. If we choose between George Croft Cell and Father Maximin Piette, we shall have a caricature of greatness. Neither alone, but both together, and corrected by each other, give a truer characterization. Indeed, the adequate appraisal of John Wesley has yet to be written, and it may well have to wait until we have re-married, in the experience of Methodist worship, those two elements which God joined together in the eighteenth century and man allowed to drift asunder in the nineteenth. When the day comes for that full-orbed biography to be written, an appropriate frontispiece would be a picture of the memorial carving in Wesley's Chapel.

Finally, it is essential to remember that the reason for this concern is not an interest in either ancient documents and traditional rites, but a desire to discover more of the purpose of God when He raised up John and Charles Wesley. We do not ask of Wesley, 'What wilt thou have me to do?' in the twentieth century; we ask Wesley's Lord as we seek a truer understanding of what He accomplished through His servant. On 15th November 1739 Wesley wrote in his *Journal*: 'In the afternoon I exhorted four or five thousand people at Bristol neither to neglect, nor to rest in the Means of Grace.'

If Methodism's present danger be the neglect of the Means of Grace, without which the Church's devotions are so unordered and unrewarded, we nevertheless do well to remember Wesley's word of caution: 'neither to neglect, *nor to rest in* any means'. Let us therefore recall his own words:

'It behoves us always to retain a lively sense that God is above all the means. Have a care, then, of limiting the Almighty. . . . In using all means, seek God alone. In and through every outward thing, look singly to the power of His Spirit and the merits of His Son. . . . Nothing but God can satisfy your soul. Therefore eye Him in all, through all, and above all. Remember also, to use all means *as means*; as ordained, not for their own sake, but in order to the renewal of your soul in righteousness and true holiness.'

Only last week I received a letter which will form a contemporary and relevant conclusion. My correspondent, a young Methodist missionary, writes from Central America, and says:

'On Wesley Day, while you were holding your celebrations at Wesley's Chapel, I was in the process of being appalled by Roman idolatry at the Corpus Christi High Mass celebrated by the Archbishop of Mexico in the largest church in the new world. . . . However, that same night when you were all in bed, I went to Iglesia Metodista in Central Mexico City and thirty people came forward to make their decision for Christ. So Wesley Day was not forgotten in the depths of Latin America even on the great Roman Catholic feast of Corpus Christi.

'Our new Methodist Church in Belize is now built and opened and has 791 members. At the first Service over 400 received Communion at 6 a.m., and at 7 p.m. the same day there were no less than 229 decisions for Christ. Scores are seeking membership and we are putting them on trial in the Society Classes. Our choir is robed and we use the Office of Morning Prayer, and for the Lord's Supper John Wesley's Order always. So you see liturgy and revival go hand in hand.'

The revival of ordered public worship and deeper private prayer, of Bible study, the Class Meeting and the calling of sinners to repentance— *all* this together is, I affirm, the Methodist tradition and our task in the world today.

THE LIFE OF FELLOWSHIP

An address delivered by the REV. Dr F. GERALD ENSLEY, *North Broadway Methodist Church, Columbus, Ohio, U.S.A.:*

Dr John Simon, in his monumental study of Wesley, tells us that the founder of Methodism had a 'fixed idea'. It was not 'evangelism', though he was perhaps the first evangel of his century. It was not 'missions', though he literally took the world for his parish. His fixed idea was not 'conferences', though a Methodist preacher is a cut flower without a conference.

The notion which obsessed Wesley from the dawn of his ministry to its close was this: Christianity cannot be promoted effectively without small societies supplementing the regular services of the Church where opportunities are given for intimate spiritual fellowship. For Wesley there could not be a vital body of Christ without living cells of comradeship, little clusters of serious-minded individuals who prayed, sang, searched the Scriptures, and edified each other by religious conversation. Wherever he went he organized Class-Meetings, prayer-bands, 'select societies'. When by the natural process of growth they got to the point where eye-to-eye, heart-to-heart fellowship was endangered, he would divide them anew. While Wesley believed in the power of preaching to awaken and to convert, he looked to the 'two or three gathered together' as the real growing edge of Christian discipleship.

The words which the New Testament most frequently employs to describe the early Christians in their corporate capacity are *ecclesia* and *koinonia*. *Ecclesia* is the Church as an organization; *koinonia* is the Church as a fellowship. And the history of Christianity may be written as an account of the interaction and relative emphasis of these two conceptions within the life of the Church. Both are essential: a community cannot live effectively if it fails either to build an organization or to establish an inner bond of fellowship. An organism requires both a skeleton and a vascular system. The differences in the Church arise from the measure in which the one or the other predominates. The New Testament community was primarily *koinonia*, and only secondarily *ecclesia*. But the Anglican Church of Wesley's century was mainly *ecclesia*,—a creed, a building, a discipline, orders, liturgy—and, very secondarily, *koinonia*. The Methodism movement may be described as an exercise in correction, an attempt to supply the ecclesiastical body of the eighteenth century with a heartbeat.

The most characteristic form of religious fellowship was the class-meeting, which Dr R. W. Dale of Birmingham once called Methodism's 'one striking and original contribution to the institutions of the Church'. The ideal was to divide each Methodist society into groups of twelve persons in charge of a leader. When the class-system was inaugurated in 1742, the 'General Rules' listed the business of the leader 'to see each person in his class once a week, at the least, in order—

'To receive what they are willing to give toward the relief of the poor.
'To inquire how their souls prosper.
'To advise, reprove, comfort, or exhort as occasion may require.'

The weekly visitation soon proved unfeasible: it took more time than lay men who had a living to earn could devote; many of the first Methodists were domestics whose masters did not relish their being visited; often differences arose between members which could best be cleared up by their confronting one another face to face. Thus, there gradually emerged the characteristic class-meeting. It was directed toward the personal religious growth of the Methodists through fellowship. The weekly meetings lasted an hour or two on a weekday evening or a Sabbath before or after the preaching service. They were spent in song, confession of faults to one another, composure of differences, sharing of religious experience, exhortation—to use the quaint Wesleyan language—'provoking one another

114

to love and good works', and never closing without prayer for one another. Wesley repeatedly offers his emphatic testimony to the worth of these little cells of informal fellowship in the development of Methodism.

We have called this emphasis of Wesley's a fixed idea. It was not fixed in the sense that he committed himself to a precise and rigid form. It was a fixity in that he refused to give it up, recognized no circumstance in which it would not work, accepted no excuses from evangelistic-preachers who contended they could get along without societies. When even Dr John Fletcher of Madeley, Wesley's heir-apparent in 1782, complained that he could not prevail on the people of his parish to join in society, Wesley went up and preached a strong sermon on 'Awake thou that sleepest,' persuading over ninety persons to join!

How did the founder of Methodism come to his idea? What 'fixed' his mind on the necessity of small units of fellowship? Certainly he had many precedents. The New Testament *koinonia* must have been of limited dimensions: 'the upper room' of Pentecost could not have contained many souls, and Paul refers in his letter to Philemon to 'the church that is in thy house'. The Roman Catholic Church had long encouraged molecular fellowship in its monastic orders. The Church of England had its intimate societies for the cultivation of religious devotion: Wesley's father had been a warm supporter of them, while Susannah held informal religious meetings in the Rectory kitchen at Epworth. Wesley himself had been active in a small 'Holy Club' here at Oxford. Had he been a worshipper of precedent, he could have justified his fellowship societies with good conscience.

But the history of Christianity till 1742 hardly explains the form which Methodist fellowship took. Nor does it account for the passionate defence which Wesley made of it, nor his almost stubborn refusal to compromise on the principle. If we are to understand his 'fixed idea' we are to look not so much to the history as to the psychology and philosophy of religion. As Wesley started out to fulfil his avowed purpose of spreading Scriptural holiness across the face of England, he ran into several considerations whose convergence was the small society for religious fellowship.

The first is the fact that Wesley was attempting to spread a *Scriptural* religion. Early in his ministry he had entered into conversation with a casual acquaintance who dropped a remark which never left him; 'Young man, the Bible knows nothing of solitary religion. You must find companions or make them.' Wesley was committed to a religion whose conception of God—the Trinity—was social. He was the follower of the Son of Man, 'who came eating and drinking', who began His public ministry at a wedding and closed it with the fellowship of a sacramental meal. Wesley was the heir—as a Christian minister—of a long tradition of corporate religion. He was, thus, the purveyor of a social product. The very logic of his task would have carried him into fellowship.

In the second place, Wesley was attempting to spread *holiness*, religious excellence. We rarely look to the large group for excellence. It is the small fellowship to which we turn for standards. The small group in every realm is the seed-plot of the higher life. It is a commonplace of literary history that the best writing comes not from the solitary author. Original thought and art are the work of the individual, to be sure, but the individual in touch with fellow craftsmen who keep him up to the mark with the criticisms and put heart into him with their encouragements. Even a genius like Shakespeare, the most recent lives are reminding us, did his work in a community that included dramatists of the first order—Marlowe, Beaumont, Fletcher, and Ben Jonson. We are discovering that the large lecture courses—which have been so much in favour in our universities—

115

are pedagogically unthrifty. They must be supplemented by the quiz section, the tutor, face-to-face interrogation, if the purposes of the broader instruction are not to seep away. A. D. Lindsay, Master of Balliol, has celebrated the thesis that a healthy democracy requires not only a debate of public issues in the Houses of Parliament or Congress, but a steady discussion of the same themes in the voluntary small groups of the commonwealth—clubs, lodges, societies, and informal groups in the kitchen and around the stove of the country store. Hence, Wesley's very task of promoting religious excellence entailed, human nature being what it is, cultivation of the small group.

Once more, Wesley was a *spreader* of holiness. He was an evangelist. He was engaged in extending religion. As he entered upon his work, he soon discovered the polarity which exists in life between extension and intention. 'Lengthen your ropes', cries Isaiah to the men of his time, 'and strengthen your stakes.' The figure is meaningful to every camper. If you lengthen your ropes but do not bother to strengthen your stakes, before you know it the tent comes down upon your head. The extra strain caused by extension must be compensated by deeper anchorage. As Wesley, therefore, multiplied his numbers, there had to be a supplementary process of cultivation of converts or his effort would come to naught. He found early that the heavenly showers of preaching soon ran off if there were no cisterns in the form of societies to conserve them. He discovered that it was futile to lead men to religious decisions and let them wander back into their old ways for want of training and moral reinforcement. Hence, the class-meeting.

Again, Wesley came to grips with a fact about the human make-up—namely, that communication is necessary for the growth of a human soul. Psychology teaches that thought depends on the power of expression: it is only by learning to speak that we learn to think. Human intelligence rises above animal intelligence step by step with the development of language. Only as a person has a language whereby he can distinguish the objects of his experience and classify them does he have a tool whereby he can increase his experience. A person who grew up without anyone to talk to would attain to only the most rudimentary levels of intellectual life. The same principle applies to the things of the spirit. A religious mute is likely to be a religious moron. Probably Wesley never philosophized about the matter, but he saw intuitively, as he laboured with his converts, the need for religious expression as an avenue to religious growth. The class-meeting was a remarkable answer to the problem posed by his task.

Finally, Wesley was confronted by the deep hunger of the human heart for community. It is not good for man to be alone; no normal person wants to be alone. He has the impulse to share his other values; it is to be expected that he would want to enjoy his religious experience with his fellows. Particularly the people of the Wesleyan Movement—those who had been looked down on, neglected, and left out—craved fellowship. And the religious society was Wesley's response to their needs. But it was more than that! It met Wesley's own need for fellowship. He says of the 'Select Society' which he formed in London, after paying tribute to its value for its members, that it gave him also 'a select company, to whom I might unbosom myself on all occasions without reserve'. The loneliness of leadership meets its anodyne in the religious society!

It is no secret, however, that the small religious group, so dear to Wesley's heart, has gone into eclipse in these later days. I cannot speak for other than American Methodism. But in the United States the class-meeting is practically non-existent: it is not even cited in the index of the

116

1948 *Discipline*. The prayer meeting enjoys only a precarious existence. The adult Sunday-school class, one of the last opportunities for lay conversation on religion, has lost ground. We still have much sociability in our churches—good in its way—but it isn't religious fellowship in the Wesleyan sense, where men meet to 'pray together, to receive the word of exhortation, and to watch over one another in love'.

Why has religious fellowship declined in our churches? First, because of what has happened in our world. Irreligion has slowly but inexorably devoured us all. The increasing chill of secularism has invaded the house of God. There is not much call for society to share religious experience where there is no experience to share. The world is organized, too, without a thought to religious convenience. Anyone who tries valiantly in these days to keep the altar alight within his own family in the face of the multiple distractions of the time can fathom what has overtaken the larger religious group.

Secondly, something has happened to the Methodists; and I do not speak disparagingly. We have changed. We have, generally speaking, climbed the social ladder, and many of the needs for fellowship which the class-meeting met in the earlier day are fulfilled at other levels. Our tastes have changed. We are gun-shy of the soul-barings in which the earlier Methodists revelled. In 1738 Wesley drew up a set of five questions to be asked at each weekly meeting of the religious societies. They were:

'What known sins have you committed since our last meeting?
'What temptations have you met with?
'How were you delivered?
'What have you thought, said, or done, of which you doubt whether it be sin or not?
'Have you nothing you desire to keep secret?'

Can you imagine a quicker way to depopulate a meeting today than to insist on answers to such queries?

Not only have our tastes changed, but our American churches are much larger than the old-time Methodist societies. Some of our city churches run to 5,000 and 6,000 members, scattered widely over a great metropolitan area. I submit that fellowship is a different matter in such circumstances from the days when the Methodists totalled a few score souls in a quiet village.

Finally, something happened to the class-meeting itself. It fell prey to its own inherent weaknesses. It was a hotbed of contentiousness, even in Wesley's time. Its emphasis on confession often led to exposures to a group of things that should have been reserved for the ear of God alone. There was a certain subjectivity about it, a preying into the affairs of a brother, that has not the mark of mental healthiness. And not least of all, the class-meeting was an open invitation to the religious crank, the 'screwball', and the chronic grinder of axes to relieve themselves. Professor Edward A. Ross, the distinguished American sociologist, once likened the small American town to a fished-out pond, from which the game fish were gone, with only 'the suckers and the bullheads left'. So the class-meeting in some churches became the reservoir of the religiously difficult—the negatives, the 'stingers', the unco-operative! It died for want of re-stocking —and fresh water!

Well, what are we to do? Try to revitalize the old Wesley societies? Bring back the class-meeting? Speaking only as a representative of the American Church, I do not think it can be done. They do not match the mood and temper of our day. Shall we then write off the attempt to build

117

fellowship and concentrate on *ecclesia*—preaching, liturgy, church administration, mass effort? I doubt that, too. When William Temple went to Geneva in 1932 to preach before the international Disarmament Conference he wrote to his friend, G. F. Bradby: 'I suppose that no sermon preached to a crowd ever did much good. Some have had a great effect —one launched the First Crusade—but then I think it was a bad effect. *Good spiritual work is done on one person or a dozen at a time.*'

There is a more excellent way than either to restore the Wesley mode of fellowship or to give it up altogether. It is to repeat what the Church has done again and again in its long history—to lay hold of the vision, the essential ideas, of its saints and express them in the idiom and method of the new day. The considerations which drove Wesley into building the small religious fellowship are as valid now as then. The social nature of Christianity, the need for intension to balance extension, the demand for standards and for self-expression, and the hunger of the human heart for community are as insistent in 1951 as in 1751. Our task, if we would provide what Elton Trueblood, the Quaker scholar, has called an 'alternative to futility', is somehow to turn the 'one or the dozen' to religious account. Here is the creative opportunity for Methodist churchmanship in our day.

What form will such religious fellowship take? Frankly, I do not know. The field invites experimentation. The student 'cells' of the college, the Bible-reading group meeting in a home, the post-sermon seminar, where the congregation gets a chance to talk back, the neighbourhood zone group in the large city church are all attempts to find a method. The important thing is to feel the urgency. In human affairs, spiritual as well as mechanical, the tool awaits the demand. When once we see how intimately the earthly destiny of the Church bound up with the small unit of fellowship— as Wesley saw it—the means with us, as with him, will be forthcoming.

G. F. R. Henderson, the English military analyst, in his classic study of *Stonewall Jackson and the American Civil War*, makes a penetrating observation. One of the basic differences, he tells us, between a green recruit and a seasoned veteran in combat is this: Under danger the recruit tends to move away from his unit. He becomes an individualist and hopes to find safety in dispersion. The veteran, in contrast, feels safest in the ranks, and the greater the danger the more pertinaciously he clings to the group, the more closely he draws toward his comrades.

With two centuries of churchly experience behind us, we Methodists should qualify now as veterans. With the enemy pressing us from every quarter, our hope lies not in dispersion, but in a closer unity. If we see that and implement it, perhaps it is not too late, with God's help, to win a victory in the Church's ageless struggle with the world.

The Ecumenical Council met in the afternoon.

At 5.15 a lecture on *Christianity and Totalitarianism* was given by the Chancellor of Boston University, Dr Daniel Marsh.

CHRISTIANITY AND TOTALITARIANISM

A lecture delivered by CHANCELLOR DANIEL L. MARSH, *of Boston University:*

By Christianity I mean essential New Testament Christianity, which is the most democratic of all religions. By totalitarianism I mean a highly centralized government under the control of a group which allows neither

118

recognition nor representation of other parties than its own. Its political form was seen in Fascist Italy and the Nazi régime in Germany, and is still seen in Franco's Spain and in Russian Communism, which is the pseudo-religion of today. There are also some ecclesiastical forms of Christianity which are totalitarian.

There are three points of apparent similarity between real Christianity and totalitarianism. They both require supreme loyalty and allegiance to a person, they both bear fruits, and they both demand total commitment to a cause. The contrasts are found in the person upon whom loyalty is focused and to whom allegiance is yielded, in the kinds of fruits that are born, and in the cause to which total commitment is made.

I

Totalitarianism requires supreme loyalty to a person, the dictator, who not only prescribes what his people must do, but also denies them the right to refuse to follow him. Therein is a marked difference between Christianity and totalitarianism; for Christianity inspires free men with a feeling of moral obligation to follow Jesus. Christ makes men free with the liberty that implies the absence of arbitrary restraint, but which does not imply immunity from responsibility or regulations.

Christianity, in its essence, is devotion to Jesus Christ. It is more than a system of doctrine; more than an ethical code; more than a redemptive social force. It is incarnate love; but we cannot love an abstraction; we cannot love a thing. We can love only a Person. Christianity reveals in the heart of history this Divine Person, and shows that love for Him is to be the motive power of the Christian's life. St Paul said, 'I know whom I have believed'—not what, but *whom*. His faith was not in a thing, but in a Person; not in a religious system, but in a Redeemer; not in a 'plan of salvation', but in the living Saviour; not in a creed, but in Christ. It was faith in Christ as a Person. 'Christ in you', said St Paul. 'Christ in you, the hope of glory.' Christianity is the active and energetic contact between the person of Jesus Christ and the human persons who follow Him.

This makes Jesus alone Lord of the conscience, freeing us from the intolerable bondage of fear on the one hand, and of hierarchical dictation on the other. In contrast to totalitarianism, Christ's appeal is always to reality, and His powers are characterized by sweet reasonableness. In loyalty to Him, we never substitute theories and traditions for truth. Totalitarianism dethrones the conscience and shuts the mind up in a mental concentration camp. But the inherent right of a Christian in any controversial matter is always to ask, What does Jesus say? This means that we have a right to build our faith at first hand on the words of Holy Scripture, and not on extra-Scriptural authority or tradition. Christianity is but the overflow of Christ's Sermon on the Mount. Christ included in His Kingdom—in the Kingdom of the Beatitudes—every person who is like him in character, or is of His mind.

This leads naturally to Christianity's making persons the norm of values. Not so in a totalitarian system; for there a person is nothing more than a cog in a wheel of a vast machine that ruthlessly grinds and grinds for the corporate State or organization or system. But true Christianity teaches that all values, in the last analysis, are personal and that only persons can value. The loyalty we give to Jesus as a Person leads us on to all things true and beautiful and good, ennobles and enriches life, and gives meaning to it. Christianity views the whole universe as a society of persons. It takes into consideration the sum total of experience. Its sovereign test of every experience is: What kind of person will this make? By this standard must be judged educational processes, industrial affairs, social contacts, political movements, international relations and everything else.

II

The sharpest contrast between totalitarianism and Christianity may be seen under the light of Jesus' dictum: 'By their fruits ye shall know them.' Whenever a totalitarian individual or social institution (civil, political, economic, or ecclesiastical) lays claim to a man's soul, all his freedoms of thought, conscience, speech, assembly, and all the rest are specifically vetoed. You can no more gather good personal character, good government, or good civilization from totalitarianism than you can gather grapes of thorns or figs of thistles. Its blossom is 'the crimson bloom of battle', and its fruit is bigotry, intolerance, persecution, bloodshed, conquest, and tyranny.

The fruits of Christianity are manifold, multifarious, and multipotent, but always good and only good. The Kingdom of God is a heavenly claim, a sacred sovereignty of ideas, ideals, impulses, purposes, and intentions of the most lofty sort. Christ 'rules the world by truth and grace'. His kingdom is a human, universal, spiritual emancipation. It establishes and expands itself as an incessant and ever-increasing inspiration, as leaven interpenetrates the meal, or as the seed which the sower goes forth to sow culls material from soil, air, and water, and transmutes it into a goodly harvest. The history of totalitarianism's spread is written with the point of the sword dipped in human blood, but the spread of Christianity may be likened unto the seed-sowing of Johnny Appleseed and Timothy Hanson. Do you recall the story of Johnny Appleseed? He was a New Englander who was regarded as queer by his neighbours. They said his queerness was the result of having been kicked in the head by a horse when he was a boy. If that is so, I know some persons whom I would like to see kicked in the head by a horse; for his queerness took the form of unselfish service. He envisaged the transformation of the Middle West wilderness into a great empire. Therefore, he went around among his New England neighbours and collected quantities of apple seeds. These seeds he carried across country, sometimes on foot, and sometimes on horseback, to the Ohio River, down which he went, by canoe or by flatboat, until he reached Ohio. There he left the river, and in a constant noontime gloaming, he threaded the forest paths. Whenever he came to an open space which had been cleared by fire or by the Indians for their corn patches, he planted his apple seeds—all through what are now the States of Ohio and Indiana. Years afterwards, when the settlers pushed through the forest primeval to establish their homes, they found apple orchards already bearing fruit.

And Timothy Hanson? Do you know how this coarse fodder grass that is called timothy got its name? There was a young man by the name of Timothy Hanson who, noting that this grass was good both for grazing and for hay, collected bushels of the seed, and then went down into the southland, and all through the longitudinal mountain valleys of the Carolinas, Tennessee, and Kentucky he sowed the seed. Years later, when the settlers pushed over the mountain ranges into the valleys, they found rich grazing land for their herds and meadows of hay to fill their new-built barns. They had forgotten the family name of the man who had sowed the seed, but they remembered that his Christian name was Timothy, and so they called the fodder grass timothy.

120

Not contrariwise, followers of Jesus have gone up and down the world, sowing the seeds of those virtues and blessings for which men have hungered and striven from time immemorial, and for some of which, such as freedom and democracy, millions have dared to die even in our own generation. Jesus was not a politician, but freedom and democracy sprang from His example and teachings; He was not a philosopher, but metaphysics grew out of His truth; He was not a moralist, but He was the inspiration of the finest ethic; He was not a theologian, but vital and intelligent creeds grew out of what He said. Wise old Benjamin Franklin, in a letter to the French Assembly, declared that 'he who shall introduce into public affairs the principles of primitive Christianity will change the face of the world', and Daniel Webster, in his address at the Centennial of the landing of the Pilgrims in Plymouth, thundered that 'whatever makes men good Christians, makes them good citizens'. It is the verdict of history that Christianity, wherever truly practised, has made new creatures, new lives, new functions, new relations, and new destinies. It is unique in its power to culture the soul, to discipline the will, to stir the whole nature into benevolent impulse toward other men. The irrefutable argument for Christianity is the glorious things it has done for the world.

All you need do to convince yourself of the present vitality of Christianity is to take out of the world, by imagination, all the fruits of Christianity—all the charity, the philanthropy, the social advance, the morality, the unselfishnesses that have been inspired and supported by Christianity—and see what is left!

Freedom is a fruit of Christianity, but the fruit of totalitarianism is subjection, thralldom, enslavement. Totalitarianism is of a hypnotic character which depends upon complete absence of critical dissent. It demands the mobilization of all psychological techniques to guarantee conformity—all of which is contrary to the spirit of Christianity; for freedom, in the modern acceptation of the term, is a product of Christianity. Jesus said: 'Ye shall know the truth, and the truth shall make you free.' The truth gives us freedom from error for the reason; freedom from constraint for the affections; freedom for the will from the tyranny of evil desires.

Academic freedom is indispensable to true education. Academic freedom means that each professor or student is free to seek the truth in his own way, to form his own opinions, to arrive at his own conclusions, and to announce his own convictions. He is not to be limited by patented dogma, faint-hearted consideration, inherited tradition or acquired prejudices. He does not need to bend the knee to error, nor to fawn before flattery, nor to cringe before denunciation, nor to yield to the lawless impulse of his own self.

Political freedom means that the people are free to govern themselves, free to live their lives in their own way, free to choose their own officers, free to hold those officers responsible for the conduct of government, and free to dismiss them if they fail to serve the best interests of the people. True political freedom makes freedom of enterprise far more than a shibboleth or catch-phrase.

The spirit of Christianity demands religious freedom also—freedom of conscience, freedom to worship God in one's own way. This spirit judges and condemns as un-Christian the totalitarian ecclesiastical system which, through the Inquisition, shackled the mind and conscience of Europe with fear and hatred. The Inquisitors, in their effort to crush heresy, stopped at nothing: confiscation of goods, torture, death. The Inquisitors claimed that the end they sought was the glory of God—and argued that the end justified the means!

Bishop G. Bromley Oxnam is but expressing the true Christian conviction when he condemns any present-day Church that does not believe in religious liberty or in the separation of Church and State, that rejects the democratic principle in its own organization and practice, and that insists upon being both a State and a Church, or which holds that it is the only organization authorized by God to teach religious truth and to conduct public religious worship, or which regards the existence of any other Church as opposed to Christ's command. 'A man who takes his religion from an authoritarian Church may be so conditioned to totalitarianism that he will take his politics from a totalitarian party and his economics from a totalitarian class.'

Totalitarianism in religion is a terrible thing. When any man says that he is as God upon the earth, or that he alone is the vicar of Christ, he lies and the truth is not in him. When any man says that he is infallible, he blasphemes.

Freedom of faith means the right not only to worship undisturbed, but also to propagate one's religion. It means freedom from a dictator in any ecclesiastical system, freedom from the burning of proscribed books, freedom of access for everybody to the open Bible, and freedom from interference with the pronouncements of the pulpit.

Protestant Christianity is not a break with the real Church of Christ, but rather a return to the primitive Apostolic Church. One can be sure that Jesus, who had combated the priestcraft of his day even unto death, would not build up a new priestcraft more dominant than the old. His teachings, including such beautiful parables as the lost sheep, the lost coin, and the lost boy, stress the sacred significance and value of the individual person. He taught that the truth made men free. He emphasized all those verities that not only create but undergird democracy as an attitude of mind, a spirit, and a way of life. Protestantism is a return to the Christianity of Christ. The Latin term from which our word 'protestant' is derived does not mean to protest against, as it is commonly used: it comes from the word *protestare*, which means to testify for the truth, to be a witness for some truth, some person, or some thing. The Reformation set the minds of men free from the totalitarian dictatorship of the hierarchy. It showed men that they could be saved by faith; that they had the right of private judgement; that they as individuals could consult the Bible; and that every believer became a priest.

The Rev. Robert J. McCracken, pastor of Riverside Church, New York, recently preached a sermon about 'The Dogma of the Assumption of Mary', in which he deplored the dictatorial control of the mind by any Church, pointing out that it is a claim to an absolute authority which extends to a man's thinking, and denies the rights both of reason and conscience. It threatens penalties which are more terrible than the threats of political totalitarianism, for the latter penalties extend only to this life, while totalitarian ecclesiastical power threatens consequences which reach out into eternity. 'Faith cannot be compelled. Spiritual life depends utterly on freedom. It is extraordinary and terrifying that this is so often overlooked.... As William Temple put it: "To use, in the name of Christ, any other means of persuasion than spiritual appeal and rational coherence is to betray His first principle of action." '

True Christianity not only undergirds freedom, but it warns us not to forget the responsibilities of freedom, recalling the words of St Peter: 'As free, but not using your freedom as a cloak of wickedness, but as bond servants of God.' Freedom is independence from unjust restraint, not independence from properly constituted authority. A sense of responsibility is to freedom what a trellis is to a vine—restraining it in order that it may rise. Christianly speaking, freedom means that a person is free to do what is right; but he is not to confuse liberty with licence, nor freedom with irresponsibility, nor human rights with their perversion. He is free to be the bond-slave of Truth and Right. Freedom is never an end in itself. It is but a means to an end. The end of academic freedom is the discovery of truth and beauty and goodness. The end of political freedom is the living of the good life. The end of religious freedom is the worship and service of God.

Democracy is a further fruit of Christianity. The fruit of totalitarianism is dictatorship, the elimination of dissenting minorities, and violent revolution; but true Christianity involves government founded on the consent of the governed, protection of dissenting minorities, and peaceful change through education, persuasion, and reconciliation. Since progress and democracy are both found in the Christian conception of the capacity, the dignity and the infinite worth of every individual, it is proper, I say, to list democracy as one of the fruits of Christianity.

The best definition of political democracy ever uttered was given by Abraham Lincoln: 'Government of the people, by the people, for the people.' Political democracy means that a just government is established with the consent of the governed, and is under their control; that government is the servant of the people and not their master, and that government is by law and not by men. Thomas Jefferson reminds us that 'governments are republican only in proportion as they embody the will of the people and execute it'.

To Lincoln's compact definition of political democracy, we need to add the ethical conception of democracy expressed by Theodore Parker who said that 'Democracy meant not "I'm as good as you are", but "You're as good as I am" '. Democracy implies equality before the law and also equality of opportunity. It expresses itself in brotherhood, especially brotherhood as interpreted by the Golden Rule.

Therefore, we crusade not only for political democracy, but also for the ethical conception and implications of democracy. This includes democracy in education; for when a people undertake to be their own dictators, they assume the responsibilities as well as the privileges of the function. Hence education must be as widely diffused as the right of suffrage. When the people are ignorant, they become an easy prey to greed and corruption, and quickly accomplish their own debasement and ruin.

We believe also in democracy in religion. That is the essential idea that underlies the doctrine of the priesthood of all believers—that every man has access to the throne of God.

Democracy, rightly understood, means brotherhood. Christianity unites men: it never antagonizes them. It points the way to brotherhood, mutual confidence, reciprocal honour, common interpretation of motive and purpose, and united action in a common spirit of loyalty. It is opposed to all limitation, narrowness, intolerance, bigotry, and exclusiveness. It is achieved when society is permeated with the spirit of Christ, when all men, great and small, here and there and everywhere, apply their hearts and minds in honest and passionate devotion to this goal. The very essence of democracy is the consciousness of the individual's responsibility.

Rights, in the Christian sense of the word, have their origin in the nature of our relation with others. In a totalitarian system, rights are conferred by the State or the hierarchy and reside in the State or the hierarchy. In a

Christian system, there are human rights which may even be against the State or hierarchy. They are God-given, and inherent in man. In recognizing these rights, and in responding to them, we fulfil the law of righteousness. For instance, every man has a right to merciful treatment by others. It is Christianity alone, in all the history of the world, that guarantees such a right as that. In a totalitarian system a thing is accepted as right because it is ordered by the dictator or has been legally enacted by the totalitarian group in power. In the Christian conception of things, authority comes from a centre and source of moral authority, implanted within the soul by a hierarchy of ideals, with the Lordly ideal of Christ at the top.

Power—and the way it is used—is one of the surest means of revealing whether or not a system is Christian. The human heart harbours an inextinguishable love of power, and the love of power easily degenerates into lust for power. Rulers become dictators when they grasp power that belongs to the people or to the people's representatives. Lord Acton, the British historian, said: 'All power tends to corrupt, and absolute power corrupts absolutely.' For confirmation of that statement, simply read the history of dictators across all the ages.

Totalitarianism worships force. It believes both in the physical force and violence of war, and also in the various kinds of forces—mental, emotional, and otherwise—which were used by the Inquisition. Totalitarianism acts as though the only way to get rid of an idea is by killing the person who holds it, while Christianity relies upon 'the expulsive power of a new affection', as Chalmers expressed it, and the creative power of a new idea. The way of Jesus is to see the truth clearly, to express it courageously, to live up to it faithfully. In the Christian sense, power must always be subordinated to persons, no matter whether power is intellectual, financial, political, military, or any other kind.

Since any victory of Christianity is the triumph of right over wrong, it becomes the moral substitute for war; for every victory of Christianity implies a long siege, stubborn hostility, inveterate prejudice, and the triumph of good over evil. Christianity makes its appeal not to physical force and violence, but to reason, and conscience, and heart, and moral persuasion.

A spiritual conception of life is an energizing fruit of Christianity. Totalitarianism grows out of and runs into a materialistic conception of life. Between the spiritual and the materialistic conceptions of life there is an irreconcilable divergence. On the one hand, you have materialism which regards the universe as a machine without a machinist, a mechanism without a mechanician. It regards man as an animal, and only an animal. It holds that there is no such thing as a code of ethics; that what man does, he does as the result of physical stimuli, or of glandular secretion, or the results of the fulfilment of desire upon himself as an animal organism. The grave is a blind alley, and death ends all.

On the other hand, you have the spiritual conception of life which holds that back of the visible phenomena of the physical universe is a personal God, who knows Himself, and knows what He is about. It insists that while man is a part of the animal kingdom, yet he is more than an animal: he is a living soul. It proclaims that there is such a thing as a code of ethics, and that there is an everlasting difference between right and wrong. What man ought to be, he can be, and what he ought to do, he can do. Man is an immortal child of God. This conception makes the grave a thoroughfare leading to the fields of light and life beyond.

Whenever men accept the materialistic conception of life, they act like animals, horning and shoving their way into the trough, engendering struggle and strife and a recrudescence of the jungle. But when men accept

124

the spiritual conception of life, that a Christ-like God is leading us on to all things good and true and beautiful, ennobling and enriching life and giving meaning to it, then they are likely to act as children of God ought to act, and we may hope that they will become builders and makers of a new world.

> 'Beat down yon beetling mountain,
> And raise yon jutting cape:
> A world is on the anvil,
> Now smite it into shape.

> 'Whence comes that iron music
> Whose sound is heard afar?
> The hammers of the world's smiths
> Are beating out a star.'

Note the opposing attitude towards the weak and unfortunate. Totalitarianism is hard, cruel, ruthless—the tortures and deaths inflicted by ancient inquisitions and the persecutions sanctioned by present-day ecclesiastical totalitarianism, and the outrages perpetrated by the secret police, the concentration camps, and the firing squads of modern political totalitarianism tell the story of total unkindness, malevolence, hardness of hearts, and demoniacal cruelty. For illustration, take Nazism. It could not tolerate democratic Christianity. Thus the Nazi book, *Gott und Volk*, says: 'We realized for the sake of Germany that there was no other way out than to drive Christ from our hearts in order that Germany may fill the whole place. . . . Christianity is the religion of the small and the weak, the religion of cowardly and pitiable people. . . . The God of Christians is a God of love, but love cannot be the essence of divinity. . . . It is the strong who rule, and the weak who should be ruled.' Therefore much of German Christianity was perverted into the deification of the State. *Mein Kampf* was substituted for Holy Writ, and the swastika crowded out the Cross. Hitler himself said in his 10th December 1940 speech: 'Two worlds are in conflict, two philosophies of life. . . . One of these two worlds must break asunder.' Dictators glorify the strong and kill off the weak. The world, uninfluenced by Christ, is described in the words of the poet Burns:

> 'Then, horn for horn, they stretch an' strive
> Deil tak the hindmost, on the drive.'

But the whole ministry of Jesus, both by teaching and example, emphasized the protection and kindly treatment of the poor and the weak and the underprivileged and the dispossessed. His life made forever luminous the text of His first sermon: 'The Spirit of the Lord is upon Me, because He hath anointed Me to preach the gospel to the poor; He hath sent Me to heal the brokenhearted, to preach deliverance to the captives, and recovery of sight to the blind, to set at liberty them that are bruised, to preach the acceptable year of the Lord.' His spirit was expressed in the apostolic injunction that 'we that are strong ought to bear the burdens of the weak', and that we should 'remember them that are in bonds, as bound with them'. This ministry of sympathy is Christian to the core. Christianity is described at this point by the little girl's definition of sympathy: 'Sympathy is *your* pain in *my* heart.' One of the greatest of our more recent American poets was Edwin Markham, and his favourite of all his own poems was this Christian plea:

> 'I dare not ask your very all,
> I only ask a part.
> Bring me when dancers leave the hall
> Your aching heart.

125

'Give other friends your lighted face,
The laughter of the years;
I come to crave a greater grace:
Bring me—your tears!'

Was it not Lord Chesterfield who said that 'a Christian is God Almighty's gentleman'. Christianity proves its divinity by its beneficence. It is a religion of refinement and subtlety of spiritual excellence. It looks out with sympathy and kindness from honest eyes, and shines understandingly through the facial tissues, and transforms sullen sourness into radiant beauty. It softens the raucous voice, and changes cruel arrogance into gentle tactfulness.

III

Absolute commitment to the cause espoused by the dictator is a requirement of totalitarianism that is most reprehensible. The Napoleons, Mussolinis, Hitlers, Francos, and Stalins, and all their ilk, require their followers to give away their inherent selfhood. The incompatibility of totalitarianism with Christianity was expressed by Hitler thus: 'One is either a German or a Christian. You cannot be both.' Hermann Rauschning declared: 'As long as youth follows me, I don't mind if the old people limp to the confessional. But the young ones, they will be different. I guarantee that.' Hitler's terrorism reached its ultimate when he said to the German people: 'It is your souls we want.' That was the negation of freedom.

Christianity, rightly understood, means the absolute commitment of the Christian to Jesus. But Christ never compels our submission. He always leaves it as a matter of choice of will with us. Moreover, the cause for which the commitment is made is the salvation of the world, the redemption of human society, the benefit of mankind. It is a commitment in the interest of true freedom, democracy, human rights, and the salvation of individuals and society.

Christianity demands sacrifice. It is a more stirring call to the heroic than the words with which Winston Churchill challenged British devotion: 'I have nothing to offer but blood, toil, tears and sweat.' Jesus offered the strait gate, the narrow way, self-denial, and the cross.

Carl Carmer, in his radio drama on V. E. Day, said that it was not the time to 'blow taps', or to assume that war was over, even though the victory was won. Concerning the evil that still existed in the world, he cried:

'Blow bugles—but not taps—blow
. . . the call, the charge—and we shall strike
And strike again until the world is ours,
And we may live in dignity and truth.'

Christianity has to battle as well as to inspire. It demands noble temper, high behaviour, faultless constancy, invincible fortitude in the hour of trial. It is a hallowing of all human interests and occupations. All life, all endowments, all gifts and talents are equally claimed by our Lord. Our learning, virtue, and piety are all His. He says that His followers are to 'Strive to enter in by the narrow door' of renunciation. All moral life involves a choice between two distinct alternatives. The follower of Christ must choose the rough and difficult pathway of duty.

Our commitment to Christ must be so complete that it will mould our character and determine our destiny. As Harry Emerson Fosdick says: 'The sacred elements in life are those concerning which we feel, not so much that they belong to us as that we belong to them. They are not our servants, but we theirs. They have a right to our utter loyalty, and we find life's true meaning in giving it. It is not what we command, but what commands us that determines our destiny.'

And so we come back to the place where we started: Christianity is loyalty, devotion, allegiance to Jesus. He stands alone, without a rival for our loyalty and our love. At the World's Fair in Chicago in 1893 there was what was called a Parliament of Religions, which had been assembled on the recommendation of William Fairfield Warren, who was at that time President of Boston University and one of the greatest educational statesmen America has ever produced. In that Parliament of Religions there were representatives from all the great peoples of the world, and from all the religions of the earth, and each one sought to present a physician who might cure the deadly disease of sin. At the close of a debate which had been going on for two days, Dr Barrows, who was presiding, turned to Bishop Arnett, a Negro minister from the southland, and said: 'Bishop, what do you think about the great men of the world as compared with Jesus Christ?' And the good Bishop replied: 'I feel like singing the Old Methodist hymn:

> ' "Jesus! the Name high over all,
> In hell, or earth, or sky;
> Angels and men before it fall,
> And devils fear and fly." '

Then Dr Joseph Cook, a distinguished Boston preacher and lecturer of that day, said, speaking of the great certainties of religion, 'Lady Macbeth hath bloodstains on her hands', and he asked the representatives of each religion what they could do to remove those stains. He waited a moment for an answer, and then solemnly said, with an emphasis that those who were present reported they could never forget: 'Nothing but the blood of Jesus!' The vast audience broke forth into applause—a reverent, rapturous applause—agreeing that no one has an absolute claim upon our loyalty and allegiance but Jesus only.

Confronted with the necessity of choosing between Jesus and totalitarianism, our answer is furnished by Watson Gilder:

> 'If Jesus Christ is a man—
> And only a man—I say
> That of all mankind, I will cleave to Him,
> And to Him will I cleave alway.
>
> 'If Jesus Christ is a God—
> And the only God—I swear,
> I will follow Him, through heaven and hell,
> The earth, the sea, and the air.'

     .   .   .   .   .

In the evening of 31st August the delegates attended a reception at Rhodes House. In the absence of the Vice-Chancellor, Dr John Lowe, the guests were received by the Warden of New College.

FIFTH DAY

Saturday 1st September

MORNING devotions were conducted by Bishop Eleazar Guerra of Mexico. The address was given by the Rev. Dr Gordon A. Sisco, of the United Church of Canada. After reading Ephesians 3[14-21] Dr Sisco affirmed the belief of Christians that the disorder of the world would eventually be resolved. That was why Christ came in the flesh.

'Three basic declarations underlie the Epistle to the Ephesians', he continued. The world is a place of discord, but it is the will of God that harmony should be restored through Christ, the Incarnation of divine love, and the Church is God's agent in this restoration. In seeking to accomplish His purpose, we must not only acquire knowledge of the peculiar treasures of other denominations or confessions, but must realize that love is more than knowledge, and true knowledge is unattainable without love.

The theme of the morning session was *Methodism and Other Churches*. The two addresses, delivered by the Rev. J. S. M. Hooper, of the Church of South India, and by the Rev. Dr Lynn Harold Hough, sometime Dean of Drew Seminary, New York, dealt with two aspects of the subject: the contribution Methodism could make to other communions and the lessons she could and should learn from them.

METHODISM AND OTHER CHURCHES

I. WHAT METHODISM HAS TO OFFER

An address given by the REV. J. S. M. HOOPER, *of the Church of South India:*

The implications of our subject this morning are clearly of vital importance. There can be no doubt that Methodism in the eighteenth century arose in response to a pressing need; in the days of John Wesley it was used of God to do things that the Church without it was failing to do. The question for us to face is whether there is still justification for the Methodist Church to retain its separate existence: today, what calls for defence is not union of the Churches, but their remaining distinct from one another. What then has Methodism to offer that is not otherwise fully to be found in the great Church of God?

It is not out of place to remind ourselves that Methodism does not claim, and never has claimed, that she has a monopoly of the truth; she looks upon herself as part of the holy catholic Church. If there is anything of value that is peculiar to Methodism, she does not regard it, whatever it may be, as of the *esse* of the Church—though she may well hold it to be of the *bene esse*. She dare not be guilty of the presumption of consigning Christians who are not Methodists in faith or order to 'the uncovenanted mercies of God'. Between us and those Churches or groups of Christians

128

which make such claims there is a great gulf fixed, and no man has yet found the bridge to cross that gulf. We have our rules of Church order for the right governing of our own Church; but we un-Church no one who holds the Faith that Jesus Christ is God come in the flesh, and in the Lord's Supper we welcome as fellow guests at the Table of the Lord all communicant members of any branch of the Christian Church.

With this joyful and humble recognition that we belong to the great and varied family that is the Church of God, we can yet see in some of our emphases things that we are glad to be able to offer to our fellow Christians. We have been enriched by these things; we are eager to share them with others, no less than to receive from others their peculiar treasures.

During the past few days we have been left in no doubt as to the traditional doctrines of the Methodist Church, and of the place of Methodism in the catholic Church. We have been reminded of the characteristic Methodist way of life, and of the marvels of Methodist organization. From various angles the same things have naturally and inevitably been stressed. So in what I am to say there will unavoidably be a saying again of what has already been said, with a difference. Today it is my privilege to represent the Church of South India, which includes in its membership nearly a quarter of a million people who up to 1947 were members of this Methodist Church, an offshoot of British Methodism. I am thus to deal not with theories of what Methodism ought to be able to offer, but with the testing of our theories and of the present validity of our traditions by facts of recent history and by the demands of a concrete situation. We of the Methodist Church in South India joined in forming the Church of South India without capitulation, not by way of absorption, but on equal terms with Congregationalists, Presbyterians, and Anglicans, and each group, consciously to some extent, but perhaps far more unconsciously, carried with it into the united Church the riches of its own inheritance. Much must be left unsaid; but we are to try to see part of what the distinctive Methodist contribution has been and continues to be in that great adventure of obedience, and soberly to appraise it: it may help us to see what Methodism may be expected to bring into that fuller ultimate union of the whole of Christendom for which we pray—that they all may be one, as the Father and the Son are One, that the world may believe. . . .

Spreading Scriptural holiness has always been recognized as the business of Methodism: a strong evangelistic emphasis, as of the essence of the Church, a going to those who need us, and to those who need us most, is a duty and a privilege that has never been forgotten among us, however it may have been neglected. But to suggest that in overseas work Methodism has this emphasis to give as its special contribution to the common stock of Christianity would be untrue. All the great missionary societies have been stirred by the same impulse and are doing the work they are doing in obedience to the same loyalty. In the overseas work of the Church the awakening for which, in God's mercy, John Wesley was so largely responsible here in England, with its world-wide effects, is now shared by all the Evangelical Churches. But in parts of the overseas Church the perils of a Christianity of the second and third generation begin to be felt, and in many lands the Church is tending to become a self-contained and self-satisfied little group. It is thus necessary, there as here, for the evangelistic motive to be kept in the forefront of the thought and life of the Church. We may be thankful that Methodism has not been less zealous than the others who have come together into the Church of South India in emphasizing that no man can truly be said to have the mind of Christ who does not share in His redemptive Passion; He came into the

129

world to save sinners, and the Church is in the world, as His Body, to
carry on His work. The Church of South India is essentially and consciously, a missionary Church.

In the proclamation of this gospel of reconciliation by the Methodist
there is, I think, a quality of peculiar value. I am not denying it to others,
but it is eminently characteristic of Methodism. It may be summed up
in one line of our hymn: 'O let me commend my Saviour to you.' The
gospel that we preach is the Faith of the Catholic Church through the ages,
based upon the New Testament revelation of God in Christ, purged of
superstitions in the Reformation; but we proclaim it not because it has the
authority of the early Christian centuries and is embodied in the great
Creeds of the Church, prescribed for our acceptance. No, our witness has
more immediacy and irresistible urgency. 'Because in my desperate need
I have been saved by Jesus and am being saved by Him I must introduce
Him to you in your need.'

> 'My heart is full of Christ, and longs
>   Its glorious matter to declare!
> Of Him I make my loftier songs,
>   I cannot from His praise forbear.
> My ready tongue makes haste to sing
> The glories of my heavenly King.'

In the New Testament we have found full support for what we have called
the doctrine of assurance; it is that reality of the personal experience of
the saving power of Christ which has been the driving force of Methodist
evangelism.

So, too, our first concern has been with individuals, to bring them one
by one to Jesus Christ, for Him to do what He wills with them. We have
been sure that His will for men is nothing less than perfect love and
holiness. We have been compelled to accept this standard for ourselves,
as a necessity for honest and effective evangelism.

> 'That I Thy mercy may proclaim,
>   That all mankind Thy truth may see,
> Hallow Thy great and glorious name,
>   And perfect holiness in me.'

That which we know to be His will for us we have not dared to refrain from
preaching to others; the relentless demand of the gospel, that we should be
perfect as our Father in Heaven is perfect, was accepted by Paul, whose
declared aim was to present every man perfect in Christ (Colossians 1[28])
and we too must accept it. It is only not a word of presumption, or of
despair, because in Jesus Christ we know that God is Love.

> 'Yield to me now; for I am weak
>   But confident in self-despair;
> Speak to my heart, in blessings speak,
>   Be conquered by my instant prayer:
> Speak, or Thou never hence shalt move,
> And tell me if Thy name is Love.

> ' 'Tis Love! 'tis Love! Thou diedst for me!
>   I hear Thy whisper in my heart;
> The morning breaks, the shadows flee,
>   Pure, universal Love Thou art;
> To me, to all, Thy mercies move:
> Thy nature and Thy name is Love.'

This gospel of the redeeming love of God in Christ, offered to all men and making its inexorable claim upon all men, has been the centre of our witness, and we proclaim it with certainty:

> 'What we have felt and seen
> With confidence we tell,
> And publish to the sons of men
> The signs infallible.'

To conclude, however, that a purely individual salvation is a characteristic Methodist emphasis would be a misreading of Methodist history. It is true that in some other communions the doctrine of the Church has been more fully elaborated; but nowhere has there been a stronger emphasis than in Methodism on the fellowship of believers as a means of grace, linking the Church of today with the Church of the New Testament. The Church as a whole is in urgent need of such fellowship, and Methodism, by its history and experience, is surely called of God to make this contribution to the Church's enrichment. The small groups in which in the early days the Methodist Society used to meet—the Class Meetings, the band meetings, the Love Feasts—familiar terms within the Methodist family, strange though some of them may sound in other ears—were under God the specifically Methodist means of grace for our fathers; in the intimacy of their fellowship, the fruit of the Spirit was richly grown, and Christian character and knowledge were firmly nurtured. From these little meetings arose a great succession of class leaders and local preachers, laymen, and women, versed in the ways of God's dealings with the human soul in every kind of need, and able as under-shepherds of the Great Shepherd to lead wanderers safely into His fold. Within the local Church such cells of vital Christianity have nerved the life of the whole community, not only of the Church: they have been the outstanding feature of Methodist life and witness. In extension of this, the same spirit, showing itself naturally in circuit, district, national, and indeed world-wide organization, has created throughout Methodism what I believe to be an unparalleled sense of brotherhood in Christ: the very itinerancy of our ministers, the very fact that our Missionary Society is the whole Church in its overseas work, and not merely one sectional society within the Church, have contributed enormously to this intimacy of knowledge, this sharing of one another's burdens and joys, that are of the very essence of the Christian life. . . . I said when I began that I was to speak of facts, of contributions actually made by Methodism in South India to the united Church that came into being there in 1947. I believe we have made this contribution; but there, as here, our fellowship is not of the strength and infectious vigour that our history would lead us to expect. There is urgent need for the revival among ourselves of this precious thing that has been given to us, this frank, fearless, intimate fellowship, if we are not to betray God's trust by our failure to bring it in fullness of health, and in forms suited to 'serve the present age', for the enrichment of the holy Catholic Church throughout all the world. There is widespread hunger for it among men and women; it will be well for them, and for the Church, if they can satisfy their hunger within the fellowship of the Church rather than have to seek for it in groups in any measure isolated from the main body of the Church's life.

With these doctrinal emphases, and with the unique place we have given to fellowship in our Church life, I would name one other thing, which seems to me to condition and to give its peculiar quality to all that Methodism stands for. The *Methodist Hymnbook*, and, more specifically,

131

the hymns of Charles Wesley, are our special heritage. (I would not forget John Wesley's own great translations.) Everything I have said this morning has been tinged, or rather deep-dyed, with it. 'Methodism', says the Preface to the 1933 Hymnbook, 'was born in song. Charles Wesley wrote the first hymns of the Evangelical Revival during the great Whitsuntide of 1738, when his brother and he were "filled with the Spirit", and from that time onwards the Methodists have never ceased to sing.' Such singing in itself is a natural expression of the varied experiences of the Christian life, and our habit of interspersing the business of our Synods and other formal meetings with hymns is a good thing which we have handed on to the Church of South India; it is a constant reminder that all our business is 'begun, continued, and ended' in Him, and that of it all it should be possible to say with the early Church and every decision that is made: 'It seemed good to the Holy Ghost and to us.' In the meetings of the Synod, the governing body of the Church of South India, the hymnbook chosen for our use is the Methodist book; in no other are the deeps of Christian experience so sounded and the wealth of brotherhood in Christ so explored.

For it is the content of the hymns rather than the mere fact of singing that is significant in Methodism. John Wesley asks, in the familiar words of his Preface of 1779: 'In what other publication of the kind have you so distinct and full an account of Scriptural Christianity? such a declaration of the heights and depths of religion, speculative and practical? . . . so clear directions for making your calling and election sure; for perfecting holiness in the fear of God?' I think his claim still stands: it has stood the test of 170 years since he made it. The Hymnbook has been the Methodists' great devotional manual, and in all devotional literature I know nothing more searching, nothing more uplifting, than many of these hymns. It is in Wesley's words that the Methodist has recognized the expression of the deepest experiences of his own life, and in them he has found satisfying exposition of Christian truth. If the Methodist in the pew is in any measure a theologian—and I think he is, though in many cases he would with modesty, if not with horror, repudiate such a label—if he is able to give a reason for the faith that is in him, it is because he has been praying and singing and unconsciously absorbing theology in Charles Wesley's hymns: a theology completely delivered from the sterile abstractions of the classroom, transfused by Wesley's genius to be emotionally alive and obviously related to everyday life. It is very far from being mere sentiment, because always the hymns are based firmly on the Scriptures, with an amazing range of easy knowledge and use; but it is all aglow, with the authentic glow of New Testament devotion, recalling us again and again to the great doxologies of St Paul. His theme and Wesley's are the same: 'In all these things we are more than conquerors through Him that loved us. I am persuaded that neither death nor life nor angels nor principalities nor things present nor things to come, nor powers, nor height nor depth nor any other creature shall be able to separate us from the love of God, which is in Christ Jesus our Lord.'

> 'Captain of Israel's host, and Guide
> Of all who seek the land above,
> Beneath Thy shadow we abide,
> The cloud of Thy protecting love;
> Our strength, Thy grace; our rule, Thy word;
> Our end, the glory of the Lord.

'By Thine unerring Spirit led,
　　We shall not in the desert stray;
　　We shall not full direction need,
　　　Nor miss our povidential way;
　　As far from danger as from fear,
　　While love, almighty love, is near.'

In the advertisement to a very different collection of Christian verse, itself destined to wide usefulness—Keble's *Christian Year*, published in 1827—we find the following cautious statement: 'Next to a sound rule of faith there is nothing of so much consequence as a sober standard of feeling.' I would set by the side of that John Wesley's closing words in his Preface to the 1779 Hymnbook, with their characteristically clear perception of the importance of bringing the rule of faith into the central springs of will and imagination and emotion: 'I would recommend this collection to every truly pious Reader as a means of raising or quickening the spirit of devotion; of confirming his faith; and of kindling and increasing his love to God and man.' That, by the grace of God, is precisely what these hymns have done in Methodism for 200 years. I greatly rejoice that we have been able to bring this gift as part of our Methodist contribution to the Church of South India both in its original English form, and also in some measure through translation into our four main languages; it is a gift that has been valued aright, and that is being increasingly used by people of every tradition in that Church.

Let us then continue to sing our theology—and let us never be afraid of the Evangelical fervour that breathes through the hymns; let us never become so respectable that we are ashamed of singing, with passionate desire and humble thoughtfulness:

'O let Thy love my heart constrain!
　　Thy love for every sinner free,
　　That every fallen soul of man
　　　May taste the grace that found out me;
　　That all mankind with me may prove
　　Thy sovereign everlasting love.'

II. WHAT METHODISM CAN LEARN FROM OTHER CHURCHES

An address given by DR LYNN HAROLD HOUGH *of New York:*

We must appropriate at once a principle growing out of the thought of Aristotle. Any organism and any institution lives and grows truly only when it is loyal to the deep and defining meaning of its own life. Its true development is always according to its own genius. You cannot ask any institution to accept that which contradicts its own essential quality. It is the genius of Methodism to represent man's living experience of God in Christ so possessing him as to dominate all his thought and action. Other communions, of course, have not been without this quality. But in Methodism it has come to a certain uniquely commanding emphasis.

To be sure, Methodism did not spring full-grown from the heart of a man blazing with the fire of God. In a sense, the whole Christian past was in its blood and effected its life. In a large and generous sense, John Wesley was a scholar, and he tried to listen to all the true voices of the Christian past. In a sense, he was a university don and a prophet and a practical politician all made into one. So it is often true that when we ask

Methodism to learn from other Churches we are asking it to accept something which was at least implicit in the large and generous activity of Wesley's mind. None the less, it is true that every great communion has worked out a witness which is its particular contribution to the universal Church. And the processes of cross-fertilization are good for them all.

Moving along these lines, what are some of the things which Methodism can learn from the other Churches?

I

Since the sixteenth century it has been easy to think of the Latin Communion simply in terms of protest and hostility. And no doubt the friendly spirit is always at its best when it is checked and guided by a cool and critical spirit which saves it from unintelligent hospitality. At the same time the trunk of the tree contained that which may well be found in all of the branches. It is said that once, standing under the dome of St Peter's, Mr Gladstone was profoundly moved by the thought of the imperial quality of the Church. That the principle can be misused is clear enough. That it can be used rightly is also true. Indeed Christianity is less than itself if it is not thought of in imperial terms. In any particular place and in any particular time, it may be true that only a persecuted minority represents Christian truth. But the Church, according to its very idea, is a vast empire of the spirit happily commanding the worldwide loyalty of men. This idea must never be lost. It must be maintained as a dream and a hope even when it cannot claim to be an actuality. Christ has a right to reign over the minds and the consciences of all men. And His right to universal sovereignty must never be forgotten.

Then the belief that reason as a divine gift and revelation as a divine gift can work harmoniously together—a belief nobly emphasized by the great Neo-Thomists—is one which has meaning for us all. 'Come, now let us reason together' is always the true Christian attitude. 'Come now, and let us throw away reason in the name of faith' is never a true Christian position at all.

II

The great Lutheran Churches were founded upon a great act of faith in which the past and the present and the future were gladly and fully thrown upon the arms of God. Perhaps this principle has sometimes received more verbal than real honour as the centuries have passed. But there it is at the very heart of the Protestant revolt. It may well be said that it is the heart of Methodism too. But the reader of the great Lutheran writings will come to see that there it has an emphasis which we may well study and from which we may well learn. That man has his true life only in God and that his supreme act is that in which he gives himself completely to God cannot be kept too clearly or constantly before our minds. Luther, with a stifling self-contradiction, completely denied man's freedom in order as he thought to give the deepest significance to his faith in God. The follower of John Wesley keeps the faith, but he bases it upon a free and responsible act of man, and thus gives it true validity and permanent significance. It remains true, however, that the particular Lutheran sense of the faith which is the living nexus between man and God deserves our profound and repeated consideration.

The relation of the Lutheran Churches to the State is not without meaning for us all. To be sure, when that relation is essentially political it comes to rest upon a completely false foundation. But there is something

134

in the idea of the Church as the State worshipping which cannot be entirely cast aside. It must be made thoroughly spiritual and it must be completely separated from political entanglements. But it remains a witness to the fact that the State must not be allowed to become a merely secular and materialistic institution.

III

The Reformed Churches have made for themselves a place of ample dignity and power in the life of the world. Their emphasis since the time of John Calvin upon a clear and coherent theology is something which must be made a feature of the witness of all Christian Churches. To be sure dialectic as the rational expression of the vital is one thing. And dialectic as the barren setting forth of dead relationships is quite another. The Reformers' witness has not always been able to resist the temptation to fall into a scholasticism of its own. On the other hand, the non-theological Church is always a decadent Church. The Christian religion must be made intellectually commanding if it is to be morally compelling or spiritually satisfying or socially effective. There was more theology in the little finger of John Wesley than there has been in the loins of some of his followers in later centuries. And so the Reformed theology may well remind us of a heritage which we should make our own so far as belief in coherent thought is concerned, though we are by no means committed to all of the assumptions or to all of the conclusions of Reformed processes of thought.

The profound conviction of the sovereignty of God has received full and notable witness in the Reformed faith. It can be set forth in such a fashion that it sees a hard and arbitrary will at the heart of the universe dispensing decisions without moral basis or moral conclusions. No end of the best Reformed thinkers have turned with uneasiness and something not unlike distaste from such positions. But the sovereignty of God may be interpreted as His complete and eternal loyalty to His own nature, which is in its essence the perfection of moral goodwill, of ethical love eternally alive. It is not an irresponsible thing. It is perpetually responsible to that goodness which is the very genius of God's own eternal life. So interpreted, the sovereignty of God has an inevitable place in the ecumenical faith.

IV

The Baptist emphasis upon adult decision in respect of the Christian verities is of permanent importance. It may not effect the Methodist attitude toward infant baptism. But it will remind us that the parents' consecration of a child must be reaffirmed by the child himself when he comes to years of discretion. The solidarity of Christians in a corporate spiritual life is never to wipe out the sense of individual responsibility. In Christian baptism there is claimed for the child its heritage through Christ as part of the Kingdom of God. But the validation of that claim by the responsible adult decision of that child in later years is a matter of the greatest and most pivotal importance. Without discarding our own position, we can thus learn something from the Baptists. And a certain robust energy comes from this position of the Baptists which we can all well make our own. Those who confronted the virile personality of Dr Clifford must have felt that they had much to learn from him. I once heard Dr Jowett characterize him as a man of war from his youth. And it is easy for us to see how the Baptist tradition helps to make the Christian warrior a man of personal commitment to his cause.

135

V

There was a day a little before our own when every vital and vigorous young Methodist minister was a proud reader of the writings of Dr R. W. Dale. Indeed I remember once hearing Dr George Jackson pay tribute to the influence of Dale upon Methodist theological thought. His book on *The Atonement* and his book on *The Living Christ and the Four Gospels* became a part of the inheritance not only of Congregationalists, but of the whole Christian Church. When one thinks of Dale in his great days at Carr's Lane Church in Birmingham one feels in the presence of something very massive and very compelling. In him the rather patrician, intellectual tradition which has characterized Congregationalism at its best became stoutly Evangelical. To follow the Burke-like flow of Dale's nobly urbane sentences, in which lofty thought receives royal expression, is to feel that the best is none too good for the commending of the great evangel to the minds of men. Dr Peter T. Forsyth, who is so happily coming to his own again, put a flashing and epigrammatical dialectic at the service of the gospel. In his case paradox was never a method of escaping intellectual responsibility, but was rather a method of expressing Christian insight. In such men as Dale and Forsyth the Congregational tradition came to fine flower. And from them all of us have much to learn.

VI

The Society of Friends if in a sense we may refer to the Society of Friends as a Church—has had a place of its own in the religious life of the world since the seventeenth century. The very pronouncing of the name Quaker suggests the opposition to war of this small but influential group. It is not always realized that the guidance of the inner light is even more fundamental. If a young man feels that the inner light leads him to take part in military activity, he can become a soldier without losing his place in the meeting house to which he belongs. There is a creative and far-reaching quality about this principle that our positions must be submitted to the test of the deep religious experience in the soul of the Christian. At this point we come upon a note which has its importance for all of the Churches.

VII

We have up to this point said nothing of the ancient and significant Greek Church. We may now take time to remind ourselves that if the emphasis of the Latin Communion has been on the Cross, the emphasis of the Greek Church has been on the Incarnation. When we follow the tradition back to Clement and Origen and Athanasius, we find ourselves in the presence of a central consciousness as to the person of Christ. That the flesh was of such stuff that the Word could become flesh was the important matter in the thought of Christians of the Greek tradition. All diseased and unhealthy conceptions of human nature fall before this belief. Sin can now be seen to be what Wesley called it—the voluntary transgression of known law. It is the deed of a creature made for God who by the misuse of his freedom has turned from God. You can only understand humanity when you see what it became in Jesus Christ. These conceptions have tremendous relevance for the thought of the Church today.

VIII

Doubtless Satan, the adversary of the Book of Job, if he is still interested in such things might suggest a study of the Churches for warning as well

136

as for inspiration. We may study certain aspects of the life of various Churches in order to learn what not to think and not to do and not to say. Without any damnatory clauses addressed to particular Churches, we venture several remarks along this line. Whenever the political usurps the place of the spiritual, the Church is taking the wrong way. Whenever intellectual analysis takes the place of Christian experience and Christian action, the Church is moving upon a false path. When Church feeling is made a substitute for Christian action, the Church itself suffers from a process of emasculation. The history of all of the Churches is full of warning as well as of inspiration.

All that we have said comes to this: every Christian communion has its own significant witness and has made its own contribution to the thought and action and to the experience of the Christian religion. And so it is well for each communion to study with deep and critical friendliness the genius and the history of all the rest.

IX

There is one more necessary word. We have said nothing of the great communion out of whose life Methodism came. The relation is so deep and so intimate that it requires a consideration which is all its own. There are to be sure many things to be said about the Anglican witness. Two of them are particularly relevant to our discussion. The first has to do with the sacramental view of life. Put briefly, this can be expressed by saying that it is of the very nature of the physical to be the livery of the spiritual. The physical finds its true meaning as it is shot through with the splendour of the spiritual. The physical is its own true self as it becomes the vehicle for the commanding power of the spiritual. The principle is deep and far-reaching, and Methodists have a right to make it their own.

Then there is the emphasis on Christian Humanism. A few months ago, Dr W. R. Matthews, the Dean of St Paul's, wrote: 'There are eminent Christian apologists who write as if Humanism were the enemy of Christianity and simply the supreme manifestation of human pride. Such indiscriminate denunciation, however, is unjust and dangerous. Surely the better course would be to show that there is a Christian Humanism which exalted the dignity of man while insisting firmly upon his dependence on God.' And in that very important book, *The Recovery of Man*, Dr Frank Russell Barry, the Bishop of Southwell, declares: 'The great task of the Church in this savage era is the rehabilitation of Humanism.' He says, further: 'If the Church is to play its true part in the redemption of this post-war world and not to be overwhelmed beneath its ruins it must be as the champion and protagonist of Christian Humanism.' No communion is in a better position to unite this emphasis with the profoundest sanctions of the gospel of salvation in such a fashion as to produce an Evangelical Humanism which will bring a new power to the thought and experience and action of the Christian Church, than is that which inherits the tradition of John Wesley. The Christian Humanist can combine the profoundest elements in the thought and life of all of the Churches with a searching proclamation of the utter dependence of men upon the grace of God brought to us in Christ.

X

A man only becomes a full man when he becomes conscious that he is a part of something larger than himself. A particular communion of the Christian Church only becomes the full possessor of its own life as it

137

realizes that it is a part of something larger than itself. There is even solid basis in the New Testament for the assertion that Christ must surrender His authority to the Father that God may be all in all. So the final contribution which a study of all of the Churches can make to Methodism comes with the vision of that larger fellowship in which the good and true elements of the witness of each communion are gathered up in the fullness and the finality of the Church as it exists in the purpose of God and will one day exist as the final achievement of His grace. In the meantime, each communion must perfect its own instrument to make a fit contribution to the music of that orchestra whose vast harmonies give forth the noblest symphony which this world affords.

These two morning addresses were followed by group discussions, the findings of which are included in the summary on p. 289.

A Plenary Session of the Conference was held at Wesley Memorial Church at 5.15.

In the evening a lecture was delivered by Bishop Charles C. Selecman, of Dallas, Texas, on *Francis Asbury and the Advancement of Methodism in America*. The lecture had been arranged by the International Methodist Historical Society, of which Bishop Paul N. Garber is President, and the Rev. Dr Elmer T. Clark (New York) and the Rev. Frank Baker (Cleethorpes) are the Secretaries.

The Rev. Dr Leslie F. Church, Connexional Editor and ex-President of the British Conference, presided, and Dr Elmer Clark conducted the opening devotions. In a short statement on the work of the Society, Mr Baker said it endeavoured to link together those who sought to gather, classify, and study source material for the writing of Methodist history. They were concerned not only with the preservation of local records, but also with the presentation of Methodism as a living whole. The securing of Asbury's cottage home, for example, was the kind of service he felt might be multiplied. 'We believe not only in the preservation of relics', he said, 'but also in helping people to see how it is all related to our modern Methodism.'

Introducing the subject of Francis Asbury, Dr Church referred to his *Journal* which was a classic second only to the *Journal* of John Wesley himself. It contained an entry written on shipboard as Asbury sailed to the New World on a voyage which began in 1771 —a voyage as important as any ever undertaken: 'Whither am I going? To the New World. What to do? ... If I know my own heart ... I am going to live to God, and to bring others so to do.' It was in the strength of such a purpose that Francis Asbury made his momentous decision to remain in America rather than to return to England when war broke out. The vision of that lonely figure setting out, amongst the tumult of battle, to conquer a continent in the name of Christ is one of the highlights of history of tremendous importance to World Methodism. His attitude was not without its influence on the future of the English-speaking people and certainly on the growth of the whole Christian Church.

FRANCIS ASBURY AND THE ADVANCEMENT OF
METHODISM IN AMERICA

A lecture delivered by BISHOP CHARLES C. SELECMAN *of Dallas, Texas:*

John Wesley was addressing the Methodists at Bristol, England, in 1771. The occasion was the meeting of the Conference of the Wesleyan Connexion. Captain Thomas Webb, the fiery, eloquent evangelist who had travelled and laboured in America, had urged the great need and marvellous opportunity for additional help in the New World. Mr Wesley's appeal was: 'Our brethren in America call aloud for help; who will go over and help them?' Five men responded. Only two were accepted. They were Francis Asbury and Richard Wright. Soon after this, on 4th September 1771, Asbury sailed from Bristol, England, landing in Philadelphia on 27th October, and at once began his matchless itinerant career. From 4th September 1771, when, a penniless volunteer missionary twenty-six years of age, he presented himself in Bristol, to the day in March 1816, when the feeble saint was lifted from his carriage near Fredericksburg, Virginia, to spend his last few days in the home of George Arnold, he laboured, preached, prayed, and suffered as few men have ever done for the cause of Christ and His Church.

Francis Asbury is known as the Prophet of the Long Road. It has been aptly said that 'He printed the map of his ministry with his horse's hoofs'. For travels he even surpassed John Wesley, and that in an undeveloped country. 'Asbury outrode Wesley. All in all, it has been estimated that he covered 275,000 miles. He crossed and recrossed the Allegheny Mountains more than sixty times.' From his *Journal* it has been gleaned that 'He went into New York State more than 50 times; New Jersey over 60; Pennsylvania, 78; Maryland, 80; North Carolina, 63; South Carolina, 46; Virginia, 84; Tennessee and Georgia, each 20; Massachusetts, 23; and in other States and Territories with corresponding frequency'. He preached 16,000 sermons, an average of one a day for half a century. Once in Philadelphia he said: 'My brethren seem not to know the way to the country, and I think I shall show them the way.' On and on he rode, in feeble health, in 'pain, pain, pain', as he once wrote in his Journal. He rode until age and infirmity made it necessary for him to have a travelling companion. On he rode, preaching mostly to small groups, until within a few days of his death.

When on his way to America, he wrote in his Journal: 'Whither am I going? To the New World. What to do? To gain honour? No, if I know my own heart. To get money? No; I am going to live to God and to bring others so to do.' American Methodism is what it is today largely because of Francis Asbury.

Small wonder, then, that we read such sincere and eloquent tributes to his saintliness of character, his dauntless courage, his steadiness of aim, his persistent industry and his unselfish leadership as the following:

'Francis Asbury is the most distinguished man that the Methodist Church has ever produced and the most important ecclesiastical personage that our country has ever seen.' President Calvin Coolidge wrote: 'Who shall say where his influence, written upon immortal souls, shall end?' And Dixon, in his *Tour in America*, says: 'The most important actor who ever appeared from England in America took his place on the continent —Francis Asbury.' Bishop Bashford writes: 'His common sense and administrative abilities have never been excelled in America, either in

Church or state. Even Lincoln had not so long and full a test as Asbury.'
Curlock said: 'Asbury was the master builder.'

Fitness and Preparation

By a strange combination of circumstance, training, and temperament, this man of no great flashes of genius, and of very limited formal education, was fitted to be a great ecclesiastical leader and statesman in the New World. One British author, Dr James Lewis, has this to say of Asbury's contribution to American Methodism: 'Francis Asbury was the chosen leader . . . who laid the foundations and determined the structure of the Methodist Episcopal Church of America. What Washington is to the political realm, Asbury is to the ecclesiastical—a star in the Western Hemisphere that dwells apart.' Dr Lewis quotes with approval Macaulay's comparison of Asbury with Richelieu.

The cruel beatings of a brutal schoolmaster drove him from the classroom when just a lad, and as his father was a gardener of small financial resources, Francis soon became acquainted with toil as an apprentice to a saddler. In this period, too, he became deeply impressed by the preaching of the early Methodists and became active in the religious meetings held in his home and the homes of neighbours. Before volunteering for America, he became one of John Wesley's circuit preachers and for five years laboured on circuits, during which period he studied Christian doctrine, Methodist standards, and even Latin, Greek, and Hebrew. The titles mentioned cover poetry, history, politics, biography, philosophy, and theology. The consciousness of his lack of early training more often produced humility rather than self-assertion, 'The cloak generally employed by little minds to hide their nakedness'.

He was much impressed by the Methodists. 'Now behold! They were singing hymns', he writes, 'sweet sounds. Why strange to tell! The preacher had no prayer book and yet he prayed wonderfully! What was yet more extraordinary the man took his text and had no sermon book.' As the record unfolds, as told by his Journal, we shall see how God was taking the weakness of such a man to confound the mighty. The Wesleys, Whitfield, Coke, and Fletcher were all men of culture, products of university training. Asbury lacked this background. But his very lack may have fitted him to adjust himself to the problems of an untrained ministerial leadership in an undeveloped land.

John Wesley took a long step in using lay preachers whose only ordination was 'the mighty ordination of the pierced hands'. Such men as John Nelson and Thomas Maxfield were used by him as flaming witnesses of the gospel of grace. Just what he would have done at Lovely Lane Chapel, Baltimore, in 1784 with sixty uneducated itinerant evangelists, not one of whom was college-trained, is another question. Robert Strawbridge, an untutored Methodist immigrant from Ireland, administering the sacrament of the Lord's Supper, would probably have invited an open break. Asbury undertook to put the Irishman under the rules. 'But Strawbridge could not yield the point, and Asbury was constrained to tolerate the innovation.'

Methodist Itineracy

DuBose declares that the history of American Methodism really begins with the arrival of Francis Asbury in Philadelphia in 1771. 'To his ideal and to his tireless labours to realize it the Church owes the itinerary. He was the first preacher in America to form and regularly travel a circuit.' Preachers were appointed to definite places and instructed 'to cultivate all the land possible'. Wright was given New York; Pilmoor, Maryland and

140

Delaware; Boardman, New England; and Asbury was to have Philadelphia. The entire preaching force consisted of Richard Boardman, Joseph Pilmoor, Francis Asbury, Richard Wright, Philip Embury, Robert Strawbridge, Captain Webb, Robert Williams, and John King. These were shut up for the most part in Philadelphia and New York. Asbury's Journal reads: 'I have not the thing which I seek—the circulation of the preachers.' In barns, taverns, court-houses, prisons, at public executions and in the open, he proclaimed the gospel. 'I humbly hope that about seven preachers of us will spread seven or eight hundred miles and preach in as many places as we are able to attend.' Thus began the 'Trail of the Circuit Rider', born in the mind and heart of Asbury and boldly sketched by his own travels and labours. 'Daily', writes DuBose, 'at the gates of prison, at the doors of comfortable houses, in school houses, in family circles, by the river and baysides, to friends, to strangers, to masters, to slaves this tireless itinerant opened the word of Life.' His Journal relates that at one place the schoolhouse would not contain half the people. So he stood at the door and the people without. Another entry concerns a 'family meeting' where he spoke 'separately and privately' to all, both black and white. Again he preached in an unfinished church, without windows or doors. It was cold and he pitied the people. After an hour's intermission, 'The people waiting all the time in the cold', he preached again. Thus by laborious example and by the use of a combination of brotherly constraint with episcopal authority, Francis Asbury literally hewed and hammered out the Methodist itineracy, perhaps the most distinctive feature of the development of the Methodist Church in America. In the *Minutes of the Methodist Conferences annually held in America from 1773 to 1813 inclusive*, the following appears in the record of 1779:

'Question 6. Who of the preachers are willing to take the station this Conference shall place them in and continue till next Conference?'

The list of those signing this agreement is headed by the name of Francis Asbury. The profound significance of this lies in the fact that Asbury conceived his relationship as that of a yoke fellow, never demanding of the rank and file of circuit preachers an obedience of which he himself was not a willing subject or a service which he was not ready to render. So long as the preachers and lay members of the great Methodist Church discover this sacrificial spirit in our episcopal leaders, we may be assured that there will be little chafing under episcopal authority and leadership.

The apt description of the adjournment of the Christmas Conference which appears in the recently published *Endless Line of Splendour*, by Halford E. Luccock, is an appropriate conclusion of this all too brief and imperfect discussion of the itinerant system as it involves both pastors and general superintendents:

'One of the most impressive things about the Conference was the rapidity with which it dispersed. The appointments were made; the final prayer offered; and it was almost as though some of the men leaped through the windows of the chapel on to their horses to be on their way. The King's business required haste—and got it. The day after the Conference Asbury rode fifty miles, through frost and snow, to Fairfax, Virginia, and Bishop Coke began a six months' preaching tour of the South.'

Evangelism

The early Methodist movement in America was above all else an evangelistic movement. In many ways it partook of the methods, signs, and results similar to those of the spiritual awakening in England under the Wesleys and Whitefield.

141

Francis Asbury was a product of that movement. He came to America with the message, the experience, and the tempo of the Wesleyan Revival firmly fixed in his mind and heart. The doctrines which he had laboriously studied and preached on the circuits for five years in Britain were those which Captain Webb and the early missionaries were proclaiming in the colonies. Wesley had commissioned George Stafford: 'Publish your message in the face of the sun and do all the good you can.' Whitefield had answered one inquiry as to his work in America by saying: 'I am roaming and ranging the great American wilderness in search of lost souls.' One Anglican churchman, the Rev. Mr Jarrett, was largely instrumental in promoting the Virginia revival. Mr Asbury visited him and the two held several meetings together. This began a friendship that lasted many years. Jarrett came to be known among the Methodists as 'the American Fletcher'.

In co-operation with the Presbyterians, Asbury entered into the camp meeting revivals, that often attracted many hundreds of people and lasted for two weeks or more. These camp meetings were often scenes of great joy, excessive emotionalism, loud demonstrations, and even physical convulsions and trances. In these he was a steady balance between overwrought emotionalism and icily cold formalism. It is related that once he was met in the wilderness of Pennsylvania by some inquiring souls who told him that in certain meetings the spirit would grapple with men and women and cast them prone on the ground. 'Do you think that is the work of God?' they inquired. Asbury's laconic and wise answer was: 'Let us wait and see what they do when they get up.'

Bishop Holland N. McTyeire forcefully expressed a great truth when he wrote: 'It was not new doctrine but new life the first Methodists sought for themselves and for others. To realize in the hearts of men the true ideal of Christianity, to maintain its personal experience and to extend it—this was their design; and their system of government grew up out of this and was accordingly shaped by it.' Methodism owes the force which has made it progressive and historic to an experience.

If John Wesley had not felt his heart 'strangely warmed' in that humble meeting in Aldersgate Street on 24th May 1738, the world would not have known a pre-eminent Wesley, the man of fire and zeal, the man of pentecostal experience and power, nor would eighteenth-century England have known the quickening of the Wesleyan Revival, nor perhaps any equivalent of it. If the Spirit had not in a similar manner, some two and twenty years later, visited the heart of Francis Asbury, 'Wesley's few sheep in the American wilderness' might have perished or gone astray for lack of leadership. In that case it is not difficult to think of the New World as having been left without its most distinct and potential evangelical force. It is thus that the fate and welfare of nations turn upon the things which God brings to life in the awakening of the hearts of those whom He calls to be His saints. 'It is thus that conversions become more decisive than battles and revivals of religion more determinative than political revolutions. It was thus that the name of Francis Asbury came to be illustrious; it was thus that he of the humble beginning and the humble faith was, at last, given so large a share in settling the life of a continent and in influencing the destinies of mankind in general.'

It frequently has been observed that the visible results of Whitefield's vast labours in America soon disappeared. He himself referred to his labours as 'a rope of sand'. Not so Francis Asbury. He travelled, preached, exhorted, prayed, and led souls to Christ. But he did far more. He and his preachers organized new societies, demanded strict discipline, built

142

'meeting houses', formed new circuits and districts and Annual Conferences. He lived to see a small band of ten preachers and 1,160 members in 1773 grow to 678 preachers and 214,807 members in 1813.

The rate of this growth is graphically illustrated in the following table:

Date	No. of preachers	No. of members
1773	10	1,160
1783	83	13,740
1790	227	61,631
1800	287	64,894
1805	433	119,945
1810	635	174,560
1813	678	214,807

During all this time Asbury had been the official head, the inspiring leader, and the most prodigious labourer of the advancing hosts who had set out 'to reform this continent and spread Scriptural holiness throughout the land'.

As I have said elsewhere: 'Such a multiplication of disciples has seldom been known in the history of the Church, since the marvellous expansion in the first centuries of the Christian era. In this way the Lord of the harvest set His seal upon His faithful ministers. In the ardent language of their time, they were "given souls for their hire". Most of them succumbed to the hardships of the wilderness, to exposure, fever, and other maladies and went early to their graves. But they faltered not. "God buries His workmen, but carries on His work" was the maxim oft upon their lips. They followed the trail of the pioneers, the woodman's axe, the farmer's plough, and on this virgin soil they scattered the seed of gospel truth, the harvest of which is our heritage today, the Methodist Church, 11 million strong.'

The Elective General Superintendency

When Thomas Coke came to America in 1784, he carried a letter from Mr Wesley dated 10th September 1784: 'To Dr Coke, Mr Asbury, and our Brethren in North America. By a very uncommon train of providences many of the provinces of North America are totally disjoined from the mother country and erected into independent States. The English government has no authority over them, either civil or ecclesiastical, any more than over the States of Holland. A civil authority is exercised over them, partly by the Congress, partly by the provincial assemblies. But no one either exercises or claims any ecclesiastical authority at all. In this peculiar situation some thousands of the inhabitants of these States desire my advice, and in compliance with their desire I have drawn up a little sketch. Lord King's account of the primitive Church convinced me many years ago that Bishops and Presbyters are the same order, and consequently have the same right to ordain. For many years I have been importuned from time to time to exericse this right by ordaining part of our travelling preachers. But I have still refused not only for peace's sake, but because I was determined as little as possible to violate the established order of the National Church, to which I belonged.

'But the case is widely different between England and North America. Here are bishops who have a legal jurisdiction. In America there are none, neither any parish ministers; so that for some hundreds of miles together there is none either to baptize or administer the Lord's Supper. Here, therefore, my scruples are at an end, and I conceive myself at full liberty,

143

as I violate no order and invade no man's right, by appointing and sending labourers into the harvest. I have accordingly appointed Dr Coke and Mr Francis Asbury to be joint superintendents over our brethren in North America, as also Richard Whatcoat and Thomas Vasey to act as elders among them by baptizing and administering the Lord's Supper. And I have prepared a liturgy, little differing from that of the Church of England (I think the best constituted National Church in the world), which I advise all the travelling preachers to use on the Lord's Day in all the congregations, reading the litany only on Wednesdays and Fridays and praying extempore on all other days. I also advise the elders to administer the Supper of the Lord on every Lord's day.

'If any one will point out a more rational and Scriptural way of feeding and guiding these poor sheep in the wilderness, I will gladly embrace it. At present I cannot see any better method than that I have taken.

'It has indeed been proposed to desire the English Bishops to ordain part of our preachers for America. But to this I object: 1. I desired the Bishop of London to ordain one, but could not prevail. 2. If they consented, we know the slowness of their proceedings; but the matter admits of no delay. 3. If they would ordain them now, they would expect to govern them. And how grievously would this entangle us! 4. As our American brethren are now totally disentangled, both from the State and the English hierarchy, we dare not entangle them again either with the one or the other. They are now at full liberty simply to follow the Scriptures and the primitive Church. And we judge it best that they should stand fast in the liberty wherewith God has so strangely made them free.

'JOHN WESLEY.'

In this famous letter, in addition to authorizing them to 'follow the Scriptures and the Primitive Church', he boldly states: 'I have appointed Dr Coke and Mr Francis Asbury to be joint superintendents over our brethren in North America, as also Richard Whatcoat and Thomas Vasey to act as elders among them by baptizing and administering the Lord's Supper.'

When Coke unfolded this plan to Asbury, his sensitive soul and good judgement prompted Asbury to decline the general superintendency without election by the whole body of his fellow itinerants. Both Wesley and Coke had difficulty in understanding the spirit of their American brethren. Coke once assumed authority to change the date of a Conference while absent from the country. As a result he was forced to sign a humiliating agreement not to undertake to exercise such authority again. At the Baltimore Conference, 'The arbitrary action of Bishop Coke in changing the date of the annual sittings brought this whole matter to an issue. The contest was sharp, and for a time "The Little Doctor" attempted to justify his course. "You must consider yourselves my equals", he retorted sharply, upon which Nelson Reed, one of his aggressive critics in the Conference made the spirited reply: "Yes, Sir, we do; and we are not only the equals of Dr Coke, but of Dr Coke's king." '

With Asbury, whose growing sympathy with the colonies caused him to refuse to return to England along with other British Wesleyan preachers during the Revolutionary War and who even expressed gratification in his Journal when the Colonies gained their independence, the reaction was quite different. His refusal to become Mr Wesley's deputy superintendent marked him as a man of sound judgement and fraternal spirit.

'He showed his prescient grasp of the new situation in America, and his power to deal effectively with it, when he deliberately decided that no such episcopal authority as Wesley could have had him exercise would he dream of accepting, without first having it granted to him as a sacred trust by the deliberate vote of his ministerial brethren. This was an act of divine wisdom and prudence. It is quite certain that Wesley, with his imperious will and Tory principles, combined with his High Church views, could not have done what his peasant lieutenant so wondrously accomplished. Asbury studied, not only Wesley's discipline, but the temper of the men (and their fundamental ideas on all government, whether in State or Church) among whom he applied it, and, before issuing orders, ensured by his good judgement and tact that they would be obeyed. In the long run he performed something like a miracle in government, for what seems an aristocratic and monarchical ecclesiastical power was enthusiastically obeyed in the American Methodist Church, by men who had put down State Churchism, and had triumphantly asserted, as against the tyranny of the King and the British Parliament, the principle that all men are born free and equal, and that the people are not governed from above, nor from outside, but by themselves, through their own freely chosen and appointed representatives. What a king Asbury was among his daring fellow itinerants! He held at one time what seems almost an absolute autocracy among them. One gasps at reading that in one of the Conferences they resolved that, "on hearing every preacher for and against, the right of determination was to rest with him." The greatness of their trust was matched by the audacity of their action. Asbury, of course, was too shrewd and wise and humble to take advantage of all that they would fain give him. Cromwell refused the crown, and gained a greater thing, the Protectorship. Asbury governed by consenting to be governed. A free people under a strong episcopal authority was ably and successfully controlled, and a royal highway was blazed and built through a perfect jungle of thorny difficulties. Often Asbury's despair led him to write: "The Lord must see to His own Church." And He did, through patient modest Asbury.'

Asbury, knowing the American conditions as his long and frequent travels and close contacts with the people made possible for him, understood readily that an absentee control was neither desirable nor workable. One significant entry in his Journal runs: 'I do not think it practical expediency to obey Mr Wesley at 3,000 miles' distance in all matters relative to Church government.' At another time he asserted that his authority rested upon '1. Divine authority. 2. Seniority in America. 3. The election of the General Conference. 4. My ordination by Dr Coke. 5. Because the signs of an apostle have been seen in me.'

Results and Developments

If the limits of this paper permitted, it would be both appropriate and engaging to denote the beginnings of the outlines of Church life and institutions that had their origin under the guiding hand of Asbury. We mention here the (1) Elective General Superintendency; (2) the District Superintendency; (3) Appointive Itinerant Ministry; (4) an aggressive Evangelism; (5) the Constitution; (6) the Delegated General Conference; (7) beginnings of Boards and Institutions.

As early as 1789 this entry appears in the Minutes: 'What has been contributed for the Superannuate Preachers and the widows and orphans of Preachers? Answer 65L. SS.' When McKendree and Soule advanced to places of leadership and responsibility, Asbury happily adjusted himself to their wholesome advice and co-operation. Due in no small measure to his reasonable, calm, and patient controls, Methodism was saved from reverting to formal intellectualism on the one hand or plunging into an era of shallow and noisy emotionalism on the other.

Largely also by his guidance, message, and example, there was established a wholesome balance between the individual and the social gospel. This entry appears in his Journal: 'What absurdities will not men defend! If the Gospel will tolerate slavery, what will it not authorize?' The Conference Minutes contain repeated references to the iniquity of human slavery. Only the patient forbearance of Asbury prevented a division of the Church over this vexing question, but he never at any time compromised or toned down his personal views. In respect of other moral issues, such as drinking and drunkenness, gambling, racing, and Sabbath desecration, the early American Methodists maintained high ethical standards.

It is not our object or intent so to exalt Asbury as in the least respect to take from other noble leaders their due credit for their matchless record or service and sacrifice. There were such lofty souls as Pilmoor, Rankin, Strawbridge, Whatcoat, Jessie Lee, John Dickens, Freeborn Garretson, William Watters, Ezekiel Cooper, William Kendree, Joshua Soule, and many others whose names are in the book of life, including Black Harry. But our task and privilege has been to tell of the one man whose devotion and wisdom welded together these various personalities into a force of spiritual unity and ecclesiastical progress.

Francis Asbury, the typical itinerant, the Bishop on horseback, will ride at the head of the advancing columns of American Methodists until they shall be disbanded when the final victory of the militant Church shall bring the kingdoms of this world under the dominion of the risen, reigning Son of God.

'There he goes—an embodied itinerancy, a Bishop whose episcopal throne is in the saddle, whose diocese is a continent.'

If the Spirit of God that so wonderfully anointed, inspired, and sustained Francis Asbury and his comrades of the Cross would come in like manner upon the ministry and membership of our great Church today, world-wide Methodism would write a new and glorious chapter in our noble history. We would then go forth to reform all continents and to spread Scriptural holiness, brotherhood, justice, and peace throughout this troubled world.

'Lead on, O King eternal,
The day of march has come.
Henceforth in fields of conquest
Thy tents shall be our home.'

'For he was a good man full of the Holy Ghost and faith and much people was added unto the Lord.'

SIXTH DAY

Sunday 2nd September

THE Sunday sessions of the Conference began with the celebration of Holy Communion at Wesley Memorial Church. The service was conducted by the Rev. Walter J. Noble and Bishop Ivan Lee Holt was the preacher. Some of the ministerial delegates assisted in the service and the large number of communicants represented Methodism in all parts of the world.

THE FORWARD LOOK

A sermon preached by BISHOP IVAN LEE HOLT:

Text: 'We are saved by hope' (Romans 8^{24}).

In the summer of 1937 the Archbishop of Canterbury preached at St Paul's Cathedral. It was a Sunday between the Oxford Conference on Life and Work, and the Edinburgh Conference on Faith and Order. In the congregation were the delegates to those two conferences coming from forty different lands and a hundred different communions. The Archbishop announced as his theme 'Looking Forward', and took as his text 'Speak unto the children of Israel that they go forward'. What a difference there is between the temper of our times and that of the summer of 1937! Reading over that sermon now, one realizes how much our thinking has been changed within these fourteen years. To a much older message I turn this morning for guidance, but to one which seems in the sweep of its thought to possess the element of timelessness, the Epistle to the Romans. The author of that Epistle was a realist. He never buried his head in the sand, but looked straight at the facts of life. No one could accuse him of shallow optimism. The pain and tragedy of the world were ever before him, and no theologian was ever more vividly aware of the sinfulness of man or the prevalence of evil. 'The whole creation groaneth and travaileth in pain together until now.' Yet Paul was so sure of the transforming power of God, through Christ in human life and in this world that he could write with confidence: 'We are saved by hope.' 'If God be for us who can be against us?' 'Tribulation worketh patience; and patience experience; and experience hope.' In directing your thinking to 'the Forward look', it is to the twenty-fourth verse of the eighth chapter of Romans I turn for our text: 'We are saved by hope.'

In an admirable biography of Christopher Columbus called *The Admiral of the Ocean Seas*, we are told that the explorer often recorded in his diary the prayer: 'May Jesus Christ go with us on the way.' Then at the close of each day, whether the sailing was pleasant or the sea was rough, whether the crew was co-operative or mutinous, he wrote at the end of the entry the word *'Adelante'* (Forward).

When the Children of Israel journeyed to Canaan, they came to a mountain that blocked the way. Some voices called them back to Egypt, where they had food and shelter even if they were slaves. Some voices insisted on waiting for a miracle that would remove the mountain as the sea had opened to let them pass. But the leader called: 'Turn you and

147

take your journey and go.' As an obstacle blocks the way, those three voices can always be heard: 'Turn back to yesterday'. 'Wait for God to work a miracle.' 'Go on.' It is God's command that we go, and advancement is His will, was the word of the Hebrew leader.

Unfortunately, we are living in a time when the idea of progress is challenged. (1) A young man says to me on a train: 'Youth wonders why there should be effort in college when the graduate exchanges his diploma for a rifle. (2) A lay churchman from England, at a luncheon in New York is sure that hosts of people in Europe have ceased to believe in the possibility of progress. (3) With the vast manpower of Communist groups, the determined opposition of Communism to Christian civilization, and the fear of devastating attacks from the air, there is such uncertainty about the future as to produce terror. As I began my ministry, we were anticipating the speedy coming of the Kingdom of God. Then came the first world war. There followed great dreams of peace, and suddenly a second world war shattered hopes of a better day.

Of course, there were in the early years of this century prophecies of doom. Oswald Spengler, in his *Decline of the West*, previewed the advance and failure of numerous civilizations, finding in their reasons for decline the same situations as in his contemporary West. Brooks Adams, in the *Law of Civilization and Decay*, argued that every prosperous nation becomes too cruel and greedy to last. However, our Christian faith in the social gospel, the creation of the League of Nations, and the signing by fifty-four nations of the Pact to Outlaw War kept our hopes high. When Dean Inge, the gloomy Dean of St Paul's, preached his farewell sermon, he voiced the desires of a great section of the Christian world: 'We are living in a perplexing age, perhaps the most perplexing the world has ever known, but, to quote Meredith, "We must not lose the value of the forward look".'

But this is another time, and the most widely discussed Christian interpretation of our world expresses pessimism as to the outlook in any world order. The neo-orthodoxy of Kierkegaard, Barth, and in the United States, the brilliant Reinhold Niebuhr points to the sinfulness of war and ridicules the idea of progress which was for so many years the preachment of theological liberalism. Says Niebuhr: 'There is not a single bit of evidence to prove that good triumphs over evil, in this constant development of history.' Another thought of his is this: There are some things the Christian can do to bring in more of freedom and justice in a better brotherhood, but 'even the inborn man in whom the spirit of love has become the new way of life still lives in a world which contradicts that love, and the conflict is never resolved in this life, even within his own soul'.

In his searching analysis of man's plight, Niebuhr regards 'the doctrine of original sin as a myth which is absurd to reason and necessary to faith'. He says that we are finite creatures living our lives in the insecurity, the mystery of nature and history. 'As finite creatures, we become anxious in the face of perplexities. Anxiety is temptation to sin, to take flight from the self or turn to pride in which we make ourselves more secure than we have a right to be.' Those thinkers among us who have turned so eagerly to Kierkegaard and Barth and Niebuhr for intellectual support of their positions had better read more carefully or think more deeply about where these theologians are taking us. They stress war, barbarity, and sin as continuous evidences of human failure. There is no hope in their thinking of any growth of a Kingdom of God on earth. The Kingdom is an eternal one and is not of this world. Man can do nothing to create a better world here. That must wait for God's good time!

Such a belief as this is a thoughtful challenge to the old liberalism. While there is too much of a tendency in contemporary pessimism to stress the shallowness in the optimism of yesterday, there is no doubt that many humanists were too sure of man's progress through his own efforts and that liberal theologians were a little too confident of the growth of love and brotherhood. Great books which ushered in the preaching of the social gospel were Canon Freemantle's *The World as the Subject of Redemption* and Rauschenbusch's *A Theology for the Social Gospel*. Neither book was shallow; neither ignored the fact of sin; neither failed to stress the need of God's grace. However, much of the preaching which flowed from them was so optimistic about a new Jerusalem on earth that it needed the correction of the emphasis on sin and tragedy in this world.

One of the most thoughtful books of this whole present-day discussion is *Agape and Eros*, by Bishop Anders Nygren of Sweden. *Agape* and *eros* are the two Greek words for 'love' in the New Testament, and in his study Nygren sets forth the fundamental motif of Christianity, the answer which it gives to the most important questions which can be asked concerning the way of salvation. *Nomos* (or law) is the motif in Judaism, and there man becomes acceptable to God through conformity to God's law. In Hellenic philosophy and religion it is *eros* as love which leads man to God. But *agape* is a New Testament word for love, which indicates the forgiving love of God poured out for the redemption of man. Man is incapable of *agape*, and thus the whole conception of man's love for God becomes a puzzle in Nygren's interpretation.

Daniel Day Williams, in his lectures on *God's Grace and Man's Hope*, feels that Nygren has overstated his case. He is sure that much of what liberalism stressed is of value. He is sure that there is possible a transformation of man through God's grace that promises a better world here. In this neo-liberalism we are much closer to our Methodist and Arminian tradition than in the neo-orthodoxy of Kierkegaard and Barth and Niebuhr. Their position is much more basically Calvinistic, and in the addresses at the first Assembly of the World Council of Churches this point of view was so frequently presented that a letter calling attention to the Calvinism in the utterances was sent to each of our preachers in the United States who received a copy of the proceedings of the Assembly. We are not shut up in our thinking to a choice between an old liberalism which neo-orthodoxy attacks and neo-orthodoxy itself. We recognize the fact that neo-orthodoxy is making a fight for Christian faith right up to the gates of Hell, but we can honour its spirit without accepting its conclusions, if our own liberalism comes to deeper evaluations of grace and love.

Let us turn from the theological controversies of our day to the original sources of our faith, the Holy Scriptures.

The Old Testament has a philosophy of history—prosperity, sin, punishment, repentance, prosperity! There are two emphases in all prophetic interpretations: (1) God is always near, and (2) there is a new order to come. The priest and the seer found different ways out of difficulty and perplexity. The Old Testament prophets wrestled with the very problems of sin and God's Providence, of failure and man's hope, which disturb us. They never came to a perfect solution. But Jeremiah came to a new experience of God when the God he had preached seemed to have failed. The great Prophet of the Exile lived in a dark night, and the world was devastated as it is now. But he clung to faith in a Creator God, a God who brings nations to judgement, and a God whose forgiving love can make new men and a new order of justice and righteousness. In the New Testament the historical perspective is shorter, but there too God is ever

149

near; the Kingdom of God is within men; and a new society of new creations is possible. To Jesus God is Creator, Companion of the way, and Guide into the future. For Paul the ministry of Jesus closes the door of the old house where a man has lived, through God's forgiveness; it is such a stay in life that no calamities can separate one from the love of Christ, it brings an assurance of man's redemption here and hereafter. Paul was aware—*vividly* aware—of man's sin, and the groaning of creation; evil is present with the good. Nevertheless, he looks for such transformations as he had known. The New Testament Church was certainly more than a spectator in an age of change: it was an agency because it had Paul's great concepts of its mission: 'Ye are the body of Christ.' 'We are a colony of Heaven.' 'Ye are Christ's and Christ is God's.'

Turning back now to our contemporary world, there is a contrast between the Catholic and the Protestant concept of the Church's mission. The one emphasizes tradition and the other experience. In a widely read study of spiritual movements within the Church called *Enthusiasm*, Monsignor Ronald Knox calls attention to the fact that Wesley's heart-warming experience brought to the Church a revival which reached thousands of people, but that such outbursts of religious enthusiasm were known before Wesley's day. All through the history of the Church from the early days there have been vivid experiences of religion which have led men to impatience with the Church as it is. Sometimes these men and their movements have been incorporated in the Church, as was true in the case of St Francis. Sometimes there have been breaks from the Church and new organizations. Through the years the Roman Catholic Church has stressed tradition, and has been the haven of refuge for distressed and troubled souls. Perhaps a Church may some time stress both interpretations of the approach to religion, the historical and the psychological.

Are we too bold if we emphasize the fact that the Methodist Church has both approaches to religion—the historical and the psychological—not enough emphasis on tradition to satisfy the Roman Catholics or some Protestants of the extreme right, nor the kind of emphasis on experience to satisfy some of the newer sects and Protestants of the extreme left? Neo-orthodoxy commends itself to the extremists of the right and the left, but for the great middle group to which Methodism belongs neo-liberalism offers, in my thinking, a much more congenial interpretation. The thing which concerns me deeply is that we should find a faith realistic enough to face facts, but one also which can save us from pessimism and hopeless despair about our present world! I want that for pulpit and pew!

The prophet Habakkuk, challenged by those who asked, 'Where can God be in a world like this?' flung the challenge into God's face and had the answer: 'The righteous shall live by his steadfastness.' A Methodist layman in Great Britain, commenting to me on the picture of John Wesley preaching to the miners in Cornwall, said: 'The tears on the miners' faces are not only tears of repentance because Wesley talked to them about their sins; they are tears of joy because he assured them that, though they were not welcomed in great houses, they were children of a Heavenly King. They are tears of gratitude because Wesley preached to them of God's love which could redeem, and change.' Methodism's great mission has been to *see that no one misses the grace of God*, and Methodism has that word for these days. We can, with God's help, serve to recapture for a despondent world the 'rapture of the forward look'.

We face the future not as a Church which identifies itself with the Kingdom, nor one which feels itself a small remnant of the faithful in perpetual conflict with an alien universe. 'Our hope sees beyond the years

150

and we live in this demanding present under the everlasting assurance of God's love.' Close each day with the entry '*Adelante*', beloved Church, that at the beginning of each day may be heard God's voice: 'Turn you, take your journey and go.'

This does not mean that we support the philosophy of long-run optimism by which we believe in the certain progressive elimination of sin and evil. We must resist the temptation to accept that philosophy as we reject the pessimism of neo-orthodoxy. We voice our faith for the future in these words: 'Christian hope for human society is based on the fact of God's creative and redemptive working which is woven through the whole fabric of life. . . . Today to establish the City of Man on anything else than faith in God is to build on quicksand.' Those words of Williams set forth our faith, as do these sentences: 'Paul's faith that love hopeth all things is not sentimentality. It is the affirmation which Christian faith must make about what it means to trust in God.' 'For we are saved by hope.' 'If God be for us, who can be against us?' 'Tribulation worketh patience; patience experience; and experience hope.' That is the faith and must be the faith of Methodism.

On Sunday afternoon a Women's Service was held in Wesley Memorial Church, Oxford. The Chairman of the Women's Fellowship of the Methodist Church in Great Britain, Mrs D. H. Stoate, of Bristol, presided. The speakers were Mrs Franklin Reed, of New Jersey, President of the World Federation of Methodist Women, and Mrs Ladlay of the Mission House, London.

I FOUND METHODISTS HERE

An address given by MRS FRANKLIN REED, *President of the World Federation of Methodist Women:*

One of the writers in a recent issue of the *Saturday Review of Literature* states that there are certain points which we should bear in mind when we study the news coming out of the Far East, and after listing them he warns us that otherwise we cannot understand the complex challenge of Asia, where half the human race lives.

As I return from my visitation to the ten countries of Latin America where Methodism is at work, and attempt to share with you some of the great inspiration which came to me, I feel sure that here too there are certain facts which we should bear in mind if we are to understand the tasks which the Methodist women in those countries are undertaking as they try to lift their own people from shocking misery and paralysing despair.

For one thing, in spite of their national differences, there are in each country just two classes of people. This is one thing they all have in common. There is a very small ruling class made up of the educated and the privileged, and the other made up of hoards and hoards of the poor, hungry, and ignorant. The small class is called 'white', and is made up of pure Spanish, mixed with some white and other strains. The larger class is mostly Indian. The proportions differ, of course, in the several countries, but in a country like Bolivia, for instance, the figures show 20 per cent white and 80 per cent Indian.

So that when we add them all together, we may say: most of the people in Latin America live in grinding poverty, most of them cannot read or write, most of them have never seen a doctor.

Another fact which we should bear in mind is that although these ten nations are called republics, their presidents have been and are what we in America would call 'dictators'. So that again when we consider them as a whole, we can say that most people in Latin America have never known civil liberties and most have never heard of democracy.

A third fact is—and this is our great challenge as missionary women of the Church—this larger class oppressed now by poverty and disease has in many places a high cultural heritage and very real innate capacities. Many of these Indians are the descendants of ancient Incas and other high civilizations. So as yet they are merely undeveloped; and in sharing with them our Christian experience and scientific knowledge, we shall have much to gain as well as to share.

And, of course, we all know that we can say in general of these ten countries, most of the people are Catholic, and that the Roman Catholic Church makes the task of the Protestant very difficult.

I did not go to Latin America in an administrative capacity. The Woman's Division in the U.S. has work in only six of these countries, but the Board of Missions does carry on work in all ten. My first purpose was not to visit the Methodist schools and churches; nor even the missionaries, although I must pay the highest tribute to the warm welcome and help which they gave me. No, I went to visit the organized, Methodist, national women, of both classes, those who have come to know Christ and are now trying to share what they have found—to make Him known. Just how difficult their task is you will realize from the facts which we have been mentioning, and it was told me while I was there that if each Church member in North America (and I feel that the same could be said for this country) brought just one other person to Christ, the task of evangelism would be practically accomplished. To achieve a similar result in South America, each one would have to win 100 new members.

Passing very briefly over this part of my journey, I will say that it was rather strenuous travel for nine weeks, flying up and down and across the Andes, and by train, bus, and jeep into the isolated places as well as the large cities. But at each journey's end from sea-level up to 13,000 feet I found Methodist women there.

This is as good a place as any to say that the ten national groups which I visited in Latin America are only about one-third of the number of units of the World Federation of Methodist Women. The remaining twenty or twenty-five are in the countries of the Far East—the countries of Scandinavia, Central Europe, and the islands of the sea. And there may be a few people here who do not know that the idea for the Federation did not originate in the Church in America. Rather it grew out of the need of some of the smaller groups of Methodist women around the world, who asked for a closer contact with the large group in America and with each other.

Like most other bodies, it did not spring into life in any Minerva-like fashion, fully grown and ready for action. It was first called a sisterhood or a fellowship, and as it grew it became 'The International Department of the W.F.M.S.' Then, at the time of our unification in America, it was so large and so important, that it was made an agency of the General Conference and launched in 1940 as 'The World Federation of Methodist Women'. It has always been ecumenical in character, and from the very beginning its constitution provided membership for any group of Methodist women in the world, of whatever communion, if that group could subscribe to the common purpose of 'knowing Christ, and of making Him known'. The world has ever been its parish.

Well, I visited, then, ten nations of the Federation and stayed about a

152

week with each. Usually, because they were expecting me, a group of the national officers would be assembled for a meeting or a luncheon or dinner, according to the time of my arrival. We talked over their national problems, and mutual questions were answered. Then, usually on the second day, I began the visitation to their centres, where the women's groups were holding their meetings. Some of these corresponded to our district meetings at home, and often they were single groups, and, of course, I was always supposed to speak. Naturally, it was necessary to use interpreters, and in the case of the Indian women, who did not know Spanish, there had to be two interpreters: one changed my English into Spanish and the second changed the Spanish into Indian dialect. Some few times, as in the large cities of Montevideo and Buenos Aires, I met with English-speaking groups; and it was possible to speak to them in my own mother tongue, and I assure you I was much more relaxed.

It is obviously impossible to begin with Brazil, which is the country I visited first, and continue through the others, telling of each of my many wonderful experiences. So much must always remain unsaid! But if we here at Oxford today shall understand just a little more clearly the conditions and problems under which our sisters in Latin America must work, these thirty minutes will have been well spent.

I came home with these women on my heart, and my remembrance of them is never so vivid as when I sit in a group of privileged women like this and those in my own country.

I can so easily see the group of twenty-five Negro women out in the hot, humid rural country of Panama. I drove out to their meeting and found that they had no church building, but were meeting in a house built high upon stilts. When I had climbed the swaying flight of steps, I found them standing around a long home-made table, singing in Spanish their welcome song for me, and clapping their hands to its rhythm. As the roll was called, each answered to her name by telling what she had done for others that week, because they meet weekly.

One had gone every day to the prison to read the Bible to the prisoners. Another had stayed up all night with a friend whose husband had been violently drunk. And yet, in response to my simple talk about the needs of the world, they would ask: 'What can we do?' And all over Latin America I found women on fire to be doing something, so keenly did they realize world conditions and those of their own under-privileged masses.

Just so did the cultured and privileged women in the large cities ask the same question; and once in a while, an emotionally stirred single woman would say: 'What can I do?'

Amusing incidents happened constantly. One day in a rural church in Argentina, a large, buxom, and energetic woman came up after my address and said that she approved of my message, was thrilled with the World Federation, and certainly believed in the world Church, but she knew that there was just one way to bring the nations into unity and that was for me to go home, to go before Congress, and insist that learning Spanish should be a 'must' for every American boy and girl.

I had to smilingly assure her that to get before Congress was almost impossible for a woman; nor could any such reform come about that way. Here was a woman, however, who possessed the courage to attempt it.

And I can see the group which, I believe, is unique in the whole Methodist world. Twenty-four nurses in training, native girls in our beautiful Pfeiffer Memorial Hospital, have formed a Woman's Society. Somehow they are finding time to maintain a programme covering five departments—spiritual, missionary, social action, literary, and cultural.

153

One very interesting feature of their work is the placing of invitations on the hospital trays, inviting Catholic and Protestant, white class or Indian, to meet with them. Many avail themselves of this privilege while convalescing and are spiritually strengthened.

And I must squeeze in somehow what I consider my prize story.

I went overnight way down into the south of Chile, and then by jeep far out into the country to work being done among the Indians there. The missionary who was guiding me insisted that I meet and talk with an Indian who had been converted and was an active member of his Church. When I asked why he wanted me to meet a man when my object was to meet the women, he smiled and said: 'I want you to hear the story he has to tell in his own words.'

This man could not speak English, of course, but when translated, it was something like this, although it is impossible to reproduce his earnestness and his gestures:

'When I joined the Church, I found out that older Churches have Sunday-schools for children, so I started a Sunday-school and made all the children go.

'Then I heard that even women had societies of their own, so I said we will have one too. So I made all the women come, and told them what we were going to do, and I said not one of you can read so you can't be the President yet, but I will be your President now. And for two years I was the President of the women's society.'

I have saved the time to tell you of the group which is, in all Latin America, probably the most neglected. These are the Indian women high on the Altiplano, or 'high plain', of Bolivia, 13,000 feet above sea-level.

When a speaker at an earlier session spoke of a large group which had recently been discovered and which no one had ever known existed, I thought of these women. There they have been for centuries, treated like animals and exploited by their Government. In their land-locked country, held high above all others by snow-capped mountains, they can only look up at the sky and raise their eyes to the hills waiting for someone to help them. But there are organized Methodist women there. No one in their society can read or write, but they insisted upon singing a song for me which they had learned by heart: 'Jesus loves me, this I know.' Grandmothers singing this little child's song. And when I tried to tell them about the World Federation, they wonderingly asked: 'Are you sure *we* belong?' They could hardly believe it; they who were so accustomed to being 'passed by'.

The Methodist women in Bolivia have decided to start a campaign for literacy among their people, and are going to make it a rule that each woman who joins must be taught to read.

I came across the following letter which Dr Laubach, the great missionary 'literacy' expert, wrote at the time of his visitation to these Indians in 1942. He said:

'Tonight I had a spiritual experience which will echo through the rest of my life. It was an Indian prayer meeting in the Inaker church. After a long talk by the Pastor, the congregation knelt to pray. Everyone prayed aloud at the same time. It began with a murmur, then women's plaintive wails began to be heard above the rest, and presently they could be heard weeping. I heard the terrible cry of ages rising to God from broken hearts; and behind them I heard the bitter cry of all the illiterates in the world, the oppressed, the blind, the hopeless.'

Do you remember the startling figures which were given us at the time of the Madras Conference? How, 2,000 years after Christ had been on earth, one-half of His children were hungry, two-fifths of His children were illiterate or had only elementary educations, four-fifths of His children had no adequate medical care? Do you remember the call which came to the women from that same Conference in 1938? It was this: 'Women of the Churches are called upon to co-operate in promoting Christian action in reference to great common causes.'

Privileged, cultured women of world Methodism gathered here today, these contrasts which we have been considering (and which certainly exist all around the world) put upon us inescapable responsibilities. These are surely 'great common causes'.

And there are already many organized groups of Methodist women who ask to be allowed to stand by our sides and to do their part in bringing in a better world.

An address given by Mrs Ladlay, *of the Methodist Missionary Society, London:*

We have possibly interpreted the words of John Wesley, 'The world is my parish', in a wider sense than he could have intended, and it is improbable that he saw the people called Methodists so widely distributed throughout the world. But Wesley also wrote: 'In whatever part of the world I am I judge it meet, right and my bounden duty to declare unto all who are willing to hear the glad tidings of salvation.' We know therefore that he would have rejoiced to think that his followers would indeed take those glad tidings to so many; that from the ends of the earth a company like this could gather; and that it could be a company of women.

In a conference like this we cannot help but think of those early days when so many who had been converted under Methodism went overseas during the times of emigration from Europe. In addition to the great names, shipwrights, soldiers, merchants, artisans—in some cases, their wives—founded small Societies for their own spiritual well-being and were constrained to witness, to commend their Saviour to those amongst whom they found themselves.

Before the eighteenth century ended there were Societies in the West Indies, in many parts of the North American continent, in Gibraltar and West Africa. Why West Africa?

From Nova Scotia ex-African slaves who had been converted under Methodist preaching there went with others to the new settlement of Freetown and there established a Methodist Society. But the Society dwindled, and when the leaders were old men they appealed to the Church in Britain to send pastors for the flock, lest when they died the sheep should be scattered.

The care of the flock. The preaching of the Word: These are the two necessary parts of Methodist fellowship.

We have seen it go on for nearly 200 years, and we thank God for what He has done with the people called Methodists. How it warms our hearts to share this precious fellowship and to be with those who think and speak the same.

For two Sundays recently I have been in a small Swiss village. When the church bell rang I followed the people to church. How different from the church where I worship in England! The building was plain; the benches were hard; the singing was slow and restrained; the hour-glass attached to the pulpit filled me with alarm.

The sermon was the main part of the service: it was practically un-intelligible to me. Then came the feeling of being outside; but a few words were said which I understood, if I interpreted them correctly. At any rate, I suddenly knew that I was inside; I was in fellowship with these people speaking a strange language. Here was the flock of Christ and here the Word was being expounded. I was in the company of faithful believers and truly at home. For a Methodist is more than a Methodist: he belongs to the holy catholic Church.

Two words opened my heart and made me remember why I was in fellowship with the people. They were 'mystery' and 'sacrament'. For fellowship is so much more than the cosy feeling of belonging. We use the word so much in these days, and sometimes very lightly.

There is mystery in this fellowship of the people of God. We have it written for us in St Paul's Epistle to the Ephesians: 'Each one has been chosen by God—the very adopted child of God with full rights as an heir. Each one is allowed to know the secret of God's plan: that everything will find its perfection in Christ and all human history will be consummated in Him. Each one has a share in all that belongs to Christ. Each one possesses a bill of redemption like slaves set free. In Christ I who was dead now live.'

All this is God's free gift to me: nothing that I have done or could do earns it for me. Here is the mystery of God's regard for each one. And though it is so intensely personal, yet it may be the common experience of us all.

I was reading recently a comment on the hymns of Wesley. We sing:

'And can it be that I should gain
An interest in the Saviour's blood?'

Why can we sing so personal a sentiment without embarrassment? It is because those amongst whom we stand feel exactly the same; it is a shared experience.

'Sacrament' was the other word I heard, and I remembered that it meant originally the solemn oath of allegiance which a Roman soldier swore. It bound him to the service of Emperor and Empire. Each of us may accept the wonder of God's love and bind ourselves to His service: and in the doing we find ourselves in the company of others and are in fellowship.

But it is more than a promise on our side. We enter into a Covenant relationship with God, who promises us the strength to serve Him. God has bound Himself to us. He enables us to do His work.

Here, then, is our fellowship:

We are bound together because of the mystery of God's purpose for us and His gifts to us; we have a life to live in Christ; a service to give; a goodness to achieve. It is only real fellowship when we live close to Him.

So we must not narrow or restrict the meaning of the word. Youth fellowships, women's fellowships—by all means; but they are only part of a whole, and any separation will weaken the whole. Each has a special work to do and a service to give which enriches the whole.

What is our life in fellowship?

We are part of the company of people who believe on the Lord Jesus. Our fellowship transcends name and sect, colour and race, age and sex. We who are so happy in our world-wide Methodist fellowship know that it is not enough: we belong to the whole Church.

But from that same Methodism there is much to learn and a tradition to follow and honour.

The Society in Freetown asked for pastors to care for the flock and

156

preach the Word of God; otherwise the Society would die. Each of us is in a community called to share in the redeeming work of Christ whoever and wherever we are. Our relationship with each other is important. Our responsibility for each other is binding.

There is an intimate society in which we live as Christ's own people. There is a larger society composed of those we shall never see and never know. In both our fellowship involves us in the care of the flock. Each of us must find our particular duties.

One example will serve to show how widespread is our pastoral responsibility.

We cannot forget in these times those separated from us in a physical sense in a land like China. They are of our fellowship, although now we cannot meet them or send them tokens of our love. As we bring them into Christ's presence and intercede on their behalf, we exercise our pastoral responsibility. As in loving understanding we name their needs and problems before God, we are caring for them, and we and they remain in a fellowship which nothing can break.

Those early Societies in America and Europe and Africa were begun by ordinary men and women, often in their homes; they spread and grew because they also accepted the responsibility to declare the glad tidings of salvation to all who were willing to hear. We also know that our fellowship is sadly lacking unless others are being called and won.

We realize our strength in meetings like this, *but* we are well aware of the threatening hosts of evil without. Three things are necessary for each part of the Church in all the continents: that our inner life should be stronger; that we should build each other up; that we should witness boldly by life and by word.

Here is an incident from my missionary experience in Africa which may serve as a parable and sum up something of what I have been trying to say.

Leprosy is still a scourge in some parts of the world and nowhere more than in eastern Nigeria. When we first went there we saw many afflicted with the dreadful disease. We were able to offer no hope of physical relief.

One day my husband and I were visiting one of the villages in our Circuit. A leader in the church came with the sad news that he was afraid he had the disease. Fear was in his face, and a great sorrow. It meant that he was indeed an outcaste from society. For the well-being of his wife and children, he would have to leave home and live apart. But we had a word of hope for him that day! A doctor would come, bringing a healing medicine.

So Elijah was an early resident in the Leprosy Colony at Uzuakoli. After some time there he came one day to visit us. We inquired about his health. There was no fear or sorrow now in his face: there was joy and a wonderful peace. He said: 'When I first knew that I had leprosy I was very afraid and unhappy. I used to long for Heaven: I thought about it always. What is Heaven like? When shall I go to Heaven? I don't think about it now! I have found it: it is up there in the Colony.'

You can see what had happened to him. The burden of his fear and sorrow had been taken from him by the healing hands of the doctor. He was no longer an outcaste: he was wanted. There was work for him to do. He was a carpenter by trade, and he was helping in the building of houses for others who would come to share in the life and the salvation to be found in that colony. He was in a redeeming community; a colony of heaven!

We can apply the meaning of that simple story today:

157

'Be heaven, e'en now our soul's abode,
Hid be our life with Christ in God,
   Our Spirit Lord, be one with Thine:
Let all our works in Thee be wrought,
And filled with Thee be all our thought,
   Till in us Thy full likeness shine.'

He was in a redeeming community: a colony of heaven!

In the evening Divine Worship in the Wesley Memorial Church
was conducted by the Rev. Dr Oscar T. Olson, and the sermon was
preached by the Rev. Dr H. Watkin-Jones, President of the British
Conference.

A sermon preached by the REV. DR H. WATKIN-JONES:

Text: 'The Spirit himself beareth witness that we are children of God'
   (Romans 8[16]).

It is helpful for us to keep in thought Chapters 7 and 8 together. In Chapter
8 St Paul is probably taking a retrospective view of an earlier state of
spiritual frustration. He used to do what he loathed doing; he was powerless to do what he longed to do. His detestation of the bad and his longing
after the good were both of no avail, in view of what he describes as 'a
different law in my members, warring against the law of my mind'—in
other words, a sense that he was possessed by evil powers, 'world rulers of
this darkness'. He felt in bondage; he *was* in bondage. 'O wretched man
that I am! Who shall rescue me from this dead body?' But before Chapter
8 begins, he sets down the answer: 'I thank God through Jesus Christ our
Lord.' He was out of the prison house—on the hills where the winds of
God blow, out of dark bondage into 'the liberty of the glory of the children
of God'.
               'I woke, the dungeon flamed with light;
               My chains fell off, my heart was free. . . .'

When God sets a man free he knows it. So did Paul. He was now 'in
Christ Jesus', and there was therefore 'no condemnation' for him. It was
this sense of freedom through the Holy Spirit about which he writes in
Chapter 8.
   The adoration of God is the first claim of religion on any man. No less
is the Gospel of God's Son an offer—an offer of Himself, than which there
is no better 'News' in all the world. So, if the question ever presented itself
to us, is it possible to revel in a vital spiritual experience which will keep
our souls in peace, fortify us against all lower lusts, and change mere
existence into 'life—more abundantly'? the answer is here. So asserts the
holy catholic Church throughout all the ages. Here is the transforming
friendship in which all things become new.

               'Heaven above is softer blue,
               Earth around is sweeter green.'

And this new life, eternal and present, in Christ is sure and steadfast, for
time and eternity.
               'This anchor shall my soul sustain,
               When earth's foundations melt away.'

   At the foundation of such an experience is this text, a favourite one of
John Wesley's. His reference to the Spirit's witness is to 'an inward
impression on the soul of believers, whereby the Spirit of God directly

158

testifies to their spirit that they are the children of God'. This can only mean that every person who has this experience *knows* that all his sins are forgiven, and that he is completely reconciled to God. That experience came to Wesley on 24th May 1738. Two months earlier, on 27th March, before he himself entered fully on that experience, he was enabled to help a condemned prisoner into it. After prayer with him in Oxford Castle, Wesley described in his *Journal* the outcome:

'After a space he rose up, and eagerly said, "I am now ready to die. I know Christ has taken away my sins; and there is no more condemnation for me." The same composed cheerfulness he showed, when he was carried to his execution; and in his last moments he was the same, enjoying a perfect peace, in confidence that he was "accepted in the Beloved".'

Not as yet did that prisoner's guide know this for himself, but, when he did come to know it thus, he was convinced that God intended it to be the normal experience of Christian people. Surely, if condemned felons could have it, why not everyone? Hence, it was not for emotional fanatics who were 'made that way'; neither was it a mark of presuming persons, if only because pride would, of all things, ensure its impossibility. So we may declare that the recovery of this evangelical truth as the privilege of all believers was Wesley's most notable contribution to the faith of the Church. That this was the plain fact must have brought some regret to him, for he insisted that this truth was upheld by the early Fathers and also in the Articles and Homilies of the Church of England. At first he asserted that unless one had this experience one was not saved by Christ. This mistake on the part of both Charles and himself he readily admitted: 'I wonder they did not stone us.' But his more mature judgement that the witness of the Spirit is the *privilege* of believers became a firmly rooted conviction from which he never moved. Surely St Paul had meant precisely the same—namely, that we may possess an utterly transforming experience, not on the ground of our imagination, still less on that of our own merit, but on that alone of the Divine salvation. 'For other foundation can no man lay than that which is laid, which is Jesus Christ.'

I alluded to Wesley's *recovery* of this truth. Indeed, it would appear that, until Wesley's time, hardly anybody would believe it—certainly in the wide sense in which he was sure that the Apostle wrote. Little encouragement was given to it by the Papacy. An accustomed example of this is a letter written to Pope Gregory I (the Great) by a lady of the Eastern Emperor's Court at Constantinople, who declared that she could have no peace of mind until she knew from him that her sins were forgiven. To this the Pope replied that she had made an unprofitable request, 'because', in the translation usually given, 'thou oughtest not to become secure about thy sins except when, in the last day of thy life, thou shalt be able no longer to bewail them. But, until that day comes, thou oughtest, ever suspicious and ever fearful, to be afraid of faults and wash them with daily tears.' It is significant that the Pope did not deny the reality of the Spirit's witness, but he so narrowed its scope as almost to deny it. Only on the last day of one's life, and even then not to every dying Christian, might the Witness be granted.

This is by no means surprising where the authority of the priest is particularly stressed. In a sacerdotal system the priest, after hearing confession, may declare that the penitent is absolved from his sins. But where the belief prevails that the Spirit of God directly assures the penitent of his present salvation, what is the essential need of the priestly pronouncement? The New Testament speaks joyously of the former, and nothing of the latter.

The Reformers were not so encouraging as might be expected concerning this subject, largely on account of their belief in predestination. That great herald of the Reformation, John Wyclif, strongly denied any consciousness of one's acceptance with God—no, not even on the part of a Pope. A Pope might be 'a limb of the fiend', for all he knew! Luther always believed in Assurance on the ground of one's baptism, faith in Christ, and membership of the Church. The teaching of the Roman Church to which allusion has been made he characterized as 'pernicious' and 'devilish'. At the same time, where predestination now and again intruded as the skeleton at the feast, there could hardly have been, in the official Lutheran theology at least, the glad certainty which later caused the Methodists to rejoice. In any case, as Luther came more and more into contact with 'certain proud fanatics' who did 'arrogantly and presumptuously boast possession of the Holy Spirit', something of his earlier emphasis on Assurance seemed to slip into the background.

In Calvin's teaching, God gives a 'peculiar testimony' to His elect, who have a 'sure ground of confidence' imparted to them by the Holy Spirit. This is confirmed 'if we are in communion with Christ', and strengthened by our part within His Church. Further confirmation is derived from the Word and the sacraments, as we give heed to the former and partake of the latter. With some believers there is a perpetual struggle with their own distrust, yet, says Calvin, they are victorious because they have recourse to faith. It is as well, then, for believers in Christ to assume that they have been elected! Little wonder that the Methodist Church historian, the late Dr H. B. Workman, declared that 'with Calvin a logical doctrine of Assurance is impossible; for inasmuch as the source of salvation is external, in the immutable decrees, the certitude of salvation must take the form of a special external revelation'. In other words, we are once more thrown back on the Romanist position, with its insecurity and possibility of illusion. A similar outlook characterized much of the thought of English Calvinists. Faith is the gift of God; of a surety it is. But to say that if a man has not faith God never intended to give it to him—this is a position impossible to be reconciled with the gospel.

Before the time of Wesley we find an exception to prevailing English belief in that of John Bunyan. We remember how, in *The Pilgrim's Progress*, burdened Christian came in his pilgrimage to 'a place somewhat ascending, and upon that place stood a cross'; before that cross the burden fell off his shoulders, tumbled down the hill into a sepulchre, and was never seen by him again. We may remember that, at the cross, Christian received from the Third Shining One (manifestly the Holy Spirit) 'a mark upon his forehead' and 'a roll with a seal upon it, which he bid him look on as he ran, and that that he should give it in at the celestial gate. . . . Then Christian gave three leaps for joy, and went on, singing.' Clearly, the 'roll' stood for the Witness of the Holy Spirit in his heart. Next, the pilgrim loses the roll as he sleeps the sleep of spiritual sloth. His joy is gone, he cannot go on without it; then he retraces his steps to the place where he slept, and recovers it. 'Who can tell', Bunyan comments, 'how joyful the man was when he had gotten his roll again? For this roll was the assurance of his life, and acceptance at the desired haven. . . . O, how nimbly now did he go up the rest of the hill!'

The Hill Difficulty is steep. It may have differing gradients for different people, but it stands full in the way of all. No one can by-pass it. Yet God never meant people to be weighed down by the burden of sin in addition. That is why Bunyan makes his pilgrim see the cross before he sees the hill, and at that cross the burden vanishes. It has gone, and well he knows it

160

has. Then, with the assurance of forgiveness in his heart, he climbs 'nimbly'.

Such is the picture of radiant Christianity. What a commendation of the gospel this is! Local churches here and there would not feel driven to attract 'outsiders' by betaking themselves to doubtful expedients if their members possessed it. The 'pearl of great price' is its own best recommendation.

But is there no peril in all this? Certainly there is. In the seventeenth and eighteenth centuries in England there was a name for it—'enthusiasm', by which was meant fanaticism; and it was duly abhorred as such. John Howe, Puritan divine and domestic chaplain to Oliver Cromwell, asserted that the new life in God did not mean any 'enthusiastical assurance'—to the exclusion of external revelation or the exercise of reason. And he was right. But there is no need to exclude either; indeed, it were fatal to make the attempt, for the assurance that Christ is one's Saviour must be based on the revealed Word of God and appropriated by both mind and spirit. Yet what misunderstanding there was in England about this, even on the part of wise and godly men! 'Sir', once said the great Bishop Butler to John Wesley, 'the pretending to extraordinary revelations and gifts of the Holy Ghost is a horrid thing, a very horrid thing.' But, when Butler came to die, he sought for something of the very Assurance he had so seriously doubted years before. To his chaplain he said: 'Though I have endeavoured to avoid sin, and to please God to the utmost of my power, yet from the consciousness of perpetual infirmities I am still afraid to die.' 'My lord', said the chaplain, 'you have forgotten that Jesus Christ is a Saviour.' 'True', said Butler, 'but how shall I know that He is a Saviour for *me*?' 'My lord', replied the chaplain, 'it is written: "Him that cometh to me I will in no wise cast out." ' 'True', said the Bishop; 'and I am surprised that, though I have read that Scripture a thousand times over, I never felt its virtue till this moment; and now I die happy.'

Now let us come to the classic example of John Wesley's own experience. We remember how, on that evening in May 1738 he went, as he says, 'very unwillingly', to a Religious Society meeting in Aldersgate Street in the City of London at a spot now marked by a tablet outside a bank. There, while someone was reading Luther's Preface to the Epistle to the Romans, he realized the saving power of God through faith in Christ: 'I felt my heart strangely warmed. I felt I did trust in Christ, Christ alone, for salvation; and an assurance was given me, that He had taken away my sins, even mine, and saved me from the law of sin and death.' Was this a delusion? Definitely not, as is proved by what was next recorded: 'I began to pray with all my might for those who had in a more especial manner despitefully used me and persecuted me.' If any of us is not prepared to do the latter he cannot rightly lay claim to the former.

I can picture that little man, five feet and five inches in height, humanly defenceless, going out to the rough colliers of that Bristol suburb of Kingswood whom the citizens dared not visit, standing among them and teaching them to sing his brother's hymn:

'My God, I *am* Thine,
What a comfort divine,
What a blessing to *know* that my Jesus is mine!'

As they sang it the tears welled out of their eyes, and made white channels down their grimy cheeks.

I wonder if any may say: 'I wish I could feel like this. What am I to do?' There is no better answer than that which St Paul gave to the Philippian jailer: 'Believe on the Lord Jesus, and thou shalt be saved.' It is important to remember that salvation is not by feeling, but by *faith* —by what our fathers used to call 'a recumbency on God'. As we cast our all upon Him, we are saved for Christ's sake, for it is God who in Christ reconciles sinners unto Himself. The feeling of joy we can again trust to God to give us, and trust implicitly, when once the deed for us and in us has been accomplished. In Wesley's case, before he returned home that same night from Aldersgate Street, he was called upon to face that very issue: 'It was not long before the enemy suggested, "This cannot be faith; for where is thy joy?" Then was I taught, that peace and victory over sin are essential to faith in the Captain of our salvation; but that, as to the transports of joy that usually attend the beginning of it, especially in those who have mourned deeply, God sometimes giveth, sometimes withholdeth them, according to the counsels of His own will.'

The same temptation came again on the morrow after he had heard a joyous anthem at St Paul's: 'The enemy injected a fear, "If thou dost believe, why is there not a more sensible change?" I answered (yet not I), "That I know not. But this I know, I have 'now peace with God'. " ' There is enough here to know; and God will do the rest.

The Assurance, even though God gives it, is of deliverance from *present* sin. It brings no guarantee of its continuance, however our spiritual life may fluctuate. We may need to test its presence by our study of the Bible, by our own conscience, by the fruits of our character, by the experience and guidance of fellow Christians. But let us realize that we are saved far more by God's hold upon us than by our hold upon Him. It is the sure knowledge that Christ is All in All to us which brings the sense of triumph and peace. Joy in God, overwhelming, indescribable, is only for those who cast away their pride, and taste to the full His infinite mercy.

Meetings were also held in Reading and Swindon on Sunday evening.

A Youth Service in Whitley Hall, Reading, was conducted by the Rev. Leonard P. Barnett, Methodist Youth Department, London, and the speakers were the Rev. Harold Ewing, Director, Youth Department, Methodist Church of America, and Dr O. K. Ogan, of West Africa.

OUR LIVES: THE LEAVEN

An address delivered by the REV. HAROLD W. EWING, *Director, Youth Department, Methodist Church of America, at Reading:*

These are days of unparalleled crisis for our world and all who live in it. This is an inescapable fact which no one can avoid. It screams from the headlines, it roars from the radio, and you can't gather with your friends for a few minutes of casual conversation without the talk turning to the perilous times in which we find ourselves, the new world crisis, or the haunting danger in which we all live.

In a recent issue of the *Saturday Review of Literature*, the Editor, Norman Cousins, out of his rich background of observing the complexity of human events, wrote: 'The human community today is in one of those rare pivotal points in history. A wrong turning now would mean that nothing on earth will become cheaper than human life . . . but a proper

162

turning now could mark the beginning of a vast upward surge in human history, infusing life with enriched purpose and meaning. There is a precarious balance between terror and hope, both of which have their legions and their momentum.'

As civilization stands at mid-century, the tempo of the day has become one of emergency, crisis, danger, hazard, concern—and it is our world! We see it reflected in the taut faces of our friends and find it mirrored in the tense human relationships of everyday life.

What are the elements that contribute to this day of doom in which we live? For it is important that we understand the factors which create this era of crisis. An important factor in this crisis of our time is the un-abashed, unmoral standard in many sections of so-called smart society and the flagrant immorality which parades through every community, every school and campus, and through many of the homes of the world. We have come to the place that many believe 'the sky is the limit'. People now have the idea that if they can 'get away with it', their conduct, therefore, must be all right. We are well aware of this condition in which we live, and many of our people with Christian courage hold to their standards. But, indecency, divorce, gambling, delinquency, the breakdown of the home are all symptoms of the fact that the basic moral foundation of society and of individual life is all together lacking or rapidly giving away. The stark fact is that the world is attempting to build without moral foundations.

There are many historians who attribute the fall of France to the moral decay within the very life of France and not the threat of the *Panzer* movements of the German armies. France thought herself to be im-pregnable within her Maginot Line, the finest defence ever built by man. But when the fall came it was not by breaching the Maginot Line, but by the moral and spiritual capitulation of the French people. This is not an isolated condition. Within the past week the public Press has reported the elder statesman of the United States, former President Herbert Hoover, as saying, 'Our greatest danger is not from foreign armies.... Our dangers are that we might commit suicide from within by complaisance with evil, or by public tolerance of scandalous behaviour or by cynical acceptance of dishonour. These evils have defeated nations many times in human history.'

Another significant element in the crisis of our day is that we have given God the back seat in our lives, or, to be more honest, we have actually shown God the back door. This secularism denies God, ignores Him, or declares Him to be irrelevant to the affairs of our daily life. It is the spirit of our time which enhances things and ignores persons; that enshrines tangibles and mocks the intangibles; that glorifies science and belittles spiritual elements of life. This is an easy attitude for a scientific world which only recently unlocked the secret of nuclear fission and un-leashed the incredible power of the atom. It is an easy attitude for a civilization that feels it has become too big for God. But the very growth of secularism has undermined the foundations of stable living.

A haunting witness to this growing secularism comes from the lack of participation in our services in the Church. In the United States socio-logists tell us that there are at least 15 million youths under sixteen years of age who have never been inside the door of the church. At the Toronto Convention of the World Council on Christian Education the pre-conference discussion guide stated: 'The Churches have never really had the youth.' In a recently published study by Bryan Reed, made of the youth of Birmingham, England, and entitled *Eighty Thousand Adolescents*, he concludes that 75 per cent of the youth of Birmingham are out of

163

touch with any form of organized religion. Growing secularism has led to the hardening of the arteries of the spiritual lives of millions of the world's peoples.

Our society became jittery with fear and suspicion. So saturated has it become that many keen observers say that society has developed a neurosis of fear and hatred that renders it incapable of sustaining normal relationships of goodwill and brotherhood. At one time we were content to confine our suspicions to those in far-removed places. But rapid transportation and instantaneous communications have wiped away the barriers, and now we even suspect those among whom we live. Our next-door neighbours, friends in our own social group, our teachers, our students, our government officials—all of them are subject to this spreading neurosis of fear that grips much of life. It becomes a vicious chain-reaction as the atoms of hate are broken with explosive brutality. So insidious does it become that even generous deeds prompted by honest and sincere motives become suspect as the poisoned minds of individuals and nations seek to find an ulterior motive. The growth of this cancerous spirit renders nations incapable of working together in the parliament of mankind.

The fourth factor in the crisis of this century is the weakness of the Church. It is not that the Church has failed, but rather that the Church has been unable to make a sufficiently strong impact upon the world this century. At the recent meeting of the Central Committee of the World Council of Churches at Rolle, Switzerland, we were in conversation with a number of the Church leaders. Upon one point they agreed: that the Church is under the judgement of God for not being able to remove the conditions which have led to two major wars in one generation and sustained international unrest through this century. Too many are not giving strength to the Church in this day of crisis. They support the Church, but feel that God's purposes will be fulfilled as the staff of the Church, the clergy and educators, carry on the work of the Church. They serve the Lord by proxy. They feel that they discharge their obligation to God by giving financial support to the kingdom's causes. Others in this day have retreated into a crisis theology which places all of the responsibility for building better relations between mankind and averting the crisis of these days in the province of God. They enrich their own personal religious lives and are content to sit by the hearth in their rocking chairs, waiting for God to take over. Neither position was shared by the Master, and neither will cause positive, militant work to be done in the name of Christ in this needy day when the world is looking to the Church for leadership.

This is not a bright picture, but it *is* the world in which we live painted with the colours as we see them. For one of the qualities of youth is to want to face the facts of their life as they are without artificial colouring. These are the frightening, grim, fearsome facts which are the substance of daily life which have caused the thinkers of this day to sound a warning to the Christians and non-Christians alike in the world. Elton Trueblood, Professor at Earlam College in Richmond, Indiana, writing in one of his recent books, declared that civilization is in a race with catastrophe. Looking carefully at the facts as he sees them, he feels that there is very little hope for averting the catastrophe unless the Christian Church takes firm and immediate steps to make Christianity the power in life which it can be.

Centuries ago Jesus looked out at His world and saw many of these same factors. Time and again He was filled with despair, but through all of His experience there was a note of hope. In speaking to His disciples, he said: 'The Kingdom of Heaven is like unto leaven which a woman took and hid in three measures of meal till the whole was leaven.' It is my firm conviction that the youth of the Methodist Church constitute the agency for carrying that leaven to the Church, the community, and the world in these days of crisis. I recall my grandmother, in Ohio, preparing the dough for the good home-made bread. In the early evening she would place all of the ingredients into the large wooden dough-tray and with experienced hands knead them into a graceful, symmetrical lump. Just before completing her task, she would slip out to the spring-house and bring in a pinch of yeast—the leaven for the lump—and knead that pinch of leaven into the lump. Spreading a clean white cloth over the huge dough-tray— with its small lump of flour and water and yeast—she would place it on the floor behind the old wood stove and slip off to bed. As the fire died out of the stove the heat would begin to fill the dough-tray and warm the lump of dough. In the morning, long before the family would be stirring, Grandmother would come to the kitchen and look into the dough-tray. The magic of chemistry had been at work—just as Jesus had seen it time and again—for the small lump of dough had risen until the cloth had raised off the tray and some of the sticky mass had oozed over on to the floor. The magic of chemistry, expanding each small cell, had caused the dough to increase in size and grow until every segment of the dough now had the property of the pinch of yeast Grandmother added the previous night. Jesus was saying to His followers that His Kingdom grows like that —heart touches heart, and life touches life with the divine alchemy known to God alone; and His cause is spread as the eternal laws of God operate in human life.

For the past eight months as I have moved among the youth of the United States, I have asked them: 'What should be the message to the youth of the world in this day?' I have received answers from hundreds of them, and they have expressed a message of realism, yet of hope, for this day. This message is really the message of youth speaking to the youth of the world. In the world of crisis and despair I find hope in the youth of our Church as they dedicate themselves to His purposes and go forth to serve their God.

In the lives of youth I see signs of hope as youth turns to God with deepened and renewed faith. In an atomic age of science and pseudo-science men have become dazzled by their own brilliance and the unfolding of scientific discovery until they believe themselves to be the masters of all of life. Men pride themselves and become vain in their power and say, 'God is but a figment of the imagination' and 'We have no need for faith and superstition'. In the delirium of their new power they forget that the power of the atom is but the power of God and the processes of science are but the processes of God. The greatest need of this century is for a return to a firm and unshakable faith in God; for the renewal of the stabilizing trust in the infinite power of God. A few years ago a prominent American magazine took a poll of American public opinion to ascertain the percentage of persons in America believing in God. Following the poll they made the astounding announcement that 94 per cent of the people believed in God. Regardless of one's attitude toward the reliability of opinion polls, the thinking person immediately rejects the conclusions: 94 per cent of the American people could not believe in God and have the kind of attitudes which American people have toward moral standards, home and family life, Church responsibilities, vocational ethics, international relationships, and a dozen other areas where one's faith becomes

165

operative. I am confident that a similar conclusion could be drawn from other countries where the Methodist Church is at work. A man cannot behave like a practising atheist and then affirm his faith in God. There is a need for a renewal of what George Buttrick calls the 'dangerous venture of Love' until we know from the very depths of our beings that God is, and is concerned about us as individuals. There is need for far more than the intellectual consent which pervades many of our universities. We are in need for seeking after God until, as a profound personal experience, we know Him as a companion and guide.

John Wesley had been raised in the spiritual environment of the parsonage home, had disciplined his mind in the studies of his University, and had sought the further discipline of the spiritual fellowship of the Holy Club. Yet through all of these experiences, while serving for ten years as a priest of the Church of England, he was preaching without faith and living without the strength of a personal relation to God. It was only after the heart-warming experience of Aldersgate that the founder of our Church found the spiritual power to kindle the hearts of men with a holy light.

In a recent conversation with Bishop Richard Raines, the Chairman of our Committee on Youth Work, I asked him what was the vital message for the youth of the world in a day like this. Without hesitation, he replied: 'Regardless of how long life may last, whether it be long or whether it be short, the most important thing is a deep faith in God. Through it life can be beautiful and fine and good. The security which former generations found in their surroundings we can find with greater certainty in a deep faith.'

When Job, of a far-away day, found that life was going against him, his fortunes vanished, his family taken from him, his home gone, and his health destroyed, his friends counselled him to 'Curse God and die!' But through the grim experiences runs a note of hope which nothing could extinguish for Job proclaimed from the depth of his perplexities: 'I know that my Redeemer liveth. . . .' Fortunate is the one who has made real and intimate a firm faith in God. In such there is hope.

In a German community we had the privilege of talking with a German youth who is preparing for the ministry. He had been a member of the Hitler Youth and a soldier in Hitler's armies. Four days after he had surrendered to the Allied forces, an irate soldier without provocation shot him in the back. It was only after a long period of recuperation and the loss of one lung that he recovered. During these long, lonely days he went through a spiritual and mental anguish, but emerged with a radiant, militant faith which will send him into his homeland to serve God. In our conversation he said: 'I can hold no bitterness in my heart for the man who shot me. I would like to hunt him up and thank him. For it was through those bitter days that I found my faith in God. It is that faith that makes life worth living and the road ahead bright.'

If the youth of this generation are to have in their lives the leaven of God's Kingdom, it will come as they acknowledge the sovereignty of Jesus . . . the Kingship of Christ. In these days youth are being called to give their loyalty to political doctrines, social panaceas, economic nostrums, and philosophical speculations. The Christian life becomes real to the individual as he surrenders his will to Christ and recognizes His will and way in life. Christ will give to those who acknowledge Him joy and peace and life in abundance. In the fifth chapter of Matthew are the glorious teachings of the Beatitudes. Since the day three centuries ago when they were translated into the beautiful language of the King James Version some of the language has lost its meaning and no longer communicates the strong teaching which Jesus gave to His disciples. 'Blessed are the meek, for they shall inherit the earth' is such a Beatitude. One of the New Testament scholars has taken the original Aramaic which was spoken by Jesus and has brought this misunderstood Beatitude down into the venacular of our day. In Christ's words: 'Blessed are the God-guided, for they shall inherit the earth.' What is needed in this day are God-guided youth who will follow Him as their Lord and Master in social education life, in work and in recreation, in private and in public life. Only as youth give themselves in glad surrender to Christ can the leavening process work through them.

In talking with the youth of America, the one point upon which they all agreed was that there is need in this day to make Christian love a real factor in human relations. In a world set aflame by hate, the Christian can once more prove the power of love with a new demonstration of its meaning in daily life by putting into practice a Christian concept of the brotherhood of men. The Church has for centuries proclaimed the Fatherhood of God and the inestimable worth of the individual, but at the same time has failed to speak out in public utterance to counsel the State and private agencies which have violated the logical conclusions of this teaching in a practical working brotherhood. Of all institutions, the Church should be the pioneer in a fellowship which knows no nationality, no race, no class, but holds ever highest the one condition—a love for Jesus and a desire to serve Him. Can a Church hold spiritual leadership which proclaims that all men are created by the same Creator and then, by specious reasoning, justify procedure for excluding racial or social groups from our fellowship. It is time for a serious facing of the question as to the place of leadership of the Methodist Church in the twentieth century. Our Church should proclaim the message of Jesus to all people of all classes, all races, and all nationalities, and welcome them to our fellowship as brothers.

In a world where suspicion divides groups and hatred springs to devour those who are separated by small differences, the Church can build strong bridges of understanding, goodwill, and reconciliation if we will sincerely serve in the name of the One who said: 'Come unto me, all ye that labour and are heavy laden, and I will give you rest.'

Ten days ago several of us stood in the Marx-Engels Platz of East Berlin as onlookers at the World Festival of Youth sponsored by the F.D.G., the German Communist Youth Movement. For five hours we watched the youth as we strolled around the east sector. Huge banners, thirty feet high, proclaimed peace in every tongue of the human race. The flags of all nations, in glorious display, announced the slogan of the Festival, *Freundschaft*—friendship. The greeting between the hundreds of thousands of youth who gathered from every corner of Germany and from many foreign countries was *Freundschaft*. Youth desire peace and friendship. Their idealism carries them far in their dreams of peace and brotherhood. Will the Christian Church in the twentieth century permit the Communist Party to become the active apostle of peace and brotherhood. It is rather the province of the Christian Church, following the Prince of Peace, not only to proclaim brotherhood, but to make it an ever-present reality for all to see in every community where Christian youths live and serve. In such practice of Christ's example lies hope for brotherhood and world peace.

There is further hope for averting the catastrophe which threatens our civilization if the youth of this generation will, with whole-hearted enthusiasm, join in strengthening the Church in its fundamental purposes. There have been those who have looked upon the Church as a social agency where all the 'right people' joined in a very shallow type of fellowship. Some youth have looked upon the Church as a canteen where recreation and a quick snack could be obtained. Still others have thought of the Church as a place where an occasional charity was supported or a basket of food sent to the poor. It is small wonder, in the circles where such false conceptions prevail, that the Church has had little strength and that many youths have not been attracted to it. The Church in the earliest days was referred to as the *koinonia*, the redemptive fellowship. In every age it has been the fellowship of those who had faith in God, love for Christ, and a desire to work with other Christians for the building of His Kingdom. Such a dynamic fellowship cannot be conceived in shallow or small terms, but only in the greatest of concepts of work, sacrifice, witness, and service for our Lord and Master.

Paul, in describing the Church (1 Corinthians 12), refers to it as the Body of Christ. For such a sacred function, the Church is set aside to preach and to teach; to serve and to labour; and to be a continual voice of eternal truth to the world. This is the mission to which the youth of the Methodist Church at mid-century are called. The free Church is not the agency of any State, class, economic view, or political party, but is the Body of Christ, humbly serving in His stead.

What a glorious institution it is. To be certain, it is filled with human frailities and imperfections. But, as in every age, God has achieved extraordinary results through ordinary men, women and youth. Critics can pick it to pieces and sceptics scoff, but whatever is good in your country and in your community has come as the direct result of the work, the preaching and the prayers of the Church of God. You can check them one by one: whatever makes life good and fine in your land and mine has come out of the work of the Church.

But even so, in a world where ignorance, hunger, disease, injustice, intolerance, and hatred still work their fiendish damage in the lives of individuals and the corporate affairs of mankind, the Church stands in judgement of not doing enough. At the meeting of the Central Committee of the World Council of Churches at Rolle, Switzerland, last month we were talking with one of the delegates about the world conditions, and he said: 'With all that the Church has done, it stands under the judgement of God for not eliminating the conditions which make hatred and war possible.' But in the strength of the Church and the sincere work of Christians is the hope for this day.

This is the day when the youth of the Church should move forward to give the best of their idealism, their devotion, and their strength to making the Church strong for this hour of challenge. In the words of the hymn:

'Rise up, O men of God,
The Church for you doth wait;
Her strength unequal to her task.
Rise up and make her great.'

Within recent years there has grown up a mighty movement within Christendom, as well as just the Methodist Church, which is known by a rather frightening term—the *ecumenical movement*. The ecumenical movement is a move to bring into close fellowship those many branches of the Church of God which for so long have walked their separate and very independent ways. We have, through the years, been so absorbed with the peculiarities of our faith in the various denominations and even within the various branches of the Methodist Church that we have failed to share in fellowship in the vast areas of common faith and communion.

168

Many Christians and non-Christians have been justly critical of this scandal of the Church. Each has prized its nugget of truth and each has enhanced its view of reality, and frequently has looked down its noses at other groups and has been critical if not openly scoffing of their practices. It is significant that in this age into which you are coming as leaders of the Church the ecumenical movement should be moving ahead so rapidly. We have recognized that God's laws are universal. No one group or nationality has a corner on the hypotheses of geometry or the conclusion of science. They belong to all and are clearly recognized as such. The principles of art and music cannot be monopolized, for they too are universal. No one denomination has a monopoly on spiritual truth, nor does any sect have exclusive right to the gospel of Jesus. With the growth of our understanding of each other's position and a closer fellowship in the herculean tasks of serving our Lord, we have learned that there is far more that unites Christians in their service than separates them. Within our own Methodist Church there are, I understand, more than forty separate groups who call themselves Methodist, with no organic fellowship to unite them. What a significant step it would be if Methodists, around the world, could move closer together in fellowship and on into organic unity that our witness might be united in every land and to all creatures. A step can be taken in this direction by Methodist youth in sharing opportunities for fellowship and by bringing the work of the youth in sharing opportunities for fellowship and by bringing the work of the youth of the various branches of the Methodist Church, working in every continent, into close relationships for exchange of leadership and fellowship experiences. We must take advantage of every opportunity to strengthen the fellowship of the people called Methodists for the service of our Lord.

Youth can lead the way, as Methodist youth in Malaya, Africa, England, France, Germany, Switzerland, Ceylon, China, India, the Philippines, Mexico, Canada, South America, the United States, Australia, and other nations of the world, representing multiplied millions of youth, can join hands and hearts in dedication to Christ and the building of God's Kingdom.

It is not enough to have an ecumenical movement within the Methodist Church. It is important that we join hands in common cause with other Christians of many denominations. It was a thrilling experience to sit in on the meeting of the Central Committee of the World Council of Churches recently at Rolle, Switzerland, and see there an Anglican bishop presiding, with a Methodist secretary, a Dutch Reformed executive officer, and a Greek Orthodox making a statement from the floor. There in one room, planning the work of the World Council, were leaders representing 150 Churches around the world united in the fellowship of holy service.

As the world stands at mid-century in the gathering gloom of despair, with pyramiding problems on every hand and the potential catastrophe becoming more real each day, it is the youth of this age who can open their lives to Christ, and in complete dedication to Him and His Kingdom become the instrument through which the leaven can permeate the whole lump of our civilization. *These are not days of despair, but, with a strengthening of the ecumenical spirit, a reinforcing of the Church, a truer application of love in the affairs of men, the acknowledging of the kingship of Christ and a deepening of our faith in God, there will be hope and courage for the days ahead.*

169

Address at a Youth Rally in Whitley Hall, Reading, given by DR O. K.
OGAN, *of W. Africa:*

May I begin by saying how very happy and thrilled I am to be amongst
such a large crowd of young folk.

During the past week, as you are fully aware, there has been a sort of
'gathering of the clans' of world-wide Methodism at the Oxford Methodist
Ecumenical Conference. Of necessity, the majority of the delegates have
been men and women of the higher age groups, but here at Reading
tonight we appear to have come into our own, in that the young people
are in the overwhelming majority; and this is most refreshing.

I remember one occasion, nearly fifteen years ago when I went with a
party of Boy Scouts for a day's outing at the beach. I was then at school
in Lagos, a big seaport town, and the capital city of my home country,
Nigeria. As you approach the entrance to Lagos Harbour, you notice a
mole or breakwater on either side, solid walls of rock extending out to the
Atlantic Ocean for nearly a mile, so as to stop the fury of the breakers and
provide calm anchorage for the ships in the lagoon. On the seaward side
of one of these breakwaters there is a lovely bathing beach known as
Tarquah Bay, where lots of people are to be seen surf-riding or enjoying a
long walk along an endless tract of lovely white sea sand, all the year round.

For our day at the beach we had picked a day in October, because the
seasons very conveniently divide themselves into dry and wet, and we've
none of this business of the B.B.C. forecasting, 'Generally fine weather,
perhaps, with a few scattered showers in most places . . .' or some such well-
known cliche with which it attempts in vain to cope with the unpredictable.
We all looked forward to lots of fun and games, perhaps a game of
rounders when we weren't bathing, or a spell of just basking in the pleasant
sunshine gazing at the stately coconut palms swaying gracefully in the
breeze overhead, or watching some of our number climb these trees and
vie with one another as to who could collect the largest number of
coconuts.

As you will know yourselves, there is always something that stands out
in your memory through the years in connexion with an outing, a holiday,
or a picnic. Perhaps it's something about the food. It may have been bad,
or you didn't get enough to eat, or some clumsy person spilt paraffin oil
on the sandwiches, or the bright spark who bought the sardines left the
tin-opener behind. Of course, if you'd been unfortunate enough to be
sharing a room or a tent with a chap who snored, then you had infinitely
greater cause to recall many things, lying awake!

Now, as I look back upon our visit to Tarquah Bay, what I remember
most vividly is a lighthouse—Lagos Lighthouse, which stands on that
beach, towering high above. You can imagine the thrill with which we
surged up the spiral staircase of Lagos Lighthouse on this our first visit,
climbing higher and higher, our curiosity sustaining us even when our
knees felt they had had enough, and then, when at last we got to the top,
Oh, how utterly lovely it was. On each side was a vast expanse of land on
the one hand, and sea on the other, separated by a coastline extending for
miles and miles for as far as eye could see. And right at the very top was the
lamp. The lighthouse-keeper was a pleasant faced old boy, looking most
distinguished—a grizzled white beard sticking from his chin. He took great
pride in showing us round the lamp-room, for everything was spick and
span. The glass-work glistened and the metal work shone, and there was
not a speck of dust anywhere. But the thing that intrigued me most about
the lamp was the structure of the reflector. It wasn't just one dome of
smooth glass, as you might have imagined. Rather, it was made up of

several odd pieces, varying prismatic sections all cemented together, and the whole mounted on a swivel, so that the beam of light could travel far in every direction.

I dare say that all this sounds very commonplace to you boys and girls in this country who at some time or other will have seen lighthouses at Eddystone, or Holyhead, or any other of the many lighthouses along the coastline of Britain. But for me, I am sure that the first lighthouse which I saw in my youth has never quite lost its fascination. It has always been a symbol of something high and lifted up, something that people who might easily get into trouble look out for, something they trust to guide them from danger into safety. And that brings me to the words of the thirty-second verse of John, Chapter 12: 'And I, if I be lifted up, will draw all men unto me.'

I have often thought that there was a lot in common between the lighthouse and people like you and me who are privileged to call ourselves Christians. A lighthouse does not discriminate in its service. It will guide the great ocean-going vessels in and out of Lagos Harbour in just the same way as it will serve as a beacon for the frail craft in which our humble fisherfolk venture forth to do business in great waters. Secondly, it reflects its light most effectively by virtue of every individual prism that goes to make up the whole dome of the reflector. Each of them has its own special part to play. Herein, I think, is a challenge that comes to us young people, each one of us, who, because we are followers of Christ, must together lift Him up so that all men might be drawn to Him. It is a thing infinitely bigger than ourselves, a task to which we are committed, and which we can accomplish only by working together.

There is a newspaper on the Gold Coast which bears the rather strange name *Talking Drums*. This name harks back to the more remote days before the impact of European civilization on the peoples of those territories, when roads and railways, telephones and aeroplanes were things unheard of. The early European explorers of those days soon discovered, often to their discomfiture, that they could not keep their movements secret. As they trudged about the land, they found that news of their whereabouts always went before them, flashed across the countryside over hundreds of miles by means of messages tapped out on drums. These drums were great big affairs, hewn out of whole tree trunks, and the messages they conveyed went echoing far across country, over hill and down dale, to warn the local inhabitants of the presence of suspicious-looking strangers.

We of the present age may rejoice in what we term modern civilization. Within the twinkling of an eye, we are able to waft wireless messages across thousands of miles. We can sit back in an armchair and enjoy an entertainment from the uttermost parts of the earth, or even watch it before our eyes on a television screen. But the important point I wish to bring out here is that it doesn't really seem to matter what our times and circumstances are. Our potentialities and inclinations, the inherent dangers surrounding us are for ever the same. The talking drum was equally capable of carrying a message of friendship and greeting, of warning tribesmen to organize against impending danger, as of being used for an evil purpose. With our modern, quicker means of communication and intercourse, we are as likely to communicate news of a ship in distress or relief to people in sickness or famine as we are of hastening the declaration of atomic war.

A week or so ago, I was listening to some of the radio commentaries on the recent meetings of the British Association in Edinburgh. An eminent scientist was trying to enumerate a whole series of beneficial uses to which atomic energy could be devoted—beneficial things that would make life safer and happier for all mankind. But, in spite of all this, isn't it true that the first—in fact, so far the only—use to which atomic energy has been put has been to make the fate of mankind uncertain. We live under the shadow of its hellish potentialities. How different it would be if the love of Christ could lift us up and remove from our hearts all fear and distrust of one another.

I believe that for us young people this question of personal relationships is very important, because it is the beginning of a fuller life that is more in keeping with the attitude of our Lord.

But where do we start? Where do we fit into all this? We are not in power, and the people who make all the important decisions thunder away from such giddy heights above our heads. So what can we do to alter the history of mankind?

I suggest that, as young people who own a common Lord, we start right where we are among ourselves, trying to create a better understanding, trying to do away with all sorts of prejudices and suspicion, trying to let the light of God shine through us into the hearts of all men. And all men includes everybody: Europeans, Africans, Americans, the Oriental peoples, and even the Russians—if they were to become accessible to us. I dare to mention the Russians because I know fully well that they are people who do not think the way we do. Quite rightly, we disagree with them on the way in which they have chosen to put their trust in things made with men's hands, in ideologies that reckon without the existence of God or salvation through His Son. But what hope can we have of their hearts being changed unless it is entirely by the grace of God. One of the greatest points in favour of travel is that you come to associate countries with individuals. To an African who has been in Britain and has had fellowship with the boys and girls here, England cannot mean a country populated by people who are cold and aloof. It becomes the home of Sydney and Jean and Harry, people who were his real pals. He also identifies it with John's parents, who were very nice to him and treated him just like their own son when he visited their home. In just the same way, through personal contact Americans, Germans, French people, and all nations of the earth come to mean more to us—living, vital people like ourselves, quite different from the misleading impressions we might have gathered from our conventional and out-of-date textbooks.

Finally, just one point with which I would like to close: I know that when we read the Scriptures, or consider the array of people who have been made famous in Christian history, we tend to be overawed, because we get the impression that it must be the extraordinary people only who are capable of making some impact on the Christian world. We think of Saul on the road to Damascus and the dramatic experience that he had. We recall Martin Luther's classical boldness when he pinned his denunciation of the Roman Church on the doors of Wittenberg Cathedral. We think of John Wesley, over whom there came a particular change at a specified time and place. But also we should remember Peter, and others who did the more ordinary thing, and who on occasion even did a cowardly thing. And we should think again how Peter's life became purified and strengthened, and how much more he was able to achieve for his Lord after that enrichment and purification.

Many times during the past week, I have had the pleasure of walking from one Oxford college to another, in those lovely grounds so full of history, made so beautiful by man and Nature. As I have gone from college to college, and entered chapel after chapel, each possessing its own peculiar beauty, there has been one constant feature: there has been nothing to compare with the beauty of the stained glass in the windows. One has felt absolutely enraptured by the beauty of the craftsmanship, as, gazing on them from within, the pictures they hold have been lit up by the sunshine outside. And yet when you have stood outside and looked at these self-same windows, you have not seen any beautiful pictures, because there is no sun shining through them, lighting them up in such rich variations of colour. In like manner, when we allow the light of Christ to shine through us, when we reflect His love for us by extending it to all people of every race, then Christ shines through all the dim patches, the ugly sins and shortcomings in our weak natures. Then we are ourselves lifted up, so that our efforts are worthier of our Lord, and we can be used to bring all men unto Him.

At Swindon a public meeting was held in the Central Hall and Mr David Foot Nash, of Plymouth, presided. The speaker was Bishop J. Waskom Pickett, of Delhi, India.

An address delivered by BISHOP J. WASKOM PICKETT, *of Delhi, India:*

After the order of clergymen and to insure that I shall feel at home before you, I'll take a text. It comes from the best possible source, the words of our Lord, quoted for us by St John in the fifth chapter of his record of the ministry of Jesus, verse 17: 'My Father worketh hitherto, and I work.' Because this is one of the neglected words of the Great Teacher, I am the more eager to use it on this occasion.

This statement of Jesus that God worketh hitherto is theologically significant. The Father whom He knew so well and whom He represented so perfectly that He could say, 'He who hath seen me hath seen the Father', has never finished His work and retired. He is still creating and still sustaining His creation. There are many today, as there have been many in years past, who have never thought thus of God, but have supposed that He long since completed His creation and established immutable laws for its governance, leaving Him free from any necessity to continue His work. To such people nothing is left for God to do— at least, nothing that can rightly be described as work. It is not surprising that people who think of God as having finished His work and retired do not, as Jesus did, call Him Father and do not, as Jesus did, devote much time to prayer.

This teaching of Jesus was significant in relation to the work of Jesus. He said: 'My Father worketh hitherto and I work.' This he said in defence of His right to heal on the Sabbath Day. It is as though He said: When God is at work today why should I not have done today the work of which you complain.' The Jews to whom Jesus addressed these words had objected because on the Sabbath Day He had healed a poor, impotent man who had been terribly ill thirty-eight years. In effect, Jesus was saying to them: 'You are in error in objecting to the work I have done, and the reason for your error is that you have incorrect ideas about God and His work. If you had known God as I know Him, as Father, you would have known that He works even on the Sabbath Day and that I, His Son, must work on the Sabbath, for I do the works of My Father.' Jesus taught that it is never right to ignore human need. The Father is ever ready to hear man's prayer, to heal his diseases, to forgive his sins, to cleanse his heart. The Father works at these jobs. So does the Son.

173

The world has not found it easy to accept this picture of God. The chosen disciples of Jesus did not find it easy. They did not understand that God was always at work in man's behalf—every man's behalf. They thought of God as ready on occasions to hear the prayers of some men, of those with whom He was well pleased; that He must be persuaded by obedience to His law, by goodness, and especially by prayer. Bad men had no access to God. He was against them for their sins. But Jesus said in effect: God is not against any man for his sins; He is for every man against his sins, and this is so *all the time*. To this end 'the Father worketh hitherto and I work'.

So difficult did the disciples find it to believe what Jesus taught them about God that on one ocasion He resorted to parables, and in three of them taught what God is like and how He works without ceasing for man's good. The first was the parable of the shepherd and the lost sheep. The shepherd was in charge of 100 sheep. Ninety-nine followed him to safety in the sheepfold, but one wandered into danger on the mountainside. The good shepherd would not sit down and rejoice that he had brought ninety-nine sheep to safety. Neither was he content to blame the sheep that had not followed him to the sheepfold saying: 'That wicked sheep. I taught him as faithfully as any other to follow his shepherd. Now he is lost. It's his fault, not mine, that he is not here. I'll sit down and rest and eat. Soon I'll sleep.' No, he went out after the lost sheep. He trudged over the hills and down into the valleys and finally found him and brought him in rejoicing. 'That', said Jesus in effect, 'is what God is like.'

But lest the disciples should still not understand, He proceeded to tell the second parable. This time He chose a woman as an example of God's character and work. I'm glad of that. It was a bold thing to do. His hearers didn't think very highly of women. None of their teachers had ever told them that God is like a woman. And Jesus chose an ordinary, humble woman for this purpose, not a queen, not even a woman of declared piety or wisdom, but an ordinary faithful wife and mother in a poor home. This woman had ten pieces of silver for the week's household expenses. One of these she lost. She didn't sit down and say: 'That wicked coin! Where has it gone? How did it get lost?' Neither did she say: 'Never mind! I have nine coins left. I'll economize. I'll feed my husband and children a little less at each meal, or I'll put off until next week the buying of the new shoes our son needs.' On the contrary, she set to work to find that coin. She searched in her boxes. She took the furniture out of the room. And at last she found the lost coin. 'That', said Jesus in effect, 'is what God is like. That is the way He works for man.'

And for fear some of His disciples had not even then understood, He told a third parable. God is like a loving father who had two sons, one of whom became very independent and selfish and came one day demanding that he be given his share of the family property and be allowed to go away and buy land and run a farm of his own. The father knew the boy too well to believe that he would succeed in his venture, but he loved the lad too much to impose his will upon him. He gave him what he demanded and the boy went away not knowing how badly he had hurt his father. The boy had a good amount of money and planned to buy land and make good. When he had succeeded and was very rich he would call the father and his elder brother and show them how smart and wise he was. But on his way to the far country where he would become a gentleman farmer he fell into bad company and began drinking and carousing. He didn't find a good opportunity to buy at once and while waiting for the big chance he went on having a good time. After a while he woke up to the fact that his

174

money was all gone. He was grief-stricken and remorseful. He had planned things very differently. But all was not lost. He would yet make good. He would get a job, work hard, save his money and yet be a big man. But now misfortune overtook him. Hard times came. Crops failed and famine stalked the land. He sold his good clothes for food. His friends deserted him. He got a job tending pigs and fain would fill his belly with the coarse grain he fed the pigs. Then he awoke to his folly. He remembered the goodness and kindness of the father whom he had left, and decided he would go back, humbly confess his wrong-doing and beg to be employed as a servant on his father's farm. So he started home. And his father was waiting for him, out on the road looking eagerly for the returning prodigal. Seeing him from afar, the father ran to meet the wayward boy, clasped him in his arms and loved him. 'That', said Jesus in effect, 'is what God is like. His love abides and abounds. He never ceases to seek the welfare of His children.' 'The Father worketh hitherto and I work.'

That is the heart of the gospel of our Lord Jesus Christ. It was difficult for His disciples to accept. And it is difficult for many people in the world of our day. *To the Hindu, this gospel seems incredible.* I have often had the experience of preaching very earnestly to Hindus who had never before listened to a serious exposition of the gospel and of learning that my words left them completely unconvinced, because they just couldn't believe that what I said to them was true. Just this month a Hindu ascetic—a deeply religious man who twenty years ago left home and began an earnest search for God, going on long and painful pilgrimages throughout India, walking in the broiling sun, measuring his length on the ground for many miles to sacred temples, often going hungry, begging his food from all sorts of people, tramping hundreds of miles over steep mountains and across deep valleys, nearly freezing in high snow-covered altitudes—came to me and confessed that it had all been done in vain. He had gained no light, no peace, no experience of God, no release from sin. He listened as I told him the good news that Jesus proclaimed. Now and then he seemed to hear gladly and his face shone with joy. But when I stopped, he shook his head and said sadly: 'Very interesting, Bishop! I wish I could believe it, but it isn't true. No man is that important. God doesn't care that much for sinful man. *Only those who have earned much merit can be saved.*'

As a young missionary in India forty years ago, I hoped to bring people to Christian faith by preaching. I couldn't, and I was very disappointed. It seemed that the plainer I made the gospel the less successful I was. It took me some time to discover that to those to whom I was preaching, the gospel seemed utterly incredible. Some were made angry by what I said, for it challenged what they believed. A few heard gladly, but still did not accept it as true. That sent me to a study of the ministry of Jesus, and I soon discovered that He who spoke with authority as no other has ever done didn't win many converts by His preaching alone. He didn't try. He who said 'Thou shalt love the Lord thy God with all thy mind' didn't demand that people accept His message just because He preached it. *He offered proof of what He preached. He proved His words by His works.* His mighty works drew the multitudes, and then He preached to them and frankly claimed that His works proved His word to be true. On one occasion He told them that He would heal a man of a terrible illness in order that they might know that His gospel was true. When John the Baptist was in doubt whether Jesus was the Messiah and sent his disciples to ask Jesus, our Lord replied: 'Tell John what you have seen and heard.' He knew that when John heard the report of his disciples he would

175

realize that what they had seen Jesus do was proof that what He said of Himself and about God was true—that He was, in truth, the Messiah.

In the confusions of our day we hear many strange advices. An eminent theologian is quoted as saying recently: 'The only task of the Church is to preach the Word.' Many Continental European preachers and writers have attacked what they have chosen to call the activism of British, or even more, of American churchmen. They have seen in sharp contrast the recognition of the sovereignty of God and the effort to serve the needs of men. To me it seems extraordinary that ministers of Jesus Christ can so far ignore the lessons in the ministry of Jesus. He certainly never regarded His only task as the preaching of the Word. He saw no conflict, but on the contrary an essential connexion, between preaching the Word and doing good works. He went from one to another with the utmost ease and naturalness.

Instead of making preaching the gospel the only task of His disciples, Jesus never told them to preach without commanding them to do the same good works than He did. They were to heal the sick, to cleanse the lepers, to raise the dead—in short, to make the gospel credible, to confirm it. I doubt whether any man has a right to preach unless he is ready to heal. It is appallingly inconsistent to preach what Jesus Christ preached about God and do nothing to meet the needs of man.

Jesus went so far as to tell His disciples that they should and would do greater things that He had done. He had shown them what they should do. His ministry was an example to them. He had accepted a limited field of service. He gave them an unlimited field. His ministry was confined to Galilee and Judea. They were to go into all the world. The world was their parish. They were to preach and prove His Gospel to all nations. And to make their success possible, He would go with them wheresoever they went. When, as a young missionary discouraged over the very limited success that I found it possible to win through preaching, I studied afresh the ministry of Jesus and His instructions and promises to His disciples, I came across this statement that the disciples should do greater things than Jesus had done, and it frightened me. I said: 'That isn't possible! The disciples can't do what their Lord did. How can they do greater things?' And then the Holy Spirit, the Comforter, began His promised work of leading me to Truth. I said "If Jesus is with His disciples scattered all over the world, why can they not do greater things than He did when he was a prisoner in the flesh, limited always to one place and to contact with one group of people and their needs". And I remembered that when Jesus told His disciples to heal the sick and cleanse the lepers He said nothing about the methods they should use. He never said: 'Heal the way I have healed.' He wanted a certain result, not the use of a certain method; a result that would confirm the Gospel, not one that would establish a particular system of treating the sick. And soon I discovered that what Jesus said His disciples would do, they were doing. You may not realize it, but the disciples of Jesus, the Master being with them, inspiring and leading them, are doing in the world of our day incomparably greater things than Jesus did in the days when He was limited to the use of one body in one place. For an illustration, take the cleansing of lepers. I don't know how many lepers Jesus cleansed. Neither do you, for, strange as it may seem, Jesus never appointed a statistical secretary. Shall we say fifty? Or 100? Or, to make sure none is left out, 200? But today the disciples of Jesus are healing more than that many lepers every month. Several years ago I delivered a farewell address in a leprosy home in India on the occasion when more than 100 sufferers from that dread disease were being

176

discharged to go home, taking with them certificates that their relatives and neighbours could welcome them without fear, for they were free from contagion. Or take the healing of the blind. To how many blind men, women, and children did Jesus restore sight? I don't know, and you don't know. But this I can say with confidence: that the disciples of Jesus are restoring sight to more blinded eyes in India every month than Jesus healed in His entire ministry when He was limited to the use of one body.

But the work of Jesus was by no means limited to the healing of physical diseases and infirmities. He probably worked harder and gave more time to *instructing his disciples*, changing them from what sin and error had made them into the men He wanted them to be. This, too, was a necessary proof of His gospel. The world would not believe what Jesus taught about God unless it saw evidence that men could be transformed in character, freed from their chains, and enriched in personality. What convincing proof the work Jesus did for and in those disciples provides! Think of how He changed the impetuous Simon into the stable Peter, the ambitious, self-seeking, frightening sons of Zebedee into devoted, selfless, heroic men who counted not life itself too precious a sacrifice to make for God and His Church.

No task of the Church today is of such compelling importance as presenting to the unbelieving world of our time evidence that God can, will, and does change the characters of men. A distinguished Hindu once said to me: 'The teaching that sin can be forgiven is totally erroneous and pernicious. Let a man believe that, and what is there to restrain him from wrong-doing?' I told him that if he once realized that God's love is of such perfect quality and so measureless that He is never against man for his sins, but always for him against his sins, he would not fear the effects of the gospel of forgiveness. The most powerful restraint against sin is not the fear of God's wrath or of punishment, but a sense of His love. Had my Hindu friend been willing to look for the evidence, he would have found abundant proof in his own land that men who accept Christ's teaching, as Simon and James and John accepted it, are utterly transformed, for God the Father and Jesus Christ His son are working now in India and in all the world to provide this convincing proof of the Gospel.

What has happened to many of India's depressed class sufferers, victims of Hinduism's evil concepts of *karma* and rebirth, is an oft-told story. But let me remind you of one of those sufferers, Venkayya, who, as a Hindu made to suffer ostracism and inhuman oppression for alleged sins committed in imagined previous lives, seeing no hope of escape or of easing his sufferings, became a robber and organized and led a band of robbers. Venkayya was ruthless, and under his leadership his band terrorized the population of a large area in South India. He formed alliances with the priests who would not let him enter the temples, but who for a share of the booty prayed for the success of the robbers as they went forth to pillage and to kill. At the height of his career, Venkayya lost his only son in circumstances that destroyed his faith in the efficacy of the prayers of the priests. A little later he heard of a missionary who in a city a score of miles away was preaching a strangely different religion to Brahmans. He went with seven members of his band and insisted that the missionary tell them what he knew about God. That missionary was not pleased to see them. He had been preaching to Brahmans only, because they seemed to him the natural leaders of the people, more intelligent than others, and the only ones able to understand his learned arguments. He could not imagine that it was the will of God that criminal Untouchables should be the pioneer members of the Church in that area. But the

Brahmans had not accepted the Gospel, and only that day had told him to stop preaching. These people at least wanted to hear his message. So he told them the story of Jesus, and to his amazement they responded joyfully. They were delighted to learn that Jesus chose common people for His disciples, that He healed the sick, cleansed lepers—the Untouchables of Palestine—ate with publicans and denounced the Scribes and Pharisees, whom they likened to the Brahmans. When the missionary told of the Crucifixion, Venkayya leaped to his feet crying: 'No! They couldn't kill such a good man that way.' When assured that they had, he cried out: 'Where are those wicked men? Tell me where to find them. My men and I will kill every one of them.' 'That you don't need to do', said the missionary. 'Those men have died long since. But listen, Venkayya! They killed Jesus and they buried Him. But He became alive again. He came out of the grave. He is alive now. I know him and you can know Him. He is your friend. He wants to save you. He'll forgive your sins and take the sin out of your heart. He'll change you and all your fellow robbers, if you'll believe on Him and give him the chance.' Again Venkayya leaped to his feet, saying: 'Is it true? Is it true? Then He is my lord. I'll worship Him and no other all my life.' Venkayya and his fellow robbers accepted Christ then and there and the Church in Andhra Desh was born. The robber band was dissolved and Venkayya and his associates became witnesses for Christ. Like their Master, they went about doing good. A revival began which in more than 100 years has not stopped. Today more than a million of the former Untouchables of Andhra Desh are Christians, and so vital is their experience of Christ and so powerfully do they confirm the gospel by their changed characters, their enriched personalities, and their new way of life that tens of thousands of the higher castes in Andhra Desh have joined them in confessing faith in Christ.

Recently, after I had preached at Agra, city of the incomparable Taj Mahal, 800 miles from where Venkayya lived and died, a man of the audience followed me to the Mission House where I was staying and told me this story:

'I come from Andhra Desh. When I was a boy of twelve I was given by my father into the care of a wandering *sadhu*, a Hindu religious mendicant. He put me into a *gurukul*, a Hindu school of religious instruction, where I received a sound Hindu education. I am now acclaimed as a sanskrit scholar and am one of the editors of a daily paper. Last year I went to my home, a village in Andhra Desh. I found that during my absence many of the most influential families in the village had become Christians. The rest were all Communists. Among the latter were my two brothers. They tried to make a Communist of me. I told them that I would think about it. Since then I have done nothing else much but think about what I saw and heard in my village. It seem to me that what has happened there is going to happen all over India, and perhaps all over the world. People must become Christians or Communists. The choice has to be made. I have made my choice. I prefer to become a Christian. I'd rather be one with those converted Untouchables, once dirty, stupid, and vicious, but now good and clean and intelligent, rather than with my own brothers and their fellows, who have been coarsened and made into criminals by Communist influence.'

In the Delhi area, too, far away from Andhra Desh, there have been powerful mass movements of Untouchables. The first of these also took place among criminals, a small community of Mazhabi Sikhs. They were under police surveillance. Within little more than a dozen years, all of

178

them in two civil districts were converted. Within another ten years, all were released from police surveillance and had become honest, law-abiding citizens. From among them were recruited hundreds of the pioneer preachers who carried the gospel to other districts of Uttar Pradesh, formerly called the United Provinces, and of the Punjab. Their initial successes everywhere were among the Untouchables. But working in and through them and those whom they led to faith, our Lord has confirmed the gospel for many of their neighbours, including Brahmans and landlords, beneficiaries of the Hindu system, had previously insulated against the gospel by their social and economic self-interest and pride. They were immune to preaching, but the mighty works of Christ in those whom they had despised provided proof of the blessed words of the Saviour.

Since Christmas last I have baptized over fifty high-caste Hindus and Moslems of influence. Neither of my two predecessors in the Methodist episcopacy at Delhi baptized that many new converts from those classes in all his years in the office—one twelve years, the other eight. I mention that fact only because it may help you to understand how timely it is, amid the pessimisms of today, to remember and apply to our generation those words of Him who is the same yesterday, today, and forever, words that are eternally true, 'My Father worketh hitherto and I work'; and again that you may believe that those words of the Saviour addressed to his disciples are being fulfilled: 'Greater works than these shall ye do because I go to the Father.'

SEVENTH DAY

Monday 3rd September

THE opening devotions were conducted by the Rev. E. W. Hames, President of the New Zealand Conference, and an address, based on Romans 12¹, was given by the Rev. Dr Nolan B. Harmon, Book Editor of the Methodist Publishing House, New York.

Whilst St Paul, in the earlier chapters of the Epistle to the Romans speaks of God's grace, Dr Harmon pointed out that in the twelfth chapter he turns to man's opportunity. We must insist that God's truth be applied to every aspect of man's life. It is a fine thing to have John Wesley and Francis Asbury for our spiritual fathers, but it will be a finer thing if we prove to be worthy descendants by doing in our day what they did in theirs. It is not enough to hold what our fathers have taken, as a humdrum army of occupation. Let us not try to relive the past, but to live in the amazing present, applying God's truth to life. Careful theological foundations are the basis of Christian action.

The theme for the morning sessions of 3rd and 4th September was *The Social Witness*. The first two addresses were delivered on Monday morning. In the absence of Bishop Hazen G. Werner, the Rev. Dr Maldwyn Edwards, of the Central Hall, Birmingham, spoke on *Marriage and the Family*, and Mr Donald W. Hughes, Headmaster of Rydal School, Colwyn Bay, delivered an address on *Education*.

THE SOCIAL WITNESS

I. MARRIAGE AND THE FAMILY

An address delivered by the REV. DR MALDWYN EDWARDS, *of the Central Hall, Birmingham:*

A hundred years ago the Great Exhibition was opened in Crystal Palace, London. It was dedicated to the cause of peace, progress, and plenty. It rested on a belief in man's ability to save himself. Now there remains only charred and blackened ruins. The pomp of yesterday is one with Nineveh and Tyre. All is not lost, however. The curious who visit the South Bank Exhibition may see a representation of the opening scene. They will discover that on the outskirts are soldiers, statesmen, and divines. In the centre, however, there is the Royal Family. The Prince Consort stands beside Queen Victoria and their children are grouped around them. That is altogether fitting, for the family was the very centre of Victorian life. We are no longer tempted to look with patronage upon the Victorian Age. Lytton Strachey and his school are themselves debunked. A long series of books has re-established the Victorians, and now we look with wonder and a little envy at the strength and solidity of their family life. What was the principle of authority? All power was vested in the father. The patriarchal principle dies hard. In Oliver Goldsmith's *The Good-natured Gentleman*, Leontine says to his father, 'An only son can expect

180

some indulgence', and Croaker replies: 'An only father can expect some obedience.' The Victorian father both expected and received obedience. When Mr Barrett, the father of Elizabeth Barrett Browning, spoke to his sons, they clicked their heels and said 'Sir'.

On what basis did this authority rest? Firstly, there was the economic position of the father. He was in truth the breadwinner of the family. The woman's place was in the nursery and in the kitchen. It is true that children went out to work. One reason why the Industrial Revolution resulted in an increase of population is that children were found to be economically profitable. It is significant that when education became compulsory and children had to be maintained longer at home, the birth-rate began to decline. Yet even though children earned money, it went to the father. He was the dispenser of the family purse. Secondly, it rested on the social position of the father. The nineteenth century was the century of the male. The woman's status was inferior to that of her husband. She had no freedom in the disposition of her own property. In the words of Blackstone's *Commentaries*: 'Upon marriage her legal existence was suspended, and incorporated and consolidated into that of the husband.' She had no political suffrage. Except in rare cases, no career was open to her. In like manner, the child in Victorian England was expected to be 'seen and not heard'. Already his physical well-being was being secured, but no attention was yet paid to his own distinctive personality. Lastly, authority rested on the religious position of the father. Until the beginnings of the Darwinian controversy, the generality of people accepted a literal view of the Bible. The Old Testament had equal importance with the New Testament. They were familiar, therefore, with a patriarchal society. In any case, the Bible spoke of 'the Father of our Lord Jesus Christ, of whom every family in heaven and on earth is named'. Religious sanction was therefore given to the authority of the father as the undisputed head of the family.

In time the bases of this authority were undermined, and with it the power of the father collapsed. It is to the disappearance of this principle of authority that we owe much of our present distress. How did it come about? In the first place, the economic status of the father changed. With the passing of the years, and more especially in the accelerated tempo of two world wars, women began increasingly to earn their living. There are now as many careers open for girls as for boys. In very many instances a woman still maintains her job even after marriage. Though children stay at school for a longer period, when they do begin to earn they no longer pass their money automatically into the father's purse. He is no longer the dispenser of the family fortune. It is much more a matter of common agreement. In the second place, the social position of the father has changed. The nineteenth century was one of individualism. In one aspect, it was the fight for freedom in many spheres, and not least that of the freedom of the woman. By the Married Women's Property Acts, 1870-93, women attained complete economic independence. She had the full right of disposal of her own property. In the next century she attained political self-expression. Today it is virtually true that there is sex equality. Lastly, the religious sanctions for the father's authority were undermined. In his book, *Science, Religion, and the Future*, C. E. Raven has spoken of the Darwinian controversy as a 'storm in a Victorian teacup'. One may be pardoned for misquoting Churchill and exclaiming: 'Some storm, and some teacup.' For many it seemed that the whole authority of the Bible was destroyed. If the story of Creation as told in Genesis was not true, what assurance was there that the rest of the Bible was true? Gradually

181

doubt began to chill the hearts of men. Tennyson is supremely the people's poet, but even in so religious poem as *In Memoriam* he could say:

> 'Thou madest man, he knows not why;
> He thinks he was not made to die:
> And thou hast made him; thou art just.'

He could only trust 'that somehow good would be the final goal of ill'. After years had gone by this doubt hardened into unbelief. Thomas Hardy could speak in *The Dynasts* of the drowsy knitter who knits in skilled unmindfulness. The two world wars hastened this process of unbelief. For some war may bring God closer, but for the majority it makes belief in God more difficult to accept. In the disregard of human life, in gas chamber and concentration camp, people find it difficult to believe in a beneficent purpose behind all things. It is not surprising that in the aftermath of the second world war we should have the vogue of Existentialism with its catch-cries of anguish, abandonment, and despair. Some, of course, can deny God and still keep cheerful. The scientific humanist can dispense with God and still assert the unity and intelligibility of the universe. The average man, however, is more logical. He believes that if God goes, cosmos goes. The race goes to the swift, the battle goes to the strong, the weakest goes to the wall, and everyone must fend for himself. We must eat, drink, and be merry, for tomorrow the undertaker comes. In such circumstances there is no objective standard of values. A man does not ask what he ought to do, but what he wants to do. That is why the family suffers. There is no longer any sense of family obligation. A man thinks in terms of what the family can do for him, and not what he owes to the family. With such a self-regarding attitude, the very existence of family life is challenged.

In the present circumstances what ought we to do? There are three possible attitudes one can take. In the first place it is possible to have a nostalgic longing for the past. This means that one is always reminding children of what one's parents used to expect, and telling them of the good old days when their grandparents were young. It is, of course, an entirely unrealistic attitude to adopt. The sun only stood still for Joshua. History will not go back on its tracks. How foolish it is to suppose that change is necessarily for the worse.

> 'New occasions teach new duties,
> Time makes ancient good uncouth,
> They must upward and still and onward
> Who would keep abreast of truth.'

The second attitude is sheer opportunism. It regards the family in the light of personal convenience. The sex instinct is divorced from its social function. It is not integrated into the structure of family life. Since it is used only in the interest of individual seeking for pleasure and fulfilment, it makes a mockery of family ties and community obligation. It means that one can indulge in sex relations before marriage and be unfaithful after marriage. The only criterion is not what one ought to do, but what one wants to do. Already this selfish, individualistic attitude has resulted in mounting divorces and legal separations. It is obvious that the Church must oppose such behaviour strenuously. Yet mere protest is not enough. One does not get a man to Heaven by telling him that he is going to Hell. For our comfort, we need to know that in God's universe ultimate satisfaction only lies in going God's way. The universe is only open to one-way traffic. In consequence, the people engaged in irregular sex adventures do not even find the fulfilment and satisfaction they seek. They deprive family life of its true significance, and by their behaviour they constitute themselves the enemy of the child. At this present moment irresponsible conduct has gravely weakened family ties, and hundreds of thousands of children are growing up against the background of broken family life. This is an untolerable handicap. They are the problem children of today; and the problem child of today becomes the problem adult of tomorrow. When we condemn sexual irregularity, we are only echoing the denunciation of God Himself.

The third attitude is to re-establish the authority of the family. This can be done, not by resting it upon the authority of the father, nor upon the authority of the mother, and most certainly not upon the authority of the child. (There is no tyranny like the tyranny of the child.) The new authority rests on the family as an organism. It is father, mother and child as a living society. This is in accord with the philosophy of the age. We have passed from the era of unregulated individualism to an age in which we speak of social democracy. In the flashing phrase of Edmund Burke, we desire 'the living partnership of the governed'. We seek the general will in the service of the common good. In precisely that sense, we desire not the self-assertion of the different members of the family, but their co-operation in the interest of all. Each must bring his own gift to the common treasury. This is the true Biblical view of marriage. It is instituted of God, and it signifies the mystical relation that is between Christ and His Church.

How can this authority of the family in its modern setting be maintained? There must be, firstly, the use of external aids. In the Pauline philosophy of the State, it is most clearly affirmed that the State cannot produce the good life. It can only make the good life possible. It can remove hindrances and create the right conditions for every man to enjoy the good life. In exactly the same way, the State cannot make the good family, but it can help to make the good family possible. It can do this by coming to the help of the family on those occasions when help is most needed. That is why for effective conditions of family life there must be some form of social insurance. Help must be given at times of sickness, childbirth, old age, and death. There must be the provision of full educational opportunity. Most certainly there must be family allowances to assist the parents in the rearing of the family. A vital task of the State is to see that accommodation is provided for married couples. The urgent need is for houses, houses, and still more houses. It is intolerable that so many married young people have to live for years with their in-laws. This is a most fruitful cause of marital unhappiness. No Church will command the ear of the public if it shows itself indifferent to this most pressing problem. By every means open to us, we must seek to give the need for houses priority in all discussion of marriage and the family. The State must incessantly strive to secure a stable international order. Whilst young couples look anxiously at a threatening sky and listen to men speak ominously of an uncertain future, they will have no encouragement to develop a normal family life, crowned with the happiness of children.

Secondly, the authority of the family depends upon its internal resources. The danger is not that the partners expect too much from each other, but that they expect too little. If the authority of the family lies in its wholeness, then the husband must expect everything from the wife, as she must from the husband, and as both must from their children, and their children from them. Perhaps the finest compliment ever paid to a woman was paid by Sir Richard Steele. He said: 'To love her is a liberal education.' In the highest form of family life there ought to lie the liberal education of all its members.

All this means that the authority of the family must rest on a spiritual basis. Daniel Niles, in one of his trenchant epigrams, said: 'Man is not willing to be waited upon by God.' There are many, of course, who have no belief in God and therefore seek nothing from Him. Many Christians, however, only want to do God's work. They are willing to give, but they are not willing to receive. They will fight for Him, but they will not allow Him to minister unto them. Yet the whole genius of the gospel is in the symbol of empty and outstretched hands. That is the innermost meaning of the drama of the Lord's Supper. It is only when our hands are empty that we can receive the body and the blood. It is so easy to give good advice to married couples and to urge upon them the virtues of tolerance, good humour, sympathy, and forbearance. Yet these virtues are only possible through divine enabling. It is significant that in the New Testament even the smallest actions are set against the largest background. Jesus, knowing that all authority had been given unto Him, and that He came from God and went to God, took a towel and girded Himself and washed the disciples' feet. When Paul wanted to urge people to be lowly minded, he spoke of Jesus, who, being on an equality with God, was willing to humble Himself as a servant. For the smallest tasks of family life, we need all the help of God. It is only by God's grace that the family can find its true source of peace and power and joy. The family that is waited upon by God is the salt of the earth, for it is the pungent preservative of society.

II. EDUCATION

An address delivered by MR DONALD W. HUGHES, *Headmaster of Rydal School, Colwyn Bay:*

'Education' is a dangerous word. Like that other dangerous word, 'science', it covers a wide field and is used commonly with such a fatal lack of precision that it is gradually ceasing to have any real meaning. Label a man a scientist and he will be listened to with respect on any subject that can be termed scientific—astronomy, for instance, or marine biology, though his expert knowledge may be limited to some narrow field of inorganic chemistry. Label a man an educationist and he will be listened to with respect on such questions as juvenile delinquency or the proper way in which to organize a nursery school, though he may be a university professor, a tutor in a theological college, or merely the headmaster of a Methodist boarding school. The term 'educationist' seeks to mean so much that it is coming to mean nothing at all.

I sometimes wonder whether the word 'education' is any more precise than the words 'human life'. If you say of a man that he is an educationist, have you really defined him any more exactly than if you had called him a human being? We who work in schools and other factories of knowledge need to remember that a great deal of education is carried on outside our walls and that some of the external agencies of education are a good deal more powerful than our own. There is the home, for instance. Educational theorists are always being rude about parents. Indeed, when Plato proposed to remove children completely from the pernicious influence of those who had brought them into the world, and when Swift said that parents were the last of all people to whom children should be entrusted, they were only anticipating what thousands of school-masters have said, and are still saying, on the same theme. But if we are

184

to do what we are constantly urging our pupils to do—that is, to face the facts as they are—we had better recognize that parents are a far more powerful educational factor than we can ever be. We may flatter ourselves that we speak the last word, but the parents speak the first word, and that is the word that counts. And if we are wise enough, and humble enough, we shall not only recognize the fact, but welcome it.

I wonder whether you will agree with me when I say that we in the schools are in danger of becoming arrogant about the work that we do. This arrogance is well illustrated by the comment of a young Englishman who was invited to read *Crime and Punishment* and then say what he thought of it. His comment was: 'All this would never have happened if they had been educated at an English public school.' Educational arrogance is understandable, of course. Education has been the Cinderella for a long time; now her time has come and she is the belle of the ball. Every schoolmaster who can hold a pen writes a book about the subject; people preach sermons about it; politicians have become aware of it and have produced, in this country at any rate, a lot of legislation to prove their interest in it and, incidentally, their ignorance of it. The teacher, it appears, now holds the key to the future. He is moulding the character of the rising generation; he is preparing it for society, for citizenship, for the State, for life; and he is carrying out this arduous task practically unaided. It is a bold claim; fortunately for the community, it isn't true. It is salutary for us to remember, from time to time, that we do not command the child's undivided attention, but only such time as he can spare from his home, his newspaper, his wireless set, his cinema, his television set, his Church (if he goes to one) and from all the other influences which bring powerful pressure to bear all the time in this strident age in which it is our lot to live. When I call myself an educationist, then, I apply to myself a label to which editors, radio comics, film stars, parents, preachers, and popular athletes are all in their different ways entitled. Perhaps I may be excused, then, for saying that the term lacks precision.

My brief is to speak on education for about twenty minutes. You won't expect the subject to be dealt with exhaustively. Let me define the limits within which my experience entitles me to speak. I am concerned with a Methodist boarding school for boys between the ages of thirteen and eighteen. Our curriculum is academic and we try to encourage all the athletic, cultural, and spare-time activities which are traditional in the English public school system. We believe in the training of character, but we are not quite sure how it is done: we hope that it is a kind of by-product of all the things that we do deliberately. This is the only section of education about which I know anything. I hold strong views about all sorts of educational questions, just as a zoologist might hold strong views about the Milky Way, but there is no reason why anyone should take any notice of what I say outside my own sphere. When I talk about education, as I am going to do now and for the rest of this paper, you will understand, I hope, what sort of education I am talking about. If anyone complains that I don't know anything about girls' schools, she will be quite right.

Our concern here is, I think, to consider what contribution Christian education can make to enable young people, and especially Methodist young people, to grow up in this difficult world which is the best that we can do for them by way of a legacy. I believe that we need to distinguish three different tasks, which we often tend to confuse, and in each of them, I am convinced, the school has a very important contribution to make. I would define these tasks as the preservation of Christendom, the propagation of Christianity, and the preaching of Christ. You will, I am sure,

185

appreciate how inadequate and sketchy must be my attempt, in the time at my disposal, to grapple with these three tremendous themes.

First, the preservation of Christendom. I wish that we used this word more often and cherished more intelligently the conception for which it stands. We should be saved from a good deal of loose thought and muddled talk. In the great issues which divide the world, men on this side of the Iron Curtain talk as if it were the Kingdom of God which we are building up our armaments to preserve; we spend our working hours equipping ourselves with aeroplanes and tanks, taking time off on Sunday to sing 'Sufficient is Thine arm alone And our defence is sure', and we have to endure thinly disguised pep-talks urging us to rise in defence of Christianity. It is only too easy for this kind of thing to be answered in the words: 'My kingdom is not of this world, else would My servants fight.' On the material plane, Christianity is indestructible and therefore indefensible. It has survived the catacombs before, and would survive them again. But these arguments are not appropriate, because they deal with the wrong things. It is not Christianity which is at stake, but Christendom, a system of civilization, rooted in Christian values, which has been laboriously built up over the centuries, often by men who seem to us to have been quite unconscious of its roots. It is in Magna Carta, and in the French Revolution, in the Declaration of Independence, and in the conception of the Welfare State and of the United Nations. It has undoubtedly been both extended and preserved by the use of force, both in the remote and in the recent past. It has always been imperfect, of course, and has been defended by unworthy champions, but in the last analysis it has stood for a conception of God before whom ruler and ruled must ultimately come to be judged, and therefore for a certain fundamental respect for personality which guarantees to the individual at least certain minimum rights. I believe it to be true to say that it is this cause that we are called upon to take up today, and I wish that we could learn to call it Christendom. The British character, or the American way of life, is not really an adequate substitute; as a rallying cry, they tend to leave intelligent Europeans and Asiatics somewhat cold.

Now, clearly this conception of Western civilization as inherited Christendom is something which education ought to be concerned to inculcate. To say that our attitude in the contemporary conflict is too negative is a truism. We counter Communist propaganda by giving a list of the evils from which the totalitarians suffer and from which we do not suffer, but we never seem to have a list of our own virtues to present, and our young people seem to be left with the choice between the virile fanaticism of the Marxists and a tepid preference for something which we call 'democracy', which is apparently vague enough and elastic enough to embrace Marshal Tito and General Franco and everything in between. They must be taught, and we must teach them, that the right name for the precarious fringe of civilization which men have managed to construct on the verge of barbarism is Christendom. They must learn that the respect which the scientist has for absolute truth, the determination of the historian to be loyal to the facts as he sees them rather than to be the slave of policy, the appeal of the artist to his own inner light, the instinctive demand of the ordinary citizen for an area within his own personality which is inviolable—all these things, which we take for granted, have been won and kept for us by men who had learnt that there are things which belong to God over which Caesar has no claim, and that there are contexts in which we ought to obey God rather than men. There is no time for me to develop this theme as it ought to be developed, but I would suggest to you that there is not a subject in the academic curriculum which we could count on having taught without distortion if the modern barbarians were to have their way. We know that the arts and biology have already felt the whip; a little imagination will tell us what would be the fate of literature, history, and all the subjects linked to them. I suppose that the last subject to be interfered with would be atomic physics. In our teaching of these things, I believe that we can do much for the preservation of Christendom —even if we teach no more than that there is such a thing to be preserved.

Secondly, the propagation of Christianity. With a different audience I should say a great deal more on this subject, but I imagine that there will be little disagreement here with what I have to plead, and it is never very stimulating to preach to the converted, either for the preacher or for the congregation. Quite briefly, what I have to say is this. Christianity is a system of thought, based on dogmatic religious belief. It is a historic religion and its development can be traced by a historical study back to the words and actions of men who lived at an ascertainable time in world history. Our civilization pays lip-service to this faith, at any rate sufficiently to date its history from the Founder of Christianity. Many of our schools are religious foundations, and in this country the State has given its blessing to activities which are known as 'acts of worship and religious instruction'. So it would seem that the situation is pretty favourable for the propagation of Christianity by means of education. All that we have to do is teach the facts and proclaim the creed.

But this is not true, for two reasons. First, there is the belief which is fashionable in advanced educational circles that it is wrong to inflict dogmatic teaching on the young; and, secondly, there is the whole climate of the society in which they are growing up outside the school. I will deal with these two problems separately.

The advanced educationist has found out that dogma is authoritarian and undemocratic. The child, it appears, has a thing called an 'ego', which is very easily upset; and nothing upsets it so rapidly or so fatally as dogmatic teaching. This, of course, is the type of outlook which drives me into verbosity, and I have already promised that I will not waste your time in arguing with absent opponents. But if I may indulge in one brief moment of shadow boxing, I will say only that the choice is between one dogma and another, not between dogma and no dogma, and that I have never encountered anything more dogmatic than the typical ego-merchant in defence of his theories. And the dogma which I choose is the one which has stood the test of time and is still truer to life as we know it than any other system of belief and conduct. And I affirm, dogmatically and unashamedly, that schools ought to be places of true religion and sound learning, and that it is our educational job to propagate the Christian faith, by preaching and teaching, not only in the teaching of Scripture— though certainly in that—but in all the considerations of philosophy and ethics which are the important by-products of the teaching of such subjects as literature, history, current affairs, and so on. I would also affirm that it is more democratic to let children know where you stand and then teach them dogmatically than to wrap yourself in a cloak of bogus neutrality and try to pretend that you have no beliefs.

My other point concerns the climate of the age. We have to propagate Christianity in a sub-Christian environment. The ethos of the newspaper, of the cinema, of Father's business methods, it may be, and of mother's shopping strategy is very far removed from the standards of the Gospels. Jesus said that the meek should inherit the earth, but Humphrey Bogart at the Odeon last night managed to inherit a good slice of it by being a little tougher than most, and the modern equivalent of 'meek' is 'sucker'. Jesus said that we ought to render to Caesar the things that are Caesar's, but Father was telling us during the holidays of a new method which he had learnt of outwitting the rapacious representatives of the Inland Revenue. Jesus said that we ought to love our neighbour as ourselves, but Mother has found her way to the back door at the butcher's, and by paying a little extra she can now provide a better joint than any of the people who stand there meekly in the queue. If you think that I am laying this on rather too thickly, let me tell you of a successful business-man who sent his son to the school in which I work, but before he sent him he said: 'Remember, if you want to get on in life you've got to look after yourself, and the weakest goes to the wall, so don't take any notice of the things they tell you in chapel about turning the other cheek.' There is nothing exceptional about the attitude, though it is not often expressed so crudely—if you like, so honestly. In the face of this sub-Christian climate, it is our duty, not only as Christians, but as educators, to propagate Christianity. I have already said that I am suspicious of the exaggerated claims which we make for the importance of our job, but I believe that, at any rate as far as this country is concerned, unless we can do this job in our schools, and in our Sunday-schools, we shall have little hope of arresting the fall in standards and of coping with that particular aspect of original sin which is known nowadays as juvenile delinquency.

I have said that this proposition will meet with little opposition here. We ought to recognize that it meets with a good deal of opposition outside, not only with the empirical neglect which I have described, but also with powerful intellectual hostility. In a book called *The Content of Education*, published in 1945 as the interim report of the Council for Curriculum Reform, the following words were quoted with approval in the chapter on religion and ethics. They were written by Professor Julian Huxley in a work called *On Living in a Revolution*. 'The Christian ethic and Christian doctrine, though they have left an indelible mark on our Western civilization in their insistence on the overriding value of the individual personality, on the necessity for sacrifice, and in many other ways, are no longer a primary or an essential part of its framework. New attitudes, new values, new needs have come into being. It is incumbent on the Churches to recast their theologies in forms acceptable to the new phase of the Western world.' I will not insult this audience by pointing out in detail the danger of this woolly heresy, quoted from the writing of an influential intellectual. It is clear that we are asked to abandon the defence of Christendom and the propagation of Christianity in favour of some new so-called synthesis—and you can get away with any nonsense nowadays as long as you remember to call it a synthesis—which will aim at being contemporary today and succeed in being out of date tomorrow. I know that this attitude is being answered in our theological colleges. Are we answering it on a less esoteric wavelength?

Lastly, the preaching of Christ. On this, of all themes, there is very little need for me to dwell here, for the thing that we all have in common is Methodism, and whatever else we may think about our Church we know that if we lose our evangelical urge we lose our *raison d'être*. But before I come to the end I want to make it clear that I do not regard the preservation of Christendom, or the propagation of Christianity, as being at all the same thing as the preaching of Christ. They are dependent on it ultimately, of course. If Christ is not preached, we shall soon have no Christianity to propagate and no Christendom to preserve. That is obvious. But what is not so obvious is that this, too, is an educational task which we cannot properly leave to be done 'by the Church', as we say when we want, as we constantly do, to pass the buck to the clergy. For one thing, all children go to school, but most children do not go to church; for another, if it is really true that man is an imperfect creature in need of a saviour, and that God loves him enough to have made provision for that need, and if it is really true that the secret of living is to be found in a spiritual experience, then what sort of education is it which leaves these facts out of the picture? If it is right for us, in the name of education, to try so to influence the emotional development of adolescents that they may be led to the feet of Shakespeare and of Bach, ought we not to seek also to lead them to the feet of Christ? We are fond enough of the cliche about education being a preparation for life. Should it not be a preparation for life abundant?

There is no doubt about the answer that we should give to these questions. Let me finish by asking that we should face soberly the fact that we are not achieving our aim. It would require greater powers of self-deception than I possess to conclude that Christ is being effectively preached in our schools: that children are growing up in the knowledge that in the scale of values the religious ranks higher than the academic or the athletic. The great wave of apathy which submerges religious feeling in the Western world at this time, and which is a far greater threat to what I have called Christendom than any menace from outside, has not, of course, left the rising generation untouched. Christ must be preached to these inheritors of what has been called a post-Christian paganism. I am not speaking primarily about sermons in school chapels, though these have an important place in the evangelical strategy. What I think is required is that the minds which train these developing minds in adolescence should be Christian minds, and that Christian lives and characters should give expression in their daily environment to the standards and values of the kingdom of God. It is from good teachers that the young catch all their really creative enthusiasms.

I began this paper by confessing that the schoolmaster's job is not as important as he often makes out. Is it really inconsistent that I should end on an apparently contradictory note? Here is a great mission field, a generation growing up in an atmosphere of materialism and spiritual ignorance. If Christendom is to be preserved, they will preserve it. They will not be able to do this, as I believe, unless the propaganda of Christianity is spread amongst them, and this can be done only by those who are resolved to devote their lives to the preaching of Christ. There have never been enough Christians to go round, I know, and there are not enough now, but does not spiritual strategy dictate that Christian schoolmasters and schoolmistresses should, at any cost, be provided? And can the Methodist Church play her rightful part in helping to make that provision?

Group discussions followed the address. (See p. 289.)

The afternoon lecture, in the Examination Schools, was delivered by Dr C. A. Coulson. The Co-Treasurer of the Ecumenical Council, Dr M. S. Davage, of Nashville, Tennessee, presided.

SCIENTIFIC HUMANISM

A lecture delivered by DR C. A. COULSON, F.R.S.E., *Professor of Theoretical Physics, King's College, University of London:*

One of the books which I have at home, and value more than most, is a copy of John Wesley's *Primitive Physick*, or, as the sub-title puts it, *An*

Easy and Natural Method of Curing most Diseases. It has, for me, an interest by no means limited to the information, kindly provided on the fly-leaf, that the book was sold by George Whitfield at City Road, and could be bought at all the 'Methodist Preaching-Houses in Town and Country': nor yet for the happy discovery, surely not without significance in this present gathering, that diseases 'among the Americans . . . are exceeding few', and are generally cured by drinking 'the juice of some herb'. No; it lies in a remark first introduced in the edition of 1760, where Wesley discusses electricity, and 'intreats all those who are well-wishers of mankind to make full proof' of it, claiming that 'it comes the nearest an universal medicine of any yet known to the world'. The claim is substantiated many times over in the list of prescriptions that follow, where we can often read the simple instructions, 'Be electrified', followed by the equally simple, yet devastatingly scientific comment, 'Tried'.

Why does this interest me? First, because even the word 'electricity' was still a relatively new one (William Gilbert, its originator, had died only at the beginning of the previous century); and, second, because Volta, whose experiments with frogs showed how significant electrical influences could be for living matter, was only fifteen years old when this advice of John Wesley was first published. This is important because it shows Wesley grappling with everything that was, as we say, 'in the air' at the time. Science—modern science—the revolution which Herbert Butterfield describes as the greatest landmark since the Birth of Jesus Christ, and which 'reduces the Reformation and the Renaissance to the rank of mere episodes, internal displacements within the system of medieval Christendom'—this revolution had just got under way. *Primitive Physic* (and other books too) remains a witness to the catholicity of John's thought, reminding us that the 'people called Methodists' started their corporate life prepared to understand, and to accept or, if necessary, to refute, all elements of the contemporary mental climate. I should like to think that the same was true of us, now, who are heirs to his high tradition of thought.

I can only bring to such critical commentary my own experience as a professional scientist. But I think it is important that we should discuss scientific humanism while we are here together, because in the last fifty years it has become one of the regulative factors in people's conduct. Both as a creed, and, perhaps more effectively in the form of unspoken presuppositions, it influences behaviour all round the world. It is as much at home in the doctor's surgery as the housewife's kitchen, the politician's office as the pub. This arises from the fact that science and scientific products have dominated our Western civilization. The doctor, the housewife, the politician, and the man in the pub see this every day in their lives. No wonder then that there springs up the claim, often made and far more often implied, that scientific humanism is able to fashion for us a satisfactory way of life.

I want, straightway, to dispose of technology. It is, of course, important and I think future generations will take some pains to stress the manner in which the forms of technology have prescribed corresponding forms of community. But I am anxious to avoid the easy and popular, though quite absurd, mistake of equating science with technology. Technology is, at best, a tool which can be made to respond to any hand that pulls the levers in the right way. In its essence, therefore, it is neutral, even though the penalty that we now pay for its empiricisms and opportunism since the Industrial Revolution should give us pause. Science, on the other hand, makes claims about the nature of reality. It cannot possibly be neutral to the Christian. I think it would be fair to say that there is a large body of

190

public opinion, at heart non-materialist, often (though not always) anti-Communist, who believe that within science there may be found such conceptions of man's place in the whole economy of life, such standards of conduct and behaviour, such success in understanding the world around us and its historical development, such power to create and to destroy, that it seems to them big enough to provide a sufficient basis on which the life of man can be built.

We who are Christians have not played fair with this conviction. Partly through fear, partly (I would like to think, most often) through ignorance, we have tried to laugh it out of court, to speak of its bankruptcy, to sneer at the so-called 'scientific view of man', to pretend as if science itself were one of the Devil's trump cards: when all the time the number of science students at universities and colleges is increasing fast, and our judgement is shown to be so far wide of the mark that the most important new ideology of the day claims the sanction of being scientific (I refer to Marxism). When shall we remember that the scientific revolution which lit up the mind of John Wesley with an almost prophetic glow when he spoke of electricity in the service of man was itself a child of Christian thought, cradled in the Christian tradition? Many of those seventeenth-century scientists, men like Robert Boyle the chemist, John Ray the botanist, Isaac Newton the physicist, all of them early members of the Royal Society, seem to have felt that Creation itself would have been imperfect and the rationality of God in doubt if the physical universe could not be envisaged in terms of scientific law. Even in the Middle Ages men had been aspiring to discover the very kind of laws which took shape ultimately in the theory of universal gravitation, and interpreted for us the motions of the heavenly bodies. It is not hard to show that religious minds were hankering after laws and rationality even before the modern scientist had perfected an adequate technique whereby the form of these laws could be discovered. If now we are too glib in our condemnation of scientific humanism, and liken it to eating the fruit of some forbidden tree, we should do well to recall that this particular tree was not only planted, but also tended, by us.

The Scientific View of Man

The central claim of scientific humanism is that a sufficient view of man, his purpose, his functioning, and his control, can be obtained from scientific study. It will help us to get this clear and in its right perspective if we realize that until quite recently no one would have thought of distinguishing a 'scientific' view of man from any other view. They would have regarded it as one facet of a greater whole. The very possibility of making the distinctive claim for science lies in the disintegration—or, perhaps better, the atomization—of knowledge.

There was a time when religion, morals, science, and aesthetics all owned one common discipline. But these realms of thought are now distinct. 'Geometry, as its name implies, originated with the priests of Egypt to meet the difficulties of the measurement of land following the Nile floods; astronomy in Babylon arose to fix the times of the sacred festivals. In England medicine and nursing was the work of monks and nuns, and St Bartholomew's is the oldest hospital. Poor relief was administered at the monastery door, and the rubric in the Prayer Book still refers to the collection at the Communion Service as "the alms for the poor".'

All this has gone: and the differentiation of function which accompanied the rise of civilization led to the growth of many separate disciplines, where one had served before. It was, indeed, a necessary stage in our intellectual development that this specialization should intervene to break the previous unity. It was necessary, in the same way, that even in the field of science itself, the different disciplines should separate from each other, so that, until recently, there has been little or no speaking ground where, to name but two branches, physicists and psychologists could converse with one another.

I must not labour this point. But I do not believe that we can properly address ourselves to our main task this evening until we recognize how deeply the current of this division runs through our habit of thought. Last summer the Town Planning Institute held its summer school at Nottingham, and heard with evident approval an account of 'biological man's primary activities'. The doctrine of 'economic man' and 'political man' goes back beyond Karl Marx to Aristotle and the Greeks. And now 'scientific man' takes his place, perhaps more self-confidently than the others, as the latest arrival in that procession.

The Three Strands of Scientific Humanism

The time has come for me to say something more specifically about scientific humanism. What is it? On what does it rest? Only by answering these questions can we see its true relation to our Christian faith. It is not easy to define it, for the simple reason that it is woven out of several distinct strands of thought; its strength and its weakness both lie here. For the 'scientific view of man' is a kind of umbrella under which there shelter several apparently unrelated disciplines, each with their corresponding 'view' of man. I must make my case here quite clearly, and, with your permission, will pick out as illustration three of the main strands which together comprise the scientific view. For convenience of classification, I have called them the determinist, the sectional, and the functional. The labels are not entirely happy, and there are many more than these three strands. But these will do.

The Deterministic View. The very word 'deterministic' suggests that this view originated, though it certainly did not remain exclusively, with the physicists. Physics was historically the first science to develop in any thoroughgoing manner, and strict laws were found with a generality that seemed to have no limits, and which appeared to govern all observable phenomena. As Laplace, the French mathematician, said in his famous *Essay on Probability*, if there were a wise and sufficiently industrious mathematician, solving all the equations of motion for every particle in the world, then 'nothing would be uncertain for him, the future as well as the past would be present to his eyes'. The world is a great machine, and, as for God, well 'we have no need of that hypothesis'. If He exists at all, His office is restricted to winding up the Universe when it first started moving. But now He is out of the machine, and the second law of Thermodynamics bears silent witness to the inescapable running down of the works. If it was from the earth that man came, it must surely be to the earth that he returns: for, as Leibnitz, another of the great mathematical physicists said, everything that takes place in the mind and body of a man was as mechanical as what went on inside a watch. No wonder that Descartes had to localize the soul. For if it could not be localized, it could not exist: and, being localized, it became subject to universal physical and chemical laws that tumbled the apple to the ground and fixed the lunar month.

This point of view stretched beyond physics and soon invaded biology. Malthus, Darwin, and Huxley, vitamins, glands, hormones, and genes—

I do not need to trace the story, for it is so well-known. The processes of the natural order are 'explained' and brought under control. The primrose by the river's brim is not just a yellow primrose: it becomes a delicate, carefully balanced mechanism requiring potash, phosphates, and nitrogen in definite proportions, and a fit subject for the laboratory, to see if by suitable cross-pollination its colour can be changed. I remember clearly how, when I was a research student at Cambridge, a friend of mine proudly explained to me that he had devised and grown a blue strawberry. People who think and work like this soon get carried by the very momentum of their activity into strange fields. It is not surprising that only a century ago Engels could define life as 'the mode of action of albuminous or protein substances'. So history gets its new interpretation. For the career of Henry the Eighth is determined by the condition of his thyroid gland, and Churchill's conduct of the last war follows from the shape of his figure!

This is, of course, just a little exaggerated. But we must beware of disregarding the considerable element of truth that it conceals. To a very large degree our actions do follow deterministic laws. And the physical nature of the brain does influence behaviour most significantly. Thus, in the operation of pre-fontal leucotomy, where, following sleepy sickness, the surgeon cuts certain large bundles of nerve fibres connecting the front part with the rest of the brain, we know that the condition of a man's personality is much improved; and we know enough about the electrical aspect of the transmission of sense-data by nerves to recognize a large and fundamental importance of the purely physical in the behaviour and the nature of man. The same is true for much of his psychological behaviour. We disregard it at our peril.

The Sectional View. This leads me to the second strand in the scientific view, which I have called the sectional. According to this, the world of human experience can be thought of in certain non-interacting categories or spheres. In part this is a reflection of the atomization of science, but in part also it bears witness to the integrity and good faith which play so central a part in the Western scientific tradition. For if I am a physicist, then my whole life almost must be sacrificed at that particular altar, and I shall be most unlikely to understand you who are a physiologist or a psychologist. But just as my own scientific standards of honesty and faithfulness to observation are as absolute as they can be, so I must attribute the same fidelity to you. Thus, if physics is my pigeon, psychology is yours: both are valid, by mutual consent, but both are quite divorced from mutual interaction. One has only to look at a gathering of scientists at a scientific congress to realize how clearly there is a physical world, or a chemical world, or a psychological world. (And—may I say it?—a theological world!)

This view of the nature of our universe and of man has recently developed at an alarming rate. I pick out two examples to show the sort of thing I mean.

The first is the growth of what we may call the theory of the physical basis of life. Thanks to the labours of people like Haldane, Bernal, and Darlington in this country, and Oparin in Russia, it is possible to hazard a very sound guess—or series of guesses—regarding the way in which life appeared on this earth out of the primordial dead matter. Thus we start by noticing that only about thirty types of chemical molecule are needed as bricks out of which the larger biological materials are constructed. These are sugars, purines, and amino-acids: and they are quite small, with between four and forty atoms in each. In fact, all the proteins that

193

we know involve only some twenty amino-acids. All these molecules are compounded out of carbon, nitrogen, phosphorus, oxygen and hydrogen in suitable proportions and geometrical relationship. If we get started with these, it is a safe bet that the rest of living biological material will follow. I have no time now to outline how this occurs: how, as the earth cools a certain amount of water vapour appears, and how the ultra-violet radiation from the sun, far more powerful than we find it at the top of the Alps now, and the alternating hot and cold of day and night, pulverizes the barren rocks and leads to the formation of clays and an atmosphere of oxygen; and how the clay particles act as a kind of organizer to hold the component atoms in the right positions to form the fundamental molecules necessary for the emergence of life. It may take a short time, but it will be more likely to take a long one: yet the aeons of time available, some 3,000 million years, are such that it is almost sure to happen some time, when chance brings together the first necessary conglomeration of atoms, just as three or four friends on holiday in Oxford quite independently must inevitably meet if they stay there long enough! Biologists like Darlington go further and say that once the drift towards life had started, it is very likely to end in human beings, not unlike ourselves; and he is led to wonder whether the arrival of some denizen from another habited world might not result in his mating with a woman of this world.

There is much that is speculative in this, and many gaps. That does not matter for our present purposes. What does matter is that life can be discussed in such physical terms and with such completeness. It is probably with such theories in mind that the Russian Hierarchy at the Kremlin has just ruled, for the benefit of the faithful, that life has been generated out of matter by technological means which very soon will be available in the laboratory.

My second example is closely linked with the first. A little while ago the Third Programme of the B.B.C. organized a most interesting series of talks, now published as a book under the title *The Physical Basis of Mind*. How suggestive this is as a title, almost prejudging the conclusion to which several of the contributors came: that mind could be discussed in these physical terms.

The comment which I want to make on all this is that, if they are not exactly correct, they are all so nearly correct that the difference is scarcely significant.

The Functional View. I must pass to the third of my strands of scientific thought—the view of man as functional, and therefore to be regarded, and if necessary exploited, in much the same way that we exploit the natural resources of the mineral rocks. This is the point of view when we speak of operatives, and not working men and women; of so many hands to be employed, or of so much redundancy in the labour force. We see it reflected every time that industrialists speak of 'machinery for collaboration' or 'machinery for settling disputes', as if the physical nature of the machine and the daily labour of the workman were almost indistinguishable in function. It is to be seen in those dreadful words uttered by one of our most distinguished atomic physicists when he said: 'Our civilization is founded on technology, and technology is founded on science.' In a recent newspaper I read the observation by a leading representative of the Road Haulage authorities as he tried to initiate action against certain private hauliers who fail to conform to the pattern of the union: 'The individual does not count; it is only the big thing that matters.' But perhaps the most remarkable description of this functional view is found in that novel, *Arrival and Departure*, by Arthur Koestler. Will you forgive me quoting it to you? It is a most vivid portrayal of the spell of the 'power state' to neglect the human side of man. One of the characters is speaking: 'Close your eyes. Imagine Europe up to the Urals as an empty space on the map. There are only fields of energy; hydro-power, magnetic ores, coal seams under the earth, oil-wells, forests, vineyards, fertile and barren lands. Connect these sources of energy with blue, red, yellow lines, and you get the distributive network. Draw circles of varying radius around the points of intersection and you get the centres of industrial agglomeration; work out the human labour required to feed the net at any point, and you get the adequate density of population for any district, province, or nation; divide this figure by the quantity of horsepower that it produces and you get the standard of living allotted to it. Wipe out those ridiculous, winding boundaries, the Chinese walls that cut across our fields of energy; scrap or transfer industries which were heedlessly built in the wrong places; liquidate the surplus population in areas where they are not required; shift the population of certain districts, if necessary of entire nations, to the spaces where they are wanted, and to the type of production for which they are racially best fitted; wipe out any disturbing lines of power which might superimpose themselves on your net, that is, the influence of the Churches, of overseas capital, of any philosophy, religion, ethical or aesthetic system of the past.'

It is a grim picture—and overdrawn. But it echoes much that we know to be true of the planning of our day, on both sides of the Atlantic—planning which claims above all else the sanction of being scientific in its view of man. And the peculiar irony of it all is that most of what it says is correct; if we neglect it, our civilization will perish.

Comments on This View. I hope I have not spent too long in describing those three elements in the scientific view of man. Granting these, and others which I have not described, what are we going to say about them?

First, that each of these views holds a large measure of truth, with an undeniable authenticity. The whole edifice of science, with its various compartments, is too solid, too austere, to be disregarded. There can be no possible hope for Christianity if it essays a head-on collision with this body of established truth. Bearing in mind the way in which modern science grew out of religious conviction, this should not surprise us.

Second, we must notice that to some extent these separate elements appear mutually incompatible. If, for example, it is once admitted that the determinist view of man enshrines the whole truth about him, then any other view, such as the functional one, is quite impossible.

Scientific humanism represents the attempt to make these separate views whole and coherent, under the axiom that by this means we can get a sufficiently complete view of man.

Let me say at once that with much of this I am in complete agreement. For the more we know about man, from every angle, the more possible it becomes to serve his best interests. There are insights which are not given to the theologian, but which are given to the scientist. This is why I welcome the work of all genuine scientists, and believe that anyone, be he politician or churchman, who attempts to impose any restriction from outside on the work of the scientist, blasphemes against the Holy Spirit. Even the functional view of man, frightening as it is, has much that is true in it. The grim state of the Balkans, the stark poverty of India and the astonishing progress of certain parts of Russia, bear incontrovertible witness to the essential need for improved technology, including the most efficient use of manpower, if we would encourage the full development, not only of the land, but of the people who inhabit the land.

There are some among us to whom what I have just said must appear heresy. I think they are people who have misunderstood John Wesley's injunction to spend our whole time in 'saving souls'. For souls are housed in bodies, and bodies live in a physical world, obedient to physical laws. So we cannot separate the two; and the scientific view of man is good in so far as it reminds us of this. The Universe speaks to us through the scientists, often enough God's unknowing mouthpiece. I should like, here, to adapt some words from our most modern prophet, George Macleod: 'When we realize that all our scientific discoveries are sacramental unveilings of the Body of our Lord; when we realize that we cannot lift a stone to build a fortification but the presence of God moves in to occupy the hole that we have made; when we grasp that the houses men live in (and not just the men who live in them) are offerings for His glory; and that the food men eat (and not just they who eat the food) are aspects of His presence; when the angels reveal (as science, that modern trumpet of the angels, does reveal) that the "fulness of the whole earth is His glory" ', then we begin to know what it means that 'The Word became Flesh'.

The scientific humanist is halfway there. He can supplement our Christian experience: do not let us therefore despise him. For as he brings his element of understanding, so we bring ours—our theological insight into the fact of Christ, which is necessary if we would avoid becoming what would otherwise be pantheist or animist. He sees, as in a glass, that God is in the stone, the tree, and the clod. We supplement his indistinct vision because we see God in the very soul of man, and in our Saviour Christ.

Difficulties

Of course, there are difficulties in scientific humanism. Some at least of them are known to the scientist, and he accepts them as a transitory stage, similar to that through which most scientific theories must pass before they achieve their final status. If, as I hope, we point out these difficulties, and try to make capital out of them, we must do it with sensitiveness. One example will show what I mean. There is a very real sense in which, for us, the revelation of God in Jesus Christ is final and complete. But we must be extremely careful not to confront the scientist too brusquely with this finality and this completeness. (Indeed, in passing, it seems to me that our revelation acquires its authenticity for us as our own life proceeds and deepens.) To the scientist it is absolutely ridiculous to deny a progressive revelation. It is so obvious to him that all his science progresses. We shall only do harm if we object. I am reminded of the way in which, as a result of his continued study, the French entomologist Fabre came to see 'a sublime law of sacrifice' running through the animal world: and of how, from the other angle, St Paul spoke of a 'groaning' in the whole physical creation, as if it waited for something. The scientific humanist, at his best, may put us in the way of beginning to understand what all that means. I should be sorry if we antagonized him so much that we never learnt the lesson he can teach us.

I said there were difficulties for the scientific humanist. And now I am thinking more particularly of the true scientist. The non-scientist, the second-rater, the camp-follower of science, he may see things much more easily than the real scientist does. May I mention, all too briefly, the nature of some of these difficulties? These it is which present us with our opportunity.

First, I shall mention the view, widely accepted till recently, that these several disciplines all start with man as he is, and, because they accept no presuppositions about his nature, possess an objective validity. This is plain nonsense nowadays; and practically every branch of science confirms what I say. The psychologist, for example, knows that it is impossible even to ask a question about a person's mind without, in some degree, influencing that mind. Einstein once said, in relation to another great physicist, Max Planck: 'Most people think it is the intellect that makes a great scientist. Not at all. It is his character.' And oddly enough, physics, that apparently most impersonal of all disciplines, has been having a laugh at us. 'Give me a place to stand', said Archimedes, 'and I will move the world.' Modern physics has shown that there is no need for such a place: and that we are, for better or worse, inescapably part of this world, not only physically, but also mentally. Practically the whole of the later life of Sir Arthur Eddington was spent in showing how the nature of our mind, its way of thinking, and the very experiments that we devise to explore the natural world, to some extent predetermine the kind of answer that we get. There is one of his witticisms that is worth repeating, because it shows what I mean. It exaggerates, but never mind. 'Lord Rutherford', he said, 'is usually credited with having discovered the nucleus in the atom. I think he put it there.' The so-called objective character of the world is transformed into something where personal judgement, and imagination, and even metaphysics begin to intrude. Thus Jeans can write: 'The Universe has become more like a thought than a thing: a thought in the mind of a thinker who is a mathematician, who has left the imprint of his mind in the Universe.' And Bronowski can say: 'It is the unity of nature, living and dead, for which our thought reaches. . . . Science cannot exist without judgements of value.' The most recent book published in this country on the nature of science (J. L. Synge) says: 'Measurement without imagination is but an empty sieve.' So we must stress to the scientific humanist that he has got so far as he has because he has inherited an essentially religious tradition. I should like to develop this further, but must just hint at it. He believes—though he cannot prove it —that there *is* a truth, which is accessible to all people alike. And as for many of the basic virtues—charity, fair-mindedness, truth, tolerance, humility, responsibility, co-operation—these are familiar to him and to his work as being the foundation on which he must build. If all these are not presuppositions, linking him more closely than he usually realizes with our Christian faith, and in some senses reflecting an essentially religious view of man, then I am ignorant of what religion means. Theodor Mommsen's famous phrase—'science without presuppositions'—is now outmoded. Even when devising his scientific theories of man, the scientist is responding to something beyond science; and occasionally glimpsed, as when Jacobi made his famous retort to Fourier—we do science 'for the honour of the human mind'.

The second omission in scientific humanism with which I shall be concerned is equally simple. It does not do justice to our own experience as human beings. The Bishop of Bristol tells how one day he was sitting in a London tram when a very immaculate gentleman entered, resplendent in his pin-stripe trousers, black coat, bowler hat and tightly-rolled umbrella. A small boy, sitting opposite, eyed him most suspiciously for a minute or two, and then, in that high-pitched, querulous tone of voice which small boys reserve for really important occasions, he turned to his mummy and said: 'Mummy, what's that man for?' He was right. There are questions about man that do not come into the categories of science—perfectly

197

valid questions, which do not allow those people who have once perceived them to rest until some satisfying answer has been given. We might say that there was something extra needed, not to change the previous answers, but to supplement them, to interpret them, and to enhance their significance. In Samuel Butler's words: 'The highest thought is ineffable. It must be felt from one person to another, but cannot be articulated—our profoundest and most important convictions are unspeakable.'

Examples crowd themselves upon us. In music, for instance, why does the octave sound pleasant to us? If we say that it is because the two frequencies are in the exact ratio two to one, we do not give a satisfactory answer, though it may be a correct one. When two lovers meet, shall we merely describe the event in terms of an accelerated release of adrenalin into the blood? It's true, but how pitifully inadequate! When we see a mother caring for her child, shall we speak only of the preservation of the race? When we think of the powerful mind of the President of our Conference, is it nothing more than an intricate network of nerve endings and innumerable pulsating electrical circuits that we envisage? It is all this, without a doubt. But all these things—and others too—keep on telling us that what we have been saying about them is true, but it is not enough: that man lives in two worlds (or perhaps more); and that there is a field or world of science in which questions posed in scientific terms get scientific answers, and another world, where words like 'belief', 'love', 'splendour', and 'majesty' have meaning. This other world refuses to be shut out of our experience; and if men try to do so, then even what they have discovered will be taken from them.

Yet these worlds impinge: they are not disparate. When, at the end of his *Origin of Species*, Darwin speaks of the 'grandeur' of the economy of life that he has been describing, when one of the section leaders of the British Association this year chooses for the title of his Presidential Address, 'Organic Design', we ought to see a reaching out to something beyond. When Huxley and Darwin try to interpret whole realms of biological activity under the title 'struggle for existence', we should be willing to recognize kinship with at least one of the main themes of religious thought. When this year's Reith Lecturer, J. Z. Young, speaks of man as made for co-operation and communication with his fellows, he is glimpsing something of the Christian experience of fellowship and the Christian doctrine of Heaven. When Jeans writes of the 'mysterious Universe', and when Fred Hoyle speaks of its 'fineness', both 'in concept and design', they are not far from the Kingdom.

This has brought me to the third—and last—line in which we want to carry the scientific humanist further on his way. I am thinking now of the fact, historically demonstrable, that without a transcendental element in his life, man never achieves stability. Was it not Kierkegaard who said: 'Let the race, let the individual, make the experiment of doing without the unconditional—it is a whirlpool and remains such. For a longer or a shorter period it may seem otherwise; it may seem like stability and security; but at bottom it is, and it remains, a whirlpool. Without relating himself to the unconditional man cannot, in the deepest sense, be said to "live".' When we compare that with the famous canon of Lloyd Morgan, which has dominated psychology for these fifty years—'In no case may we interpret an action as the outcome of a higher faculty if it can be interpreted as the outcome of one which stands lower'—we shall realize that the Christian faith so far transcends the scientific humanist's belief that some sort of 'jump' has to be made if you would pass from one to the other. It is as much part of our job as it ever was in the days of Aristotle that we should 'live eternally in the midst of time'. There are glimmerings of this even in the solid edifice of science: but they are yet only glimmerings. One of our chief tasks, particularly for those of us who are both Christians and scientists, is to lay bare the existence and relatedness of that eternal world of which we are personally aware; and the awe-ful exhilaration that comes to those who know themselves to be *sub specie aeternitatis*. If we can do that, then it will be seen that scientific humanism is a halfway stage, serving a double purpose. On the one hand, it leads to that richer life of faith which is God's intention for all human beings; on the other hand, it adds to the richness and vitality of our worship because of the insights that it gives us into one aspect of the nature of God. To see the splendour of the world revealed by science, to recognize it as fulfilling a purpose mightier than we could have guessed, or even dreamed, to glimpse the almost unthinkable possibilities for human life which are the gift of God to this generation, to know the God thus revealed to be the same as the God and Father of our Lord Jesus Christ, this indeed is to grasp eternity in a moment of time, and 'be lost in wonder, love and praise'.

In the evening a public meeting was held in Wesley Memorial Church. The subject was *The Christian in the Changing Social Order*, and Mr C. C. Parlin, of New York, presided. In his opening remarks, the Chairman pointed out some people believed social justice would be achieved through private enterprise, others through nationalization, and yet another group thought it could only come through the abolition of the profit motive and the establishment of the Marxist State. History would regard some of our experiments as tragic. The speed at which great problems were solved varied. These had been a racial question in America before the Negro came. At first the American Indian had been misunderstood, but the years had revealed his unsuspected qualities. Race relations had changed and were still changing. People were today praying for a new world order. What should the Church stress in such an hour? Perhaps in the Ecumenical Movement there might be an emphasis on world order which rose above race and nation.

The Chairman's address was followed by two speeches. The first, on *Vocation*, was given by the Rev. E. Benson Perkins, M.A., of Manchester, and the second, on *Personal Relationships*, by Dr Dorothy Farrar, of Ilkley.

THE CHRISTIAN IN THE CHANGING SOCIAL ORDER
I. VOCATION

An address delivered by the REV. E. BENSON PERKINS, *ex-President of the British Conference:*

In my student days, we were reading the books of William James and discussing his philosophy of pragmatism. Curiously enough, a footnote on a page of one of his essays fastened itself in my mind and has often recurred through the years. It runs thus:
'The whole defence of religious faith hinges upon action. If the action required or inspired by the religious hypothesis is in no way different from that dictated by the naturalistic hypothesis, then religious faith is a mere

199

superfluity better pruned away, and controversy about its legitimacy is a piece of idle trifling unworthy of serious minds.'

I have little doubt that John Wesley would have accepted that statement, but only, I think, as part of the truth. Action by word or deed is more than just a defence or a test of faith. It is an essential part of the life of faith. The word John Wesley uses is 'fruits'. He held that where the desire to be saved from sin is 'really fixed in the soul, it will be shown by its fruits': not therefore just a test of faith, but the fruit of faith—the fruit being an essential part of the tree itself.

From the beginning, this has been a Methodist emphasis in relation to the Christian life. There was a time in the earlier period of John Wesley when the fruit of faith seemed almost more significant than the faith itself, but there was never a time when the fruit in active living was absent. This emphasis can be indicated by three references to Methodist history:

(1) The name we bear originated, as we are so well aware, in a sneer at the little group of Charles Wesley and several of his friends at Christ Church College, known as the Holy Club. Later John Wesley became their Leader. They observed a rule of life, bringing all the actions of the day under review and seeking by service which involved self-sacrifice to help others as well as themselves. When in 1738 both John and Charles entered into the rich experience of the living presence of Christ, this new experience did not in their thought or interpretation abrogate the meaning and significance of the discipline of those earlier days in Oxford.

(2) Still more significant are the *Rules of the Society of the People called Methodists*. This document, drawn up in 1743, had a powerful effect on Methodism in that early and formative period. The late Henry Carter, in a book called *The Methodist*, analysed the *Rules* under three headings which it will be helpful to use:

(*a*) *The Christian Negative.* 'Doing no harm, avoiding evil in every kind.' Much of the detailed exposition under this heading reads rather quaintly and must, of course, be set against the background of that century. Even so, it is not without direct reference to life today. Such phrases as 'buying or selling spirituous liquors, or drinking them except in cases of extreme necessity—buying or selling uncustomed goods—doing to others what we would not they should do to us—taking such diversions as cannot be used in the name of Christ—softness and needless self-indulgence—laying up treasure on earth'—these are not so antiquated in their reference as is often supposed.

(*b*) *The Christian Positive.* 'Doing good of every possible sort and as far as possible to all men.' This means doing good to their bodies—to their souls—to members of the household of faith, and indirectly by diligence and frugality, that the gospel be not blamed.

(*c*) *The Christian Dynamic.* 'By attending upon all the ordinances of God'—such as public worship, ministry of the Word, the Supper of the Lord, family and private prayer, and the like.

Here is the Methodist rule of life, embodying a standard of reference and indicating quite clearly that sense of vocation which has an abiding significance. One amongst many incidents related to the *Rules* from the early story of Methodism may be quoted. John Nelson, the stonemason who became so great an evangelist, dismissed from the Society a woman who was later charged before the York Assizes for a capital offence. He was subpoenaed to appear as a witness and asked the reason for his dismissal of the woman from the Methodist Society. John Nelson referred to the *Rules*, and at the Judge's desire they were read in open Court, leading to the comment by the Judge: 'Gentlemen, this is true Christianity.'

200

(3) It was the year after the Rules were framed when John Wesley preached his famous sermon in the Church of St Mary the Virgin, Oxford, on 'Scriptural Christianity'. He described it as beginning in the individual, spreading to others, until at last it covered the earth. In the latter part of the sermon he said, 'Let us stand a little and survey this strange sight, a Christian world', and, after indicating what a Christian world would be like—where there was no din of arms, no country or city divided against itself, no oppression or extortion or injustice—he asked: 'Where does this Christianity now exist? Is this city a Christian city? Is Christianity, Scriptural Christianity, found here?' Having regard to the condition of Oxford, as well as of the country, at that time, it is not surprising that John Wesley was never again allowed to preach before the University. His words were too pointed in the realm of actual living, describing as they did the real vocation of a Christian.

This sense of vocation is an essential part of John Wesley's understanding of 'Scriptural Holiness'. As he said in one of his sermons: 'Christianity is essentially a social religion and to turn it into a solitary one is to destroy it.' He was against that type of piety or quietism which turned one's thoughts inward instead of outward. Giving his *Plain Account of Christian Perfection* in 1777, he said: 'A Methodist is one who loves the Lord his God with all his heart, with all his soul, with all his mind and with all his strength . . . and loving God, he loves his neighbour as himself, he loves every man as his own soul.' Here is the safeguard from that type of so-called perfect love which is a state of mind and heart detached from the life of the world—a kind of personal monasticism. There are two elements which meet in the true understanding of Christian holiness, and they are personal conversion to the religion of love, and the social obligation of Christian discipleship. As John Wesley put it in one of his own hymns:

> 'Inflame our hearts with perfect love,
> In us the work of faith fulfil,
> So not Heaven's host shall swifter move
> Than we on earth to do Thy will.'

The two truths of inward holiness and social activity were held as of equal obligation. It was the filling of the heart and mind with love which led inevitably to a real concern and obligation 'to serve the present age'. One of Wesley's famous sayings was: 'Love is the never failing remedy for all the ills of a disordered world.' By that he meant, to quote him again, 'pure love, filling the heart and governing all the words and actions'.

The whole history of Methodism demonstrates the truth of the Christian vocation—the calling of the Christian to a life of active love. Wesley the citizen is as true a picture of the great man as is Wesley the evangelist. Both aspects belong to the one life. The British historian, C. M. Trevelyan, declared that 'Methodism in one form or another inspired most of the philanthropic work of the century that ended with Wilberforce' (died 1833). The story of Methodism on the American continent records how Francis Asbury and Thomas Coke, before any other religious leaders, attended upon George Washington, the first President of the United States of America, to convey the wishes and prayers of the Methodist community. In effect, they were saying that the Methodists recognized the obligations of their citizenship.

Passing over so much of interest in this connexion which is found associated with the life of Wesley—his work for education, his interest in the bodily health of the people, his philanthropic work for orphans and destitute people, his concern for political wellbeing—let us note that the

201

following century in Great Britain saw the Methodist people living out their faith in relation to the changing social order. It is not the truth to say, as do Mr and Mrs Hammond in their study of the early nineteenth century, that the Methodist movement made saints and not citizens, that in fact Methodism had no contribution to make in respect of the social conditions which were the outcome of the Industrial Revolution. Let one or two familiar facts speak for themselves.

There are certain very significant dates in the early nineteenth century. The year 1832 saw that interesting group known as 'The Seven Men of Preston' taking the first total abstinence pledge against all alcoholic beverages under the inspiration of their Methodist experience of the love of God. It was a step requiring courage, and was taken not for themselves merely, but out of concern for those who were suffering in body, mind, and soul as the result of alcoholic indulgence. The following year, 1833, came the declaration of freedom for slaves in British territory. It should be recalled that John Wesley's last letter, the week before he died, was written to William Wilberforce, who had begun the agitation against slavery, which John Wesley described as 'that execrable villainy which is the scandal of religion, of England and of human nature'. That was on 24th February 1791. Forty-two years later, the year of the death of Wilberforce, the victory was won.

The next date, 1834, is associated with a group of Methodist farm labourers in the village of Tolpuddle in Dorsetshire. A deed still intact and associated with the first Methodist chapel in that village bears the signatures of George Loveless and Thomas Standfield, two of the members of this group. Out of concern for their fellows, they formed an association with a view to working out means to improve their lot. They were arrested on the ground that they had formed a seditious society, and in the year 1844 were deported to Botany Bay as convicts. The country rang with indignation, and four years later they were given a free pardon. It was, however, their action and their suffering which established the right of trade association and made possible the development of trade unionism, which, in spite of whatever mistakes may have from time to time been associated with it, was a great factor in the improvement of social conditions in England during that century and since.

For another set of facts coming later in the century, we may turn to the historian of the trade union and Labour Movement, Lord Passfield, better known as Sydney Webb. Let his own words speak for themselves:

'Into a community, ignored by the statesmen of the time and virtually given up as hopeless by cleric and philanthropist alike, there came between 1821 and 1850 two inspiring influences, religion and trade unionism. First to be named must be the Methodists, notably the humble, unschooled but devoted "ranters", carrying gradually from village to village the Gospel of Salvation. . . . What they aimed at was primarily the salvation of the soul. But the change of heart which accompanied conversion was habitually marked, though often with backslidings, by a change of life. . . . Family after family became thus transformed to serve in its turn as a centre of helpful influence. . . . It is the men who are Methodists, and in Durham County especially the local preachers of the Primitive Methodists, whom we find today taking the lead and filling the posts of influence.'

Those Durham miners whose hearts and lives the Lord had changed had no doubt about their vocation, and bravely did they serve their generation. It was such men who were the pioneers of what is known in Great Britain as the Labour Movement. Morgan Phillips, the Secretary of the Labour Party, said in a recent conference that the Labour movement owed its chief debt, not to Marxism, but to Methodism. That is not to make Methodism responsible for all the political actions of that Party, but it is to recognize the spiritual impulses moving in the hearts and lives of men which found expression in leadership for better social and economic conditions—a sense of vocation indeed. It is in fact regrettable that the spiritual impulses of the social advance at the end of the nineteenth and early twentieth century came to be ignored or forgotten by many in the later generations of Labour leaders, though, we may be thankful, not by all.

What, then, is our vocation as Methodists in the changing social order of our time? Before I endeavour to answer that question, I must point out certain dangers or hindrances.

In the first place, the scale of world change and world confusion tends to remove our thoughts from the local and the immediate. We tend either to conclude that the canvas is too vast for any effort of our own, or we satisfy our sense of responsibility by somewhat vague generalizations. Quite often our general talk becomes an escape from immediate personal responsibility in respect of our neighbours and our neighbourhood. It is not wrong that we should discuss the settlement of world issues, but unmistakably wrong to let that take the place of a true sense of our personal vocation—our calling to serve this present age where we are placed and in relation to our own immediate environment.

Then another frequent mistake is the tendency to equate Christianity with a particular economic or political system, particularly the system operating in our own community. As the first Assembly of the World Council of Churches at Amsterdam pointed out in the report of one of its commissions, the constructive reply to Communism is not the precious *status quo*. As this report indicated, while Communism offers what is supposed to be justice while at the same time denying freedom, *laissez-faire* capitalism claiming the privilege of freedom of action often denies justice. We must not accept this easy and superficial solution, but realize that Christianity impels us further and deeper than we often suppose.

It is not only that we have to note the tendency to associate Christianity with a particular system, but we must acknowledge that unless the Christian recognizes a personal vocation, any and every system will be bound to fail. Many have hoped in recent years that in some form of economic Socialism the true ideal might be realized and both freedom and justice be secured. Sir George Schuster, in his recent Beckly Lecture, *Christianity and Human Relations in Industry*,[1] says: 'Every form of human system will be liable to abuse as long as men seek selfish ends.' He added: 'I believe that the power motive or the publicity motive might be even more dangerous than the profit motive.'

These points call for much further discussion than is possible in this address, and I can only note them in passing. It is particularly important, however, that we should recognize that we can neither escape from a personal responsibility by generalizations about what politicians and governments should do, nor by resting satisfied with the conditions of life with which we are familiar.

In the endeavour to be definite about the question of vocation, I can only deal with it along one or two lines by way mainly of illustration and without attempting anything in the way of a complete statement. I suggest that in the main our vocation can be summed up in the classification of John Wesley's *Rules of Membership*, to which reference has already been made, particularly in the Christian negative and the Christian positive.

(*a*) Turning first, then, to the Christian negative. It is sufficient to recall

---

[1] The Epworth Press (1951), 6s. 6d.

that one serious and regrettable phase of the life of the world today is that of self-indulgence. A story told during the latter part of the war recalls the incident of a girl in a railway carriage being invited by the three other occupants, who were American soldiers, to accept a gift of gum or a cigarette or a drink from the silver-stoppered flask, and refusing on the ground that she did not take any of them. She affirmed in answer to the question that she was neither addicted to chewing, smoking, or drinking, and one of the Americans said: 'Then I guess you must be a Methodist.' It would, of course, be absurd to suppose that this is a true description of a Methodist, but it is equally false to take the line that there are no negatives in human life. The true discipline of refusal is involved in our vocation. It is clearly set out in the New Testament, where the one who would follow Christ must, as it has sometimes been translated, 'say No to self'. At the present time the better life of England, to illustrate from one country, is being debased by indulgence. The drink problem is not at an end because drunkenness is not so frequently seen on the streets, and associated with indulgence in drink is that of drugs, which if report is to be relied upon, is affecting young people in more than one country. Then, in this country gambling is a growing menace, so much so that a Royal Commission has been recently examining this problem at the instance of the Government. It is not only the gambling which takes place on racecourses, but the gambling which is entering the homes through the post in the form of football pools. A Commission representing a section of the Church of England issued a report recently which on the basis of casuistical argument declares that gambling is not wrong in itself and is all right if it is merely an amusement. I mention this to indicate that it is necessary not only to stand against the practices themselves, but also to resist the false arguments of those who justify a measure of such indulgence. In still another direction, a book recently published, *English Life and Leisure*—the result of research by Seebohm Rowntree, so well known in this field—contains a number of case histories which present a terrible picture of sexual looseness. Then, too, the use of money has become a matter of carelessness and indulgence. Professor Zweig of Cracow University has been studying conditions in England, and points out that there are many working men who spend half their wages every week in drink and gambling and smoking. The sense of responsibility in the use of money seems to be lacking, and the more so as wages increase. The real tragedy is not the material and financial considerations merely, but the hurt to the souls of men and women as a result of this self-indulgence. A joyous self-discipline is a contribution which the Methodist people, in a peculiar sense, can and should make. It is indeed part of the true vocation of the Christian and part of that vocation which Methodist life and history has strongly emphasized. It is to be found in Charles Wesley's hymns:

'Superior sense may I display,
By shunning every evil way,
And walking in the good.'

'The secret pride, and subtle sin,
O let it never more steal in
To offend Thy glorious eyes.'

This part of our vocation should never be a matter of self-satisfied pride that we are free from these things, but a deep concern, arising out of our love, that no stumbling block should be placed in the way of our brethren in Christ.

(*b*) The Christian positive calls for an exposition far beyond the opportunities of this address. It is a part of our vocation which is not to be exhausted by philanthropy. The very conditions of life and work claim our thought and service. As William Temple said, 'The Church cannot abandon its task of guiding society', and, as we have so oft reminded ourselves, the Church means the members of the Church. There was a time when the needs of the poor and neglected cried out for assistance and help. To some extent, and in some communities to a considerable extent, the action of the State has eliminated much of this grinding poverty and many of these evil conditions. The Welfare State is being realized, and in this connexion the State can be regarded as the handmaid of Christianity. Further, in the realm of political and economical action, the Christian cannot stand aside. State action in Western civilization determines very largely the distribution of the gifts of God and the ordering of the life of the community. Seeming restrictions upon an unfettered freedom are really in many cases the means to secure a larger freedom for a greater number. In all these endeavours, the Christian must support that which makes for righteousness and justice, while at the same time declining to be the slave of a party or a system. The World Council of Churches talked about the 'apostolate of the laity', and one part of that surely is found in the service which the laity can and should render in the life of local and national government. These responsibilities should be accepted as opportunities to live out and work out the Christian life of love. It may well be that out of regard for personal comfort and freedom from irritating discussion too many have stood aside from the opportunities presented by official action and official position in the governing bodies of the community. This is unquestionably for some their Christian vocation.

In the last analysis, it is persons in themselves and their relationship one to another which matter most of all. Schemes and policies will fail unless these personal contacts are inspired and directed by love. There are many who consider that the nationalization of some if not all the public services and some of the industries may well point the way to adjustments that will be helpful to the life of the community, but it was Mr Herbert Morrison, the present Foreign Secretary in Great Britain, who pointed out not long ago that changes in the social and economic order are not sufficient unless also there are changes in men and women. We need the best possible system. Kind-heartedness is no substitute for inefficiency. But having the efficient instrument in the realm of social and industrial life, we have not solved our problem. Strained human relationships and antagonism between management and workers do occur under both nationalism and capitalism. Whether as manager or worker or in any other field, the Christian finds his more immediate vocation at his point of contact with his fellows. The real answer to the dominance of merely material interests is love in human relationships, and no mere economic system, however desirable in itself, can create those true relationships. External measures are not enough unless they are governed by the right spirit on the part of those concerned at every point. Only love in human lives will suffice, and that love need not wait until the perfect scheme or plan has been devised. Here is the immediate vocation of the Christian —here is the field where Scriptural holiness finds its opportunity and true expression.

Quite often we are inclined to doubt the value of one person with one narrow range of influence. In fact, no limits can be set to the ultimate results of personal influence, however simple in itself. If I were inclined to doubt the power of personal influence, I have only to recall an incident in my own ministerial life when I was Superintendent of one of our Central missions. It was at the time when unemployment was rife, and a girl of sixteen, sadly needing employment in order to help in the home, was sent by the Labour Exchange to a job of work at a printer's. She found when she got there that it was where football pools were being printed and issued—in fact, part of the organization of gambling. Without hesitation, she refused the work, and in reply to the angry retort of the Manager declared that she was bound to do so as a Methodist. She was reported as having refused work, her unemployment allowance was stopped, and she was called upon to attend before the Court of Referees. I was able to be her friend and to argue the case before the Court, and ultimately to take it up with the Ministry of Labour. The final result, was a clear and emphatic verdict that any young person was entitled to refuse such work. It happened that it was the first case of that kind which had been challenged, and because of that case word went to the Labour Exchanges throughout the whole country making clear the right of any young person to refuse an order to work in connexion with the organization of gambling. Rosie had no conception that she was doing anything particularly important, but was just standing for those principles she had come to know and understand. In doing so, her influence spread throughout the land. This must ever be the case when moral decisions are made, and the love for God and for one another operates in all the activities of life. It begins and centres in the experience of salvation and passes out into the life of the whole community. Here pre-eminently is the vocation of the Christian amid all the changes of the social order.

It has often been said that the most thrilling of the national songs is the 'Marseillaise', and Heinrich Heine described one of the songs of Luther as the 'Marseillaise' of the Reformation:

> 'Ein feste burg ist unser Gott,
> ein gute wehr und waffen.'

Someone has described one of the songs of Charles Wesley as the 'Marseillaise' of Methodism:

> 'A charge to keep I have,
> A God to glorify,
> A never dying soul to save
> And fit it for the sky.

> 'To serve the present age
> My calling to fulfil,
> O may it all my powers engage
> To do my Master's Will.'

Could the Christian vocation be indicated more accurately?

II. PERSONAL RELATIONSHIPS

An address delivered by DR DOROTHY FARRAR, *of the Wesley Deaconess College, Ilkley:*

It is usually considered necessary at a conference of any importance that the speakers should have some knowledge of their subjects; if possible, they should be experts. In the matter of personal relationships our need for help is so great that many people have become specialists in different aspects of this subject. Indeed, the number of specialists is perhaps the measure of our defeat. There are those who can advise in relationships

206

between husband and wife, parent and child, teacher and taught, nurse and patient, management and employee, and so on. I am not one of them, and do not therefore intend to speak as an expert. In any case, there must always be a question mark even against experts. What about the problems of the expert himself? Have there been no disasters in the lives of those who advise others on marriage? Can that problem child really belong to a child guidance specialist? Can it be that some psychological and socio-logical knowledge is, as John Wesley says, only 'Splendid ignorance, pompous folly, vexation of spirit'?[1] It would seem that there is only one safe place from which to start, however much or little knowledge one may have: the standpoint of one who recognizes the fact of sin in all our human contacts. Behind all that I say tonight is the confession and prayer: 'In all matters of personal relationship, God be merciful to me a sinner.'

I. Our Defeat

In our changing social order there are, of course, many relationships which are creative and enriching and we all thank God for those which He has granted to us. Yet we cannot deny that we live in an age of nervous tension, uneasy friction and personal loneliness which seems to us to be unique. We have a tendency to see our personal contacts as potential problems containing alarming possibilities of abnormality. This is no doubt brought into prominence by the changing pattern of our society, when conditions which seemed stable have crumbled, many bonds have been broken by war and violence; when many people who might never have been aware of one another have been forced into daily contact in camps, cramped living quarters resulting from lack of houses. Our theatre, radio, magazines, and the daily Press present us hourly with stories of poignant failures between persons, in homes, communities, and even Churches. Add to this the life stories of the human beings each of us know, stories which have never been made public, then is it any wonder that we are frequently hurt and painfully aware of defeat?

This sense of defeat is frequently expressed as a sense of isolation. It is so hard to reach one another. We seem unable to make and keep a living connexion with another human being which goes deeper than mere super-ficial contact. We are uneasily aware that we do not really know one another. It is not for nothing that one of the words of Scripture which has most deeply moved men's minds is 'Behold I stand at the door and knock . . .', for each one of us knows that we truly live alone in the house of the soul, and if the door remains closed we are prisoners. This has been stated for modern readers by a character in Arthur Koestler's novel, *The Age of Longing.* She thinks of each person as 'living in his own portable glass cage. Most people she knew did. Each one inside a kind of invisible telephone box. They did not talk to you directly but through a wire. Their voices came through distorted and mostly they talked to the wrong number.' So often in the literature and life of today there is a strange hunger for some half-imagined personal deliverance which will lift the burden of loneliness. For instance, there can be a crushing sense of anonymity in modern industry. This particularly was noticed by the Roman Catholic priests who are working among the dockers of Marseilles, but it is not only at that level. A girl who had been employed in a small, homely business took a post in one of the subsidiary companies of a big corporation. One day she said to me with a kind of fear in her voice: 'You know, I don't know now who *really* employs me.' Even in the Christian Church there can be a loneliness which should not be there. A minister

[1] Sermon on Scriptural Christianity.

207

can be lonely in his congregation, and a visitor to his church may be lonely too. How can these 'Christian solitudes', as one writer has called them, succeed in coming together? If we cannot find a solution how can we hope to reach the vast working population which in so many of the world's great cities seems to be outside the reach of the Christian Church?

We claim that the Christian Gospel has an answer to this tragedy of isolated persons, but talks, lectures, sermons will not convince us, still less the perplexed and hungry society outside. Canon Warren, in his book, *The Truth of Vision*, has said: 'Here our task is one of demonstration that we do in fact possess the answer to the needs and problems raised by human relationships.' There must be something for men to see and understand. Wesley said: 'Love cannot be hid any more than light. . . . As well may men think to hide a city as to hide a Christian.'[1] The showing forth of our answer is not for our comfort or convenience, but for a more important end: nothing less than our power to evangelize is at stake. When we quote 'That they may all be one that the world may believe' we think rightly of the re-union of divided Christian communities. But it is not enough. No real union is possible without a firm network of personal relationships. Two alienated churchgoers in one street can obstruct the witness of the Christian community in that locality as effectively as two estranged congregations can do in a town. Is not God calling us to draw near to one another at a deeper level, to reverence one another—yes, to love one another? Here we do well to pause for we find ourselves at a point where all our thoughts are drowned, for we are brought face to face with an amazing possibility.

> 'Love divine, all loves excelling,
> Joy of heaven, to earth come down;
> Fix in us Thy humble dwelling. . . .'

II. The 'Threefold' Relationship

We who are Christians have never considered deeply enough the fact that in our personal relationships there is present One Other. There can never be a relationship between two personalities for there are always three, never a contact between two minds but three. This is true whether we speak of husband and wife, parent and child, foreman and worker, friends and colleagues. Whenever a Christian is in contact with one or more people there is always present and active, God Himself, whether we think of Him as the Holy Spirit or as the Lord Jesus Christ. We do not think of Euodia and Syntyche being of one mind; they are of one mind *in the Lord*. The Christian Church affirms this truth in its services. The Marriage Service declares that the union of a man and woman is not their private concern, or even the State's concern; it is in Spirit. Baptism, among other truths, declares that the new situation in the home does not involve father, mother, and baby, but father, mother, and baby—and God. There is no better testimony to this fact than that given by Professor John Bailie in *Our Knowledge of God*, p. 4: 'As little can I reach a day when I was conscious of myself, but not of God, as I can reach a day when I was conscious of myself but not of other human beings. My earliest memories have a definitely religious atmosphere. They are already heavy with "the numinous". They contain as part of their substance a recognition, as vague and inarticulate as you will, yet quite unmistakable for anything else, of what I have now learned to call the divine as a factor in my environment. I cannot remember a time when I did not already feel, in some dim way, that "I was not my own" to do with as I pleased, but was claimed by

[1] *Sermon on the Mount*, IV.

208

a higher power which had authority over me. . . . For as far back as I can remember anything, I was somehow aware that my parents lived under the same kind of authority as that which, through them was communicated to me.' This awareness may not be the lot of all children, but its presence or absence does not alter the fact of a relationship indwelt by God. All this was summed up for me in a profound simplicity by a fine old Christian man, who, when he and one friend wished to embark on a new venture of fellowship, was met with the remark: 'But there's only two of us.' He replied at once: 'No—you and me and the Master.'

This is not a matter of conventional prayer for those with whom we have contact, or of trying laboriously to obey Christ's commands about loving our neighbours, but the recognition of a profound truth about the relationship between persons. There is One actively present, perfectly loving in our imperfect human contacts. C. F. Dodd, in his *Commentary on the Johannine Epistles*, says: 'The energy of love discharges itself along the lines which form a triangle whose points are God, self, and neighbour.' This fact seems to have been grasped more surely by theologians, at least in theory, than by psychologists. Of course, one would not expect an examination of family relationships, 'social interest', etc., by non-Christian psychologists, to reckon with this fundamental truth, though, in so far as it is ignored even as a possibility there must be some distortion in thought. It is amazing, however, that psychologists professing some Christian faith can in practice ignore it. They are concerned with the wrong attitude of an individual towards other individuals and can see active in that defective relationship a father-figure, a mother-figure, but rarely does one feel that God Himself is thought of as active in the tangled situation. There is open a strange gap in our thinking. As Koestler's heroine says: 'For the place of God had become vacant and there was a draught blowing through the world like an empty flat before the new tenants have arrived.' A draught indeed—and the New Testament has something to say about the possible new tenants of empty houses. It may be that in theory we all believe in an active love, not our own or our neighbour's, present in our human encounters, but even in pastoral work, counselling or whatever it is called, we all tend to forget it in practice. If Christians are to be experts in personal relationships, surely it is at this point that we should be more expert than those who have no faith, even though our knowledge be held with a trembling hand, for we confront a mystery of God.

III. Results of the Threefold Relationship

The fact that the relationships of a Christian are in and through Christ has certain inescapable results. These results are understood in so far as they are accepted by the individual. The presence of active holy love in our relationships means just that our poor attempts at loving are always under judgement of that love. I do not mean that there is a constant condemnation which leaves us helpless and guilty, for if that were the case we have no message of salvation. Judgement involves a showing forth of truth, a diagnosis of our condition, and surely we need to know the truth in our personal relationships. We see in Christ where our love fails, where it is tainted by self, where it is twisted and marred by hitherto unrecognized factors. The Christian can pray, 'Search me and know my heart', and can come to welcome the searching judgement of perfect love. As we turn thus to Him for mercy, we find not only that we are welcomed, pardoned, cleansed, relieved, but that through that deeply personal transaction with Christ we have learned how to forgive others. Paul did not learn that 'love never faileth' from his own affections, nor from any other friend, but only because he was constantly met in his need by a love that never has failed nor can fail. The injunction to forgive means little till we have actually experienced it, so we forgive others as Christ forgave us, comfort others as God comforts us, love one another as He loves us. The very pattern of right relationships is set up in our minds because they have happened to us, not because we have read or heard about them. Our human contacts are caught up into the realm of pardoning love and we can pardon and be pardoned in Christ. Our brother is transformed because he becomes the brother for whom Christ died. We can say: 'Love to the uttermost is literally taking place here and now in my relationship with my nearest and dearest, and in my contacts with the derelict, the repulsive, the complacent.'

As there is judgement and mercy ever present, so also is holiness, and the perfect love of Christ through the Spirit sanctifies. John Wesley points out: 'God builds up His children, by each other.'[1] We cannot be made holy in some mysterious inner way while our human relationships remain unholy. If sanctification is 'perfect love', then it is plain that it is in our relationships that it will be seen. We are sanctified with and through our brethren, and we look towards 'loving every soul which God hath made, every man on earth as our own soul.'[2] The most difficult of our personal relationships interpenetrated by the perfect love of our Lord may be the greatest instrument in our sanctification, for not only does His love penetrate the 'dumb region of the heart in which we dwell alone', the hidden man of the heart, but in doing so breaks the 'glass cage' and sets us free to be in community with our fellows, and that community is the 'medicine of life'.

This mutual human love shot through and through with His love must have a discharge in action; emotion is not love. The problem of the Church today is often that this discharge is remote from its object. For instance, our evangelism can be remote: we pray that others may be trained and sent to reach people thousands of miles away, or even three miles away in a down-town mission. It becomes unreal unless as well as the necessary giving we are sharing in the personal cost by trying to reach the people we know. Money has been given and is, thank God, being given for the feeding and clothing of stricken people, but sometimes it can be a means of salving the conscience and keeping the distressing problem at a distance from one's mind. The 'Love in action' of which John Wesley speaks should mean direct evangelism, the giving from person to person involving understanding as well as remote giving or there is no real discharge of love. Contacts leading to friendship are what we need especially between Christian and those who seem remote from the Church. If our love is also Christ's love, it will be expressed as He expressed love, through care for each person without patronage, by concern for both body and soul, by seeing people as they can be, through spending and being spent for them. When the world can see Christian love demonstrated, not merely talked about or discussed, they will have the chance of believing which they can never have when we 'unsay with our lives what we say with our lips'.

IV. Renewal of Relationships

Personal relationships are often costly in nervous energy. In such a gathering as this most people must know what it is to have a great number of superficial relationships—too superficial, perhaps—which are exhausting by reason of sheer number, but also those which demand much

[1] *Sermon on the Mount*, XIV, p. 265.
[2] Quoted, Henry Carter, *Methodist Heritage*, p. 177.

patience, alertness, and long-suffering. Contacts with those within and outside the Church who are neurotic and unstable can leave us drained. Writing to the *Christian Frontier*, Sir Arthur fford remarks on this 'drain on the personality', the necessity to 'replenish the reservoirs'. Is there a remedy?

First there is the renewing power in the deep fellowship of a small group who can meet for 'the interchange of thought and the community of prayer'. Sir Arthur fford found this in the Christian Frontier Council; the Methodist Church in the Class Meeting or, earlier, in the more intimate Band Meeting. In some mysterious way, the contact of personality at a deep level, interpenetrated by the active presence of the indwelling Christ is not demanding, but refreshing, and seems to bring the water of life to parched minds. Our relationships are the poorer without this fellowship, and some are too difficult for us to sustain creatively. Especially is this true of relationships with the hostile or indifferent third-generation pagan or with the emotionally disturbed.

The other and more generally accepted way of renewal is in the complete withdrawal which our Lord practised. In Wesley's *Sermon on the Mount*, IV, where he stresses the fact that Christianity is a social religion, he says: 'Not that we can in any wise condemn the intermixing of solitude or retirement with society. This is not only allowable, but expedient, nay it is necessary. . . . It can hardly be that we should spend one entire day in a continued intercourse with men without suffering loss in our soul and in some measure grieving the Holy Spirit of God. We have need daily to retire from the world at least morning and evening to converse with God. . . . Nor indeed can a man of experience condemn even longer seasons of religious retirement.' While Charles Wesley experiences the same thought in Hymn 598:

> 'All Thy life was prayer and love,
> Such our whole employment be,
> Works of faith and charity;
> Works of love on man bestowed,
> Secret intercourse with God.'

This principle of alternation called by Arnold Toynber and later by Max Warren 'withdrawal and return' is not strange to us in theory, but is it in practice? How long do we spend in secret intercourse with God? And if we hold what we call a 'retreat', is it often a retreat from talking in one place to talk in another? We cannot detach ourselves sufficiently from the claims we make on one another so that the reservoirs may refill. We are not good at saying to our neighbour: 'I cannot for this hour, day or week give you the attention which I am usually glad to give, for I must be alone with God.' That should not be the word of the crank, but of the ordinary Christian. It is not a devotional luxury but as necessary for our inner life and to our real life among people, as food and sleep to our bodies. We Methodists shall have taken a step further on the road of creative personal relationships. God knows and He alone, how long each of us spend in real converse with Him and whether we can say any other than 'God be merciful to me a sinner.' We have not failed in the art of prayer: we have failed our friends, for we are poor when we might have been rich, strained when we might have been serene, blind when we might have seen.

Our relationships in Christ can never be stale or ordinary because they must bear the stamp of eternity upon them. They must always have in them a hopeful looking forward to a fullness of joy which will crown our love for one another in Him. In the translation of Kittel's *Bible Key-words*, in the article on 'Love', we can read the following: 'Love is the power of the coming age already breaking into the world'; and again, love 'means glowing with a passion for God, the passionate eagerness to suffer that characterizes the little flock which hold on faithful and undismayed. . . . Until He comes whom they love.' Another writer speaks of the looking forward which will bring us 'at once into a closer unity with the loving Lord and so with one another'. The desire for a deeper understanding of the consummation which of God's purpose pervades so much modern writing is not irrelevant here. If the active presence of a Living Lord is at work in our relationships, they can never be static, never merely a collection of precious memories, for the fulfilment is yet to come. Our Lord is present, but He is also coming. When St Paul describes love as present reality he also points to a relationship with the Lord, 'face to face', as yet to be. When that day comes can we doubt that with all the separations of earthly life of the body ended, we shall also see each other face to face and find in that knowledge, not a problem, not a heart-break, but the joy unspeakable and full of glory?

We are here together in Oxford, a company of Methodists concerned about our witness, our fellowship, and in some degree our organization. Let us now face the fact that unless in Christ we can demonstrate to the world a building up of stable personal relationships which show that the love of God is indeed shed abroad in our hearts, we shall fail. To you Americans, do the British ever irritate you? To you British, do you ever become impatient with Americans? To you from the East, do you ever despair of the blindness of the West? To you of African blood, do you ever resent us? If so, is it experts we all need? Or a common penitence? If we are to draw nearer and the glass cages to which we can withdraw are to be shattered, we need to ask our Living Lord to enter again into every contact we make. Not America and Britain, but America, Britain, and Christ, not India and Africa and Australasia, but all three in Christ. He is between us, not as a barrier, but to join us together, for in His love alone can we rightly see each other and love one another. Together we can say, 'God be merciful to me a sinner', and enter afresh into the peace and pardon of our God.

212

EIGHTH DAY
Tuesday 4th September

THE OPENING devotions were conducted by the Rev. H. D. Leigh, Superintendent of the Oxford Circuit, and an address was given by Bishop J. Waskom Pickett, of the American Methodist Church in South Asia. 'Religious revivals release energy', he said, 'and genuine Christian revivals direct the energy they release into channels of service.' Jesus not only preached; He healed and ministered to human distress, frankly arguing that His works proved His gospel. St Paul said we are saved by hope, and the writer of the Book of Revelation gave a prescription for the discouraged Church or individual—a tonic to strengthen hope. The epidemic pessimism of today must be met by our confidence that man's needs can be satisfied in Jesus Christ. As God's grace is working in modern India, so it works in all the world.

The morning session continued the theme of the previous day— *The Social Witness*. The first of the two addresses was given by the Rev. Edward Rogers, Secretary of the Christian Citizenship Department of the Methodist Church in Great Britain. His subject was *The Economic Order*. The second speaker was the Rev. E. W. Grant, ex-President of the South African Conference and President of the Christian Council of South Africa, whose topic was *Inter-Racial Relations*.

THE SOCIAL WITNESS
I. THE ECONOMIC ORDER

An address by the REV. EDWARD ROGERS, *of London:*

I assume that the title of the subject allotted to me was chosen for its brevity. I wish it were as neat and tidy as the phrase 'The Economic Order' suggests. How pleasant it would be to analyse that order, assess it in the light of the gospel, and so solve the economic problem before we adjourn for coffee. It would be less pleasant, but equally simple, if I could argue that there was nothing but chaotic disorder in the economic world. Then I could survey it with a few well-chosen words of woe, leave it to the wrath of God, and adjourn for two cups of coffee to cheer us before the crash.

The fact is that the economic world is a variegated patchwork of competition and co-operation, of freedom and planning, of nomad, peasant, semi-industrial, and industrial communities; with industrial enclaves in peasant societies and peasant corners in industrial societies just to make the whole thing more difficult. As this is a world conference, I cannot be locally parochial in my view. I must take the whole confused medley— which means that I shall have to be dogmatic, something stating a case that ought to be argued at length, and indicating answers rather than expounding solutions.

The economic order I will roughly define as the constantly changing and infinitely complicated social organization by which men seek to provide the necessities, conveniences and comforts of their material and terrestrial life. It is not always easy to see the social significance of a particular job, especially in the man-made artificiality of mammoth cities. It is obvious enough in the work of a farmer or a miner, not quite so obvious in the daily toil of an average-adjuster, and almost microscopically imperceptible in the arduous enterprise of the man who counts the laughs in a Bob Hope programme. But always the economic organization, and the work of individuals within it, is directed to the production and distribution of the goods and services needed or desired by the community.

The system will not stand still to be examined at leisure—a fact, incidentally, which gives the planners their biggest headache. At the end of the eighteen months or so which it takes to compile and correlate economic statistics, the planner is left with impressive statistical analyses of yesterday to deal with the urgencies of today. The economic order is continually changing, either by slow decay and ingenious patching or by sudden revolution. It changes because it is an imperfect order with which men are never satisfied. On occasion it fails to provide even bare necessities for millions, and they die of starvation. For the great majority of mankind it provides no luxuries—which envious human nature might more easily endure if some did not live in comparative comfort and a few in ostentatious luxury. Every new idea, every refinement of an old technique, contributes to the change. In our generation, less settled than any preceding generation, the poor and relatively stable peasant communities of Asia have surged into revolutionary activity, the end of which no man can foretell. Africa is stirring. There are no simple solutions to the economic problem.

Economics is reputed to be a dismal science because it says just this. Except when interpreted by some politicians, it tells us the unwelcome truth that if there are only four apples, five people can't have one each. They may all want one, but they can't all have one. You can't have your cake and eat it. You can't keep your coal and burn it. You can't run a harvester-combine on a two-acre holding. Economics is anchored to reality, and cannot be ignored. Let me make two brief preliminary observations which relate it to Christian social witness. The first is that the world economic order, and every change in it, directly affects the total life of every living person—which means that it is a religious concern. Only those who are blind to the brutalizing power of grinding poverty and inhuman toil can be indifferent to it. The second is that the appeal of Marxist Communism lies in its confident claim to have discovered the technique of progress to a perfect social order through an understanding of the economic motives of social life—a claim which casually and contemptuously dismisses God as a hypothesis no longer necessary.

The first challenge was pricking the Christian conscience in the nineteenth century, but the second has got home to all of us today. In the patient providence of God, His wandering people are continually prodded back to the fullness of His truth by the spread of heresy when some aspect of that truth has been long ignored. Marxist-Leninist dialectical materialism has much to say that is pointedly relevant about material necessity, economic motive and social strife. The Marxist over-simplifies. He distorts or omits inconvenient fact. But he deals vigorously with basic problems that ought to have been and were not Christian concerns. The great heresy of Communism, essentially a clever adolescent parody of Christianity, is compelling us to consider again the realm of economic life which we had handed over to others.

214

Methodism, in common with all other Christian communions, has until latterly had little to say about economic order. If I had followed the example of some of my brethren here, and confined myself to what John Wesley said about my subject, my address would have been so remarkably short that I should have been the most popular speaker at this Conference except with the officers. We have said much about how a man ought to live in the existing economic order. We honour our ardent social reformers, who strove to remove some of its more hideous excrescences. We proudly boast of the Tolpuddle Martyrs, quietly forgetting the cool and distant reserve of official Methodism at the time of their martyrdom. Let us be honest about it. There were such exceptions as the fiery heroism of Primitive Methodism in Durham and the Christian defence of the Maori in New Zealand, but, generally speaking, Methodism and the whole Christian Church took it for granted that the shattering disturbances and miseries of the Industrial Revolution in the West were none of their business.

I wonder if we are quite sure now. Ought we to be concerned, for example, with the aims and methods of trade union organizations? Are the mysteries of price-fixing and wage-fixing, the incidences of taxation, the balance between agriculture and industry, or the legal rights of property any business of ours? To put it bluntly, is the economic world independent of the Kingdom of God?

Superficial reasons for our reticence are not hard to find. The problems of the economic order are desperately complicated. For instance, the tenuous link which joins the curiously assorted economics of the world is money; and in a world of gold standards, gold-exchange standards, controlled currencies, frozen assets, liquid reserves, gold credit, bank credit, inflation and deflation and barter, no one—not even the financial experts, and I am tempted to say, especially the financial experts—knows just what is going on. The most valiant travelling preacher, who can dispose of most things in twenty minutes, would hesitate here.

Again, our Churches are so geared to the economy of the societies in which they live that we tend to regard the local manifestations of economic order as the natural economic order and so to leave it unexamined. John C. Bennett has a pungent word relating to this in the third of the volumes prepared for the first meeting of the World Council of Churches. Referring to the practice of the Church as an owning, investing, or employing institution, he says: 'The fact seems to be universal that the Church as an institution is not easily distinguished, so far as the moral sensitivity shown in its practices is concerned, from institutions that have less moral pretensions.'

Yet again, because the nexus of the economic world is monetary, and therefore impersonal, nobody feels any particular responsibility for it, so that a Christian probing into the relevance or righteousness of any particular aspect of the economic set-up is bound to irritate some very sensitive spots—to wit, pockets and purses—and to evoke correspondingly vigorous and pained reactions. A rousing attack on the intellectual sins of Antinomians or Predestinarians is perfectly in order, if imperfectly understood; but we feel that we must handle much more delicately the vocational sins of shop stewards or company directors.

The real reason for our reticence, however, lies deeper. It goes back to the unfortunate and unscriptural division between the material and spiritual obligations of man which developed in thirteenth century thought as a way of escape from the arrogant pride of a powerful and politically ambitious Church. For seven centuries it has put political and economic

215

thought on the wrong track, and split truth into fragments, until the politician came to think that he could build a sound secular order without God and the religious came to think that politics was a low and vulgar pursuit irreconcilable with his high calling's glorious hope. In both secular and religious post-medieval thought the Kingdom of God was so dematerialized, so tenuously spiritualized, that it became meaningless save as a personal spiritual discipline. The time came when good men regarded it as a sign of grace that the Church should look away from earth to Heaven. We have entered into the inheritance of those who held it as an axiom of religion that economic business was not the Church's business —held it with an incredible unawareness that a Church which is silent is not keeping out. Silence before manifest injustice, though the injustice be defended—as was the labour of six-year-old children in mines and factories —by the mathematics of secular economists, is as great a commitment as speech.

We may give our humble and penitent thanks to Almighty God that He did not consider our world, in all its relationships, to be outside His redeeming care. 'God so loved the *world* that He gave His only begotten son.' 'God was in Christ Jesus, reconciling the *world* to Himself.' The triumphant faith of Paul catches joyously the petitions of the Lord's Prayer. 'Thy will be done in *earth* as it is in Heaven. Give us this day our daily bread.' God loved the world, not a part of it, and God loves man as man, at worship or play or work. He made man a unity who, if he tries to serve two opposed masters or to seek two disparate ends, becomes less than man; a divided creature who can yet be made whole by faith in Christ. The rebel against God lives in a world which is under God's rule. In this present world he can find God and serve Him. The good news of the gospel is that there is no impassable gulf between life in Christ in this world and life in Christ in the world to come. There is no realm of life independent of the justice and grace of God.

What I am trying to say so hurriedly is that in ignoring the economic order we have failed to proclaim or live the fullness of the gospel. We know perfectly well that it would be a travesty of our faith so to over-exalt the importance of the economic world as to suggest that the chief aim of man should be a secure and comfortable secular society. I shall return again to consider that danger. My point now is that it is not good enough to preach the gospel as far as personal justification and conversion, and then to halt at what after all is not the end, but the beginning of the Christian Way. Nor is it sufficient to be content with the good work, the ambulance work, of binding up the wounds of the victims of the economic order, if we can prevent the infliction of the wounds.

The operative motive of the Christian, according to the gospel, is charity: the love of God shed abroad in our hearts. Though we have built our hospitals and orphanages, and cared for the prisoner, the outcast, and the starving, the measure of our failure to meet the basic problem of the economic order is seen in the degradation of the lovely word 'charity' till it smells damply of disinfectant and doles. In sober truth, loving your neighbour as yourself involves every human relationship, and therefore involves the structure of every human relationship. We tend, I think, to forget that the more civilized our society becomes, the more its relationships are humanly constructed. The farmer and the fisherman must of necessity adapt themselves to the inevitable conditions of Nature; but the community life, and economic foundation, of the Empire State Building or the Old Kent Road is not of the same order of necessity. In so far as the economic order is a human creation it will reflect the nature of the

216

humans who create it, which not merely gives a hope of transformation, but indicates also the way. The first clear word of Christian social witness to men trapped in economic mazes is that no purely secular politics, no ingenious economic plan, can give us the sort of world of which we dream. Only love in action, only seeking first the Kingdom of God and His righteousness can transform the economic order.

That premature peroration sounds suspiciously like pulpit prestidigitation, where the slickness of the speech deceives the mind. To test its truth, I turn again to the actual economic order, beginning with the unpalatable fact to which I have already briefly referred: that the purpose of economic organization is to produce and distribute scarce goods. There is no bottomless well or horn of plenty from which we can draw inexhaustible supplies. Unhappily, there is a steady shrinking of arable land on the face of the globe to supply a rapidly increasing human family. The population of India, now over 400,000,000, is mounting at the rate of 6,000,000 a year, and better medical services, housing, and feeding would augment the rate of increase. The population of Japan has grown from 35,000,000 in 1870 to over 80,000,000 today. In three centuries the world population—the people to be fed and housed and clothed—has multiplied fourfold. Even in Europe, excluding Russia, despite the ravages of war and anti-Semitic savagery, the population increased by 11,000,000 during the war years and is expected to increase by a further 22,000,000 in the next decade. What it means in plain language we can see if we look at India. To lift her population slightly above the bare level of subsistence, she will, within the next thirty years, have to produce three times as much food as she does now. She hasn't enough land to do it. Agricultural mechanization, depopulating the villages, won't do it. And if every peasant society industrializes, and hopes to live on imported food, where is it coming from?

That sort of problem cannot be waved aside with vague murmurs about 'scientific progress'. Many a neat blue-print for a better order of society is going into the ash-can unless the peoples of the world are prepared to work hard and work together. To adapt world economy to Methodist language, we shall be housekeeping on the minimum stipend for some time to come. With good housekeeping, we shall get by. Without it we shall lurch through the sorry cycle of shorter booms and longer slumps, and may well have to face, despite the incredible patience of ordinary men, the disappointed and destructive rage of those who have been fooled, or who fooled themselves, with easy promises of a plenty that never came.

That leads me directly to Paul's shrewd comment that 'we are members one of another'. Not, you will note, that we ought to be, but that we are. We are in one terrestrial household whether we like it or not, and there is nowhere to move to this side of Jordan—at least until the interplanetary service is operating. I need not here make the speech we have all so frequently delivered on the shrinking world and the speed of modern communications. The fact is that it is easy to get on well with your relations if you never meet them; but when you and your wife and family and mother-in-law and Uncle Joe and Aunt Lucy and their children and Grandma's second cousins are all living together, you can expect trouble about the use of the bathroom and the cooker and the best armchair—unless you are a disciplined and loving family. The analogy is exact and the conclusion inescapable.

But linked with this is an aspect of the economic order strangely overlooked by Christian sociologists. The only basis of a sound economy is mutual satisfaction in agreed bargains. It is simply not true that the

217

economic world is a jungle where every man must fend for himself against a host of enemies. The normal cash transaction is a rough-and-ready indication of an enterprise in which both buyer and seller gain; and on that foundation the economic order rests. Beneath the cut and thrust of competition and the glossy glitter of advertising—the principal imaginative art of our time—is the solid and sober foundation of making something a man wants and receiving a price he is prepared to pay. Here surely is a clue to the Divine intention for the economic order. In the long run, because this is God's world, only that sort of economic relationship will work satisfactorily.

The trouble is that in the short run there are good pickings for the unscrupulous. Selfishness gives very tangible immediate rewards, and leaves the headaches to following generations. The world tragedy of soil erosion is a monument to short-sighted greed. The despoliation of the forests, the reckless exploitation of mineral wealth, the legacies of social bitterness and class hatred, the smouldering resentments of the under-privileged—these all paid good cash dividends to somebody some time. The supple and the tough, with an eye to the main chance, can feather their nests—in Britain, U.S.A., or U.S.S.R.—careless that at the same time, if you will forgive the peculiar gymnastics of the metaphor, they are poisoning the roots of the trees in which the nests are perched.

There are three economic alternatives before us. One is the way of retreat to self-sufficient little communities with a permanently lowered standard of living. Another is the way of strife till one society dominates a ruined world, keeping its goods in peace till a stronger arises. The third is the way of co-operation. Any man in his senses knows that the third is the best way. Any man in his senses knows that it is not fully possible now. Even if we are wise enough, which is doubtful, we are not good enough. We are not sufficiently fond of our relations to love them as ourselves.

The fact is that the tensions of the economic order are but one aspect of the incessant war between grace and sin. The body economic is infected with sin, and can be cleansed only by grace. The power which thwarts us is the power of sin. Greed, malice, pride, and envy pay off in tumult and sorrow and want, which could more simply be put: 'The wages of sin is death.' I would draw your attention to the salty realism of the Christian Fathers on one of the great political problems of the first centuries of the Christian era: the problem of Communism. In succeeding generations, and in widely differing circumstances, they declare with impressive unanimity that so long as man is a rebel against his Maker, so long as he rejects Divine grace, he cannot live in the good society. He will have to manage with an unsatisfactory makeshift until he comes to his senses and returns to his Father, ready if need be to be a slave in his Father's house. They were right. In our mid-twentieth century Conference we have been discussing the message for our day, and the relevance of the gospel. The message shouts at us from every newspaper we read. Man or nation or economic order: live under grace or die under judgement.

It is true that economic organization is not the only, and ought not to be the primary, activity of man. The sudden realization of a blind spot led some sections of the Christian Church in the first half of the twentieth century to an obsession with social problems nearly as bad as the neglect to which it was a reaction. There was a so-called 'social gospel', a flight from the supernatural and eternal, which offered the pallid substitute of a kingdom of man on earth, situated in the receding ranges where the sea-coast of Bohemia meets the frontiers of Utopia. I am not pleading for that, but asking that we should cease oscillating between half-truths, and proclaim the faith which firmly sets the material life of man in its proper and not unworthy place in the providential purposes of God.

What, then, can Methodism do in the contemporary situation? To begin with a counsel of perfection, we should desist from glib superficialities about profound and agonizing problems. I do not suggest that every preacher should be an economist. We have more than enough amateur psychiatrists, and amateur economists in bulk would be the last straw. But we could do with a few men who would concentrate on the study as discipline under God. A job is ready to hand. The pseudo-scientific Marxist economics, based on lopsided philosophy, specially selected history, and abysmal ignorance of the inner meaning of religion, is wide open to attack. The Communist party-line to the classless prosperity of the workers, founded on that economics, is an amalgam of clever expediency and incorrigible dogmatic stupidity which needs to be hammered hard lest men should stray to disaster and death on the promised easy road to Paradise. The men who tackle that job in the name of Christ will have to know what they are talking about. And they will have to make it clear that they are attacking a false solution to a real problem, not defending an existing order.

Secondly, when we condemn the sin of the economic order, we should remember that sin has no life in itself. Sin is sterility and death. It infects and distorts God-given life. It defaces in man the image of God, and it perverts in the economic order the intention of God. Our halting, jarring systems bear testimony, despite every grievous imperfection, to what I may be permitted to call loosely the creative genius of man. We cannot put all the tremendous achievement of the modern world down to Satanic pride. There are skills and aptitudes and intentions in man which, governed and invigorated by the Holy Spirit, would enable the daily business of the world to show forth the glory of God.

Thirdly, we should preach the gospel in the spirit of the gospel. It is true that in a society of sinful men there can be no social security or economic peace: neither in Communism, the Welfare State, nor the American way of life. But we are not to preach that simply in order to cajole men and women into our congregations with the lure of *our* plan for social security. The warning and exhortation of our Lord comes to us within the Church as well as to those without: 'Seek ye first the Kingdom of God and His righteousness.' We are not concerned with the economic order as a source of topical sermon illustration, or as a ground for rebuking sinners who wouldn't listen to us with: 'Serves you right.' We are concerned because the Lord God is righteous, and because we love those for whom Christ died and rose.

Fourthly, we should make our concern manifest, and that is where we depend particularly on our laymen. They are in the economic world at every level. They know where the shoe pinches and where the lie prevails. As J. H. Oldham says, quoting an unnamed young minister: 'The Clydeside shipbuilding apprentice, the delicatessen proprietor, the accountant, or the New York longshoreman knows in his bones more about the essential moral problems and tensions of contemporary life than the average minister can compass with his imagination.' The layman ought both to be commending his Saviour to his fellows, and bringing his job to the scrutiny and guidance of his Saviour.

You may feel that I have so far side-stepped the vital question: what is the content of our constructive witness? The answer I give, not as evasion, but as precise answer, is that we should go one step at a time with faith in God wherever He leads on the as yet untrodden way. We are in the dark, and cannot see the distant scene. As we try to imagine it, we are in the gravest peril of falling victim to the diabolical subtlety of pride. We shall be tempted to draw up detailed plans of what *we* regard as a perfect world, and submit them to God to give Him an idea of what ought to be done. God is not man's hired labourer. We are only beginning to grasp the size of the task before us. Before we can get very far, we shall have to carry the injustices and tragedies of the economic order as a fire in our bones, as an intolerable ache in our hearts, until we are driven to our knees in beseeching prayer to know God's will.

It is our Father's good pleasure to give us the Kingdom. We need a faith that believes that, a humility that waits on God, and a readiness to go where He commands. In such a faith Methodism was born. Only in such a faith can Methodism live. The mill and the mine, the office and the factory, the order which provides or withholds bread from man are waiting to be redeemed. Surely our task is so to obey the sovereign rule of God and so to proclaim His infinite grace that the kingdoms of *our* world—the kingdoms of oil and coal and cotton and steel—shall become the kingdoms of our God and of His Christ.

II. INTER-RACIAL RELATIONS

An address delivered by the REV. EDWARD W. GRANT, *of Healdtown, South Africa:*

I have been reading again a comprehensive declaration issued by the British Conference of 1950 on the South African situation, and side by side with it statements by the South African Conference of the same year and by the Christian Council of South Africa in 1949. They are one in repudiating the pernicious doctrine that any one race is inherently inferior to any other and 'incapable of the noblest human activities'. All declare in the plainest possible terms that beyond all differences there remains the essential unity of men created in the image of God; that the spiritual values of civilization can be preserved, 'not by denying opportunity to any race, but only by the fullest possible sharing by all races in its benefits'; that there is 'no Christian or moral foundation for the claim of any race to preserve itself or its traditions at the expense of other races'.

I am justified therefore in assuming that these and similar convictions are held by us all. In such a gathering of world Methodism, with its gospel of God's free grace for all men in Christ, of sonship in the family of the Universal Father, I dare not assume less. My colleagues and I accept these principles on behalf of South African Methodism, which has said these things again and again to its own people of all races and to an obdurate Government, and will continue to say them. If we hold to these principles in South Africa, where our Church's task is set on the very battlefield of racial strife, there should be no difficulty about their acceptance by Methodists in countries by whom South Africa's racial policy is, justly, condemned.

Having then made these assumptions may I bring this question before you under three main headings:

I. Methodism and the Race Policies of the State.

II. Present Inter-racial Relations within Methodism Itself.

III. The Pattern of the Methodism of the Future in a World of Intensified Nationalism.

220

I. Methodism and the Race Policies of the State

The witness of a communion such as ours may have to be maintained in opposition to the major trends of public opinion, and even to the declared policy of the State, in a given country. I was led on one occasion to say to the Methodist Conference in South Africa: 'Any efforts to renew a tottering civilization by causing it to centre around conceptions of class or race, soil or nation, which conflict with the Spirit of Christ, or any attempt to secure the advantage of any one race or section to the hurt of another must submit to be judged by a Church which is the extension of the life of Christ in the life of this present age.'

When racial discrimination, be it political, economic, social, or all three, becomes by legislation or by implication the accepted policy of any country, there is laid upon us the duty of condemning such a policy and of opposing it by all the means in our power. Together with this goes the positive duty of upholding actively the rights of under-privileged people.

If such opposition and such championship are to be fully effective, it is necessary that our Church should create a Christian conscience on this matter. This it can do in two ways.

First, *by fearless preaching*. Our people of all races must be strongly challenged to apply in all their relationships the principles of the universal gospel, of the Lordship of Christ over all life, and of His Kingdom, which knows no racial frontiers. But in these critical days even the challenge of the preached word is not enough.

There must be also *constructive and continuous teaching*. Two years ago the Christian Council of South Africa, at a remarkable inter-racial gathering in Johannesburg, discussed the place and task of the Christian in a multi-racial society. Many understood for the first time that there is a theology of race relations, and that the Church sorely needs to have that theology stated and its eternal principles affirmed. One of our findings was this:

'While acknowledging that one historic people was chosen by God to be the medium of His fullest revelation in Jesus Christ, we repudiate the claim that any other race has been so chosen, but affirm that His chosen people is now the Universal Church.'

What made that statement necessary? The fact that there are theories of race superiority which claim to be based on the Scriptures. We have one which is working havoc in South Africa today. Much more than a century ago Dutch pioneers, facing incredible hardship and danger, won through to what was for them the Promised Land by armed conflict with and conquest of the African and other primitive peoples. With a religion strongly Calvinistic in its creed and having roots deep in the Old Testament, it was not difficult for them to carry over the idea of 'election' from the individual to the community, the nation, the race. It became to them their divine destiny to rule the non-white people. The heathen were their inheritance. Their descendants find today a religious justification for keeping the African races in permanent subjection. It will seem almost incredible to many here, but this belief is actually a powerful factor in creating and maintaining the present unhappy situation in South Africa.

Such a doctrine will be rightly condemned by us with our gospel of universal grace. But let us repudiate *any* strange doctrine which identifies any race with any chosen people and claims for it a part in the divine purpose from which others are by implication excluded. The doctrine of a master race does not become less but rather more dangerous when it claims the sanction of religion by basing itself upon a false interpretation

221

of Old Testament history and an unscriptural conception of the nature of prophecy.

So much for the need for a study of the theology of race relations, to which Methodism, with its evangelical tradition and its far-flung missionary enterprise, is in a position to make a distinctive contribution.

Two principles then emerge. World Methodism should clearly set forth its convictions on matters of race relations, with the spiritual and Scriptural bases on which they are founded. Secondly, national branches of Methodism, in the varying conditions in which they are set, should accept and fearlessly proclaim those convictions, and judge each its own particular race situation in their light.

We go on to look at:

II. Present Inter-Relations within Methodism Itself

We become aware of a variety of patterns.

There are the *sending Churches*. These were once each a home base of missions, mostly of European stock, embracing a fellowship of one race only. But these familiar conditions are being modified. Our Church in Great Britain, for instance, is confronted with a new situation in that among the thousands of students and professional and other workers now flocking to this country from overseas are many who are the children of Methodist missions in Africa, India, China, the West Indies. The place which they are to fill in the fellowship of British Methodism must be a matter of grave concern for all, just as it is a matter of serious moment for those younger Churches from which they come. A disturbing factor is that here and there race discrimination begins to rear its ugly head in Britain. All honour to work such as that carried on under Methodist auspices by the Committee for the Care of Overseas Students, centring around International House.

The second pattern is found in the *younger Churches* themselves. They are composed of the nationals of such countries as India, China, and part of Africa. The general picture each presents is that of a Church with a single overwhelming racial complexion and with a greater or less—indeed, often a lessening—degree of European missionary leadership. Some are moving on quickly toward self-government, especially in countries which are becoming self-governing territories. Here is clearly seen, not only the immense effect of State policies upon race relations within the Church, but also the effect of such change of status upon the work of our Church in other territories. Many of us in South Africa, for instance, are devoutly praying that the important developments on the Gold Coast are going to be outstandingly successful. Failure would have serious repercussions in our own field. The effect would be seen both in the race policies of our Government and in that Government's attitude to the work which our own and other Churches are doing among the non-European people. So are we all bound up together, and are forced, whether we desire it or not, to become ecumenical in spirit.

A third variety of relationship is illustrated in the *Methodist Church of America*. It is a picture of a great Church, once divided racially, but now united. There is, I understand, a separate Central Jurisdiction which embraces all the Negro or Coloured churches throughout the whole country, and which is under the charge of a Negro bishop. One hears with deep interest of a growth in the practice of common worship in some areas. A South African missionary is able to sympathize with a great Church which must combat deep-rooted colour prejudice and a host of other practical difficulties as it moves steadily toward the ideal of a fully inter-racial communion. He can also rejoice in the marked progress which has been made.

The last type is that of a country with a very *mixed racial population*, of which every racial element is represented within the fold of the Methodist Church. This is the picture of South African Methodism. Its various racial sections are found in roughly the same proportions as prevail in the general population—that is, about 20 per cent of European stock and the remainder overwhelmingly African, with Coloured and Indian groups.

Here is a Church whose control is vested in a fully inter-racial Conference with complete equality of status. The same general principle applies in district synods, with modifications due to local conditions. On the plane of the circuit and the local church there is a parallel racial organization, with growing opportunity for self-expression and training in self-government and with increasing responsibility assumed by non-European ministers and laymen. The Conference is definitely pledged to create a fully multi-racial fellowship on all levels of church life 'as opportunity offers and the good of all demands'.

Common worship has been long the order of the day at conferences and synods, and in other special circumstances. There are difficulties at present in the way of its becoming a general practice in the local congregations. The race prejudice which has become entrenched in South Africa during 300 years still in varying degrees colours the attitudes of many of our European Christians—though certainly not of all of them. There are also wide differences of cultural background. There is the ever-present problem of a multiplicity of languages. God's children must be able to worship Him in their own tongue, or both they and the whole Church suffer spiritual impoverishment. Yet we must move toward the point at which common worship of the Universal Father is available for all who can share in it with understanding.

It becomes clear that history and environment have operated and will continue to operate as determining factors in shaping relations within the Methodism of a given country. How then can we approach the last of my three headings?

III. The Pattern of the Methodism of the Future in a World of Intensified Nationalism

There is no blue-print. But this very inadequate presentation will have brought to light principles capable of general application, and aims which should be common to us all. I will state them very briefly.

The Methodist witness to the world respecting inter-racial relations will be effective only as we ourselves present on a world scale the picture of a truly inter-racial Church. In South Africa for instance, we are convinced that we cannot condone within the Church a segregation which we so roundly condemn in the State. World Methodism should move steadily toward full inter-racial fellowship; not only by strengthening official and unofficial links between our Churches in different countries; but by securing in each multi-racial country a far deeper unity of the racial groups included with our Church in that country.

Where many races are in fellowship under one Conference, as in South Africa, or in the one Church under separate jurisdictions, as in the United States, steady and planned progress must be maintained toward securing an ever larger measure of *local* fellowship, due regard being had to the spiritual interests and natural aspirations of the various racial elements.

223

That is to say, the missionary ideal of an indigenous Church prevails, but the term must include every racial group in any given country.

The younger Churches must ensure that their rapid approach to self-government and the lessening both of control and of the supply of personnel from overseas shall not weaken the tie that binds them to world Methodism. The growth of nationalism in the State must not lead to isolationism in the Church.

This ideal will be challenged. It will be challenged in some countries by the prevailing race policies of the country itself. For instance, the election manifesto of the present Government of South Africa indicated that the activities of Churches which did not subscribe to the doctrine of *apartheid* would have to be 'checked'. Since then the Government has refused on several occasions to receive our representations.

It will be challenged by the demand which the spirit of nationalism brings for a national Church. African political circles in South Africa have been calling for an African National Church. Some of our leading African Methodists have strongly opposed the idea. None know better than they that a Church whose foundation is national feeling is likely to build nationalism strongly into its superstructure. In other words, it becomes more national than Christian.

Challenge also comes from that race prejudice and fear within the fellowship itself to which I have already referred—the baleful effect, in part at least, of a country's racial discrimination and of accepted conventions based on colour. There are victories in this field which must be won within the Church as well as outside it.

We are challenged too by the low degree of culture and the widespread illiteracy of the masses of many races among whom we work. Unless this gulf is bridged, fellowship on the deepest levels is very difficult. So we must raise the non-European races as a whole to the level at present reached by groups and individuals; even as we must lead our European people to be willing to share with them on the deepest levels.

What qualities are required for such a task? Primarily, endless Christlike patience; and also unfaltering and equally Christ-like purpose.

Difficulties will not daunt those of us whose work is done in countries where racial strife prevails. But those difficulties must be recognized by our friends in the Methodist family.

We must never forget that this is not a question of cold and calculating policy. It is a matter of vital human relationships which go to the heart of the gospel as Methodism understands and preaches it. What is the greatest contribution which world Methodism, with its message of universal grace, can make to the conception of a world Church? It is that of a Church in which God's children of all races, in any part of the world wherever they may be, can find themselves at home in the Family of God, because it symbolizes to its children of all colours the friendliness of God.

Group discussions followed the addresses (see p. 289).

In the afternoon a civil welcome was extended to the delegates by the Mayor of Oxford, Alderman W. O. King. 'I would like to see a great wave of Christianity sweep across the world,' he said, 'and so enable mankind to work and enjoy the fruits of his labour, to live in love and harmony with his fellows and learn the meaning of the word "peace", and particularly the meaning of that peace "which passes understanding".' The two Presidents of the Conference, Dr

224

W. F. Howard and Bishop Ivan Lee Holt spoke in warm appreciation of the hospitality afforded by the citizens, the University and the civic authorities.

The subject of the lecture, in the Examination Schools, was *The Impact of Biblical Criticism*, and the lecturer was the Rev. Dr Norman H. Snaith, Tutor in Old Testament Languages and Literature and in Homiletics, Wesley College, Headingley, Leeds.

THE IMPACT OF BIBLICAL CRITICISM

A lecture delivered by the REV. NORMAN H. SNAITH:

I must begin by criticizing the title, in particular the last word, 'criticism'. To most people that means I am starting by grumbling about it, condemning it, and saying hard things about the Committee who asked me to give this lecture. I am going to do nothing of the sort. I am using the word 'criticize' in precisely the way in which the word 'criticism' is used in the phrase 'Biblical criticism'. That is, I am going to begin by studying the phrase, examining it, and explaining it to the best of my ability.

For when we use the phrase 'Biblical criticism' we are not using the word in the ordinary common English sense of criticizing adversely. We are using the word as it is used in literary and artistic circles generally: where it involves an honest and sincere attempt to sort out the material and give proper praise where praise is due. It is unfortunate that the word 'criticism' should popularly have this adverse meaning, because uninformed people assume immediately that the aim of Biblical criticism is wholly destructive, and that its aim is to destroy the authority of the Bible. That is not true, though it would be foolish to deny that there have been scholars whose zeal has outrun their discretion. Equally it would be foolish to deny that the authority of the Bible has been weakened during the last fifty-odd years, and it is true that this has been, at least in part due to the impact of Biblical criticism.

Nevertheless, whether we like it or not, the fearless, scholarly, scientific study of the Bible has come to stay. Neither the old Fundamentalism of the last 300 years, nor the neo-Fundamentalism of today can keep it back, any more than King Canute could stop the sea from coming in. After all, if the Bible is true, it can stand up to all the brickbats of time; and further, if the Bible is indeed a lamp unto our feet and a light unto our path, the more air it gets the better the lamp will burn; and, in any case, we must keep the lamp-glass clear of cobwebs, and incidentally our own spectacles clear of dust.

I judge that my task is to discuss the effect of what is known as 'higher criticism', not Lower Criticism. This latter ('lower criticism') is concerned with the actual text of the Bible, textual criticism. This is a study that goes back to ancient times. It is embedded in the actual Hebrew text of the Old Testament itself, in the official corrections of the Scribes, which are part of the Sacred Text equally with the rest. We get it in Origen in his attempts to establish a sound text of the Greek Bible (Septuagint). The origin of the Vulgate is concerned directly with this very matter. It was because of the uncertainty of the Latin text of the time (the Old Latin Version) that Bishop Damasus of Rome commissioned Jerome to revise the Latin Bible and produce a sound, authoritative text. The study of the text goes on continually, and at the present time we are in the throes of great discussions in respect of both Old and New Testaments: for the Old Testament chiefly through the work of Paul Kahle and his school, for it is still uncertain to what extent the newly-discovered Dead Sea scrolls will solve our problems; for the New Testament chiefly in respect of the discussions concerning the value and antiquity of the so-called Western Text. But curiously, these problems of lower (textual) criticism have never caused any particular flutter in the verbal inspirationist dovecotes, mostly because, I judge, the more enthusiastic literalists do not realize the problems which are involved. Anyway, I do not pretend to explain it: I am merely thankful, and pass on.

I turn to the matter of higher criticism. I imagine it is the word 'higher' that causes most offence. I believe it was J. G. Eichhorn, a German scholar of the end of the eighteenth century, who invented it. The word is unfortunate in that it lends itself so easily to the inference that the 'higher critics' regard themselves as being 'higher' than the Bible, and so sitting in judgement on it. That is an outrageous suggestion, because the great majority of 'higher critics' I know personally are essentially devout and humble-minded men. We have to put up as best we can with the arrogant in all walks of life: there are arrogant dukes and arrogant dustmen; arrogant hoboes and arrogant commuters—but amongst Bible students it is not the 'higher critics' who are the most arrogant. In any case, higher education means more advanced detailed study, and that is exactly what 'high criticism' means.

Higher criticism of the Bible—or, to use a much better phrase, the literary study of the Bible—goes back even farther than the study of the actual text itself. Its results also are embodied in the very text of the Old Testament itself. I refer to the notes which have been inserted at the heads of some of the psalms, notes which refer the psalm to a known incident of the life of David the King, e.g. Psalm 7, 'which he sang unto the Lord, concerning the words of Cush the Benjamite'; others are 18, 34, 51, 52, 53, 54, 57, 59, 60, 63, and also 142. Eight of the twelve are found in what is known as the Davidic Elohist Psalter; three of the rest in the Davidic Jehovist Psalter. The other, 142, is one of the small collection of Davidic psalms which is found in the fifth book of the Psalter, 138-45. The conclusion from this is that, these first attempts at higher criticism are found, apart from 142, in the two earliest of the five original psalters out of which the first half (1-89) of the Psalter was formed.

A thin stream of higher criticism can be detected all down the centuries. The Rabbis (Baba Bathra, 14b, 15a; c A.D. 200-500) said amongst other things, that Joshua wrote the last eight verses of Deuteronomy, and that Jeremiah wrote Kings, whilst Moses wrote Job. Rabbi Isaac ben Jasos (d. 1057) and Rabbi Ibn Ezra (d. 1167) expressed doubts, though in careful language, as to the Mosaic authorship of at least certain verses in the Pentateuch. But the modern study of the composite literary structure of the Pentateuch (the *pièce de résistance* of Old Testament higher criticism) begins with Richard Simon, an Oratorian priest who wrote in the third quarter of the seventeenth century. His work was mostly ignored, so that it is Jean Astruc (1753) who is generally credited with being the first of the modern 'higher critics', followed closely (probably largely independently) by Eichhorn (1780-3). But neither Astruc nor Eichhorn dealt with the problem of the variety of the Pentateuch, and of the way in which the various items do not really cohere. This problem was faced by a Scotchman, Alexander Geddes, in works which were published in 1792 and 1800. This man is the pioneer of the so-called fragmentary hypothesis which has held the field from that day to this. The hypothesis was introduced into Germany by Vater in 1802-5, and it was in Germany that the hypothesis was developed, the great names being Ewald, Reuss, Graf, and Wellhausen. And so we get the Graf-Wellhausen fragmentary hypothesis of the constitution of the Pentateuch.

This hypothesis supposes that there are four main strands in the Pentateuch, designated by the letters J, E, D, and P. J was (so most scholars have said) written down in the south about 850 B.C.: Hebron is the centre, Judah is the leader, the story begins with Creation, and the general style is a straightforward, unsophisticated anthropomorphism. E was written down in the north about 800-750 B.C.: Bethel and Shechem are the centres, Reuben is the leader, the story begins with Abraham, and the style is anthropomorphic, but less so than J. Then D stands for Deuteronomy, and it comprises nearly the whole of it. Its attitude is most distinctive. There is to be one only Sanctuary, with the Levites in charge of it. It has a most marked humanitarian interest within Israel, and a ruthless, nationalistic attitude to the non-Israelite. Israel is a chosen, privileged people. The compilers of the book believed wholeheartedly in the prosperity of the righteous. The central portion was found in the Temple in 621 B.C. during the renovations of Josiah's time, and the book was subjected to the general editing of all extant sacred writings which took place about 500 B.C. And, finally, P, for Priestly Code. This has doubtless many ancient elements which have survived from a long-distant past, especially ritualistic practices. It is the product of Judaism, by which I mean the separatist movement which set in after the Exile and gained complete control. The application of 'separatist' principles to history and so forth is to be seen in the P Creation story of Genesis 1 2^{4a}, where Creation is by separation. The English versions have 'divide', but the Hebrew root is *badal*, from which the late noun *Habdalah* is formed, and this word *Habdalah* is the technical term for those separations and distinctions which form the heart of Judaism—separation between meats, days, and so forth. The date of the writing down of P is usually said to be the time of Ezra, traditionally 444 B.C., though most English scholars make it 397 B.C. For my part, I am inclined to put it rather later, more like 360 or 350 B.C. The general scheme is that J and E were joined together about 650 B.C., JED worked in together in the 550 B.C. editing, and the whole of it placed in a P-setting roughly at the time of Ezra. The scribes of that time thus combined together all the various strands to produce substantially our present Pentateuch.

I have outlined the orthodox so-called modern position in regard to these matters at some length, because it is getting somewhat old-fashioned these days, and is a starting point for new developments. As Bentzen says, 'the new documentary theory is tending towards self-dissolution'— doubtless to the great joy of the varbal-inspirationists, and with, I really believe, a certain amount of relief on the part of many of the rest of us. We were getting rather tired of these interminable alphabets. The basic facts are these: Some sort of documentary or fragmentary theory is essential. This is because of the repetitions and even contradictions. We get, for instance, the two Creation stories, Genesis 1^1 to 2^{4a} and 2^{4b} to end of 3, the double strands in the account of the Flood; the laughter which gave Isaac his name (Genesis 17^{17-19}, when Abraham laughed; 18^{12}, when Sarah laughed; 21^6, when they all laughed), the three places where it is said that the sacred name Jehovah was first used, Genesis 4^{26}, Exodus 3^{14} and 6^3, and so on—the details can be found in the introductions and the commentaries. A four-documentary theory seemed at first to be adequate, but succeeding scholars have realized that this is not enough, but that there are various strata even within these documents. So we get J^1, J^2, E^1, E^2,

D¹, D², P¹, P², P³, and so on, until it takes a good man to know when he is going or coming, and even he is not always sure. Then we get scholars like Otto Eissfeldt proposing another source, which he calls L. Pfeiffer with his S, Morgenstern with his K. On the other hand, the dates of the various documents have been challenged by such scholars as Kennett, Hèlscher, Welch, Edward Robertson, and others. All these divergencies have been due to the fact that the four-documentary theory leaves many problems unsolved.

It was the Danish scholar Johs. Pedersen of Copenhagen who first (1931) broke with the orthodox documentary theory. He says that J, E, D, and P represent collections of material which cannot be fitted into an evolutionary scheme. They are all both pre-Exilic and post-Exilic—in fact, different traditions of Israelite culture. The central theme of them all in Israel's distress in Egypt, Moses, Jehovah's fight with Pharaoh, and the deliverance from Egypt. Exodus 1-15, for instance, is not history so much as a cult-legend for Passover, reflecting the annual recounting of the events with all sorts of additions and alterations made during the years. Ivan Engnell throws the whole literary scheme overboard, and says it is a modern scheme foisted on to material belonging to a very different set-up. He thinks in terms of two different collections of material—Genesis-Numbers, a P-circle of tradition; Deuteronomy-2 Kings, a D-circle of tradition. This, generally speaking, is the position of von Rad, Martin Noth, and other present-day scholars. The modern situation is outlined in Professor North's chapter in the recent *The Old Testament and Modern Study* (ed. Professor Rowley, published by the Oxford University Press at 25s.). (Of the eleven contributors, one is an American, two are German, and three of the eight British writers are Methodists. What more could a Methodist Ecumenical Conference desire?) I think the best solution involves us in thinking of four streams of tradition, each stream with its own 'constants', names of God, religious ideas, cultic ideas, theological ideas. These four traditions (roughly represented by J, E, D, P) have each a long history, reaching back certainly to the first days in Canaan, and it may be in some cases to the very earliest traditions of the ancestors of the Hebrew people. The stories were collected mostly at the shrines, and, like all stories so told, it is not essential that the details should always agree even at the same shrine. American visitors to this country will doubtless have realized that the stories of the guides at places they visit do not necessary agree in every detail, though the main outline is doubtless accurate and substantially true. Some such theory as this accounts both for the constants within the four main traditions and also for the variations, and altogether, in the last twenty years, we are coming to a sound basis in these matters, avoiding the minutiae of literary criticism which did nobody very much good.

Similar changes have taken place in the approach to the study of the historical books. Some scholars have sought to carry J, E, D, and P right through into 2 Kings, whilst others adopt the cultic approach, holding that the stories were told at the shrines, and that it is in the traditions associated with the shrines and in the details of the cult that we must search if we would understand the details.

In the study of the writings of the Prophets, I think the most valuable contribution of recent years is the idea that what we have in the Old Testament is four collections of prophecies, known as the Book of the Prophet Isaiah, the Book of the Prophet Jeremiah, the Book of the Prophet Ezekiel, and the Twelve. Further, that there is no main body of prophecy in the usually accepted sense, but that the books are composed

228

of many separate and usually quite short oracles. Wherever possible, the passages are linked by catchwords. The best example is Isaiah 1^{4-9} and 1^{10-17}, two sections which have nothing at all to do with each other, and are linked together solely by the occurrence of the words 'Sodom' and 'Gomorrah' in verses 9 and 10. Thus the Book of Amos is composed of some fifty-nine oracles; Dr Theodore Robinson makes it fifty-eight, and Artur Weiser makes it sixty-two. It cannot be said for certain why this catchword method should have been employed, but the easiest answer is that the system was an aid to memory, and that the oracles of the prophets may have been remembered by their disciples or at some shrine, and recited from memory for a considerable length of time before they were committed to writing. Dr Arvil Kapelrud, for instance, in his recent (1948) *Joel Studies* dates the Joel prophecies themselves at about 600 B.C., but transmitted orally until the fourth or the third century B.C.

In the study of the Psalms, the whole attitude has changed in recent years, partly because of the growing conviction that they are cultic in origin and must be interpreted on that basis, and partly because of the important discoveries made at Ras Shamra in Syria, the site of the ancient Ugarit. It is quite plain that there are elements from Ugarit still surviving in many of the Psalms, and that the Hebrews took over the poetic style and many of the phrases, transmuting them into praises and prayers to the One God.

I have given a very brief outline of the position now held by Biblical Criticism in the realm of Old Testament studies, in order that it may be reasonably clear just what exactly the higher critics do say today. Further details are to be found in the book I mentioned above, *The Old Testament and Modern Study*. Actually, the modern development is the application of *Formgeschichte* theories to the Old Testament. Students of the Bible are familiar with this *Formgeschichte* approach to the New Testament, i.e. realization that what we have got in the Gospels is not necessarily the actual words and deeds of the Lord Jesus: what we have got is the Church tradition concerning His sayings and His actions, as that tradition is told in the second and third generations after His death. The first disciples were more concerned with spreading the good news here, there, and everywhere than with writing the details down; and it was only when the eyewitnesses began to grow few that the necessity was realized of committing the preaching to writing, lest it become confused and lost. It was in just such a way that the Quran was committed to writing after a period of oral transmission. At the Battle of Al-Yemana there were so many 'readers' killed that when Omar became Caliph two years later he set about collecting and recording the sacred text of Islam lest any part of it should be lost. Returning to the Gospels, it has to be recognized that in some cases we have elements due to the lapse of the years, and that occasionally the story is influenced by later experience. All this is apart of sayings to which both Luke and Matthew had access, L (Luke's own source), M (Matthew's special source, in many ways the least satisfactory of them all), and Mark's own material, as we understand, mostly from Peter himself. Then we have the study of the Epistles, problems of the order of the Pauline Epistles, and arguments as to the extent to which the Pastorals are his, and where was he when he wrote the imprisonment epistles, and whether he wrote any of the Epistle which we know as 'to the Ephesians'.

To pass on to the impact of all this on faith and religion.[1] I would say this: if we had kept to the reformers themselves and maintained their

[1] Much of what follows is based on the theme of *The Interpretation of the Bible* (ed. C. W. Dugmore), to which the reader is referred for a more detailed study.

attitude to Scripture, there would have been little to say about the *impact* of Biblical criticism—that is, in any sense of damage done or crisis created. It is the popular opinion, buttressed by the written opinions of A. F. Pollard, that the reformers and the later Protestants replaced the infallibility of the Church with the infallibility of the Bible. It is true that Wyclif sought expressly to defend the value of the Bible as the final authority, but this was against a clergy who did not possess Bibles and regarded Bible teaching as no part of their duties; and he held rightly that to be ignorant of the New Testament was to be ignorant of Christ. The reformers themselves certainly gave the Bible the chief place, but they distinguished clearly between the Word of God and the Scriptures which convey it. For instance, here is a quotation from Hans Denck, who died in 1527: 'I esteem Holy Scripture above all human treasures, but not so highly as the Word of God. . . . He who thinks that he can be made righteous by means of a Book is ascribing to the dead letter what belongs to the Spirit.' This distinction between Holy scripture on the one hand and the Word of God on the other is characteristic of the reformers. Luther could say that a boy of nine with the Bible knew more about divine truth than the Pope without it, but this did not mean that Luther held all Scripture to be of equal worth and all of it infallible. The reformers believed that God speaks through the Bible directly to the reader. Let therefore all men read the Bible. They will hear God speaking to them, and thus the Scriptures will be a lamp unto their feet and a light unto their path. Men will not find here a verse-by-verse dogmatic declaration about the nature of God and His attributes. They will find something of much more account than that. They will find God, and they can come to a personal experience of Him. There was a time when the Risen Lord walked with two wayfarers towards the close of the day. Their hearts burned within them as He opened the Scriptures to them, and in the breaking of bread He was known to them. In this Book, in the Bible, in Scripture, said the reformers, is the Word of God. What the Risen Lord was to Cleopas and another, He can be now through the Bible to the believer: our hearts can burn within us as we read. He spoke to us, and we know Him. The Bible here is plain for every man to read, and the Holy Spirit can bear witness with our spirits that here and here and here is the Word of God, that message of salvation through grace by faith. This indeed is the Word of God in Scripture. That is how I, for my part, have learned to find the Word of God in the Scriptures. The nearer any passage is to this great doctrine, the more sure I am that it is the Word of God. The farther it is away, the nearer I take it to be to those elements in Scripture which are human, unsubstantial, and non-eternal. And if you ask me how I know this, and what my authority is for saying it, my answer is that the 'authority of the Scriptures lies in its ability to produce the conviction that they declare the love of God and His power to save' (so Arthur Peel, p. 68, in *The Interpretation of the Bible*), and, further in the words of Calvin, if we are to recognize here in Scripture the Word of God, 'it is necessary that the same Spirit who spake by the mouths of the prophets should penetrate into our hearts'.

With the reformers, the authority was not the Bible, but the Word of God combined with the witness of the Spirit. Their emphasis was on the *testimonium Spiritus Sancti internum*, the inner witness of the Holy Spirit. Now I have often thought if we had kept to the ideas of the reformers, the impact of Biblical criticism would have been wholly good; it would have been the very tool we needed in order to sift, so to speak, the wheat from the chaff; it would have fulfilled its function, which is to make clear

230

the background against which every verse of Scripture was uttered. We would have seen clearly the historical setting, the cultural background, the political cross-currents, and the rest. All this would have made clear to us the human element, with the result that the truly divine element in Scripture, the veritable Word of God, would have stood out in bolder relief. But all this never happened, because at the time of the rise of Biblical criticism, the attitude of the reformers to the Bible was no longer maintained. The change began with the second generation of reformers. Possibly some excuse can be brought forward on their behalf, or at least an explanation; certainly no defence. They were fighting against the tyrannical authority of the Roman Church, that largest sect in Christendom. They had been brought up, and their fathers before them, in a world of authority, and perhaps it is small wonder that in seeking an authority on which they could rely against the authority of the Church they turned to an infallible book. It is hard to maintain a doctrine of salvation through grace by faith alone, with the authority of the inner witness of the Holy Spirit, and all the time keeping a proper balance between the words of Scripture and the reasoning of the human mind. And, further, all men yearn for something solid on which to lean, something that can be seen, or heard, or touched, so that a Book which can be handled and seen or a word that can be heard is a great temptation as against that inner witness of the Spirit, which can be maintained only by much prayer and communion both with God and with the brethren of the faith.

The net result of all this was that Scripture and the Word of God came to be exactly equated. Every verse equally came to be regarded as equally authoritative with every other verse. Whereas, in the time of the reformers, Biblical criticism would have been of very great help in making the Word of God clear out of the midst of Scripture, the actual result was otherwise. Biblical criticism was regarded as the enemy of the Word of God, and even as the enemy of true religion—and all of this actually because the successors of the reformers were not the men that the reformers themselves were.

The most unfortunate effect of the clash between Biblical criticism and the infallible Book is to be seen in the beginnings of Marxism.[1] It was in 1835 that Strauss's *Leben Jesu* was published. He emphasized the contradictions in the Gospel accounts of the life of Jesus, and argued that there were no logical grounds at all for treating them as historical narratives on which men could rely. Instead, you see, of allowing for the human side of Scripture, i.e. the processes of transmission and the variations that necessarily take place in any oft-repeated tale, he attacked (as he was perfectly entitled to do) the prevalent notions of the time and rejected the whole of the Bible story as untrustworthy. He explained the existence of the Gospel story as the result of the myth-making consciousness of the community. Christians had maintained that their religion was historical, whereas all others were made up of myths. Here comes Strauss, arguing that the historical basis of Christianity was no more to be trusted than that of any aborigine. My point is this: that, given his premises—the premises provided in part by orthodox Christians themselves—given his premises, Strauss was right. He was right because it was held that every word of Scripture was equally infallible with every other word, so that if one word went, the whole went. And this infallibility of Scripture had no place in the minds of the reformers: infallibility of the Word of God by all means, but not infallibility of the Scriptures.

[1] See *A Commentary on Communism*, by Edward Rogers. (The Epworth Press, 1951), pp. 68 ff.

This suspicion of Biblical criticism dies hard: you find it in America; you find it here in Britain. Part of this suspicion is sheer obscurantism, but not all. Some of it is due to a real fear of its destructive results, and much of this type of suspicion is justified. There are modern scholars who commit the same mistake as Strauss, but in reverse: they also have been unable to distinguish between Scripture and the Word of God, and the result has been that they have relegated the Bible to the standard of other books (e.g. it is equally helpful to read any other book in Church services, since all good books are inspired equally with the Bible), and, more seriously, they have substituted their own spirit for the inner witness of the Holy Spirit as the final test. The net result has been a humanistic religion which bears little resemblance to the faith delivered to the saints. I do not wonder that some verbal inspirationists are up in arms against some liberal theologians and Bible scholars. I have met theologians like that and Bible scholars like that both here and in U.S.A., and I must say that in these cases my sympathies are with the verbal inspirationists. Both parties have got Scripture and the Word of God confused, but the verbal inspirationists do hold on to both, whereas these particular liberal scholars have neither: they have failed wholly to interpret the Bible as the Word of God. There are few greater crimes than that.

I have spoken so far, for the most part, as though Biblical criticism was more sinned against than sinning, suggesting that if the successors of the reformers had kept a proper distinction between Scripture as a whole and the Word of God in particular all would have been well, and the effect of Biblical criticism would have been wholly good. But this is only part of the truth. It is probable that a great deal of damage to the Christian faith would have been done by Biblical criticism in any case. And yet here again it was not Biblical criticism itself that did the damage so much as the assumptions, mostly tacit and assumed, of the literary critics themselves. All this is set forth in a lucid and helpful manner by Professor T. W. Manson in his lecture 'The Failure of Liberalism to Interpret the Bible as the Word of God', an essay which appeared in 1944 as one of the 1943 Edward Alleyn Lectures, under the general title, *The Interpretation of the Bible* (S.P.C.K., ed. C. W. Dugmore). The assumptions which lie at the root of the trouble come from two sources: (1) the philosophy of the end of the eighteenth and the first half of the nineteenth centuries— namely the German idealism of Kant and his successors; (2) the scientific attitude of the nineteenth century. From Kant and his successors we get the idea of religion based on reason and having three essentials: the nature and existence of God, the moral freedom and responsibility of man, and the immortality of the human soul. From the scientific approach we get the insistence upon the paramountcy of natural law and biological evolution (see Manson's lecture, pp. 92 f.). The net result of all this has been to cut God off from the world which presumably He made. Religion becomes the story of what man has done rather than of what God is doing. It is something discoverable by man rather than a truth revealed by God. There is no such thing as any interruption or abrogation of natural law, and therefore no such thing as a miracle. It became proper to talk of Christianity as the highest form of religion which man has yet discovered, and to rewrite the Bible as the story of a more or less steady evolution from primitive notions on through the various stages of the Tylor-Frazer scheme, till finally monotheism emerges. The Bible becomes a Book about God, and no longer contains a message from God. It is not permitted to speak of God the Saviour, active in this world to save. We must talk of 'values', truth, beauty, and goodness, and God is somehow an oblong blur composed of these 'values'. Jesus becomes a quiet, persuasive Teacher, a Reformer of Judaism and its true realization. No wonder that Strauss and Marx swept all this aside as useless in the new age. No wonder they pressed on to say that all these ideas and suppositions of man could and should be outgrown.

So it came about that Biblical criticism has born the brunt of condemnation. Actually, it was a tool of modern liberalism, that modern humanitarianism which holds that man is the architect of his own destiny and that he requires no Saviour.

I come to the last stage of the effect of Biblical criticism, the stage whereby Biblical criticism has become the tool of a very different approach to the Bible. We have, in these latter days, come to realize the inherent weakness, and indeed the falseness, of the 'liberal' approach to the Bible. We have learned that in respect even of Biblical studies 'man shall not live by bread alone, but by every word that proceedeth out of the mouth of God'. This present generation has seen the rehabilitation once more of the Bible as the Word of God. We have realized (what, indeed, we never ought to have forgotten) that the Bible is not a history of a people who searched until they found God, but the story of a God who found a people, called them to Himself to be a special people, that through them He might reveal to man His own Self. The fifth book of the New Testament is called 'The Acts of the Apostles'; the whole Bible might well be called 'The Acts of God', and actually 'The Acts of the Apostles' is not so much their acts as the Acts of the Holy Spirit. We are getting away from the God of the philosophers, the Absolute who never changes—back to the God of the Bible, the Saviour-God, who never changes in the sense that He is always doing the same thing, 'coming to seek and to save that which is lost'. He has ten million ways of doing it, but He is always doing this one thing.

Most of us were brought up in a generation which for the most part may have used the word 'salvation', but did not mean it. It has taken two major wars to teach Europe, including Britain, that we cannot save ourselves, and that this much-vaunted liberalism is bankrupt. I found much more of this old-fashioned liberalism (because that is what it really is—old-fashioned, and out-of-date)—I found much more of this old-fashioned liberalism in the United States of America than there has been over on this side of the water for many years. I can understand that. I would not detract for one moment from the great and indeed decisive part which the United States has played in two wars. We are all grateful, and can never be grateful enough. But we on this side, especially in this last war, with our resources already impaired, once more were in at the beginning and, alone of all the contestants, kept on right through to the end—and we have been badly mauled. Just at present, for one reason or another, we seem to be worse off than anybody else so far as material blessings within the country are concerned. This has given us an advantage nearly equal to our German friends. We are finding ourselves driven away from the idea that we ourselves, by ourselves, can build the New Jerusalem. We have, thank God, become theologically minded. One of the most helpful books setting forth the theological approach to the Bible is by an American (honour where honour is due), Professor Ernest Wright of the McCormick Theological Seminary, Chicago. Its title is *The Old Testament against its Environments*, published in this country by the S.C.M. Press. And it has a companion, *The New Testament against Its Environment*, by a colleague of Professor Wright's, Professor Floyd V. Filson. The great emphasis in these books is that the Bible and Israel's faith 'cannot be explained fully

233

by evolutionary or environmental categories. The central elements of Biblical faith . . . cannot have developed by any natural evolutionary process from the pagan world in which they appeared.' All this is good. We are back once again at the story of 'the God who comes', always coming in every age for the salvation of His people, calling them, converting them, building them up into the Kingdom of God. This, once more, is where Luther was—with the great doctrine of salvation by grace through faith alone as the key which unlocks the treasures of Scripture, and makes clear to us what is the Word of God.

But a final word of warning. A few years ago I was privileged to visit the Ecumenical Institute founded by the World Council of Churches at the Château de Bossey, near to Geneva. I lectured there for a week or so on the Old Testament. There was a considerable number of students and young ministers there, mostly from Middle Europe and Holland, one British (and he was half-Swiss) and some half-dozen Americans. I noticed this: that whenever I referred to a passage of Scripture, the Continentals all turned it up at very great speed and peered at it, pored over it, most anxiously and eagerly. They were saying to themselves: 'What has this got to say to me now?' I said to them, 'But what about Biblical criticism and this particular passage?' To which their reply was: 'Oh yes, we know all about that. We are going on from there.' They taught me two things. The first is this: I can understand now how the apocalypses came to be written. They were written in circumstances remarkably parallel to those which obtained in Middle Europe four or five years ago. Perhaps things are different now, with the remarkable recovery which has been made in many areas over there, thanks to considerable outside help. But then, in those days nearer to the end of the war, they had no hope. They knew that if any help was to come to them, it would have to come from the skies. They lived actually in the real crisis, and that is why they were so urgent with the Word of God. Incidentally, this attitude needs to be remembered when we read the writings of Karl Barth and his friends. I do not wonder that so many in Britain and in U.S.A. find him unintelligible. I find that most of what he says means nothing if it is interpreted against a liberal, evolutionary, environmental background. But if it is interpreted against a background of crisis, where this human world is sharply contrasted with the Heavenly world, then his writings have meaning—very profound meaning. To return to the Germans and Hungarians and Czechs at Bossey. These men and women had at any rate learned to see the Bible once more with their eyes opened. Yes, they were like Elisha's young man on the hill in Dothan. Their eyes had been opened and they could see the horses and chariots of the Lord. That is all to the good, for that is what the Bible should mean to us. Here, and here and here again, I must search for, and by the insight of the Holy Spirit find a veritable Word of God for *me*, here and now.

But the second thing I learned at Bossey. It seemed to me that many of those Germans and their friends were perilously near a new sort of verbal inspirationism. I have noticed it in this country amongst some of my friends (no names, no pack-drill). The insistence on the Bible as the Word of God is leading them to take the whole of Scripture as being equally inspired; and once more allegorical and symbolical interpretations are brought into use in order to get the right answer. Biblical criticism is neglected. I think these students of the Bible are dangerously wrong. There is plenty of material in the Bible, made all the clearer by a sound Biblical criticism—plenty of material to support sound theology without resort to this neo-fundamentalism and its allegorical methods. There is

234

no need for us to be ensnared by Scylla in our zeal to avoid Charybdis. Sound theology and sound scholarship will keep us in the true path, though, as I trust we all know, nothing but grace and faith—God's Grace and our faith—will lead us safe home.

In the evening a Service in Commemoration of John and Charles Wesley was held in the ancient University Church of St Mary the Virgin. There both John and Charles Wesley had preached, and there a congregation representative of world Methodism knelt to thank God for what had been, and to pledge themselves to continue the unfinished task. It was indeed a 'Service for believers rejoicing'. The climax came in the eloquent and moving tribute paid by the Rev. Dr J. Scott Lidgett, C.H., to the founders of Methodism.

JOHN AND CHARLES WESLEY

The substance of an address delivered by the REV. DR J. SCOTT LIDGETT, C.H.:

The Conference has thanked God, the Most Holy Trinity, for the gift of John and Charles Wesley and the great Revival of religion of which they were the leaders. It is now appropriate that we should consider before God the nature and the greatness of the gifts that were brought to us by these His servants.

John and Charles Wesley were inseparable, indispensable to one another, complementary to one another; without their partnership, the Revival would not have come about as it did. They filled the eighteenth century; were subject to all its limiting conditions; they were congenial to it. Their work has passed into history with universal appreciation of its importance at the time and familiarity with its details.

Yet are John and Charles Wesley simply outstanding figures of a past age, to be studied and placed in the past and revered as men of the past? By no means. They are equally men of the twentieth century, leaders in all issues of our present life. Their energy and their reasonable faith overleapt the barriers of their time to create and establish a new epoch of spiritual and catholic history. We shall therefore now examine, in the presence of God, the modernity of John and Charles Wesley.

To begin with, religion and theology—the spring of all their work. Their teaching was not embroidered by any accretions of pious imagination. They had been reared in the Holy Scriptures and the catholic creeds, and they held by them to the end. They preached unceasingly 'Christ Crucified' —that 'Christ died for our sins according to the Scriptures'. But their doctrine of the atonement was free from misleading explanations—juridical, governmental, mercantile—which in other quarters in their day and since have disfigured the doctrine and made it incredible to rational belief.

They preached faith, but faith hand in hand with reason. This alliance meant faith and reason were in partnership, criticizing and supporting one another. They were the two bastions of spiritual life and thought.

They preached faith, but faith as the starting point of a living, spiritual process, which, assisted by the self-discipline it inspired, led on to perfect love. There is little or nothing for us to explain away or to accommodate in their teaching.

Catholicity. John Wesley said that the Methodists were 'the friends of all; the enemies of none'. This was the life-long attitude and practice of the Wesleys and the behaviour of all their true followers. They sought truth and righteousness, but with generous appreciation and concentration on the vital and essential, not the less significant details. They were never overriding. Common acceptance of the faith and agreement in it were the foundation of friendship and helpfulness. This spirit of generous appreciation is essential to unity and reunion.

John Wesley said: 'If thy heart be as my heart, give me thy hand.' The Spirit of Methodism is the spirit of sharing.

Social Service. John and Charles Wesley were pioneers in Social Service. Charles Wesley wrote:

> 'Then let us attend
> Our heavenly Friend
> In His members distressed
> By want, or affliction, or sickness oppressed
> The prisoner relieve
> The stranger receive
> Supply all their wants
> And spend and be spent
> In assisting His saints.'

A new note struck in the eighteenth century!

John Wesley said: 'I know nothing of any solitary religion.' 'The gospel of Christ knows no religion but social, no holiness but social holiness.' Without this understanding, the pursuit of holiness maims personality and becomes abstract and ineffectual. He preached perfect love.

The doctrine of perfect love demands careful study. It should, however, be considered in connexion with the Second Commandment which, as St John in his First Epistle insists, is vitally related to it. The doctrine of perfect love needs for its completion close and fearless consideration of the ethic of the Second Commandment: 'Thou shalt love thy neighbour as thyself.' Dangerous? But what great truth is not dangerous?

All their service was carried on in close contact with the people, sharing with them, intimate knowledge of them, understanding of and sympathy with their needs. It was given in closest fellowship, not from above to those below.

John Wesley had no trouble about the frontiers of the spiritual and the secular which have tormented so many people in his time and since. What is secular? All that we are pleased to regard as outside God and separate from Him. But for John Wesley there was no separate frontier or department of life. 'In Him we live, and move and have our being.' Hence John Wesley, with the utmost freedom, gave to his inquirer the instruction: 'Do all the good you can, in all the ways that you can, to all the people that you can'! And his own life was an outstanding example of this instruction, limited only by the conditions of his age.

Education. John and Charles Wesley were true members of the University of Oxford, were steeped in its thought, scholarship, and culture. They were keen in the pursuit of knowledge, as John Wesley's saddle-bags on his journey showed. These were full of the latest and most important contributions to literature. It is right and proper that this service of thanksgiving should be held in the great church of this University, in which they both preached.

And what John Wesley sought for himself he gave to his people. He was active in increasing their knowledge, and so furnished and published 'The Christian Library'. He founded schools and supported the cause of popular education. John Scott, the founder and first Principal of Westminster College, his faithful follower in the nineteenth century, truly contended that ability was common to all classes, and that because a man was poor that was no reason for his children to have a poor education. In the face of the stinginess of Parliament and the comparative indifference of the Churches, he proclaimed that 'no education could be too good for the working classes'. For the Methodist Revival faith and reason went together hand in hand. The uplifting of the spirit was attended by the awakening, the informing, and the freedom of the mind.

World Evangelism. John Wesley called the world 'my parish', and therefore, in fulfilling his mission, he had the whole world in mind. He sent Asbury and Coke to America. Asbury's marvellous mission was a mighty fact in the creation of the spirit of the United States—a fact that has been set forth by the erection of his statue, with other founders of the Republic, in Washington, the capital. And now in the light of this universality, look around and see the Methodist churches, missions, schools in every continent of the world.

Finally, John and Charles Wesley were never separatists or sectarians. John Wesley said: 'If anyone says, Why, these are only the common fundamental principles of Christianity! Thou hast said; so I mean; this is the very truth; I know they are no other, and I would to God both these and all men knew, that I and all who follow my judgement, do vehemently refuse to be distinguished from other men by any but the common principles of Christianity . . . but from real Christians of whatsoever denomination they be we earnestly desire not to be distinguished at all.'

This was Wesley's rendering of the great definition of the catholic faith, *'Quod semper, quod ubique, quod ab omnibus creditum est* ('What always, what everywhere, what by all has been believed').

This Conference and this Congregation are enriched by the presence of Dr J. R. Mott, the great leader of the Ecumenical Movement; the author of the Edinburgh Conference in 1910, which brought about a most notable improvement in the relations of the Churches to one another. Before that they were in ignorance of one another and suspicious of one another. They learnt the value and the fullness of their common unity in their confession: 'Jesus is Lord.'

Wherever that confession is truly made, there is the communion of saints. This includes the Roman Catholic Church, despite our serious differences from it. We thank God that that Church has handed down to us the Creeds, the writings of the Fathers, and has given us numerous examples of holy and effectual leadership in the pursuit of truth and righteousness, of faith, hope, and love in Christ Jesus our Lord.

All those who confess 'Jesus is Lord' belong to one another, and their catholicity is mightier than the differences which at present divide them. So Methodism, in fulfilling John and Charles Wesley, must go forth in the utmost endeavour to promote the fellowship, the unity, the eventual union of all who 'profess and call themselves Christians' throughout the world.

NINTH DAY

Wednesday 5th September

MORNING devotions were conducted by Bishop Theodor Arvidsen of Sweden, and Bishop B. W. Doyle of the Coloured Episcopal Church, Nashville, introduced the topic for the day. In his address, based on Matthew 5[13-16], he defined 'being, seeming, and doing'.

The blessedness or happiness of people possessing the characteristics described in the Beatitudes is not only an inner attitude, but an outward act, said Bishop Doyle. It may result in persecution, but it brings a definite reward. What a man *is*, he *does*; and what he *does*, he *is*. To live by the teaching of Matthew 5[13-16] will be both an attitude and act, social and individual, public and private. We shall act without conscious volition, purifying and staying corruption like salt, shining with holy radiance, reflecting the light eternal—the light of God's love.

At the beginning of the morning session Bishop Ivan Lee Holt read messages from Josef Naumiuk, representing the Polish Methodist Church in Austria, from Dr Wesley Boyd of the Primitive Methodist Church of America, and from the Secretary of the Board of Action responsible for ecclesiastical relations in the Church of Brazil.

The theme of the session was *Personal Responsibility*. An address by Mrs Frank G. Brooks of Iowa, President of the Women's Society of Christian Service of the Methodist Church, dealt with the subject, *Within the Local Church*. The second speaker was the Rev. E. Clifford Urwin, of the Department of Christian Citizenship, London, and he led us to consider our personal responsibility *Within the Community*.

PERSONAL RESPONSIBILITY

I. PERSONAL RESPONSIBILITY IN THE LOCAL CHURCH

An address delivered by MRS FRANK G. BROOKS, *of Iowa*:

In considering the subject assigned to me, I have not thought entirely of the personal responsibility of *women* in the Church. It is my conviction that the responsibilities of lay women and of lay men are, basically, the same. As Methodists, we make the same pledge when we join the Church: to uphold it by our prayer, our presence, our gifts, and our service.

Nevertheless, since I am a woman, and rejoice that I am, I am aware of the truth of the line in Alfred Tennyson's *The Princess*: 'Not like in like, but like in difference.' I, therefore, conceive a part of my task to be the presentation of some basic responsibilities of women in the Methodist Church around the world.

I recognize also that, as the only Methodist member of the Commission on the Life and Work of Women in the Church of the World Council of Churches, it is appropriate for me to direct your thoughts somewhat along

238

the channels of the thinking of that committee. We should discover whether or not the attitudes and convictions of the women and the men from other denominations on that commission are in line with Methodist thought. It is definitely part of the responsibility of all leaders in the ecumenical Methodist Church to know something of the thinking of this Commission. To that phase of your responsibility, then, I shall first direct your attention.

Christian women, from the time of Paul to the present, have realized that Christ has brought them new liberty. They have been aware also that this new freedom must be used with quiet dignity and wise discretion, even in the Church.

To study the life and the work of women in the Church, twenty-five men and women, from seventeen countries, were called to meet in a pioneering task at the Château de Bossey, near Geneva, Switzerland, 6th-10th March 1950. The people on this commission represent diametrically different viewpoints for two reasons: many of them have known only State Churches, and others of them see all problems in the Church from a theological viewpoint. Neither of these approaches is fundamentally popular with a Methodist.

The ecumenicity of the approach of the Commission to the problem of the life and work of women in the Church is, however, of special interest to Methodists. A book compiled by Dr Kathleen Bliss of England will shortly be issued. The material for this book on the life and work of women in the Church had its origin in a questionnaire which was returned from fifty-eight countries. Many of the replies were from fifty to 100 pages in length. The questions, prepared and circulated in English, German, and French, were translated into many other languages. They dealt with such problems as the following: the professional and voluntary work of women; the extent to which women's gifts are integrated in the governing boards and policy-making groups of the Churches; women's work in the Church compared with the stage of emancipation which they have achieved in different countries.

As I have indicated, this Commission is composed of men and women. I am convinced that as God created us in the beginning man and woman in His image, he intended that men and women should help each other to perform their tasks in the Church and in the world. We know that the Church has often failed to exemplify to the world the joint mission of men and women.

This commission hopes to promote within the Churches a new concern to discover what it means that men and women are one in Christ. We have set in motion, therefore, a second study which will take account of the best that we can learn from the life sciences about the nature of man and of woman. It is determined that we shall look at the practical tasks which have to be performed and try to see them in the light of biblical teaching. We are enlisting the help of theologians, Church leaders, scientists, and persons of practical experience in the working together of men and women as we pursue this study. We trust that, when these studies are published, they will be found helpful to the Churches.

In the meantime, certain ideas and trends have been studied by the Commission. Many of these—though touching almost all Protestant denominations—are of great interest and value to us as ecumenical Methodists. To two or three of these I should like to call your attention. (See *Revised Interim Report*, World Council of Churches, December 1948.)

Members of the Commission from all countries stressed the great

239

influence of women in their own homes. This statement is axiomatic—too obvious, perhaps, for notice. Yet I must report that, though we agreed there was little likelihood that women, in spite of a modern secularized society, would choose to forgo marriage and motherhood, we also recognized the fact that there will need to be an increasing sense of mutuality between men and women in carrying the responsibilities of the home as well as those of the Church.

Questions were raised as to whether or not the subject of 'The Place of Women in the Church' is a live one in various Churches of different countries; and also as to whether there is a common mind on this subject. Taking the world as a whole, it was discovered there is every reason to say that this question is indeed of great and growing importance.

The original questionnaires showed a definite similarity in the denominational responses, regardless of the country from which the reply came. These replies seem to me to be of great significance. The Congregational Churches, the Society of Friends, and the Salvation Army are all very much interested and at the same time relaxed about the matter. They have accepted as a matter of principle full equality of status and function for men and women. The Methodists veer in the direction of equality of status and function, but are divided in their thinking about so many matters of administration that their minds must be said not to be 'made up'.

In recent weeks I have been impressed by the changes in the status of women in different communions. As ecumenical Methodists, with responsibilities in our Church, we should be interested in and aware of these developments in other Churches.

The privilege of administering sacraments in the Norwegian State Lutheran Church has just been granted to a woman for the first time in history. At the recent Synod in Paris of the Reformed Church of France, it was agreed that women could be ordained 'in certain extraordinary cases'. A committee in Sweden very recently recommended that women be recognized as members of the clergy of the State Lutheran Church in full status.

When Miss Sarah Chakko of India was in the United States recently, she made a significant comment. She said: 'One is very much intrigued by the concept of "woman" underlying Church and public life in Europe. In a country like Switzerland, which claims to be the oldest democracy in existence today, women are still unenfranchised.' And then she added a statement which we should ponder: 'All this is very puzzling to one who has come from a land where the Christian conception of womanhood has served as a dynamic in social and public life. The Church in many so-called "mission lands" pioneered in women's education, gave them their rightful place in society, and offered them opportunities of service. Many of the European missionary women workers find in these lands greater opportunities for creative service than in their own home countries. Is the European attitude on the status of women truly Christian? If not, when and why did it stop moving in the right direction? Are we in Asiatic countries on the wrong track?'

In Paris, the Russian Orthodox Church (in exile) has set up a special Orthodox Women's Theological College to train women for the ministry. In Finland there has been vigorous opposition on the part of Finland's rural population to an official proposal for the ordination of women ministers by the State Lutheran Church. In the towns and cities, women's organizations have won many supporters for such an idea. To date, no decision has been reached.

In the United States, recent months have revealed some interesting action. A woman was recently named spiritual leader of a Jewish congregation in Mississippi. The Augustana Lutheran Church three months ago shattered precedent when it voted to permit women to take part in the administration of local congregations; women may now serve as trustees, who are responsible for financial and property matters. On the other hand, a movement to make women eligible for election as wardens and vestrymen in an Episcopal diocese of New York was overwhelmingly defeated.

One other matter growing out of the Commission's report is of concern to Methodists interested in the responsibility of men and women in the Church—namely, the reservoir of lay power in women's groups. It was discovered that almost every Church in the world has its women's groups. In a number of countries these groups are the only organized groups of women there are anywhere. Their activities are many: teaching, benevolence, fund-raising, study evangelism, social action.

A friend who has recently visited Greece wrote me of her pleasure in the strong lay movement there. She said, in part: 'I was greatly impressed by the vigour and vitality of the lay movement in the Greek Orthodox Church. I attended the service at their centre at Athens and watched about 600 or more young people participate in the service. The movement sponsors the publication of religious literature, and the bookshop is a busy place. Women play a significant role in the total programme. The women's organization has a membership of over 6,000 and is very active.'

It seems to me to be important for us to assume the responsibility for keeping the lay movement among women Christian. It is already strong, as one realizes from reading the daily Press reports which tell of international meetings of various business and professional women's groups, such as the one held recently in Holland.

As I have travelled in Europe and in Asia, I have been impressed over and over again by the hunger for 'fellowship' felt by women. The church must not fail to recognize this 'clubbing' instinct of women. The tendency may be over-developed in the United States, but I felt it even in as unlikely a place as North Africa. In Algiers is a woman's group, made up of well-dressed Frenchwomen, veiled Arab women, timid, unveiled Christian women, and others; it meets twice a month for fellowship and for prayer. The women do not all speak the same language, but there is a warmth of understanding and sympathy among them. They do hand-work and sell the finished products to help in a dispensary for abjectly poor folk in Les Ouadias, a village among the Kabyles. One of the interesting things about this group is that they beg to meet weekly instead of bi-weekly.

Such groups, anywhere in the world, should be guided to do more than a bit of handwork for benevolent causes. They should be led into discussion groups on international relations, United Nations, the Bill of Human Rights, and other basic subjects. Someone—and why should it not be women?—must get to work to mesh the life represented by a Kabyle woman of North Africa who knows nothing of farming save only to pick olives from a tree by hand, and the life of the Iowa farm-woman who does not realize that corn is ever picked in any manner except by machinery.

This idea, logically, seems to lead our thinking away from the broad concepts of the Commission of the World Council of Churches to the other point to which this paper should give consideration—namely, some basic concepts of the responsibilities of lay women (and to an almost equal extent lay men) in the local church. The laity, according to a report made at

Amsterdam in 1948 entitled 'The Significance of the Laity in the Church', constitutes more than 99 per cent of the Church.

It is not possible neatly to list or classify the responsibilities of Methodist women to their Church in every corner of our world parish; to say 'So far we go' or 'So much we do'; to announce 'We go no farther' or 'We do no more'. I am suggesting, therefore, only a few of the possibilities and responsibilities which seem to me to be of major significance. And, basic to the detailed suggestions, every Methodist woman has ready to offer to her God—her life, its influence, and the twenty-four hours of each day.

In the United States, in the Central Methodist Church of Kansas City, Missouri, there is a bronze plaque. It was placed in the church by a thoughtful layman, and this is what it says: 'Men may build a church, but it is the women who preserve it and keep the spiritual life within its walls.' I shall not be so positive as the good layman, but simply say one of the responsibilities of ecumenical-minded Methodist women is to help to preserve the spiritual life of the Church.

I know of no words or acts of Jesus Christ which indicate exclusion of women from any spiritual experience or office. I have just read a summary translation of a scholarly treatise by Dr Margit Sahlin of the Swedish Lutheran Church which brings this point into full relief.

To speak with authority, however, one should speak of a thing which is known by oneself. We do not bear witness in the abstract. Therefore, I point to observations which we women from the United States have made this past summer as we studied the Book of Acts in all of our summer schools. We have noted that the Holy Spirit at Pentecost was poured out on women as well as men, and that Jesus Christ is the pattern for women as well as for men.

Women seem almost to be singled out to assist the pastor in keeping the spiritual life of the Church aglow. Jesus spoke specifically to women eighteen different times. One of the missionaries to Brazil has isolated these eighteen messages and published them in a little booklet. The first words of Jesus, as they are registered in the New Testament, are spoken to His mother.

A Brazilian friend of mine told me recently that in Brazil they say: 'Mother is the heart of the home; woman is the soul of the Church.' The Methodist Church can continue to depend on its women for the strengthening of its spiritual life; but greater religious enthusiasm among all the laity must be developed.

There are certain responsibilities which can be assumed more easily by women because they have more free time, perhaps, for specific Church work than men. The type of task which I shall single out for women to achieve is equally important for men—namely, building an ecumenical mind in each individual Church. Such a universal mind within the Methodist Church—a mind common to the leaders and to the most humble member—could well be the dynamic for 1951 to 1955 for the Methodist Church. And women can unite to produce this dynamic of Christianity—an ecumenical mind in the Methodist Church.

In that same Book of Acts I find mention of three women with ecumenical minds—Priscilla, Lydia, and Dorcas. These women were sensitive to the needs of their day, with a sensitivity typical of women: one using her workshop, one her home, and one her needle. And that, to me, is ecumenicity for women: a sensitivity to the total needs of a total Church; an awareness of the specific contributions to be made by women to their own age. And one of those contributions, I repeat, is the establishment of an ecumenical mind in each local church; the giving to each small unit a sense of being a part of the world, of having similar problems and similar tasks, of feeling a sense of responsibility for world problems, of strengthening belief in the United Nations, of feeling responsibility for the achievement of human rights for all peoples in the world. That is our challenging responsibility; its accomplishment will bring the beginning of a sense of international security and goodwill on earth.

A logical corollary, following this establishment of a world concern in each unit of Methodism, will be a growing missionary spirit within the Church. It is illogical to assume greater interest on the part of women than men in the missionary programme of the Church. Yet sometimes we are illogical! In the particular Methodist *Discipline* which I know best, I read that it is part of woman's task in the Methodist Church 'to assist in the promotion of a missionary spirit throughout the Church'.

I accept the authority of this *Discipline*, and I accept it largely because I know, as a woman, that it is true that unless women are convinced and convicted of the need for mission work, men will *never* be. I believe firmly in a statement uttered so frequently that no one knows who first said it. The last person whom I heard repeat it was Dr Frank Laubach: 'If you bring a man to Christ, you bring one. If you bring a woman, you bring a whole family.'

This paper does not need to emphasize the responsibility of women for continuing to increase the missionary spirit of the Church. Their deeds bear witness to their conviction; their activities in day schools, church schools, vacation schools, in relief work, in social centres—all these are proof of their faith.

It would be the easiest task before this Oxford Conference for each delegate to begin listing the out-reach of the women of its own group. Let one illustration from a personal letter to me from the Philippines suffice:

'Perhaps you are asking: What are the women of the Church doing in the Philippines? May I say that they are an ever hard-working group of women eager to do their part of service for the Master. Some of the societies are helping in making bandage rolls for Mary Johnston Hospital. Some of the women are very active in visitation, sharing with the women in the *barrios* the "abundant life". . . . It is interesting to hear a woman tell how she is growing papaya trees and tithing the fruit. Of course, we are all familiar with the giving of the handful of rice which, in many cases, is the only gift they have to give.'

I criticize myself, as a woman interested in the establishment of a world Christian community, in that I feel so often powerless to relieve the bitterness of soul and the depth of despair that I have seen. I find myself saying: 'I am only a woman from a Church. I do not have power to do anything to change the situation in which you are.' So I would say to myself and to other women: we do have power to change situations, if only there are enough of us convinced of the need.

Some years ago I read an article in the *Indian Social Reformer*. The gist of it is this: it is in the women of faith that the real strength of Hinduism lies today. It is women who cling most tenaciously to caste, to *purdah*, to ceremonies. In Moslem homes it is the women who watch most vigilantly for any suggestion of defamation of their faith. All over the land there are many sons of India who would become followers of Jesus Christ were they not the sons and husbands of quiet women who will not allow it. If India is to be won for Jesus Christ, the women of India must first be won for Him.

My experience with Hindu and Moslem women is not wide enough for me to verify the truth of the article. But I know that women can keep

243

alive in a family almost anything they wish. If this is true, why should they not keep idealism alive? Someone must keep idealism alive if men and women and children are to go on living in a world torn between two ideologies. It seems to be woman's natural task.

This, then, I consider to be our final responsibility: to keep idealism alive in the Church, and part of idealism is vision, and part is courage, and part is magnetism to point others to the ideal. With vision, with courage, with magnetism, women must uphold in their Church—the ideal of peace. This, women can do in the humblest tent or the largest cathedral. This, too, is ecumenical!

Representatives of twenty-seven of Japan's leading women's organizations, including Church groups, have recently signed a petition entitled, 'Gist of the Hopes of Japanese Women for the Anticipated Peace Treaty'. They conclude the document with these significant words: 'We do not mean to be blind to the world crisis and speak glibly of a sentimental ideal for peace. . . . When we face the cold reality that the world is divided . . . we cannot but recognize that the way which seems too idealistic is the most realistic way to bring about world peace. . . ."

It is realistic idealism when women of the United States try to lead the women in their Churches to create a 'climate of opinion' for peace by witnessing to the Christian ethic of love in their every day living. To this end, four months ago United Church Women requested the President of the United States to give an interview to five leaders of the major Protestant denominations. This interview is pending.

These women wish to set before the President five points on which Christian women believe lasting peace can be built: praying for peace; living democracy in one's own community every day; supporting the United Nations, which, next to the Churches, is today's best instrument for peace; disciplining oneself to share the abundance of spiritual and material resources; studying and understanding the issues in the world struggle for peace. Such action is realistic idealism.

It is also realistic idealism when women in ninety-three countries around the world pray together for peace on the first Friday in Lent. This thing we have done together for twenty-five years; it is the most important thing we do together.

It is the responsibility of women to keep alive other ideals of service in the Church—basic issues with which Christ dealt and with which any seeker after the ideal of peace must deal. Jesus states them at the beginning of His ministry in Luke 4[18]: 'to preach the gospel to the poor; . . . to heal the broken-hearted, to preach deliverance to the captives, and recovering of sight to the blind, to set at liberty them that are bruised'. In the language of the laity, the issues are simply to explore and answer the problems of the disinherited, the exploited, the poverty-stricken of soul and body.

Therefore I see the responsibilities of the individual lay member in the local church to be twofold: an informed awareness of the changing position of women in the Church and a continued interest in the study of this problem. Second, an individual responsibility for carrying out Christ's programme for His Church through prayer, through extending His kingdom, and through the promotion of the ideals that make for peace. It is our task to move among a hurt humanity, to ease the pain, to serve our Methodist Church, always closely guarded and guided by God's hand. Only as each individual lay man or lay woman is a dynamic unit in the Church can God's plan as revealed by Christ restore a broken world.

244

II. THE CHRISTIAN IN THE COMMUNITY: PERSONAL RELATIONSHIPS

An address delivered by the REV. E. CLIFFORD URWIN:

The Christian in the community! Social religion, if we really mean anything by the phrase, in action in the community about us; and I begin with a twentieth-century illustration of it in practice. This old land of Britain is going through a vigorous process of re-colonization. Old wastes are being cleared away, new areas are being laid out, and new towns built, and our people being re-distributed in new communities, with all the problems which that involves of people strange to one another learning to live together. It so happens that one of the new towns—one of twelve or more planned ultimately to house anything up to 1 million of our people —is to be named after a Durham miner who was also a Methodist local preacher.

His name was Peter Lee, and that is to be the name of the new town. Why? The answer is simply that as a Christian man, devoted to the service of his fellows, especially those of the working class, he stamped his name and memory on the life of a whole county of this realm. He is one of the most perfect illustrations I know of my theme this morning: the Christian in the community, social religion in action. Living a wild and reprobate life till he was past thirty—some of it in America and other of it in South Africa—he was won back to sobriety and purposeful living by a haunting memory of his mother's religion. He joined himself to a Methodist society in the mining village of Wheatley Hill, one of those societies which his biographer describes as a bulwark of the good life. Of this society, it was said by an unwilling sceptic: 'There are some remarkably fine men in that church. Peter Lee became one of them, impressed his mind and his convictions on succeeding generations of young men, and preached the gospel as he found it in the Bible, John Bunyan and John Ruskin. He became a miners' leader, parish councillor, county councillor, and finally Council Chairman. He fought for clean streets, better houses, better schools, better sanitation, better water supplies, better wages, and the decencies of life for those he sought to serve. A typical episode was when he went to the Annual Meeting of the North Eastern Railway as a shareholder representing the Wheatley Hill Co-operative Society, and got a new station and a better roadway to it for Wheatley Hill by the simple device of moving the rejection of the Company's balance sheet. He didn't get a seconder for his resolution, but he got the new station and the better road. So, standing at one and the same time, for clean, upright and god-fearing manhood, and for juster conditions of life and work, he served his age and fulfilled his Christian calling.'

I

That story from real life which is to leave its mark upon the map of Britain helps us to apprehend the meaning of our theme: the Christian in the community. What do we mean by community? For Peter Lee, it meant first the local community life in Wheatley Hill, then the larger community life of County Durham. Stretching beyond that was the community life of Britain as a whole; and beyond that the heterogeneous community of the world of nations. What holds men in communities, local, national or worldwide? What is it which ties saints and sinners up in the hurdle of life together for good or ill, and calls for community of interest, a sense of neighbourliness, and fellowship of man with man?

For community life is hard and difficult. Even Methodists, despite their doctrine of perfect love and their talk of social religion, haven't always found it conspicuously easy to get on with one another. Human relations are shot through with strife of divergent interests and personal differences. The clash of personalities has always to be reckoned with, inducing animosities and hostilities, so that the wonder sometimes is that human communities hold together as well as they do. Our industry is disfigured by avarice, sloth, dishonesty, and frequent exploitation; infidelities shatter home life; and prodigality wastes precious leisure in profligacy. Beyond all these in our day there are the menacing shadows of world hunger, racial strife, and the war of nations. In fact, men everywhere feel more or less clearly the necessity of a profound change, a radical alteration in the way we live together, amounting to revolution. The pressure of clamant, unsatisfied material need is driving men that way, with a desperate sense of injustice in human affairs plaguing their hearts. If we do not satisfy the hunger for community, the revolution will surely come. In a blundering way, it is the sense of sin at work. Sick with longing for the beloved community of their dreams, men are driven to desperate deeds in a vain effort to compel by force. Some of our fellow Christians behind the Iron Curtain as we call it, actually live in that revolutionary situation, and others live on the brink of it, and we may wonder what is the technique Christians should pursue when so placed. That would lead us beyond our immediate task, except to say this: whatever be the peculiar difficulties of such situations, the live Christian in a sinful world faces every day the need of revolutionary change within himself, and without in the body politic.

The truth is: if man is a social or political animal, as Aristotle rightly discerned he is, intended to live in communities, then in his unregenerate nature he is inadequately fitted for it. His strongest natural aptitudes are, first, the instinct of self-preservation; next, the surging impulses of sex. Both impulses give opportunity for self-seeking tendencies which are only faintly qualified with a helpless herd instinct. The essential goodness of human nature, to the assertion of which Rousseau gave such powerful impetus, is an illusion of ungrounded optimism, disproven in the rough and tumble of human affairs. Any native goodness or kindliness of heart there is about us is the fruit of the maternal and paternal impulses, of which mother love is the basis. Even those are fitful. Sometimes mothers desert their children; fathers do it more often; brothers fall out and sisters quarrel. Some of our makeshifts in community arrangements—what a Scottish philosopher calls 'the device of government'—turn on the initial frailty of human nature. It is good Christian doctrine that 'the State is necessary because of sin', and the care for sin is redeeming grace. If unregenerate human nature is to be fitted for community life, it needs to be redeemed; and that is where the Christian impact on society begins: with the redeeming power of the love of God in the hearts of men!

II

So back to our initial question: What does hold men together in community? As I see it, there are four sets of converging interests.

The first is the tie of economics. Men are held together by the necessity of working side by side for the material needs of life. You can't solve that problem on a basis of individualism. Not one of you this morning provided your own breakfast or made your own clothes. One of the first questions you ask about any community is: What are its dominant trades and industries? So in Britain we've our mining communities, textile manufacturing areas, heavy industrial areas, railway towns, ports and shipbuilding centres, and agricultural communities. Take the staple industries away, or let them fall into decline, and the community begins to disintegrate. But what a problem it is to work with other people—either to work for them or have them to work for you! And what an ungainly strife there is all the time about the just division of the fruits of industry.

Again, a community is a place where men and women make their homes and rear families. That at least binds them in the family relationship, for the family and not the individual is the unity of society. It is difficult to assess the influence of family life in shaping community. There we receive our first impressions and learn our mother tongue, be it standard English or the strange foreign language they speak in America. The family gives us our first schooling in self-government, mutual service, and neighbourliness. There, too, we first learn our religion, if there is any to be learned. So the family is our initial training ground of community living, and the others are the school and the church. But of those three, as an influence on character, the family can beat the school and the church any day. If the family is virtuous and socially-minded, the result will be good. If not, the reverse will accrue, and the influence of the bad family will go far beyond the confines of the home.

Thirdly, this economic and family life is lived out in the framework of social custom and the system of law and order we call 'government'. That is important for community life, for without it we should be reduced to the nasty, short, and brutish anarchic life which Hobbes so tersely described. Yet the establishment of law and order is itself a source of strife and division, by reason of divergent conceptions of the basis of law, or because of the lustful struggle for power, or our anti-social, law-breaking tendencies. Both America and Britain exhibit those difficulties. Important, however, as the task of government is, modern men are inclined to be politically obsessed, and look to politics for their salvation rather than to the transformation of human nature. Yet we cannot ignore the need for government, and have to struggle to make it good government.

Fourthly, for a community to be stable, coherent, virile and enduring, it needs at least a substratum of common faith and culture. That is, it needs a common religious faith, which inspires purpose and responsibility, upholds the common life in face of difficulty and adversity, and sustains it in its common enterprises. That is the basis for its morality and its culture, and few things seem to me more demonstrable than that when a community's religion declines, its life is undermined unless the declining faith be replaced by a new and stronger one. And religious disunity can also weaken the social fabric. Consider in both connexions the moral weakness of France and the divided state of Ireland. How America holds together with its 283 competing sects and wild varieties of religion passes my comprehension!

There, then, as I see it, are the four main ties which hold community together: economics, family, law, and religion! The truth of it can be seen in any new settlement of the Far West or in any village or city of Europe. And the point is that the Christian can influence community, and enter into personal relationships with his fellows at every one of those four aspects of their common life. He will share with them in common work or professional service. He will rear his own home alongside theirs and be involved in shaping neighbourly relations. He will take his part—at any rate, in our Western democracies—in shaping government and exercising responsible citizenship. He will witness to the truth of religion, uphold his religious association, and share in the cultural and recreative life of the community.

III

What, then, is the characteristic contribution of the Christian to that multifarious community life which surges about him? To put it concretely; what better contribution does any Christian man in London, New York, or Chicago make to community just because he's a Christian? We ought to be on our guard here against making exaggerated claims. For over a good part of his life, the social obligations on the Christian are indistinguishable from those resting on anybody else. It is merely a platitude that he should be courteous to all, honest in all his dealings, upright in character, unswerving in integrity, public-spirited, conspicuous in preserving the decencies of life and making the currents of social life run smoothly and amicably. But then so should everybody else. These are just the canons of natural law, the precepts of good social behaviour, which everybody ought to exemplify. After all, did not Aristotle lay down the cardinal virtues of all good life in saying that a good man, any good man, should be wise, just, brave, self-controlled, friendly, and magnanimous? If this is all we do, what distinction have we? 'Do not even many Gentiles the same?'

What is distinct and unique is the resource which a Christian man brings to the building of community in work, home, government, and faith. For he begins his life where no one else begins it—with God, the God whom he knows as the God and Father of our Lord Jesus Christ. That is, he lives life in two dimensions, and not one only. In social relationships we live on the horizontal plane. Religion reminds us that life has a primary vertical dimension. Christians begin with love of God before they can rightly sustain love of their neighbour. We see men, then, our fellow men, with all their faults and failings, as God sees them.

And this carries with it the fact that the Christian also lives as a member of two communities, and not of one only. By the exigencies of our natural existence, we are bound to our fellows by ties of economic interest, family, law, and common culture. We Christians in Britain are tied to our fellow Britons in the social, economic, and political society of Great Britain and Northern Ireland. You from America with your fellow citizens in the U.S.A. or Canada; and you from Australasia or Africa or Asia likewise. We share the sorrows, sins, and adversities of our fellow men, and face the vicissitudes of life with them. But we are also members of a redeemed and supernatural society, the supreme creation of God, the Christian Church. Our very coming together here in Oxford shows it. Members of a redeemed society! That ought to make a difference to our life and service in the world. To use a phrase of Walt Whitman, in his dream city of Friends, it shall be seen—

'every hour in our actions
And in all our works and words.'

IV

So you come to the daily concrete problems that should vex and trouble the Christian as he shares in the life of the community about him. There is the Christian man in industry, for instance, stepping into the factory on Monday morning, after Sunday worship. Can he transform work for gain into grateful service of the community and a real brotherhood

248

of common effort? That home of his, can he make it a place where souls are nurtured in faith and parity and love? Or, in the tumultuous debate of politics, can he lift the discussion above the strife of class or party or race on to the level of a struggle for righteousness and truth and freedom and justice? Or, in the cultural pursuits of life, how can he witness for parity, truth, and beauty, and counter prodigality, in the things which make for the mind and heart's delight? I often wish that we remembered that it is in these things that the real witness to our faith is made, and prayed more for one another as we face the problems of work, home, politics, and cultural intercourse.

For there are some supreme Christian virtues we should bring to the common life which are born of faith and faith alone. When the early Christian Fathers, like Ambrose and Augustine, took over the four cardinal virtues of earlier pagan Greek thought, and said that a Christian man should be wise, just, brave, and self-controlled like everybody else ought to be, they added three others derived from the New Testament alone. They called them the theological virtues. They were faith, hope, and love! They were the virtues born in the hearts of men when they looked much on the face of Jesus Christ, and for which conspicuously they needed the constant grace of God! To be faithful, steadfast, loyal to the Will of God even unto death, as Jesus was faithful! To be perpetually hopeful, in the face of the worst that sin and evil could do, even as Jesus never gave up hope in the ultimate victory of good! To love sacrificially— the word, you know, is ἀγάπη—and that means living and dying for sinful men, even as Jesus lived and died for them! Has anyone else in this wide world such a vocation for living in community, and putting himself alongside his fellow men, the men for whom Christ died, as has the Christian?

Let me close as I began, with an illustration of the thing in real life. Some years back, I sat in the pulpit of a crowded church in the Potteries —one of the ugliest aggregations of bricks and mortar in these islands, though the people there produce some of the most beautiful creations of men's hands—waiting a brief space along with the minister before the meeting was due to begin. Suddenly he clutched my arm. 'Do you see that man sitting there?' he asked, indicating a man sitting in the end seat of the front pew of the gallery. 'Yes,' I said. 'What about him?' 'He's a man of God if ever there was one,' he replied. I pricked up my ears. 'Who is he?' I asked in turn. 'He's a working blacksmith employed at a colliery in a village which has just been taken into the city boundary,' he answered. 'But he rules the village. They love and trust him so that, when they are in trouble or sorrow, they turn to him and not to me, their minister. And when they wanted their first representative on the City Council, he was the only man anybody thought of for the position.' The Christian in the community. A man of God if ever there was one. A colliery blacksmith, but he ruled a village. Know ye not that the saints shall judge the earth?

Group discussions followed the address (see p. 289).

The evening lecture, in the Examination Schools, was delivered by the Rev. A. Raymond George, Lamplough Professor of Systematic and Pastoral Theology and the Philosophy of Religion, Wesley College, Headingley, Leeds. The subject was *Recent Theological Tendencies*, and the chairman was Dr Gerald O. McCulloch, of Evanston, Illinois.

RECENT THEOLOGICAL TENDENCIES

A lecture delivered by the REV. A. RAYMOND GEORGE:

Methodism, which was in some senses the culmination of the Reformation, has since lived through a period which started with Schleiermacher and is still very variously assessed and has very various titles; and we now live in the opening decades of yet another period which is perceptibly different in tone and emphasis. With some exceptions, it cannot be said that our scholars, at least in this country, have yet made such a contribution to the systematic theology of this period as they have to Biblical studies; nevertheless, from our distinctive standpoint, we Methodists have not merely to survey it, but to assess it, to contribute to it, and to stand under and be reformed by such messages from God as it contains. Any such assessment has inevitably a subjective element in it; indeed, one of the distinctive insights of our time is the extent to which our thought is inevitably conditioned by sociological factors; and therefore it may be well to say that even in this ecumenical gathering I speak inevitably as a *British* Methodist. Theology is indeed worldwide, and we are all influenced by the scholars of other lands. Nevertheless, it is clear that the problems would appear to me in a different perspective if I lived in a different country. I may therefore fail to do justice even to leading works of Methodist theology overseas which are scarcely known here.

Theology is so woven without seam from top to bottom that it is difficult to know where to begin or to mention one doctrine without touching on every other. I make, however, a very rough distinction between theology as a whole and certain particular doctrines. I begin with theology as a whole, and ask how our period is to be described. It is hard enough indeed to describe the last. 'Modernist', in its proper use, is inapplicable to many of its leaders. 'Critical' describes a great advance in Biblical studies which was indeed inaugurated in that period, but which has come to stay. 'Liberal', the favourite term of denigration used by its detractors, still stands, in the English language at least, for a quality of mind by no means to be despised or rejected. Many of our own Biblical scholars stand in the liberal, though not in the modernist, tradition. They would, however, admit that, partly because of their labours in unearthing the true meaning of the Scriptures, we stand now in a very different position from that which prevailed in Harnack's day. How then are we to describe the present period? The new tendency is sometimes called 'neo-orthodox', or, in its various forms, 'neo-Calvinist', 'neo-Thomist', and the like. It is perhaps significant of our moderation that no responsible writer, I think, has used the terms 'neo-Wesleyan' or 'neo-Methodist'. What of the word 'Barthian'? Professor Karl Barth, though the most-discussed theological figure of our time, is not the most typical. He represents only one wing of the movement, and it is a crude error to describe the whole tendency as 'Barthian', and still worse to judge by the utterances of a few strident extremists whom Barth himself would disown. (The Church historians of the future may indeed discuss whether Barth was a Barthian, just as we discuss whether Nestorius was a Nestorian or Zwingli a Zwinglian.) Perhaps a more eirenic phrase is the 'revival of Biblical theology', and on that broader platform we may be able to assemble not merely the neo-orthodox, the Barthians, the anti-liberals, the transcendalists, and so on, but the intellectual successors of the great critical scholars like Westcott and Hort, such as our own Dr Wilbert F. Howard.

This revival of Biblical theology, though certainly in reaction from some of the extremes of the preceding period, is not then a return to fundamentalism or literalism, though we must note in passing a considerable revival of that view, particularly among undergraduates. The lessons of the critical period are not forgotten; we do not seek to ascribe infallibility to the text of Scripture or to make the Bible a paper Pope. Yet exegetical methods vary, and the allegorical methods sometimes used on the Continent have found some favour here, notably among Anglo-Catholic scholars, who use them particularly in support of their special view of the ministry. We have not yet felt, moreover, in this country the full force of the debate which Professor Rudolf Bultmann has started about *Entmythologisierung*. Thus it would be premature to say that we have reached agreement about our way of understanding the Bible. But we are all profiting by the lexicographical studies contained in Kittel's *Wörterbuch*, and the shorter but valuable *Theological Word Book* edited by Canon Alan Richardson. But above all there is a new eagerness to know what the Bible says. A minister, not a Methodist, once said to me: 'When I was at college, we spent a lot of time studying whether this verse or that belonged to J or E or D or P. It never occurred to us for a moment to ask what the verse meant.' But now we are all eager to know.

What then does the Bible mean? A generation ago it might have been said that Paul meant this and John that. The necessary analysis of the Bible into its component parts obscured for a while its meaning as a whole. But analysis has been replaced by synthesis, and we now stress the unity of the Bible, including the Old Testament. The phrase 'progressive revelation', with its evolutionary flavour, though not wholly inapplicable, is out of favour. In the New Testament field, the work of Professor C. H. Dodd, *The Apostolic Preaching and Its Developments*, has been most influential, and has virtually given the word *kerygma* to the English language. The golden thread which holds the New Testament together is the message which the Apostles preached, to be found in the sermons in the Acts of the Apostles. The Gospels are seen to be expanded *kerygma* rather than mere biography, and the Epistles contain an element of *kerygma*, together with *didache* (moral teaching) and other elements. In harmony with this view there is a new stress on the concept of the Word of God, which has long been prominent among Continental Protestants, and on the importance of preaching in the life of the Church. This is naturally congenial to us Methodists, who in this country have volumes of sermons rather than formal articles as our subordinate doctrinal standard or confession. And the whole emphasis on the Bible appeals to us as the heirs of one who was *homo unius libri*, a man of one Book.

But what is the content of this revival? What has resulted from the renewed attempt to take Biblical theology seriously? The new insights may perhaps be summed up under the headings 'event', 'eschatology', and 'encounter'. The alliteration almost forces itself upon us; and when, at the end of my first section, we pause to consider the relation of Biblical theology to philosophy, the keyword will inevitably be 'existentialism'.

First, then, event. And here let me take another brief glance at theology since Protestant systematisers chilled the fire of the Reformers. The warmth of pietism in a period of cold theology prepared the way for Schleiermacher, who was in a sense always influenced by the pietism from which he reacted. His emphasis on the religious consciousness, or, as we should say, on experience, provided something of a theological counterpart to pietism. It has sometimes been claimed that he was but consolidating in theology that emphasis on experience which Methodism has already secured in religion. Others hasten to dissociate Methodism from pietism, and think that to us the Word of God is more fundamental than experience, and thus are quite ready to join in the present reaction against Schleier-macher. At any rate, it is clear that the word 'experience' was characteristic of a whole century of theology. This emphasis, highly congenial to Methodism in some aspects, is yet capable of degenerating into an un-controlled subjectivity, justification by feelings, and the substitution of psychology of religion for dogmatic theology. Our own century has seen the reversal of this. Sir Edwyn Hoskyns said that the chief change which he had witnessed in theology had been the shift from experience to revelation. He was thinking, no doubt, largely of the neo-orthodox revival, particularly of Barth, and there is some truth in the scheme, whereby the liberal period (if we may for the moment call it so) corresponds to experience and the present period to revelation. But a more careful analysis shows that the concept of revelation, though perhaps in a weakened sense, was typical of the latter part of the so-called liberal period, for it was characteristic of Ritschl and the Ritschlians that they thought of Jesus as Teacher and Revealer. The real differentia of the present period is not that it speaks of revelation rather than experience but that it sees revelation in events rather than in propositions. The liberal period had it in common with fundamentalism that it was prone to think of revealed *truths*. This intellectualism owed something no doubt to the idealist philosophy. These truths were eternal or timeless, and would have been there whether Jesus had revealed them or not. There was inevitably on this view the risk that like all good teachers Jesus would make Himself unnecessary. When His pupils have grasped the truths, they no longer need the Teacher. His uniqueness must lie in His unique ethical teaching—a uniqueness which tended to disappear as scholarship ad-vanced. But now the emphasis is all on events, 'the mighty acts of the Lord' (Psalm 106²). The Bible is 'salvation-history', *Heilsgeschichte*. The Gospel is not a theory, but a story. 'After all', said a reviewer, 'that is what the Biblical authors thought was happening in their work, that God was acting in his people, not that they were producing a progressively more tasteful religious literature.'[1] The Old Testament narratives fall into place as part of the one story, but its centre lies in Christ. God in Christ has not merely revealed; He has acted—decisively, unrepeatably, once and for all, 'εφάπαξ. This is expressed in the phrase *das Ärgernis der Einmaligkeit*, the stumbling-block of particularity. He has not revealed simply a time-less truth; He has altered the essential facts; He has inaugurated a New Age.

This leads us from the theme of event to the second theme, eschatology. Here again we must begin with a lighting survey of the preceding period. The this-worldly conception of the kingdom of God held by Ritschl gave rise to those familiar concepts of 'building up' or 'bringing in' the Kingdom, so congenial to what was called the 'social gospel'. But then the futurist eschatology of Schweitzer hoist a certain brand of liberalism with its own petard. The critical study of the Gospels no longer yielded simply the portrait of an optimistic Believer in the Fatherhood of God and the brotherhood of man, an Apostle of social justice and human progress. This, at least, was securely established: that the Kingdom is God's gift, not man's achievement. But the rest of the futurist eschatology was itself shattered by the work of many scholars, popularized in this country by Professor Dodd, who introduced the idea of realized eschatology—that is, that in the event of the Life, death, Resurrection, and Ascension of Christ, and the Coming of the Holy Spirit, the Kingdom of God had already

[1] *Theology*, LIV, p. 276.

come, as could be seen both by the analysis of Christ's own utterances and by the study of the apostolic *kerygma*. Yet the kingdom is not wholly manifest here and now, and we are left with the problem of the so-called Second Advent; in what sense (if any) is there to be a final consummation of the Kingdom in this world? After the coming of the Holy Spirit, what significance has the continuance of time? The Biblical conception of time has recently been investigated by Professor Oscar Cullmann in his *Christ and Time*. In general, he reasserts realized eschatology in other categories, but he gives a fuller account of the significance of time now, and so strongly emphasizes the Biblical linear view of time against the Greek cyclic view that he wishes the word 'eternity' to bear the meaning of 'extended time'. It has long been taken in the Greek sense of 'timeless', and many theological problems had seemed to be solved thereby. Perhaps they may still be solved by speaking of God's transcendence over time. We may conjecture that time will be one of the leading subjects of discussion in the next few years, in which the rediscovered Biblical view of time must confront the philosophical view of Bergson and others. Meanwhile, the problem of time is closely akin to that of history, and the relation of Christianity to history, raised by Berdyaev, Professor Tillich and many others, has been notably investigated by the Methodist Professor Herbert Butterfield in his *Christianity and History*.

Before we leave the kindred topics of event and eschatology, we may observe that we have here a reversion from Hellenic to Hebraic modes of thought, or, as Bishop Nygren would say, from *eros*-religion to *agape*-religion. This method of 'motif-research', which Bishop Aulén has applied to the death of Christ and Archbishop Brilioth to the Eucharist, is not solely Swedish. Professor Heiler had already applied it to prayer, and any history of doctrine must make some use of it; but the method has been carried further by the Swedes; and the theology to which it leads them is likely to be congenial to Methodists, for it is definitely characteristic of the current revival of Biblical theology, without going to the extremes of employing the jargon which is sometimes current elsewhere.

We come now to the third of the insights which Biblical theology has secured for us: the stress on encounter or confrontation, which is also characteristically Hebraic. This is a richer idea than that of event. God does not merely reveal Himself in decisive historical events; He confronts us personally here and now; and, incidentally, the sacraments, in which the past becomes, as it were, present, are one of the links between these two conceptions. This emphasis on encounter has affinity with many other lines of thought, such as the movement known as personalism. It was popularized in the modern world by Dr Martin Buber's *I and Thou*, but it has a long ancestry, in which Kierkegaard is prominent. How much of the history of the modern world goes back to the two chief reactions to Hegel, Karl Marx's inversion of his dialectical idealism into dialectical materialism, and this violent attack on idealism by Kierkegaard with his entirely new meaning of 'dialectic'!

This stream of thought, mainly in the form in which we have it in Kierkegaard and Barth, is well illustrated in the contrast drawn by Dr John A. Mackay in *A Preface to Christian Theology* between the balcony and the road. It is a salutary warning that prominent among 'balcony-types' is the professional conference-goer. 'No one can become so mechanical, so supercilious, and so spiritually wilted as a professional conference-monger.'[1]

[1] John A. Mackay, op. cit., p. 43.

From the fact that the proper mode of addressing God is 'Thou' and the even more important fact that God, who is always Subject, addresses us as 'thou', it is said to follow that theology is always dialectical—that is, that when we cease to address God and speak rather about Him in the third person, our thought is so broken up that many statements have to be supplemented by what appear to be their opposites.[1] Hence the current prevalence of paradox, whereby many a question is answered by the words 'Yes' and 'No', in a theology, which has for one of its watchwords 'not "Both-And", but "Either-Or" '. But this is not another paradox; it arises from the fact, not always made clear, that 'Yes and No' belongs to dialectical theology, and 'Either-or' to existential decision.

Methodism must make two comments on this. First, no lover of Charles Wesley could ever deny the place of paradox in our religion.

> 'Being's source begins to be,
> And God Himself is born!'[2]

In so far as this emphasis rekindles our sense of wonder, we rejoice. But there must be some limit to paradox. All things go out into mystery, but we must not invoke a mystery or a paradox at every difficulty. Some work on the proper limits of paradox is urgently called for. We Methodists are not prepared—if, indeed, anyone is—for the total depreciation of reason. But happily dialectical theology with all its paradoxes, is not the whole of the revival of Biblical theology. The second comment is this: is not this stress on encounter (as Professor Brunner would call it) or confrontation (as Professor John Baillie says) a reversion to our own emphasis on experience? We have already asked whether Schleiermacher was really our friend or our foe, and here we find that the very emphasis which endeared Schleiermacher to some Methodists is to be found in men like Brunner, who are his leading opponents. Here is a paradox indeed! On which side ought the Methodist to range himself? My own opinion is that on the extreme right-wing of the modern movement in theology there is a certain chill in the atmosphere uncongenial to us, but that in a more moderate form this new emphasis on confrontation gives us what we want in a far richer form than that of Schleiermacher. The German word *Erfahrung* has perhaps overtones (as the German word *liberal* has overtones) which do not exist in the English word 'experience'; and this may account for the way in which Continental theologians shy away from the word. Moreover, even the English word 'experience' has certain possible dangers; it may treat the Person experienced as an object; it may concentrate attention on the subjective feeling experienced. But the truths for which it stands, that we have no mere academic knowledge of God, no mere assent to propositions about Him, but a personal trust in a living God, and a personal assurance of His activity in our lives, that we know Him, and not merely know about Him—these are supremely important, and in my opinion are adequately safeguarded by such terms as 'confrontation'. To sum up this emphasis on the words of William Temple.[3] 'What is offered to man's apprehension in any specific Revelation is not truth concerning God but the living God himself.'

So much for encounter, the last of the three great notes of the revival of Biblical theology. I wish, however, before applying these to particular doctrines, to say a word about the new positions which theology has taken up in relation to kindred subjects, and notably to philosophy; and, as I

[1] Cf. John Baillie, *Our Knowledge of God*, p. 225.
[2] *Methodist Hymn Book*, No. 134 (British).　　[3] *Nature, Man, and God*, p. 322

have indicated, our chief theme here must be *existentialism,* which is the fashionable philosophy of our day, particularly in France. I shall not attempt to define existentialism, which exists so largely in atheistic form that some have doubted whether the phrase 'Christian existentialism' is anything more than a contradiction in terms. That is a purely verbal question, but it is quite clear that much modern Christian thought has an existentialist flavour; indeed, in what I said under the heading of 'Encounter' I was once compelled to use the term 'existential'. Now here arises the question whether we are not guilty of just that charge which we have often brought against the theologians of other centuries, and notably of the last—namely, that they thought they saw in Jesus what was actually a reflection of the world-view or current philosophy of their time. Just as the theology of the last century was coloured by evolutionary notions of progress, may not the theology of this age be coloured by various current notions—for instance, by the totalitarianism which in the political sphere the theologians of our age have so gallantly resisted, and in particular by the existentialist philosophy? There may be some who have succumbed to this danger. Thus the emphasis on 'decision' is on the whole welcome to Methodists, though it may obscure God's part in salvation; but the word 'decision' must have some content. We must give some account of the God who is calling us to decide (at the risk of being 'mythological') of the kind of communion with Him which decision will involve (at the risk of being 'pietistic'), and of the actions which He calls us to decide to perform (at the risk of being 'moralistic'). But on the whole I do not believe that our stress on encounter or indeed commitment is a backwash from the existentialist philosophy; it is too Biblical and Methodist for that. That is why I have felt justified in taking it first under the heading of Biblical theology, rather than under that of philosophy, for it is the Bible which has led us to this emphasis.

This new emphasis on encounter rather than academic knowledge has important consequences in the sphere of philosophy of religion. On the Continent the issue was for a while focused on the question whether it is possible to have a natural theology; this is now seen to be a rather ambiguous phrase, though debates on revelation, *Ur-Offenbarung,* and so forth, continue. Side by side with neo-Thomism, both Roman and Anglican, we see in books like Professor Brunner's *Revelation and Reason,* Professor John Baillie's *Our Knowledge of God,* and Canon Alan Richardson's *Christian Apologetics* a new approach to the existence of God, which is to some extent a revival of that of Augustine and Anselm. *Credo ut intelligam:* 'I believe in order that I may understand.' 'Understanding is the reward of faith.' Together with this point of view there goes a certain depreciation of 'Objectivity and Impartiality' (to use the title of a pamphlet by Professor H. A. Hodges), which sounds most dangerous, and might easily be misused, but when properly understood is an expression of the same principle. We may doubt, however, whether some of these writers give a quite satisfactory account of the importance of historical fact.

But existentialism is not the only fashionable philosophy; there is also that task of linguistic analysis popularly known as 'logical positivism.' In its customary form this denies altogether that theological propositions can have any meaning, which is clearly a view destructive of the faith. This view is not altogether difficult to refute at the philosophical level. But lately it has been suggested that there are forms of this analytical philosophy which do not deny meaning to theological propositions, and that Christians ought to come to some sort of terms with this point of view. This is not a subject which has yet engaged much attention, in British

Methodism at least, but we must be prepared here for important developments.

The attitude of theology to science is now a good deal more confident than when we reeled under the first shock of the evolutionary theory. That theology is not in principle to be subordinated to other disciplines, but is indeed queen of the sciences, we may gladly affirm; but I doubt whether we are fully aware of the force of the scientific challenge. Now that science is so complex and departmentalized that scientists can hardly understand each other, it is not easy for a theologian to grasp the points at issue, and he may easily make a synthesis at too superficial a level. Particularly we must note the rise of the new normative and human sciences, such as sociology, which raise some questions which the old descriptive sciences did not raise. An ambiguous position is occupied by psychology; this has, of course, an important bearing on pastoral theology, more explored in America than here, but also raises some doctrinal questions, more particularly about the nature of guilt and its cure.

I conclude now the first and longer part of my lecture, on the change that has come over theology in general, with the remark that there is much here for Methodism to acclaim. I have repudiated some extremes and entered some caveats, but if we consider our main points, can we not rejoice? Theology returns to the Bible; it rediscovers what the Apostles preached; it asserts that God has revealed Himself in decisive events, that the expected end has already broken into human history, and that we can personally encounter God here and now; and, fortified by the rediscovery of these Biblical emphases, it faces secular learning with a new confidence; in all this we may well rejoice.

In the second part I shall mention more briefly the impact of all this upon particular doctrines. First, on the doctrine of God. This Biblical revival, together with the decline of philosophical idealism, has led to a new stress on the personality of God. Miracle is no longer under a cloud. The remarkable revival of Reformation studies to which several Methodists have made notable contributions, especially Principal P. S. Watson in his book on Luther (*Let God be God*), has led to a stress on God's initiative, His sovereignty, and His transcendence. Writers as diverse as Rudolf Otto and Karl Barth have proclaimed from entirely different points of view that God is wholly Other; and this is all to the good so long as it does not make Him seem either remote from our needs or on the other hand arbitrary and capricious.

The doctrine of man, in the second place, is a crucial doctrine today, especially for apologetic purposes. The descriptions of man given by biology, by economics, by psychology, and even by the comparative study of religion are all inadequate. The Christian estimate is at once more pessimistic and more optimistic. Whatever opinion be held as to the historical or mythological status of the Fall story, there is a new emphasis on the truth for which it stands. The evolutionary theory of sin is felt to be inadequate, and the essence of the traditional doctrine of original sin is re-asserted by such writers as Professor Reinhold Niebuhr, under such phrases as 'corporate sin', and 'radical evil'. The discoveries made by psychology have made these truths somewhat more palatable to the modern mind; and we must also notice the re-discovery by Old Testament scholars of the Biblical idea of corporate personality, so that the individualism in which we were brought up is seen not to go much further back than Descartes and to have reached its heyday in conjunction with political liberalism. Yet we must take care that we are not too much influenced by modern collectivism or by that monist depreciation of the individual which was its philosophical ancestor. No man, according to John Wesley, is damned unless by his own choice.

Thirdly, Christology, as we should expect in such a period, has moved away from those purely human views of Jesus which were current in some circles in the early years of this century. Kenotic theories in a sense flourish, for the wording of William Temple's attack on them concealed the fact that he really adhered to a kenotic theory of the Martensen type. More recently, Professor Donald Baillie, in *God was in Christ*, has come forward with a new suggestion, which makes a perhaps proper use of the idea of paradox, relating the paradox of the Incarnation to the paradox of grace and freedom; but in the form in which it is stated, this perhaps might have a minimizing effect on the Deity of Christ which the author plainly did not intend. Meanwhile a kindred doctrine has been illuminated by Professor Leonard Hodgson in *The Doctrine of the Trinity*.

Fourthly, the doctrine of the Work of Christ has moved on from Rashdall's Abelardianism in three not easily compatible directions. Dr Brunner's *The Mediator* has been of great influence. Bishop Aulén's *Christus Victor* has revived the dramatic or patristic theory, while our own Principal Vincent Taylor in a trilogy of books,[1] following the tradition of R. C. Moberly, and making us of 'corporate personality' and new ideas about sacrifice, has given a massive exposition of the representative theory. At the moment there is a marked revival of interest in F. D. Maurice, which perhaps affects this doctrine more than any other. The idea of Christ as the Head of the whole race is in harmony with our traditional Arminian emphasis on the universality of salvation; yet we can readily understand the fears which earlier Methodists expressed lest this teaching should obliterate the distinctions between the saved and the lost and diminish the glory of regeneration.

Fifthly, while the doctrine of the Holy Spirit remains relatively undeveloped, the great experimental doctrines have received some attention from our own scholars; we think especially of Dr Harald Lindström's *Wesley and Sanctification* and Dr W. R. Cannon's *The Theology of John Wesley*. In the widespread neo-Calvinist circles outside our own communion, there is a certain tendency to dismiss us as a perfectionist and pietistic sect, though indeed the doctrine of predestination, so long a stumbling-block to us in our relations with Calvinists, has been astonishingly modified by the leading Calvinist, Dr Karl Barth, into a form of universalism. But we need to examine further our doctrine of perfection, without at all abandoning the well-known claim which Dr G. C. Cell once made for it; we need also to examine our neglected doctrine of assurance; and we need still to maintain our traditional view that it is possible to be an Arminian without being a Pelagian. Under this heading we may perhaps refer also to ethics. The abandonment of some of the presuppositions of the old social gospel has not meant, as is sometimes supposed, any escapist lack of interest in social and ethical problems; nevertheless, a good deal of work remains to be done in this field, in order to base our ethic, not simply on the traditions of our sometimes rather middle-class culture, nor on medieval casuistry, but on the Bible itself.

As I wish to leave the Church till last, I mention sixthly eschatology. It has been said that whereas eschatology, under the title of the four last

[1] *Jesus and His Sacrifice; The Atonement in New Testament Teaching; Forgiveness and Reconciliation.*

things, used to form the conclusion of textbooks of theology, now it forms the preface, and the setting of the whole; and this lecture itself illustrates that point. Yet there still remain the questions which were treated by eschatology in the old sense, not only the question of the Second Coming, which I have already mentioned, but the questions about the destiny of individuals. Popular sentiment in the so-called liberal period quietly abandoned the doctrine of Hell; but the resurgence of evil in two great wars has aided those theologians who want it back. But hardly anyone wants it in its full form, as applied, for instance, to the whole of the heathen or to unbaptized children. Many take refuge in the somewhat milder doctrine known as 'conditional immortality'. We have already noticed Barth's universalism. I shall content myself by repeating a sentence of William Temple approved by Professor John Baillie: 'There is a very strong case for thinking out the whole subject again in as complete independence as possible alike of medieval and of Protestant traditions.'[1]

Lastly, we come to a doctrine the revival of which has been a most striking feature of our times: the Church, with the ministry and sacraments. A generation ago, a liberal Protestant theological textbook would hardly mention these themes. P. T. Forsyth cried alone in the wilderness. Indeed, neither Protestantism nor Catholicism, despite many exceptions, has really done justice to this. Partly as a result of the Tractarian movement, which really affected all the Churches, partly through the necessities of ecumenical discussion, partly through the decline of individualism in secular affairs, but much more through the recovery of the Biblical viewpoint, we are now all accustomed to speak much of the new Israel, the People of God. Once it was a dogma that Jesus did not intend to found a Church. Now, especially through the book *Jesus and His Church*, by our own scholar, Dr Newton Flew, it is a commonplace among theologians that the Church was founded—not indeed by Jesus, but by God in the time of Abraham; and that Jesus came not so much to found a religion as to reconstitute a people. Methodists, who, if they have not spoken much about the Church, have long treasured and practised intimate fellowship, have every reason to rejoice in this.

There have been two consequences; first, a new confessionalism. Most of the great confessions or denominations now have conferences on a worldwide basis, such as this; and in each, though particularly among Lutherans and Calvinists, a zealous study is being made of the original formularies and writings. This is all to the good, so long as it does not lead us to harden our hearts against each other. The second consequence is the Ecumenical Movement, which William Temple in an oft-quoted phrase called 'the great new fact of our era'. (It uses the word 'ecumenical', of course, in a different sense from ours. I think we had it first.) This was making great headway on rather liberal presuppositions till the growth of confessionalism (itself in part its product) began to check it. Now, just when the progress of Biblical theology bids us to take the unity of the Church more seriously, we are faced, as at Amsterdam, with the discovery of differences even within our agreements. In this country the differences have been explored in three valuable reports, *Catholicity*, by the Anglo-Catholics, *The Fulness of Christ*, by the Evangelical Anglicans, and *The Catholicity of Protestantism*, by a group of Free Church men, edited by two Methodists, Dr Newton Flew and the Rev. R. E. Davies.

The crux lies largely in the doctrine of the ministry. There is, I believe, a new interest in episcopacy throughout the world. In this country we are faced with a new trend in Anglo-Catholicism, led, I believe, largely by

[1] W. Temple, *Nature, Man, and God*, p. 456; J. Baillie, *Our Knowledge of God*, p. 98·

Dom Gregory Dix. The much-heralded work, by this group, *The Apostolic Ministry*, edited by Dr K. E. Kirk, the Bishop of Oxford, with a new defence of episcopacy, has provoked many replies, especially *The Church's Ministry*, by Professor T. W. Manson. Some of the Anglo-Catholic points have definitely been disproved; and for the rest I will echo the words of Dr A. E. J. Rawlinson, the Bishop of Derby, that Dom Gregory's conclusions 'are not such as to be likely to convince everybody' as that the whole theory 'rests on conjecture at too many points'.[1] In fact, the book has not won the support for which its authors seem to have hoped.

There is also a strong revival of interest in the sacraments. About the Eucharist, I believe that new conceptions of sacrifice and such eirenic works as O. C. Quick's *The Christian Sacraments* have brought us within sight of, though not to the actual point of, agreement. There is also a new interest in the form and structure of public worship; and it has been re-asserted that the ordinary Sunday morning service of almost all Protestant-ism except Anglicanism and Methodism is historically and well might become more plainly the ante-Communion service. This is likely to have its effect eventually on Methodism also.

At the moment, however, the centre of interest is undoubtedly Baptism, or, as it is called, to include the question of Confirmation, Christian initiation. Professor Barth's attack on infant baptism has been met by Professor Oscar Cullmann, by a Methodist, the Rev. W. F. Flemington, and by Professor Joachim Jeremias.[2] We, of course, practise the baptism of infants; but the relation of baptism to regeneration in the customary Methodist sense of the word involves a problem which goes to the heart of Evangelical theology. Wesley struggled with it, but he left it partly un-solved. It is sometimes said that the great problems of theology have become prominent in the Church in much the same order as that in which they occur in the Creeds. If so, we are near the end, for certainly 'one baptism for the remission of sins' is hotly debated in theological class-rooms throughout the world today.

I hope I have said enough to show that, though there are problems enough before us, we live in an age when theology is alive and vigorous. God has granted to us some fresh insights into His truth; we must not proclaim them stridently as our own discovery, but hold them humbly as His gift. We must remember that our understanding of them is fallible. We must try to share them with the member in his pew, while at the same time we listen eagerly to hear what more the Spirit saith to the Churches. And for every fresh glimpse of God's glory and saving power, let us give our grateful praise to Him.

In the evening a public meeting was held in the Wesley Memorial Church. The Chairman was the Rev. Dr R. Newton Flew, ex-President of the British Conference and Principal of Wesley House, Cambridge. Introducing the subject—*Methodism and the World Church*—Dr Flew said that Methodism was already world-wide. The idea of a world Church was, as yet, only a dream to be realized in the future. There was still divisions, and the underlying unity had to find expression. To get people—especially young people —into a communion would be to take a great step towards the goal.

[1] *Problems of Reunion*, pp. 41–2, 48.
[2] Karl Barth, *The Teaching of the Church regarding Baptism*; Oscar Cullmann, *Baptism in the New Testament*; W. F. Flemington, *The New Testament Doctrine of Baptism*; J. Jeremias, *Hat die Urkirche die Kindertaufe geübt?*

Addresses were delivered by Bishop Fred P. Corson, of Philadelphia, and the Rev. C. W. Ranson, Secretary of the International Missionary Council.

METHODISM AND THE WORLD CHURCH

An address delivered by the REV. BISHOP FRED PIERCE CORSON, *of Philadelphia:*

The setting of this world conference of Methodists in Oxford has been of inestimable value for the furthering of our purpose. Coming to the homeland of Methodism we have been reminded of our distinctive land-marks; we have recalled the glowing power of our beginnings and we have been inspired and encouraged as our fathers have walked again in our midst.

One of our great English-American scholars, Dr Alfred Whitehead, said that it was 'the duty of the present to receive the past and build the future'. Meeting amid the scenes of our origins we have had an oppor-tunity to do this, and for that opportunity we express our sincere thanks to our hosts.

The subject, 'Methodism and the World Church', in discussion of which I have been asked to participate comes logically at the conclusion of such a conference. Only after our foundations have been re-examined, our past achievements reviewed and the present needs for Christianity lifted up, can we deal adequately with our Methodist part in the total Christian enterprise. Naturally, I have been looking at this relationship and its possibilities through American eyes, and what I shall have to say concern-ing it will be largely from an American point of view. I trust that it will compliment Dr Ranson's presentation so that by means of both papers *our* Methodist world Church may more completely find its place in *the* universal world Church.

A definition of terms may not be needed in this connexion, but we should keep in mind Methodism as a whole when we discuss its relation to Christianity as a whole. Methodism itself is a world Church with nearly 20 million members and 50 million constituents scattered throughout all of the continents. It has, therefore, a many-sided contribution to make to any united, universal and contemporary witness to the Presence, Power and Meaning of Christ and to the co-ordination of the various segments of that witness in effective relationships within the framework of the world Church.

I. Methodism's Ecumenical Outlook

Current Methodism comes by an interest in the world Church naturally. Because of its origins it could hardly escape an affinity for the ecumenical movement. Some Protestant Churches, I fear, can never feel this oneness with the larger movement because their development has been like a mathematical point which has position but no breadth.

Such narrow and isolated development has been avoided in Methodism. Its place of service has been sought through the spirit of catholicity, and its central concern has been, to use Wesley's term, 'To all conditions of men and to men of all conditions'.

This broad directive did not come in the life of the Methodist Church by chance nor as an aftermath. It was planted in the beginning by the founders and nurtured by those who have inherited this 'vineyard of the Lord'. A non-Methodist historian fixes its beginning in John Wesley, 'who', he said, 'was the most ecumenical-minded of all the great reformers' (quoted by Bishop Arthur J. Moore), and Dr Henry Carter points us to its nature and growth in his very able book, *The Methodist Heritage*, stating there that 'the true relation of Methodism to the ecumenical movement is to be discerned in its history'.

What John Wesley had to say about ecumenicity is of great importance because of its relevance to the need and mood of the world today. In this respect he was a prophet speaking for an era yet to be. The description of a Methodist's relation to the Church and to other Christians, as set forth in his *Short History of Methodists*, still provides the basic consideration for the wide Christian fellowship required in the world Church. In it he states the Methodist position by saying that 'we leave every man to enjoy his opinion and to use his own mode of worship, desiring only that the love of God and his neighbour be the ruling principle of his heart and show itself in his life by a uniform practice of justice, mercy, and truth. Accordingly, we give the right hand of fellowship to every lover of God and man whatever his opinion or mode of worship be, for which he is to give an account to God only.' The point of view expressed in this statement of comity has been responsible for the willingness of Methodists to lead in the Christian movements seeking wider co-operation and for the success of those ventures in union among the various branches of the Methodist family and in conjunction with other denominations.

Wesley had the world view of the Christian fellowship. In his sermon on 'The Catholic Spirit' he sensed the necessity for a double loyalty on the part of a true Christian seeking the coming of the Kingdom on earth— a loyalty to the part and a loyalty to the whole; a complementary and not a divisive loyalty both to the denomination of his choice and to the fellowship of all believers. The Methodist, he said, 'while united to one particular congregation by the closest ties' must 'enlarge his heart toward all mankind'.

This recognition of a double affection and a dual responsibility for an effective ecumenical movement, not always fully appreciated, appears more often now in contemporary discussions of the world Church.

Wesley's prophetic churchmanship was shown also in what he feared might happen to the outlook of his followers. He was concerned lest the spirit of exclusiveness and ecclesiastical snobbery displayed by others toward the Methodists might soon become the Methodist attitude toward different religious groups. His determination to prevent this was expressed in a letter to Vincent Perronet written in 1748, in which he said that 'the thing I was greatly afraid of all this time, and which I resolved to use every possible method of preventing, was a narrowness of spirit, a party zeal, that miserable bigotry which makes many unready to believe that there is any work of God but among themselves'.

If Methodism follows the path of its founder, it must move in the direction of the larger fellowship in Christ, alert to every possibility for the extension of this fellowship, yet practical in evaluating the efforts to make this wider fellowship a workable reality. The true son of John Wesley says: 'Whosoever doeth the will of my Father, the same is my brother and my sister.'

In applying the ecumenical spirit of John Wesley, Methodism has already made many notable achievements and valuable contributions. Its ecumenicity is expressed, not only in word, but also in deed. Chief among its contributions has been the hymnody of Charles Wesley. Professor Robert G. McCucheon, American authority on church music, called Charles Wesley's hymns, not only 'the binding cord of all Methodism', but the most 'profound influence on the hymnody of the Church

Universal'. It has been said that 'our fathers made singing a tool', Luther, Calvin, Whitefield and Wesley all recognizing the power which came to the early Church through song. Surely it is a tool of many uses, not the least of which is the warming and quickening of the human heart and the melting away of our sharp and often artificial lines of difference. The world Church will advance in comradeship as a singing church, gathering its music from its common and universal heritage.

Another has been in the field of publications. The wide use of the Church school literature of the American branch of Methodism, reaching now 100 million copies annually and distributed through more than thirty denominations, indicates a world view in its production. More significant still is the manner in which *The Upper Room*, Methodism's devotional magazine, has transcended denominational lines and language barriers to become a common vehicle through which God's Presence is mediated to His universal family.

In the recognition of ministerial orders and Church membership, Wesley's ecumenical spirit finds an open door for contemporary Church union. Notably, also, in missionary policy and administration the so-called younger Churches have helped the Churches in the homelands to break down the crystallization of their rigid separations.

Methodism's ecumenical spirit in America is further complemented by what is now generally expected of it in the expanding inter-Church movements. Usually it is assumed that the Methodist Church will provide one-sixth of the resources required for these enterprises, and the present mood of the Church is to go beyond this expectation.

Looking backward, Methodism's sense of mission in furthering the world Church stands forth in unmistakable clarity. But 'What can be done about it now?' is the natural and inevitable question which any group of true Methodists would next raise.

What then can Methodism contribute to the world Church which we believe is the all-embracing Body of Christ for the fellowship of His followers and the establishment of His Kingdom?

Perhaps the answer to this question can best be given through an enumeration of what would appear to be essential to the Church today in its ecumenical approach to the world. Many such lists of requirements have been compiled, some of which have confused the incidental with the essential, while others would seem to block all progress by the order they insist upon in dealing with the factors involved. No list can claim for itself much more than a beginning, and the suggestions made in this address, by the side of which we shall match the offerings of our Methodism, must be thought of as starting points rather than terminals for discussion and action.

II. A Common Basis of Accord

In the first place, the unity of the world Church without which it can exist only as a formless idea requires some common basis of accord where the differences of the participating groups can meet in likeness. Even a minimum of agreement will provide a fulcrum by which the Christian movement can be lifted to world proportions, but something commonly accepted must be underneath the lever of desire and organization if anything worth while is to happen. At times it would appear to me that we have proceeded with disappointing results because we have thought the superstructure more urgent than the foundation, and have therefore attempted to build the world Church on the moving sands of contemporary popularity and change.

262

Our possibility for agreement appears more likely when we deal directly with the fact and necessity of difference. Difference is a characteristic of life. It persists in spite of man's efforts to remove it because it is an asset in democratic life. Protestantism cannot proceed to rub it out without destroying the very principle of freedom which gives Protestantism its vitality and personality. Yet the understanding, toleration, and co-ordination of difference in human relationships is an acquired characteristic rather than an hereditary one. Instinctively we demand likeness to ourselves. I have been told that the reason why there are no *white black-birds* is not because none are born, but because *black blackbirds* won't let *white blackbirds* live. So with civilized man. Difference sets off the struggle for annihilation.

When Protestantism accepts the fact that two things may be different without one being inferior or antagonistic or dominant or divisive or exclusive, then the ground work is laid for the unity which the world Church requires and the diversity which its components bring to it. Such an understanding grows out of a deep insight regarding what is essential and where it is to be found along with an high order of Christian culture which sees and appreciates goodness in all of its myriad expressions. We are not there yet but in true Methodistic fashion let us go on toward that perfection, strive for it, and expect to achieve it in this life.

Theology, polity, ecclesiasticism and divergent cultures are the chief differences which the superficial observer is likely to look on as insurmountable obstacles in the way of a truly world Church. Such differences exist. In Protestantism they should exist, and when the world Church is really achieved they will still exist.

It is the common bond holding these differences together in organic relation and with proper co-ordination and appreciation which is the crux of the matter for the universal Church.

What Methodism brings to the world Church at this point can constitute its most significant contribution. Here again John Wesley recognized the existence and practical implications of both the fact of difference and the necessity of a common ground of accord, and with his customary forthrightness stated the Methodist position regarding both. He let it be known that the Methodists 'desired a league, offensive and defensive with every soldier of Christ', and sincere desire for the wider fellowship in Christ must be the first step toward its realization. But this desire for real cooperation Wesley did not leave in the mid-air of pious sentimentality or abstract doctrine. He tied its fulfilment to personal experience and to conduct. The condition of the heart provided the power of the bond, and the life which the heart prompted gave the proof of its genuineness.

Methodism's contribution to the common basis of accord yet to be completely attained for the world Church is in the realm of experience and conduct, the assurance of Christ's Presence in the heart and the manifestation of it in the life. Reality for the Methodist is the one basis of authority and the reality of the Person and Presence of Christ, clearly evident in the conduct of all who claim spiritual kinship with Him, provides the power in this day to attract 'men from the nations of every language, saying we will go with you for we have heard that God is with you'.[1] It may help our ecumenical efforts to remember that the burning bush, the Jordan voice, the Damascus light, the Aldersgate glow were all different, yet all alike; different according to temperament, to spiritual development, to environmental circumstance, to personal reaction, but alike in the assurance of God's Presence and the affect on life which followed.

[1] *Zech.*, 8, 23.

Here, Methodism says to the world Church, is the starting-point of that unity of spirit necessary to take the kingdoms of this world and make them the kingdoms of our Lord and Saviour, Jesus Christ. This experience in Christ is the universal binding together of the particulars. It provides the spiritual bond which holds together our human organization. It places the individual in co-operating relation to God and to each other. It takes the sentiment of the heart and makes it the action of the life.

In the research laboratory of one of our largest manufacturing plants these words are written upon the walls: 'When you find the solution to your problem it will be simple.' Perhaps amid the complication of our multiple denominational approach we will find the basis of an accord in a simple statement like Wesley's: 'If your heart is as my heart, give me your hand.'

III. The Ability to Initiate and Carry Through Mass Movements for Christianity

The tests which will determine whether or not Protestant Christianity can create and maintain a world Church lie in certain verified directions. These constitute the 'trouble spots' in consummating the Christian order of universal fellowship, and they should be considered by the denominations which must ultimately unite if the world Church is to become an effective body. One such test Bishop Francis J. McConnell indicated is the 'ability of Protestantism to affect great mass efforts and to produce gigantic mass effects'. That we live in a world that values and responds to mass efforts and effects cannot be denied. The temper and mind-set of the people are in that direction. The realization of it is responsible in no small part for the success of totalitarianism and the surging fads for which our age will be known. Communism understands this technique and its power especially with this generation of youth, as the East Berlin demonstration (1,500,000 youth) bore witness. Personally, I think a constructive, world-wide, spectacular youth movement is Protestantism's most needed project at the present time.

In a way the Protestant Churches have not sensed this susceptibility to mass efforts and effects. Perhaps the loosely jointed nature of Protestantism is responsible for what appears to be a fragmentary and desultory approach to the religious needs of the world. Its strategy seems removed from the mass approach which appears so successful in the hands of its religious and secular competitors. There is some truth in the accusation that our Protestant leaders have inclined too much to the notion that the Kingdom comes only by committees and seminars.

Protestantism which puts stress on a healthy mental approach to religion has also been stalemated by a psychopathic mass emotionalism sweeping along in the wake of two world wars. The *New York Times* (21st June 1951) recently blamed this characteristic of the twentieth century for the 'emotional landslide which is sweeping away morality, logic and common sense in its ruthless descent'.

Now the world Church, as we know it, must either capture and transform to healthy purposes this affinity of current society for mass efforts and their effects or be destroyed by it. And if historic Methodism has any contribution to make to the present world Church movement it is in dealing with the religious uses of mass emotionalism.

Looking back to our beginnings, we can see at this point some resemblance between the conditions which challenged Mr Wesley and the circumstances under which we are working. Then conditions were ripe for a mass approach to religion which Wesley and Whitefield sensed and for

264

which they pioneered in developing an effective technique. The need of men and their ability to respond were fundamental and universal. The methods to be used mobilizing these mass spiritual responses constituted the new and changing element which brought the early Methodists so much trouble. Our danger today lies in a reversal of our fathers' position. For while seeing the unmistakable evidence of this generation's susceptibility to mass effort Protestant religious groups have been slow to take advantage of it and clumsy in developing methods for a wide appeal to the various cultures and conditions of mankind.

Perhaps we have feared too much the one aspect of modern life which we must capture and use. Or it may be that the groupings of Protestants wherein the greatest power to undertake a mass approach resides are in need of a spiritual revival which will restore the flexibility and passion which, to use Wesley's expression, made them originally 'the servants of mankind'. Whatever the cause, the necessity for doing something about it is upon us and our Methodist responsibility is clearly indicated. By tradition, temperament, experience, and resources, Methodism is equipped to lead the way in a Protestant mass movement of world proportions which is the one hope for rescuing man and his world from the destroying forces of totalitarianism, secularism, and nihilism, themselves current world religions most adept in using mass effects. For this Methodism can feel an affinity with Isaiah's Israel of whom he said: 'The Eternal called me from my birth, saying, I now appoint you to bring light to the nations, that my salvation may reach the world's end' (Isa. 49[6]).

We have accepted the ensmalling of the Christian sphere in all life with too much complacency. We have submitted to the withdrawal of our freedom with a too quick resignation. We have wept by the waters of our 'exile' when we should have been fighting to save the outposts of our invaded Kingdom. 'The world is still our parish' is Mr Wesley's contention for the right to preach the gospel anywhere and to everybody. It will still respond when methods to fit the changing conditions are devised and courage to match the need is rekindled.

In at least three directions Methodism can help the world Church to claim its birthright and fulfil its mission in a mass effort for Christianity.

Through its temporal organization, Methodism can lead the way in advancing on all fronts of the Christian approach to life at one time. No war has ever been won where this strategy was not employed and it is clearly indicated in the Christian conquest of our present world. We cannot get very far in faith and order if we neglect life and work. An educational advance cancels itself out, as we have seen, unless it spreads widely the total possession of knowledge and lifts the world level of Christian intelligence. The world does not come to act on Christian principles by means of a high order of Christian intelligence in a few spots while dense ignorance of the mind of Christ exists everywhere else.

The same principle holds true with evangelism and in the realm of social relations. Spotty and fragmentary efforts, no matter how high the order, will not bring Christ or Christian relations to dominance in our world. The challenge is to relate our efforts in all fields of the Christian endeavour by all the participants and to universalize them so that the viewpoint and impact are world-wide and the effort of the smallest project and the humblest worker is consciously related to the whole.

Connexional Methodism should be in a position to work naturally in such a mass undertaking and to present the basic elements in a plan of simultaneous and world-wide activity. By organization, training and temperament, Methodists have had the preparation necessary to do this.

Our history has been made largely through the initiation of all-inclusive programmes and the aptitude for bringing them to a successful conclusion in practical results. It was the observation of the Methodists' ability to do this which led one of America's outstanding industrialists, a non-Methodist and a prominent churchman, to predict that if Protestants came together in a world Church they would not take the Methodist name, but by the necessities for doing the work they would be compelled to adapt for their uses the Methodist system. Methodism has a contribution to make through its system.

A second contribution which Methodism can make to the mass approach required for the Christianization of the world is its ability to work through the individual to effect mass changes in society. While being criticized for an emphasis on individual importance and personal salvation without a corresponding concern for social theory and its application, the history of the Methodist approach clearly indicates that its effectiveness in changing individuals for the better has always reflected itself in social improvement and in a widening outlook and outreach for the Kingdom. Our trouble today lies largely in the fact that we are attempting to build a redeemed society with half-redeemed constituents. This is certainly evident in the social amelioration which came with the Methodist circuit rider to the frontier colonization of America. It is also to be seen in the missionary motivation and results of both Coke and Asbury. The good life in society follows in the wake of redeemed men and women. Methodism, believing this, has developed an effective personal approach and guaranteed through it the redemption of society by making Christian social action an evidence of the genuineness of the personal experience. To quote Methodism's greatest contemporary social prophet, Bishop Francis J. McConnell, the larger social responsibility follows inevitably because of 'Methodism's stress on human conduct as the test of the genuineness of religious experience and profession'.

The reclamation of the importance of the person, along with a world plan for his redemption and an intellectual enlightenment which will direct the power of his spiritual transformation are the points where current totalitarian schemes present the strongest challenge to Protestantism.

Third, the world Church has a current problem to deal with in the relation which personal morality bears to social and political action. Back of this problem lies the religious question of whether or not this generation should obey men rather than God and the political question of whether or not the State creates the individual or the individual creates the State. Methodism's traditional position has been to put man's responsibility first to God and to look on the State as man's tool and not his master. These decisions made by Wesley have produced within Methodism both prophets and reformers and enabled it to be a religion for periods of upheaval and change. The price required was often heavy, but the results were correspondingly good. The Wesley movement for England, the Asbury movement for America, and the missionary expansion of the nineteenth century have all been praised for their adaptation and application of the Christian message to periods of critical world decision. Can we do this again when the dominant idea of government is that it stands above Christian morality and people—both leaders and followers—seem alarmingly complacent in face of the tragic results of such political immorality? At this point Methodism by its example can keep alive the power and value of the fearless prophet, the tireless worker, and the individual exponent quickening the conscience of the State at a time when large sections of the Christian Church suspect the world state to be spiritually impervious and morally shock-proof.

The Church's most violent maligners accuse it of being imperialistic. That is Communism's major assault upon it. I do not see how the world Church can avoid this indictment. To disavow a Christian imperialism would be to disenfranchise ourselves in the Christian Kingdom. We are committed to 'taking the kingdoms of this world and making them the kingdoms of our Lord and Saviour Jesus Christ'. But not after the manner of the Herods and the Caesars and their modern counterparts. Our conquest is not to establish some new form of government, but to put into the world governments a new and Christian spirit.

Such an effort requires united action on a world scale now.

IV. Vitality and Adaptability in Crisis

To do this, however, the primary concern for the life and work of the world Church is not resources. A review of what is available to work with would fill us with enthusiasm and hope. One hundred and fifty million members in the Protestant section of the world Church and the resources they control make an imposing and formidable impression, to say nothing of the power of 650 million members in all the branches of Christendom.

The problem centres in vitalizing and adapting these resources for the establishment of Christianity in the world now. They must be brought to new life, assume new forms, fulfill new responsibilities and meet new situations. The extent that this can be achieved will determine the limits to be imposed upon the strength and extension of world Christianity.

Any attempt to empower the individual units of Methodist or Protestant strength which does not see the advantages of ecumenicity for this purpose will fall short of the maximum possibilities. Methodist strength comes to its highest potentialities in relation to the Church universal. Likewise, it should be said that the world Church must recognize its dependence upon the individual units which comprise it for the resources of an effective impact.

We need to understand this elementary principle of social psychology and take courage from it. Our own Methodist history has verified the findings of the psychologist who said that 'as men come together in larger and larger groups the very fact of their coming together gives an opportunity for the unfolding of powers in the individual that would not otherwise arise. Contact with one thousand other men or one million other men or one hundred million other men ought progressively to unlock powers in each one of the individuals of the multitude. In the sphere of social psychology two plus two make *not* four but possibly five or even ten.'[1]

We see this principle at work when we take the particular concerns of Methodism and observe how, through our connexionalism, they come to their largest influence and usefulness.

Freedom has been a distinctive emphasis in Methodism, both as it has been applied to individual conduct and to religious thought and expression. Its understanding and undergirding in this period of attack upon it is certainly a challenge and responsibility for the world Church. Dr Paul F. Douglass has cited this interpretation of freedom in terms of religion and the struggle to maintain it as a peculiar Methodist contribution to world religion. This Methodist principle of freedom, as has been said many times, is embodied in Wesley's declaration that 'The world is my parish'.

[1] *The Essentials of Methodism*, by McConnell.

Strength to establish the principle grew out of its daring universal claims and application. Had it been circumscribed by some modern attitudes which would silence our proclamation of the gospel on the grounds that only where it is approved should there be freedom to announce it, Christianity, as we believe in it, would have lost its world significance and its power to influence world affairs. Many feel that one cause for the circumscribed power of the United Nations to establish the principle of freedom on the world level grows out of an application of this attitude of false tolerance which, according to Dr John M. Cummings, an American authority on political science, 'left out the recognition of a Supreme Being in its charter as a concession to the men who were running Russia at that time'.[1]

Religious freedom so essential to a Christian world must be maintained as the concern of all or it will soon be the privilege of none.

Another contribution which Methodism has made to the vitalization and adaptability of Christianity in a changing world scene is its revolt from a formalism in theology, ritual and practice which would put religion in a strait-jacket of uniformity. Order and propriety it recognizes, but not at the expense of vitality and service. American Methodism had to learn in the beginning that 'new world occasions teach new religious duties' or it would have died. And Protestantism in its various denominational and geographical expressions must be alert to the devitalizing inertia which comes from a slavish devotion to traditional forms, when great needs and opportunities calling for their spirit require new ways of expressing that traditional spirit. Hear an American parable for our times on how religious groups should keep their traditions fluid enough to meet human needs. In 1788 fire broke out in the city of New Orleans in the state of Louisiana. The bells of the Capuchin Monastery had always been used to spread the alarm of fire. But the date of this fire was 21st March, Good Friday, and religious tradition said the bells must be silent on that day. So the bells of the church did not spread the alarm of the danger threatening the city. The result was not only the destruction of the city, but of the monastery as well.

In its breath of human sympathies which made the followers of Wesley 'the servants of mankind', in its refusal to be confined in work by a narrow parochialism either of interest or of geography, in its separation through distinctive standards of personal conduct from the corroding secularism of its early environment, in its vision and devotion to the highest through a practical interpretation of Christian perfection, Methodism became a great religious power in a time of social and political change.

Now, bringing its experience to the service of the world Church, we raise the question: 'Has Methodism the same vitality to meet desperate crises in the present or in the future with the effectiveness with which our fathers met equally severe or severer crises in their day?'[2]

V. The Inherent Power to Transform

The answer is to be found in an examination of those inner qualities of spirit which motivate and direct the Christian world enterprise. Perhaps the greatest weakness of our movement lies at this point. Our world needs inner transformation more than outward reorganization. Yet our world in dealing with itself reflects the attitude of the mother who sent a note to the teacher of her little girl's class in physiology which said:

[1] *Philadelphia Inquirer*, 4th July 1951.
[2] *The Challenge of the Fathers*, by F. J. McConnell.

'Don't teach Mary any more about her insides.' The concerns with external organization often tempt us to turn away from the disturbing consideration of our inner spiritual state and its requirements. Yet it is the life within which determines the form without.

The recognition of this fact along with an understanding of the nature of our opposition bring us face to face with the realization that it is in the spirit of man where the Church universal must fight and win its battle. Christianity cannot be content with the role of a social or religious philosophy to which many would confine it. Christianity must be a creative movement in the spirit of man or revert to a sterile and useless form.

The Church universal must also understand the nature of its opposition in preparing its constituency to overcome its enemies. It is a battle to the death. Their purpose is to exterminate Christianity as we know it. Half the world has been aroused not simply to render Christianity inert, but, as D. R. Sharp[1] has well said, this half the world has been mobilized 'to take God out of religion, the Church out of society and the soul out of man'.

What are we to do in face of such strategy and attack? How must Methodists as a part of the Church universal meet the current, popular, secular, materialistic standards of achievement and hold the citadels of the spirit against the present concerted atheistic attack?

Surely we must keep before us and the Christian world fellowship the clear insight of our fathers who saw the final outcome in terms of the power to possess and transform the spirits of men. Our task is to remind ourselves and convince our contemporaries of the power of a Godly life and that the unusual demands of our day still give greater power to 'the man that keepeth his spirit' than to 'the man who taketh a city'. The moral imperative, the Christian ethic, and the social action lacking so often now in the responses of so-called Christian individuals and Christian nations, but necessary to the restoration of sanity and peace in the world come only as the outgrowth of the transformed heart and the experience of God in the spirit of man.

This, of course, is the centre of Methodism's life and work and the most valuable contribution it brings to the resources of the world Church. Conversion, entire sanctification, Christian perfection and 'the strange warning of the heart'—all historic Methodist terms—mean this when applied to life as it now is. A reinterpretation of them may be necessary for the purposes of understanding, but their essential power and necessity need reiteration and demonstration in the lives of those who have sought and found these experiences. Nothing short of the power to change the spirit of man into the likeness of God will be sufficient to make the world Church regnant.

Renewing the mind, converting the soul, surrendering the will are the steps which bring man to the experience of a repossessed spirit. Methodism, while claiming no monopoly or exclusive rights to this approach, has by an early recognition of its value and an experience with its application a responsibility to hold for it when the demands for a quicker method of world transformation would put it aside. Experimental religion is the spearhead of attack in the campaign for world transformation.

VI. The Universal Medium

To achieve its purpose of a world fellowship among Christians and the universal reign of Christ in their affairs, Christian forces must take into account the frame of operation to which our generation has been conditioned to respond. *Leadership* and *organization* are the key words for

[1] *Call to Christian Action.*

269

modern social achievement. Our age has been trained both in their uses and in response to their demands. The evidences of their power in misuse only strengthen the assurance of their power for good through their proper use.

Therefore, it is imperative that the world view of Methodists which this great Ecumenical Conference makes possible should see the Church doing its work in this modern setting through the widest and most effective organization and achieving its purposes through a Spiritual Personality as Leader and Lord who has already demonstrated His power to overcome the world.

Real ecumenicity comes only through the most practical consideration of the world Church as an organization and an acceptance of the practical demands which result. It is what the Church is able to do at the points of human contact on the field, often in competition with other organizations, which determines ultimately its effectiveness. Ecumenicity to become more than a doctrine must be closely identified with an exalted and practical conception of the Church at work among men. What Christians think together is of high value, but what they do together is of equal importance. It is the organized Church as a world body which presents us now with a critical situation in Christian world affairs. There seem to be so many obstacles within its constituent parts that stand in the way of its progress. How to resolve them is a responsibility for all who claim a part in the Church universal.

Perhaps the current mood of mankind to yield itself to leadership, now effectively used by wicked men for evil purposes, is God's way of pointing us to the achievement of a world unity in and through our many denominational differences. Professor William Cannon, the quality of whose mind and spirit we have had an opportunity to measure at this conference, in his book entitled *The Redeemer*, made a very discriminating observation which may help us in our Methodist relations to the world Church. He pointed out that 'the denominational segmentation of Christianity is largely ideological', but that, 'the unity of the Christian movement lies in the personality of the Leader'. 'He alone', says Dr Cannon, 'breaks across all ideological and sociological boundaries, and Christian denominations not yet ready to accept one faith and one baptism do pledge allegiance to one Lord.' Our denominational differences and the weaknesses which have grown out of our separations have encouraged us to be religious Cassandras pointing so accurately to the world's disintegration but bringing to that analysis no power to do anything to stop this downward plunge to destruction. Looking back over our many denominational pathways, the past may appear as Christianity's golden age. The revival of Wesley, the reformation of Luther, the haystack prayer meeting which inspired the great century of missions, are the peaks of experience and achievement to which we turn with longing eyes in these days of weary waiting for the visitation of our God.

Yet the unity we have in the leadership of Jesus Christ gives us hope to believe the Psalmist when he said: 'Instead of thy fathers it shall be thy children whom thou shalt make princes of the earth.'[1]

METHODISM AND THE WORLD CHURCH

An address delivered by the REV. C. W. RANSON, *Secretary of the International Missionary Council:*

A few years ago I sat on the roof of an Indian bungalow in the company of a very able and well-informed colleague who is now a bishop in the

[1] Psalm 45:16.

Church of South India. As we watched the lovely pattern of light and shade created by the brilliant tropical moon, the talk drifted on to a familiar theme. We discussed the distinctive contributions of the various confessions to the Church in India. Having disposed of all the conventional platitudes—the Anglican heritage of liturgy, the Lutheran sense of the paramount importance of dogma, the Presbyterian gift for precise articulation both in faith and order, the Baptist and Congregational emphasis on the 'gathered Church', the Methodist genius for evangelism—we really got down to business and tried to paint the picture, warts and all. I will not repeat the conversation. I have learned discretion in these latter years! But at one stage I asked my friend: 'What do you *really* think is the special contribution of Methodism?' He paused for a moment and said: 'Well, that's not an easy question. But if you want a short answer, I should say: Skill in ecclesiastical organization.'

I confess that I was rather startled by that reply. I have often thought about it since, particularly since I myself have become entangled in the machinery of the ecumenical movement. We know and value what Methodism owes to our founder's gifts as a wise master-builder. But we know even more surely that if John Wesley had been nothing more than an adroit and far-sighted organizer of his societies, there would have been no Methodism. I therefore find it a disquieting thought that modern Methodism is seen by some of our friends and colleagues in other great communions primarily as a piece of well-oiled and relatively smooth-running ecclesiastical machinery. May it not be part of the failure of contemporary Methodists that others think of them most readily as ecclesiastical engineers, and find it less easy to detect those distinctive notes in thought and liturgy and practice which should be our chiefest glory and our richest contribution to the common heritage of the universal Church?

In this Conference we have had many luminous glimpses of our Methodist heritage. We have reason to give thanks to God for its richness and variety. It is my task tonight to indicate its relevance to the world-wide fellowship of Christians and to the world Mission of the Church.

Let us glance, first, at a little history.

'I am a priest of the Church Universal', said John Wesley to Bishop Butler, who had denied his right to preach in the Diocese of Bristol. 'I look upon all the world as my parish', he wrote a little earlier to one who had questioned, on catholic principles, Wesley's invasion of 'other men's parishes'. This assertion of a universal commission was not only a challenge to the static parochialism of the English Church in the eighteenth century. It was a challenge to a false conception of the responsibility of the Church to the world which for two centuries had dominated the thought of all the reformed Churches. One of the less widely advertized results of the Protestant Reformation was the temporary eclipse in the Protestant world of the ecumenical character of the Church. That great movement of internal renewal left the Churches of Europe so preoccupied with domestic concerns, so entangled in the politics of nation states, that the vision of one holy, catholic Church was partly obscured and the sense of a universal missionary obligation was almost entirely lost. It was the forces of the Counter-Reformation which kept alive in the Church the missionary impulse which thrusts men out across the frontiers in obedience to the Great Commission. While Francis Xavier was engaged in his passionate embassy to Asia, the reformers were finding ingenious theological justification for their missionary inactivity. The command to preach the gospel to every creature, they taught, was given only to the Apostles; and it expired

271

with them. This curious price of rationalization became the stock-in-trade of some of the most eminent leaders of the Reformation. It was echoed, feebly in thought, if decisively in practice, in the Church in England. The Reformation was clearly incomplete.

The rise of Pietism in the seventeenth century helped the Churches of continental Europe to recover their sense of missionary vocation. When John Wesley was being rocked in his cradle in Epworth Rectory, the first two Protestant missionaries landed on the sun-scorched beach at Zanquibar in South India. Zuqinbalq and Plutochau were the gallant pioneers of the Protestant missionary awakening. A century later that movement began to achieve its full momentum. In the interval God had given to the Church and to the world the mighty apostolate of the Wesleys. The Methodist Revival had restored to a Church which had lost them some of the authentic accents of Catholicity. It set men singing:

'O that the world might taste and see
The riches of His Grace;
The arms of love that compass me
Would all mankind embrace.'

It has often been said that Methodism itself was the least result of the Evangelical Revival. That movement, of which the Wesleys were the chief human instruments, released into the life of Protestant Christendom new tides of the Spirit which carried all the Churches forward on the greatest wave of missionary expansion since Apostolic times. The modern missionary enterprise, of which original Methodism may claim to be one of the principal progenitors, restored to Protestant Christianity the conception of the ecumenical character of the Church, which had been obscured at the Reformation. But it has done something even more important. It has, for the first time in history, created the reality of a Christian fellowship, world-wide in scope.

It has *not* created a 'world Church'. That phrase is misleading. I hope its appearance on this programme does not mean that ecumenical Methodism is going to give it official sanction. You, Mr Chairman, as a pillar of faith and order, will, I doubt not, be on the side of those angels who have a care for historical accuracy and theological precision. In this matter they may need the support of your great learning and weighty influence.

The finish of the missionary enterprise of the last 150 years is not a 'world Church'. It is a series of supra-national Churches, widely scattered throughout the world. These Churches hold together in the bonds of a common obedience to the gospel, younger and older Churches and men and women of different race, nationality, and cultural background. This great apostolic outthrust has been a wonderful achievement. But let us not claim more for it than the facts warrant. It has happened within the historic framework of a divided Christendom. It has left upon the life of the younger Churches the stigmata of that division.

None of the great confessions is fully world-wide. When we speak of world Methodism, we are not using the language of precision, but of hyperbole. What is true of Methodism is true of the other great non-Roman confessions. But taken together—and this is of crucial significance —they form the great world fellowship which has been described as 'the great new fact of our era'.

When William Temple used that memorable phrase in his enthronement sermon in Canterbury Cathedral he understood the significance of the things of which he spoke. He knew that for many years God had been

272

raising up instruments through which the reality of the world-wide Christian fellowship might—despite its historic divisions—find visible embodiment. It is no mere accident that these instruments first developed as a result of missionary concern, and found their most powerful expression in the world mission of the Church. The International Missionary Council became, under God, the means through which the younger and older Churches of a divided Protestantism increasingly came to view their missionary responsibility as a common task. It also became the vehicle through which the ecumenical fellowship could find visible expression. This it did, not only in great world gatherings at Jerusalem in 1928 and Madras in 1938 and Whitby in 1947, but—more significantly—in its national constituent councils in all the great countries and areas of the world which function as permanent instruments of ecumenical counsel and action.

The chief architect and principal officer of this great organization—from its inception until the 1940's—is with us tonight. A simple answer to the question, 'What is Methodism's Chief Contribution to the Ecuemenical Movement?' might be: 'Dr John R. Mott!'

William Temple was also an officer of the Council for several years. Since his enthronement sermon and his untimely death, the World Council of Churches has come to birth. The representatives of the Churches assembled at Amsterdam in 1948 made the historic affirmation: 'We have Covenanted with one another in constituting this World Council of Churches. We intend to stay together!' One of the first things this vigorous ecumenical infant did was to enter into 'association' with its grandmother, the International Missionary Council. A new and more comprehensive instrument for the expression of the universal fellowship of Christians has thus been formed. A fresh impetus has been given to the ecumenical idea.

As one who exercises his ministry, for the moment, within the organized ecumenical movement, I am deeply impressed by the historic contribution which Methodism has made to the emergence of the movement. I am no less deeply convinced of the importance of that which it may still give—if Methodism is true both to its heritage and to its calling to serve the present age. There are elements in the Methodist tradition which bear a quite astonishing relevance to the contemporary ecumenical situation.

Let me suggest some of the points at which—in my view—Methodism has something distinctive to say in the present ecumenical conversation between the Churches of the world. I shall do so with almost indecent brevity. For I have sometimes noticed that the true art of being tiresome is the attempt to say everything.

1. First, in the realm of theological thought, it is frequently said that Methodism has no distinctive confessional contribution to offer. Ecumenically speaking, that is its strength and not its weakness. John Wesley was no sectarian eccentric. He was the conscious inheritor of the holy catholic and evangelical faith in its historic glory and strength. The Methodist Church still 'claims and cherishes its place in the holy catholic Church'; it 'rejoices in the inheritance of the Apostolic Faith and loyally accepts the fundamental principles of the historic creeds and the Protestant Reformation'. Other great denominations have their confessions in the form of historic documents. Dr Franz Hildebrandt has recently pointed out that Methodism is unique among the great denominations in that its official standards are exegetical documents: Wesley's *Standard Sermons* and the *Notes on the New Testament*. This direct appeal to Scripture is of incalculable importance in ecumenical relations. It is the appeal to the Word of God—above and behind the historic confessions—which holds

the Churches together in ecumenical conversation and fellowship. It is in the Living Word that they find the given unity which underlies confessional division.

Wesley's vivid sense of the unity given in the Word enabled him to anticipate by two centuries that catholicity of mind which alone makes possible the contemporary ecumenical movement. The whole spirit of the Methodism of Wesley was ecumenical. The mission of Methodists, as he saw it, was 'to spread life among all denominations'. Methodists who are asked what their distinctive contribution to ecumenical thought has been can hardly do better than point to the sermon on 'The Catholic Spirit'. This has been called 'the Magna Charta of ecumenicity'. And such it is. I know no more adequate exposition of the Biblical basis of the ecumenical movement. And what Wesley taught in theory he practised in the life of his societies.

In 1748, he wrote: 'The thing which I was greatly afraid of all this time and which I resolved to use every possible method of preventing was a narrowness of spirit . . . that miserable bigotry which makes many so unready to believe that there is any work of God but among themselves. I thought it might be a help against this, frequently to read to all who were willing to hear, the accounts I received from time to time of the work which God is carrying on in the earth, both in our own and other countries, not among us alone, but among those of varying opinions and denominations. For this I allotted one evening in every month; and I find no cause to repent of my labour.'

What John Wesley set forth by example and by precept, expressed in taut, astringent, eighteenth-century prose, Brother Charles wove into smooth, scriptural, singable verse. Thus did poetry become the handmaid of catholicity as well as piety, and Methodists learned to sing such verses as:

'Love like death hath all destroyed,
Rendered all distinctions void;
Names and sects and parties fall:
Thou, O Christ, art all in all.'

2. That leads me to the second thing I have to say. The richest treasure which Methodism has to offer to the ecumenical fellowship is in the hymns of Charles Wesley. It is a treasure which many Methodists have already bartered for a mess of inferior nineteenth-century pottage. I shall content myself here by quoting what a non-Methodist has to say on the subject. Methodism owes much to Bernard Lord Manning formerly Fellow of Jesus College, Cambridge, for his instructed enthusiasm for the hymns of Charles Wesley. Of the 1780 *Collection of Wesley's Hymns*, he wrote: 'This little book . . . ranks in Christian literature with the Psalms, the Book of Common Prayer, the Canon of the Mass. In its own way, it is perfect, unapproachable, elemental in its perfection. You cannot alter it except to mar it; it is a work of supreme devotional art by a religious genius.' Strong language that! But Manning justifies it. He identifies three qualities in Wesley's hymns which give them their distinction. They are charged with dogma—with a full-orbed and conscious orthodoxy. They represent, with vividness and power, a present experience. And they catch the glory of a mystic sunlight coming directly from another world, which transfigures history and experience and puts past and present into the timeless eternal now.

There have been other writers of dogmatic hymns (we think of the Greek Church); there have been other writers of hymns revealing a personal experience of religion (we think of the nineteenth century);

there have been other writers of mystical religious poetry (we think of the seventeenth century). It is Wesley's glory that he united these three strains —dogma, experience, mysticism—in verse so simple that it could be understood, and so smooth that it could be used by plain men. You can find a union of these qualities in the greatest Latin hymns of the medieval Church, but hardly (I believe) anywhere else.

Thus does a scholarly, perceptive and devout historian write of our liturgical heritage. If Methodists are to bring this priceless treasure to the service and enrichment of the wider ecumenical fellowship, they must first recover and possess it for themselves.

3. In thought and liturgy Methodism has something to say—or ought to have—in the contemporary ecumenical conversation. What of Methodist history and practice? Here again there are elements in our tradition which speak with piercing relevance to the new ecumenical situation. I will mention only one.

At a recent meeting of the Central Committee of the World Council of Churches, a good deal of time was given to the discussion of the Church's calling to unity and mission. That discussion was the result of a growing recognition that unity cannot be sought as a thing in itself. It is bound up with the Church's mission in the world. Unity and apostolicity are inextricably united. The obligation to preach the gospel to the whole world and the concern to draw all Christ's people together both rest on Christ's whole work and cannot be separated. Every attempt to separate them violates the wholeness of Christ's ministry to the world. 'Both of them are in the strict sense of the word essential to the being of the Church and the fulfilment of its function as the Body of Christ.' I venture to suggest that this is the most vital issue before the ecumenical movement today. It is an issue on which Methodism should have a significant word to speak.

I have already reminded you of the historical relation between the Evangelical Revival and the missionary awakening. I have hinted at the close connexion between the world-wide expansion of the Church, the emergence of concern for Christian unity, and the birth of the new ecumenical organizations. Historically, Methodism stands in the main stream of this whole movement. It is of its essence that from the beginning it has been a mission. It did not share the introversion which beset the Churches of the Reformation. It became, under God, one of the instruments of its correction. It has laid the foundation of that evangelical catholicity which has made possible an ecumenical movement. Classical Methodism has something to say to those who seek the renewal of the Church in unity and apostolicity.

What of contemporary Methodism? Has it anything relevant and distinctive to say? I am reminded once more of that conversation in the Indian moonlight. The numerical power and financial strength of Methodism as a great world-wide communion are widely recognized. It is part of our failure as Methodists that these are too often the things that most readily strike the eye of our friends. They find it less easy to see those things of which I have tried to speak tonight; and some of which I have not spoken such as the unique development of lay writers.

We shall not recover those distinctive and ecumenically relevant notes by a mere revival of antiquarianism. Still less, I believe, shall we recover them by building an impressive organization for world Methodism. We shall have to begin first within our own household of faith to learn humbly and penitently what it really means to be a Church and to be a world Church. And that is done by something more fundamental and more profound than well-oiled machinery. To concentrate on organization may be the surest road to ecumenical retrogression and confessional sterility.

To retrogression because our machinery may hamper the freedom of the younger Churches which are the real growing points of ecumenical advance. The revival of confessionalism within the ecumenical movement is in many ways healthy and creative. Its tendency to harden into organizational forms may well retard ecumenical advance where its prospects are most hopeful. The younger Churches everywhere have a concern for Christian unity which grows out of the urgency of their own situation and their sense of the magnitude of their evangelistic task. In many areas of the world they are moving steadily towards corporate union with their fellow Christians. A rigidly organized confessionalism may fasten upon them those leading strings from which it has been the grand design of enlightened missionary policy to free them. It may mean that their steps toward unity may be hampered, their action unduly influenced by the tragic deadlock in the older Christendom.

It may be the road to confessional sterility, because God has not made the kind of world in which the winds of the Spirit can be captured by building ecclesiastical machinery—however stream-lined and chromium plated. God has set us in a world in which the real points of spiritual encounter are local and personal. One of the most disquieting things about the new ecumenical enthusiasm is the way in which it is spawning new organizations. I expect to see a high infant mortality among them. For the business of working the machinery is going to wear out the ecclesiastical mechanics.

Let us beware lest we so spend our energies on organization that we have no time to seek the real springs of renewal. We may fashion an instrument to give Methodism a bigger and brassier voice only to find that the new trumpet gives an uncertain sound.

The real trumpet note of Methodism is this:

'O for a trumpet voice,
    On all the world to call!
To bid their hearts rejoice
    In Him who died for all!
For all my Lord was crucified.
For all, for all, my Saviour died!'

When that becomes once more the passion and the prayer of Methodism, in all its branches and throughout its entire membership, we shall probably talk less about our distinctive contribution to the common heritage of Christendom. But, perhaps for that very reason, we may have one to offer.

276

TENTH DAY

Thursday 6th September

MORNING DEVOTIONS were conducted by Bishop Sante Uberto Barbieri, of the Methodist Church in Central and South America. An address on the relevance of Pentecost was given by the Rev. W. L. Northridge, Principal of Edgehill College, Belfast.

In expounding the distinctive fellowship which was the direct outcome of Pentecost, Dr Northridge stressed three points: (1) Our dependence on God if we are to accomplish His work. (2) The necessity of this fellowship of the Spirit in every local church if true and continuous evangelism is to be maintained. (3) The creation of the noblest Christian character in and through such fellowship. This was the message of Pentecost to the people of today.

The morning session—memorable in so many ways—was devoted to the consideration of *Evangelism*. The first address was delivered by Professor H. Cecil Pawson, of Durham University, who spoke on *Commending the Gospel*. The second speaker was the Rev. Dr Eugene L. Smith, Secretary of the American Board of Foreign Missions, and he dealt with *The Missionary Motive* as part of Evangelism.

EVANGELISM

I. COMMENDING THE GOSPEL

An address by PROFESSOR H. CECIL PAWSON, F.R.S.E.:

It is fitting that we should focus our thought, as we draw near to the end of our Conference, on the subject of evangelism. I believe God is calling world Methodism to world evangelization on a united scale, for the sake of the world, for the revitalization of Methodism, for the blessing of the Church Universal. Further, a trumpet call to engage in an aggressive evangelistic crusade with clearly expressed aims for life here and hereafter would be the answer to the need of our Methodist youth for an adventurous, sacrificial life of action.

To begin this address here by a reference to the *Concise Oxford Dictionary* should not be inappropriate, for I was reminded in that valuable companion volume to my Bible that the word 'commend' carries with it a sense of trust and responsibility, deriving, as it does, from a Latin word meaning 'entrust'. Charles Wesley's oft-quoted lines—

> 'O let me commend my Saviour to you,
> I set to my seal that Jesus is true,'

might be considered presumptuous—especially the second line—were it not for the fact that the good name of Jesus has been entrusted to us. We are trustees before God of time and talents, material possessions and opportunities, but as Christians our supreme trust is the Gospel which,

277

stated simply and shortly, means our knowledge of God's loving will and purpose in the salvation of men, as revealed to us in Jesus Christ, His Son. 'For when the world by wisdom knew not God'—and the twentieth century, with its disciples of Karl Marx, H. G. Wells, Bertrand Russell, and Fred Hoyle, amply confirms this statement—'it pleased God by the foolishness of preaching to save them that believe.' How mistaken we are to think of preaching as being mainly a matter of pulpits and consecrated buildings! Apostolic preaching meant commending Jesus everywhere, as did Philip when he ran to catch up with a man who had driven past him seated in his chariot reading his Bible. We are not called to preach at people, but to preach Christ, who is the Gospel and to offer Him to men and women within our daily sphere of influence.

How great is the responsibility of personal testimony! You and I live in an age when millions never read the Bible and have little personal knowledge, if any, of the written Gospels. It is our major responsibility as professing Christians to use the knowledge of Christ revealed to us through all the means of grace to commend the Gospel. As Christians are in a minority in the world, we cannot say we lack opportunity.

We need more Christian propagandists. I want to rescue that word 'propaganda' from its present tainted associations. Propaganda is a good agricultural and horticultural word; it means to multiply, to spread, and all Christians are surely called to propagate the gospel. The continuity of the Christian faith depends on the blessing of God upon the commending of the gospel by Christian men and women in the Church, the home and the life of the world. We are here because of this witness, and therefore every Christian has a personal responsibility to share what he has received. Let us ask ourselves the question: 'What am I doing in a personal way to commend the gospel?' It is the question which, more than any other, should be asked by every professing Christian at this hour. For if we place this question in the setting of the need of our world today we must surely feel a sense of urgency about the matter. Nothing, in my judgement, accounted more for the success of the early Christian Church and the early Methodist Movement than a tremendous sense of urgency in commending the gospel. Is it untrue to say that in general these characteristics of evangelism, personal responsibility and urgency, are not so much in evidence in our day? Let us ask ourselves first whether our personal witness is of this character and then ask what are the reasons for this lack of a vital, continuous witness in the daily contacts of so many who profess to believe the gospel. We are told we live in a different world from that of the early Christian centuries, which is, of course, true in many respects; but it is not all the truth. There is an unchanging need in the heart of man which can only be met by the unchanging Gospel of 'Jesus Christ, the same yesterday, today and for ever'. What are our difficulties? The apathy and indifference, the mental atmosphere generated by science and pseudo-science, and the effect of wars and rumours of wars are some of them. Yet salvation is still a matter of life and death to every soul of man. Does not part of the responsibility for the widening gulf between those inside and those outside our Churches devolve on those who never consciously seek to reach those outside the Christian fellowship? We are too apologetic for our personal Christian apologetics. Are we convinced, and therefore convincing, Christians? Are any of us in as close step as we ought to be with Him who declared that He had come to seek and to save that which is lost? Perhaps our chief need is to do our part to close that gap, if we are, by God's help, to bridge the other gulf. Perhaps we need more of God in our home life, if we are to help Him in making the world

His home. More of God in us would mean more of God in the world.

How then can we commend the gospel in this twentieth-century revolutionary age? Let me remind you of *four* ways which are not likely to become out of date.

I. *Through the Written Word*

The printed Word of God, as distributed by the Bible and other similar societies, in this and other lands, should receive all the support in our power. I commend, for example, the recent attempt of the British and Foreign Bible Society to issue the Gospels in more attractive form. More than at any other time in my life, in this country, the Press is giving space for the news that can never become stale. The daily text, letters for the correspondence column, the weekly religious article and items of news covering Christian activities all contribute to the fulfilment of Paul's great desire that Christ should be proclaimed publicly by any and every means. The appointment of a Press officer for British Methodism in this country was an excellent development. We should explore and exploit worthily every opportunity of commending the gospel through these means, studying carefully and prayerfully the kind of technique most likely to interest, intrigue, and challenge those to whom the Name of Jesus is often but a faint echo of a far-off Sunday-school, and sometimes not even that.

Let us have more church bookstalls with arresting publicity for the excellent writings now coming forward concerning our faith and its relevance to the present age. If young and older Methodists are to outlive the best pagans, they must out-think them, and therefore need to know much more of their subject of theology. I suggest, too, that there is scope for further development in the production of modern evangelistic tracts or pamphlets, and more exchange of our literature. Further developments are possible, especially with the single-sheet or double-folded leaflet, designed for distribution outside our churches amongst those who can read and for millions throughout the world who are learning to read. At least once a year, every congregation should engage in house to house visitation in its area, if only to distribute a Christian message of this kind; better still if we can card-index for prayer and follow-up visits the names and needs of those who know not Christ. I rejoice in the success which has attended efforts of this kind in America and here and there in this country. The ideal for which we must continue to strive is for every local church to be a missionary, evangelistic centre, seeking by corporate and personal evangelism to commend the gospel.

Given the imagination, and therefore more financial support, I think we could do better, through the written word, on church notice-boards as well as posters in other places. When my son was about eight years old, he returned home from school one day, sat down for his meal, and then came out with this question: 'Daddy, is it true that beer is best?' He had seen on his way home one of the attractive posters through which the brewers of this country have sought, and with much success, to convert the youth of Britain to the drink habit. In my weekly fellowship, we often have a feature called 'God in the News'. It is not difficult to find items of news from the secular press which reveal the Spirit of God at work in the world, making possible things which are lovely, true, honest, and of good report. How much more could we use outside boards for such news? But let it be news which is new, instead of a torn or worn announcement of a special church event held three months earlier! Let us study applied psychology as it applies to the passer-by, and then we shall not display, week in and week out, as I have seen on one of our Northern Mission centres a word like this one: 'Strangers will be welcome.' To be reminded you are a stranger makes you feel strange.

I will mention another expression of the written word. My mother was too nervous to address a public meeting, but she was a glorious messenger of God through her letters. It is said that we have lost the art of letter-writing; we are too hurried in these days. It doesn't say much for our religion if it never gets into our correspondence, and a letter can often be more fruitful than a sermon. Religion is not something apart from life, it *is* life, and, therefore, should run through all our moments and our days.

II. Through the Spoken Word

I thank God for all that is being done and is yet to be accomplished in commending the gospel through public worship, the teaching and preaching in church and Sunday-school, broadcast talks and services, television, mobile cinema vans, and the like, but I would single out for special consideration the daily conversation of rank-and-file Christians, the unpremeditated talk of ministers and laymen alike. This last-named was the method by which the early Church grew and early Methodism spread. John Wesley visited many Societies in the area best known to me in the north of England, as well as in other parts, which he had not directly created. They sprang into being because here a farmer, there a miner, and yonder a housewife gave testimony to the saving grace of Jesus Christ and made possible the formation of a group of people saved and being saved. 'How can we recover this earnest evangelism in daily life?' is the question I suggest here. We sing it: 'Take my lips and let them be filled with messages from Thee'; but who would guess that the words we speak came from Him? Silence is not always golden, and there is a reticence which is an ally of the Devil. 'Be not conformed to this world', exhorts the Apostle, but don't we all become so, more or less, especially in our conversation? Let me remind you of what happened to a man who wrote a world religious classic in a town not many miles from here. 'I heard but I understood not, for they were far above out of my reach. Their talk was about a new birth the work of God in their hearts. They gossiped about God and how their souls had been refreshed by His promises and methought they spake as if joy did make them speak.' So wrote John Bunyan as he recalled overhearing women talking in a street. And 'To me', he said, 'it seemed as if they had found a new world'. 'Apart from singing about Him and preaching about Him, I cannot remember since my Sunday-school teaching days, His Name ever being mentioned in our church', said an intelligent young man, a member of a Methodist church with whom I spoke recently. Whatever truth there is in this assertion, here in this country is the outcome, I think, of the decline of the Methodist Fellowship meeting, where Methodists learn how to pray and witness for themselves. I have said for years, and say it here, that no Methodist is likely to bear his spoken witness where it is needed most, i.e. among unbelievers, if he has not the opportunity to speak naturally and regularly about his faith within the Fellowship and hear the experience of others. Nor can we ever exaggerate the amazing power of a prayer group, which such a Fellowship makes possible, in supporting the witness and work of individual members in winning others for Christ. No commendation of the gospel can be at its maximum which is not begun, continued, and ended in prayer. How many of us pray with people as well as pray for them and are able to encourage them to pray for themselves?

It is significant that in the important book published this year on *English Life and Leisure*, in the chapter on religion, the method the authors commend for the purpose of spreading the much-needed Christian faith is that of the influence of individual Christians, who, by meeting in small groups, would work out the relevance of their faith. I would describe that as being a revival of Methodist Fellowship and witness in daily life, for it is just that which we have sought to do in the Fellowship Group I am privileged to lead, which has met every Tuesday evening for nineteen years. Here is the finest school for training evangelists, whether for the vocation of the ministry or laity. How often do we recommend private prayer, our Church, our Fellowship, the way we find help from reading the Bible, our wonderful resources in Christ to those we meet *between* Sundays? All too often, we make the excuse that 'we cannot do that sort of thing'. My reply to that is: 'You cannot do it, and I cannot do it, but the Holy Spirit can do it through us, giving each of us the right word at the right time for the right person.' Then we shall know that His Spirit is working in us and also in those to whom we bear our witness. 'And they were all filled with the Holy Spirit, speaking God's word fearlessly.' We can claim this Pentecostal blessing. We may then discover that the embarrassment we fear we might cause the person to whom we declare our faith is, after all, the fear of our own embarrassment. Self-consciousness is often a great barrier to Christ-consciousness, and poverty of experience of God the reason for lack of a glowing testimony which ought to be more common and natural in our personal, daily life.

III. *Through the Word of Action*

'And with actions bold and meek
Would for Christ my Saviour speak.' [1]

Matthew Arnold said conduct was three-fourths of life. Christians in every country are 'living epistles, known and read of all men'. It would astonish us if we knew all the reading men do of our lives and how much of it is done between the lines. My father's favourite word for autograph books is apt at this point: 'He whose sermon is a godly life will never preach too long.' If actions speak louder than words, then how lamentable it is if our actions are not an adequate commentary on our spoken word, how tragic if they contradict them! A quotation from one of my favourite hymns—need I say, one of Wesley's—sums up for me the challenge of this way of commending the gospel:

'Hallow thy great and glorious name
And perfect holiness in me.'

The Christian life of holiness commends the gospel in a language which needs no translation. Through the personal and corporate witness of those whose lives grow in grace and in the knowledge of Christ, we have the finest commendation of the gospel. The gospel according to my life, as well as my lips, is revealed in that world of daily relationship and activity in which God has placed me. As the Acts of the Apostles, or Acts of the Holy Spirit through the Apostles, comes immediately after the gospels in our New Testament, so as we allow Christ to take full possession of us through the Holy Spirit, we shall know and witness to that active holiness which is wholeness of life. It is only when we know as an increasing experience, the truth 'I live, yet not I, but Christ liveth in me' that we can dare to believe in the glorious possibility of Paul's witness becoming our

[1] M.H.B., 291.

281

own—namely, 'They glorified God in me'. Dedicate yourself each day to the ministry of commending the gospel. Go to the people from God, with God, for God.

It must be the whole gospel we commend—that is, one which concerns the whole of man's life and therefore the whole life of the world. The glory of the gospel is that it is an all-embracing truth, which concerns everybody and everything. It will include spiritual healing and peace of mind. Has not Dr Alfred Torrie, Medical Director of the National Association for Mental Health in Britain, stated recently that one-third of all sickness in the community is wholly or mainly caused by mental ill-health? It is a gospel concerned with men's bodies as well as their souls, with a life which is abundant in a physical as well as in a spiritual sense. It is the gospel which alone can make possible the family spirit within the national community and amongst the community of nations. The answer to a godless Communism or atheistic secularism is not in abuse, but in the pattern of life revealed in true Christian community living, whereby every member has equal opportunity to experience fullness of life as a child of God by creation and a redeemed child of God by salvation. To that end, we Christians must, by God's help, go further in sacrificing that others may share, in giving that others may be enriched. Most of all, and through it all, we must commend the Gospel as the offer of life eternal. The salvation of the soul to life everlasting is the unique essence of the good news in Jesus Christ which we commend to sinful, dying men. 'Preach for souls' was the counsel I received many years ago, and that was the emphasis of Christ Himself in His teaching and preaching as recorded in the first gospels.

IV. Through the Living Word

You and I cannot convert anyone; no man can; yet conversion is our objective in commending the gospel. The Church has many ministries, but one mission to which the former make their contribution. If people are not being converted, whatever else the Church is doing, it is failing in its mission. Its ministries will languish if its mission is not given absolute priority. Yet all is of God's doing and all is through Christ, the Living Word. Paul did not make the first Christian convert in Europe when he talked to a company of women at an open-air prayer meeting by a river. It was the Lord, as they recorded, who opened Lydia's heart. Men and women are saved in the twentieth century as they were in the first Christian century, through Christ, the Living Word.

If there is a secret of the effective commendation of the gospel in every age and in every land it lies in a deep, passionate love for Christ, out of which springs a passion for souls for whom Christ died. This, in the end, is the surest way to that unity of Christians which will enable the Church to be more effective in commending the gospel. No change of thought forms, new technique, modern methods of getting the message across, important as these are, can ever be substitutes for this essential condition— to love Christ with an undivided heart. True love never counts the cost, yet if we fully commend the gospel of Him who died for us men and our salvation, we shall engage in that most costly service which shares in the fellowship of His suffering. There is no insight or ingenuity like that of love seeking to express itself. If we love Him, we shall say, when opportunities to commend Him are presented, as they are in each of our lives, not 'Excuse me' but 'Use me'—'Use even me, just as Thou wilt and when and where'. For to love Him is to share His thoughts and desires, His passion and compassion, His sight, which is always insight, and to know through Him and His power working in us and through us, ways and means of reaching men and women lost in the maddening maze of self and sin. The gospel is the good news of how men and women can be saved, and He who is the power of God unto salvation is Christ Crucified, the Risen Lord and the ever-present Saviour. He calls us to commend the gospel by sharing in His redemptive passion and purpose, His word stands for us today: 'Whosoever shall lose his life for My sake and the gospel's, the same shall save it.' His promise to those He first sent forth to preach the gospel is made to us, 'And lo, I am with you alway', and as we commend He will not fail to confirm. 'And they went forth and preached everywhere, the Lord working with them, and confirming the word with signs following', which is Mark's last word in his gospel.

II. THE MISSIONARY MOTIVE

An address delivered by the REV. DR EUGENE L. SMITH, Secretary of Foreign Missions, New York:

In this complex world, nothing is more complex than human motivation. Into the unity of each human action is focused a variety of reasons for that action. Oftentimes we are deeply driven by desires of which we are consciously unaware. Our human restlessness until we find rest in God is but a sign of our need to find a single motivation able to utilize and thus harmonize all others. The missionary is no less complex in his purposes than another person. Many desires and purposes enter into missionary activity. Love of adventure, curiosity about distant places, and eagerness for prestige, among many others, have all played their part. The missionary is not to be condemned because his desires are as complex as his brothers'. The significance of these ancillary motivations in the missionary movement is not found in consideration of their acceptability to us or of their 'orthodoxy', but of their ability to be utilized by the master motive of witness for Christ.

Missionary motivation is as inevitable as it is complex. Its inescapability is rooted in two facts. One is our nature as persons. Within us is an inner, imperative need to communicate. We cannot avoid becoming missionaries of anything deeply meaningful to us. It may be Coueism or Communism, an ethic of love or of hate, I lived in a city of maniacal missionaries of the glorious but often neglected gospel of the superiority of the Brooklyn Dodgers in American baseball. We hear much today from missionaries of the legend of Soviet supremacy in all things, from ballet to ballyhoo. The inevitability of a missionary motivation is rooted, secondly, in the nature of our society. The very refusal to communicate—a symptom of insanity— is at last the communication of an attitude. We have no choice as to whether we shall be missionaries. We can only choose the cause or the person for whom we witness.

The Christian missionary motivation, among all others, is unique in its origin and in its end. All motivations, of course, are the creation of God, and all are to some degree perverted by human sin. The impetus to Christian witness, however, as no other human dynamic, is the direct creation of the Holy Spirit. His is a ceaseless endeavour to redeem us from sin and brings us to life eternal. Integral in the experience of that redemption is the desire to share it. Christian missionary motivation is born as we experience the action of God in crossing the barriers of human sin to free us from sin. In the grateful joy of that release is an inherent desire to cross barriers to other persons with the news of that redemption. That desire is the Christian missionary motivation. Manifest supremely at the Cross,

TEC 283

it is re-created in each person who opens his heart to God. 'I labour', wrote Paul, 'striving according to His working, which worketh in me mightily' (Colossians 1²⁹). Our witnessing is integral with our salvation. Each of us can but confess with Paul, 'Necessity is laid upon me; for woe is unto me if I preach not the gospel' (1 Corinthians 9¹⁶).

Unique in its origin, the Christian missionary motivation is no less unique in its end. To the degree that any motivation is perverted by human sin, it creates barriers between persons. These barriers are thrown high today. The forces of evil have perhaps never seemed more impressive in their power than now. Yet as compared to the Christian mission their rootage is shallow and their future frail. To be a missionary of any cause or for any person except Christ is to create barriers between persons. Always there is a conflict between fraternities and fraternity, between brotherhoods and brotherhood. The barriers at last imprison their creators. The Christian missionary motivation, as no other human desire, comes from the heart of God, the Father Almighty. He will not cease his labours, nor will that motivation die in His children, until all men and all history find their consummation in Him.

Every person is inevitably a missionary. Every Christian is in a significant sense, a 'foreign' missionary. The very nature of his spiritual life leads him to cross barriers to others with the good news of Christ. In missionary parlance, the word 'foreign' has traditionally applied to crossing barriers of nationality. The significant barriers of the future may well be ideological, racial, economic, or cultural, as well as national. A chaplain to a labour union may be as truly a 'foreign' missionary from the comfortable, upper-class churches so often called Methodist as a pioneer in Pago Pago. A Christian layman crusading against a corrupt political machine may be more truly a 'foreign' missionary bearing the Cross of Christ at great personal sacrifice than a person commissioned by a board, with an assured salary, an established pension, a comfortable home, and a settled job in a distant land. We professionals in the overseas missionary movement are tempted to a dangerous Phariseeism in the claim, so often made, that there is something different—and by inference superior —in the call to witness across barriers of nationality. Our witness and our salvation are inseparable. To claim a difference in my kind of witness is to claim a difference in my kind of salvation. So the Pharisee prayed, 'Lord, I thank Thee that I am not as other men.' The importance is not found in the kind of barriers one crosses, but in the upswelling love that floods across all barriers. Wherever there is any barrier to the abundant life, the Christian becomes a 'foreign' missionary, crossing that barrier in love for those imprisoned by it.

A good test of the degree to which you and I are guided by a Christian missionary motivation is found in the reciprocity of our relationships. We are particularly tempted to pride who seek to minister in the Name of Christ. Honouring Him, the world often honours those who bear His Name. How easily we believe those honours are due us! We bear infinite treasure in our earthen vessels, but we confuse divine treasure and human vessel with a persistent genius worthy of a better cause. We see easily and preach gladly on the folly of those who believe the essence of life is found in getting. Too often we forget it is equally foolish to believe the essence of life is found in giving. So some give funds to take the gospel to the African who would be unwilling to receive the sacrament of Holy Communion from the hands of an African. I know of one instance in which churches on our western coast, rather than employ a person of Japanese blood as a Director of Religious Education, chose to take a person less competent or to have no Director at all, meanwhile giving money to missions for the Japanese.

Love is a two-way relationship. There is a grotesque hypocrisy in our assumption that we participate in Christian love in the one-way relationships so often established in our missionary work: assuming that it is ours to give, theirs to receive; ours to be gracious, theirs to be grateful; ours to bestow, theirs to be blessed. So some pastors think their job is to 'run' their churches; some missionaries their task is to lead. When thus tempted —and all of us are—let us ask ourselves why we should try to improve on the methods of our Master. We read of Him, in that luminous Emmaus story, that at supper with the disciples he 'Received . . . blessed . . . broke . . . gave'. Perhaps the central cause of many of our failures is our attempt to give without receiving. No one can minister unto others, except as they minister to him. When the Holy Spirit calls us to Christian work, He calls us to listen as eagerly as we speak, to follow as readily as we lead, to learn as happily as we teach, to obey far more than to command. Particularly in these days of the vitality of the younger Church, we are called to be pioneers in humility. The Christian life consists in crossing barriers for the redemption of others through the love of Christ. Perhaps our hardest test is to allow those to whom we minister to cross the barrier of our pride to minister in turn to us.

The Christian missionary motivation, characterized by this reciprocity in relationships, works always to the extension of that fellowship which is the Christian Church. Phillips, in his *Letters to Young Churches*, paraphrases part of the first chapter of 1 John: 'We want you to be with us in this—in this fellowship with God the Father, and Jesus Christ His Son. We must write and tell you about it, because the more that fellowship extends, the greater the joy it brings to us who are already in it.' That fellowship possesses a redemptive power explicable only as we remember that it is the creation of the Holy Spirit. A Norwegian Bishop affirmed, speaking in my church in Brooklyn, that his church in Norway discovered its real unity with other Christian churches around the world most deeply during the Nazi occupation, when the conquerors sought to sever all relationships between those people and the rest of the world.

The Christian missionary motivation and the Christian Church are both the creation of the Holy Spirit, and He has made them to be inseparable. One cannot exist apart from the other, though often we try to make them do so. An artist commissioned to paint a picture of a dying Church portrayed a beautiful building crowded with people, having a box at the door entitled, 'Missionary offering', with a cobweb over the opening for the gifts. Sacrifice has never hurt a Church, but fear of sacrifice has killed many. As absence of a Christian missionary motivation is fatal to the life of any congregation, so an inadequate commitment to the Christian Church is fatal to any missionary movement. The missionary to Africa is not called to evangelize Africa, but so to extend the Christian Church in that continent that Africans will evangelize their own people. Too little is this essential relationship of the Church and its witness realized. To report on the conception of the Christian Church held by many of us, is like trying to draw a blueprint of a fog, or make a map of a mist. When I consider my own unanswered questions about the nature of the Church, and the relationship of *ecclesia* and *koinonia*, I marvel at the capacity of the human mind to entertain confusion. One of the major needs confronting that section of our communion with which I am best acquainted is for guidance in understanding both the meaning of Christian witness

285

in the life of the Church and the incompleteness of that witness except as it builds the life of the Church.

The Christian missionary motivation is characterized not only by a definite commitment to the Christian Church, but also by a definite attitude toward history. The Christian's faith about all history is born of the experience of his own history. We enter the new life with Christ through death upon a Cross. The essence of that new life, upon our side, is the commitment of all we have and are unto God, knowing that it all came from Him, and confident that He is able to keep what we have committed unto Him against that day. When the day will be, we know not. Where our path will lead until that day, we cannot guess. Meanwhile, we walk in faith, because we trust in Him. We live between two supreme events: the Cross whereby we entered the Christian life, and the consummation of that life at last in God. As we await that consummation, we find life at its fullest as we share the fellowship we know with God the Father, and Jesus Christ his Son with others, for the more that fellowship extends the more joy it means to us who are already in it. This personal history determines our belief about all history. Mankind lives today in the era between the Cross and the eventual consummation. We have not been falsely taught to pray, 'Thy Kingdom come, Thy Will be done, on earth as it is in heaven', for so it will yet be. The questions of when and how we cannot answer, but as mankind awaits that consummation ours is the privilege of Christian witness that all men may be prepared for that day.

We are suffering from a contemporary loss of this eschatological confidence. Many of us have tried to enter the Christian life through by-passing the Cross, and because that great introductory experience has not clear meaning to us the final consummation is in our thinking equally unclear. We have watered down our Christian conception of history by a more comfortable evolutionary doctrine. This denial of the Christian truth about the meaning of history has helped us avoid many of the realities of contemporary history.

Three tremendously important developments within our own generation are powerfully influencing our history. One is the fact that through the developments of science it is now possible as never before that the burden of poverty for great masses of mankind can be lifted. A second is the conviction, new to history, to be found among the masses in every part of the world, that they do not need to remain impoverished. That new conviction is the central revolutionary fact of the twentieth century. A third is the new development so well described to us on Tuesday morning by the Rev. Edward Rogers. With the rapid erosion of the earth's arable land, the increase in the world's population and the altogether inadequate organization of the world's economy, we may confront the catastrophe of mass starvation on a scale unknown to history. Let that development occur when the masses of men are becoming convinced that starvation is not necessary for them, and the revolutions of the past will seem but child's play; the vast blood-letting of the first half of the twentieth century will seem calm and peaceful by comparison.

We confront today a world hell-bent for prosperity. Perhaps the most terrible and perilous hoax that has been perpetrated upon the human race is this expectation of *the good* through the possession of goods. Ours may be more and more the terror of dealing not with heathens who fear their gods, but with pagans who fear only their fellow men. The latter are far the more desperate and dangerous. Never has mankind so needed to hear the words: 'Seek ye first the Kingdom of God and His righteousness, and all these other things shall be added unto you.' No Christian Church can

286

proclaim that word with adequacy to this day that continues to fail as we have failed in the past to explore various economic programmes for the alleviation of poverty. That failure has caused more suffering than any of us can yet imagine. Too much we have illustrated the clever cartoon showing a well-fed pastor and gaunt and hungry widow in her pathetic hovel as she replies to his saccharine solaces, 'I know that money doesn't bring happiness, but it surely helps a body enjoy her misery in comfort.' Almost at times we justify another picture of two clergymen sipping tea in a comfortable corner as one says, worriedly, 'But, Algernon, have you ever considered what would happen to our employment if there was no sin?' Any church that ignores the passionate desire of so many human beings for a fairer share of this world's goods will be relegated to the limbo it deserves.

In this world the Communist proclaims his apocalyptic with a conviction powerfully impressing to massed thousands of men. *Vis-à-vis* Communism in this area, the Christian Church suffers a serious handicap. Under God we must explore as we have not yet the economic possibilities for the alleviation of poverty. But even when we have done that, the Christian can never say that any particular economic programme is the Will of God, the answer to all financial problems. The same contrast applies to plans for political action. The false simplifications of the Communist apocalyptic demand, if we are to present the Gospel of Christ with an urgency adequate to our day, a new sense of Christian apocalyptic. We can exert no adequate stewardship of the Christian missionary motive the Holy Spirit is placing in the hearts of such an increasing number of our people, except as we rediscover the Christian eschatological certainty. There are vast difficulties in framing a statement of history faithful to the New Testament, adequate to the complexities of history and yet simple enough to be meaningful to the masses. All great truths, however, are essentially simple in their meaning. In the rediscovery of Christian truths about history is one of the most imperative needs and challenging tasks of our time.

Three factors in the life of the Christian significantly influence the continuing development of his missionary motivation. The first is the exercise of power. Knowledge is a key to power. The Christian possesses that knowledge most needed in this weary, war-torn world in knowing that 'God so loved the world that He gave His only begotten Son, that whosoever believeth in Him might not perish but have everlasting life'. The Christian possesses that knowledge not as faith, but as fact central in all thought, the fact which gives the true meaning to all other facts. Through this knowledge as it is made known lives are redeemed, families recreated, society reoriented. Thus the Christian is steward of revolutionary power. This power operates in the most personal and intimate areas of human existence. Power often corrupts, even as it has corrupted many of us here. This corruption of pride drives out the divine power, but how often the professional religious worker continues to dabble in the lives of people, making little images of himself, ignoring the wise counsel of Emerson never to seek to make another person like yourself because one is enough. Conversely, the awareness of such influence upon persons may be a humbling factor, as indeed it has been in many who are here, leading them to a deeper dependence upon God, which then becomes the secret of deepening power.

A second condition deeply influencing a Christian's spiritual growth is the experience of separateness. Inherent in the experience of God's crossing the barrier of our sin for our redemption is an eager desire to cross barriers to others with the news of that redemption. The Christian has always a unique homelessness. By the hand of God he has been set apart, be he layman or pastor, for Christian witness. Holding his own world under the judgement of Christ, he is never completely at home in that world. Inherent in the vocation of the Christian is a witness to the unity of mankind possible only through a separation from his own segment of mankind. The life of the professional foreign missionary is a vivid symbol of the dual citizenship of every Christian. He is not completely at home in the land of his birth, or that of his service. He is not completely at home in the Church that sent him abroad, or the one to which he is sent. Within neither culture does he fully belong. He lives under two governments, serves two Churches, adapts to two cultures. Sometimes he becomes a citizen of two countries, and is claimed for military service by two governments. Fully at home in neither land, he is partly a foreigner in each. Except in heaven, he is never really at home. This tragic separateness often claims its heaviest toll in forced separation from children during years when children and parents most need each other. This separateness is a heavy cross to bear, and to some degree it is known to every Christian, as in loyalty to Christ he separates himself from his world for Christian witness. As every cross, however, it is also a key to creative opportunity.

The very separateness from the world brings the Christian closer to God. Its perspective brings new dimensions to his faith. The influence of the sacrificial missionary is a powerful factor in keeping alive the apostolic faith and practice of our Church. So every Christian is a citizen of two worlds, and the tension between the two may be the condition of his growth, or the cause of his downfall. So the cross of separateness lays its shadow upon the motives of the Christian, darkening life within its shadow but no less bringing a pattern to his very desires, until they are shaped after the desires of God Himself.

A third, powerful, moulding element in the Christian's missionary motivation is his martyrdom. The call to cross barriers in the name of Christ is always a call to martyrdom. Christian vocation begins at the Cross, and the Cross is an ever present element in that vocation. Christian vocation is made most clear in our deepest despair. In the abysmal futility of living within the barriers of sin we at last become willing to die that those barriers may be destroyed. The Christian's missionary motivation is · born of that moment when he looks at the world with the vision of a Man nailed upon a Cross. The continuing experience of the Cross for the Christian is certain, but it varies in detail. There may be literal martyrdom, for the days of persecution are again at hand. There may be imprisonment, as there is today for some I could name. Crossing the barriers may demand celibacy, and often requires long separation from families. Always it means some measure of social martyrdom in confrontation of popular prejudices against 'missionary' work, reformers, and such 'disturbers of the peace'.

The creative, universal experience of martyrdom for all Christians is suggested in the words of Paul: 'I die daily.' This martyrdom means a daily death to the world, and resurrection through the Holy Spirit. It means willingness to die not only to one's sins, but also to one's successes. It means to surrender to God each day both the causes of failure and of success, both the roots of shame and of gladness. It means to launch each day freed from the penalties both of sin and success, equipped with the tools given that day by God for that day.

This daily martyrdom is the threshold to the freedom in which Christ has set us free. In that freedom is the secret of our joy. The final seal of

288

the Christian missionary motivation is love, joy, and peace. They are the gift of God in Christ, whom we know as thus we die to all else but Him. That love, joy and peace are the sign of the presence of Him who, indeed, 'is able to do exceeding abundantly, above all that we ask or think, according to the power that worketh within us. Now unto Him be glory in the Church, by Christ Jesus, throughout all ages world without end, amen.'

Group discussions followed (see below), and at 5.15 p.m. there was an Ecumenical Council Meeting.

At 8 p.m., the Plenary Session of the Conference reassembled and heard the digest and report on Group Discussions, as follows:

Presented by the Rev. W. J. NOBLE:

I can truly say that I approached the task of summarizing the findings of the discussions in the groups with a good deal of misgiving. And that was before I had even seen the questions. When I had them, and the answers began to come in, it was not so much a comparatively mild sentiment like misgiving that flooded my spirit; it was a dark foreboding. There are forty-two questions posed, and the material that has reached me would easily form the basis for several books. I tried to catalogue them, but when I had reached a dozen quite different chapter headings, and there were still a number of questions which stubbornly refused to line up under any of them, that method had to be abandoned. There is, however, one very broad and general division. Most of the questions dealt with in the first three or four days concern, in the main, points of doctrine or experience or related matter. Those in the later part have a closer relation to the Church in the community, the nation, or the world. These divisions are not absolute, and at certain points they cross one another. But it seemed to me that to try to observe them was the best way of avoiding confusion and presenting something that at least approached a coherent picture.

It is clear that the questions, or some of them, have provoked lively discussions and the brisk exchange of complementary and even conflicting opinions. That is as it should be. Representing as we do many countries, different modes of life, varieties of social order and of political conviction, different developments of ecclesiastical and even doctrinal emphasis, it was not to be expected that there would be on all matters a precise, polite, and rather soulless harmony or uniformity. That would have defeated the purpose, or one of the purposes, which the questions had in mind. None the less, on matters which are the principal concern of the Church, there is a measure of agreement which is significant and encouraging. I cannot forbear to pay a tribute to the reporters, whose task must have been so difficult, and who have discharged it with the greatest skill and punctuality, and on the whole, a condensed brevity which is the soul not only of wit but of group reporting. I am only sorry that time does not permit here of more justice being done to them, but I hope they will be better used in the Report. I am convinced that the introduction of group discussions into the work of this Conference has proved of great value, and has abundantly justified itself. If I may be so bold as to venture a suggestion for future programmes, it is that the value would be enhanced if room were found in each session for very brief reports on the group discussions of the previous day. They are too far-reaching, too complicated, too important, too voluminous and comprehensive to be bundled together and dumped on the floor of the Conference in one brief closing session.

One more word. I am a reporter, not a commentator or a critic. Like an editor, I do not accept responsibility for the views expressed by any correspondents. Any complaints about, or disagreements with, these findings should be addressed elsewhere. The Secretaries of the Conference will, I am sure, be happy to receive them, and will know how to deal with them.

You may well think that this introduction has shied away from the questions too long. I was moved by several considerations, one of which may well have been cowardice, to give some kind of introduction to this summary. But the thing has now to be faced.

We began with questions which in broad, general terms may be said to be doctrinal. Can we today hold Wesley's doctrine of justification in its entirety? Do we sometimes interpret it too individualistically? How is it related to sanctification? Can there be such an attainment as perfection? 'Justification', it is said, is a word almost unknown to this generation. If that is so, it is not certain whether it is or is not a reflection on our preaching, and it is not for me to decide, though it is believed that we have fallen short in this, and have failed to lay proper emphasis on the two facts of sin and conversion. Some elements of a spurious humanism have invaded the Church, and have crept into the pulpit. It is necessary that this fundamental doctrine should be restated, for it is a matter not of vocabulary or terminology, but of the faith itself. That doctrine which Luther held and which Wesley preached must be restored to its supremacy. It is also true that we have been inclined to hold a too narrow view of justification, for while religion is primarily a personal matter between the soul and God, it has social implications and obligations which are ignored at our peril. There is no contradiction between Wesley's insistence on conversion and his declaration that the Bible knows nothing of solitary religion.

Justification is the prelude to, or the first step towards, sanctification. He who is justified, and continues obedient to his developing sense of the will of God, moves on toward sanctification. But there is some risk in applying a kind of time schedule to this process, such as would be observed by a student passing at intervals from class to class. The ripening of the Christian life, though it takes place in time, is affected by other considerations, and notably, of course, by the response of the soul to the Will of God. There never comes a moment when we should be wise to make the presumptuous claim that we are entirely sanctified. But unless we are to make void or limit the grace of God, it must not be thought incredible that in the growing experience of the Christian life, the dedicated soul should be made conscious of full obedience, through the movement of the Holy Spirit, to the Will of God.

That has some bearing on 'perfect love'. It is not surprising that the groups found some difficulty here, partly due to their uncertainty of Wesley's precise meaning when he used the phrase. One group raised the question whether the subconscious could be sanctified. They did not answer it, and you will not expect me to do so, for that would not only be to trespass beyond my province, but to plunge into a deep where all my thoughts are drowned. But perfect love at least implies perfect motive, and that is possible if we remember that it is the love of God that is shed abroad in our hearts. Moreover, though analogies can but illustrate and not prove, there can be something very like perfect love in the relation between child and parent, though the child is compassed about with the

290

limitations proper to its state of life and knowledge. Sin is a complete barrier to perfect love, but that ignorance which is inevitably a part of our present human experience need not be, if moment by moment, we walk in the light of God. And that love may and ought to reach out beyond the Christian fellowship to all men, expressing itself in service to those in need, in the attempt to create a spiritual atmosphere in which the gospel can have scope, in contending against every kind of wrong, in proclaiming the gospel, not least by giving evidence in our own lives to its saving power.

Passing from this, and leaving, as everywhere, many gaps, we come to some questions on the sacraments of baptism and the Lord's Supper. The latter is said to differ from other means of grace in that it is of peculiar obligations upon all Christians, that it confronts worshippers specially with the Cross and Passion of our Lord, that it employs material symbols to enforce spiritual truth, that it brings home the infinite cost of man's redemption, that, more than other forms of worship, it unites all Christians in intention, though, sadly and ironically, it has divided too many of them.

When we touch the question of baptism, and, in particular, infant baptism, we enter a field of battle. If infant baptism is not what is theologically known as 'baptismal regeneration', in what sense is it a sacrament? Some hold that it is not, being a dedication of the child to God by the Church and by parents, but a service in which the child can take no conscious part. If that be so, we may as well surrender to the Baptists with what grace we can. But powerful arguments are offered against it. In the Baptismal Service grace is imparted to the child of God. His grace can be operative, and is operative, before and apart from full, conscious response on the part of the recipient. American and British Methodism seem to differ at a rather deep level here. The former has omitted from the service the words: 'We receive this child into the congregation of Christ's flock'. The latter retains them, and I wish there were time to pursue the intensely interesting argument that arose upon this vital point, and which the reporters have expressed with so much fullness and skill. It may be relevant to observe that both the Anglican and the Methodist Churches are much exercised on this matter, and the latter has had a committee working on it for a long time. Some of the material supplied by the groups would be of interest and value to them, but to advance it intelligibly here would take all the rest of the time. It is clear to me that this is one place at which world Methodism would profit if it were thinking together, for it is surely important that on such an issue as this we should at least seek to have a uniform doctrine.

Then again, on that question of fellowship which was one of the main planks in Wesley's programme, it was felt that something had been lost in the intervening years, needed to be recovered, and was in part being recovered by means which were considered to be appropriate to the conditions of today. The traditional Class Meeting, though much reduced, still exists in British, but not in American Methodism, but there was no direct evidence from other parts of the world. It has been to some extent adapted to changed circumstances. But all were agreed that, in whatever form, and insistently in forms that involved spiritual training and the culture of the Christian life, fellowship must be brought back to its place in the Church, and it was admitted that in this there had been some failure which should be recovered.

To the question whether changed methods of communication affect the primacy of preaching, the answer is given that while radio, television, and drama are valuable for what is called 'softening up' the conscience of the unbeliever, it must be recognized that preaching is a vital part of the life

291

of the worshipping Church, and must be associated in it with prayer, Scripture, and music, and the very definite and intelligent participation of the congregation. Corporate prayer, again, should be encouraged, and appears to be increasing amongst us, partly by the use of liturgies and the better employment of our hymn books. It is one method of fostering a larger interest and share in worship.

But to turn back for a moment. Is it the fact that Methodism has no distinctive doctrines but only distinctive emphases? The answer is yes; with a rider. Our doctrines are those to be found in the New Testament, though some of them were practically rediscovered by Wesley, such as assurance and Christian perfection: not to speak of the universality of the gospel. We have also been held to have a genius for a good kind of synthesis—of the evangelical doctrines, of grace and works, of the inclusion of both Word and sacrament in worship, all of which tends to a catholicity of spirit, and saves us, it is hoped, from a merely negative Protestantism or Nonconformity.

Some kind of nationalism was implicit in the question whether there is any case for a national Church. It was agreed that unity within a given community, and distinctive characteristics derived from national cultures, may strengthen and enrich the life of the Church, but we do not believe in an established or State Church which denies complete freedom to the Church, while nationalistic and therefore separated Churches are a denial of the holy catholic Church. I permit myself here the only personal comment I am making in this report, when I remind you that no less a person than William Temple said that a national Church was a heresy—and he used the word in its full theological meaning.

Now from this point I must be selective, and touch upon only a few questions with rigid economy of words. Will closer relations with other Churches provide the opportunity for extending our social witness? That witness, for us, was derived from Wesley's own interpretation of the gospel, and made Methodism the leader in many kinds of necessary social activities. A wider union might give occasion for continuing or increasing it, but it might also water it down. We have views about gambling and temperance and some other ills of society which are by no means held so strongly in some other Churches, and that must be kept in mind in all the discussion about union or closer co-operation.

Have we any special contributions to make to Church order? Yes; and amongst them the very much greater use of laity in preaching, in spiritual leadership, in conduct of the Church's business; the circuit system; our manner of receiving ministers, from the circuit level up to the Conference, and of providing their training under supervision in and after college; the security of the ministry, and the placing of the whole ministry at the disposal of the whole Church.

On the other hand, we can learn how to enrich our worship from some other Churches, in reverence and dignity, in a decorum that is sincere and not artificial. The phrase is not in the report of any group, but a friendly critic once said that it troubled him that Nonconformists in their worship were too much inclined to 'hobnob with God'.

Some valuable contributions have been made to the discussion of marriage. How can we uphold the Christian standard in a secular society? Marriage for the Christian is more than a civil contract, and infinitely more than a physical union. But to try to impose Christian standards by civil law would be to make the State a servant of the Church. It is our task to Christianize public opinion, and not least by exhibiting in our own lives the standards of marriage which are set up in the New Testament.

There should be more explicit preaching on the nature of marriage, and more careful preparation of those about to enter upon it. It might be necessary even to contemplate the denial of marriage in Church to those who were unwilling to enter upon it in the arena of the worshipping Church, or to share in its fellowship. There is no common judgement amongst us about the remarriage of divorced persons, and I should not be adding anything to your knowledge by relating the varying views with which we are familiar.

With this is bound up the influence affecting the stability of the family, the more nomadic and rootless character of much of life today, the difficulties of collective living aggravated by lack of houses; the increasing preoccupation of women in work that takes them out of their homes, the inordinate passion for amusements that interfere with family fellowship, the loss of high moral standards in general. Against this, the idea of the home as the centre of life should be encouraged, and young people be trained to make it so. The inculcation of a strong sense of discipline in all relationships is necessary.

And that leads on to children and education. Education is a unity, and to divide it into religious and secular is to miss its purpose. It should all be related to the knowledge of God and obedience to Him. Conditions differ greatly in various countries. In Great Britain, for instance, religious educa- tion is compulsory, and through the 'agreed syllabus' is making a great contribution to the Christian view of life. That is, however, by no means the case in all countries, or in most. Where all State education is secular, as in the U.S.A., the responsibility of the Church for Christian education and Christian centres of learning is very heavy. But everywhere, the provision of an increasing number of teachers with Christian conviction is more than anything else the key to the problem.

The question on work and industry (which are not the same thing necessarily) elicited some valuable results. The Christian doctrine of work includes these elements: that the worker serves for the welfare of the community, that he believes in the dignity of work and does it to the glory of God, that he has a specifically Christian purpose, which is the redemp- tion of the whole social order through the grace of God. Therefore he scorns to do as little as possible for as much as possible, whether he be worker or employer. Some occupations are virtually impossible to a Christian, while it is difficult to maintain that sense of vocation which should govern all work in conditions of mass production which seem to depersonalize all concerned. But work, besides being necessary, must express personality and contribute to the common good. It is all service to God and our fellows. Even drudgery can be transformed. But the Church should do all in its power to conserve the truth that workers are not, in the old phrase, 'hands', but people. And at the back of it all is the fact that proper pride in one's work, a sense of social responsibility, a desire to serve, are the true incentives, and that these in any class are likely to be found only in redeemed human nature.

A related question, vast in its scope, asked what views were fostered by free enterprise, and what were likely to occur under State management. I do not know what, if anything, lay behind this rather subtle setting of the question. And what of the tension between economic liberty, social justice, and equality in reward? It was thought that unredeemed humanity, under any system, was apt to slip from under its burdens, and reach out a long arm for the available reward. It was felt that selfishness might be given larger opportunities under a State-managed economy, that political issues might be controlled by economic forces, and that there was a temptation for people to give less than their best because of the lessening of individual responsibility. If the dangers of State control are many, those of free enterprise must not be forgotten—greed and avarice, the setting of the interests of the many below those of the few, the possible tyranny of power in the hands of economic strength, and again, the control of national issues by economic forces. But in all this vast and complicated subject, it was believed to be the Church's responsibility to proclaim that human values must be supreme in any system. The profit motive is not in itself immoral, and it exists at all levels, but it must be related to reason, honesty, and righteousness.

Problems of race came under three separate questions which can be answered together. It is as undesirable as it is quite impossible that racial differences should be done away. Every race has its contribution to make to the profit of the whole. There are also differences of tradition, of culture, of intellectual achievement which must be recognized. The standard of equal opportunity for all is the Christian doctrine. Where this standard is ignored or denied, the whole life of the country is diminished and damaged. And where Christians allow themselves to be imprisoned within sub-Christian prejudices, they are not only denying their faith, but causing greivous hurt to the body of Christ. There are no easy solutions to this great problem, but none can be found at all save through the Christian spirit and approach. One group explicitly asked the Conference to adopt a resolution affirming that all forms of racial discrimination, whether in social attitudes or in the constitution and laws of a State or in their application, is non-Christian, and to declare its unalterable opposition to any such discrimination. It is not part of my duty to move such a resolution, but I am under obligation to communicate to the Conference the group's desire.

Finally, the group of questions dealt with yesterday: Is the laity given enough, or too much, responsibility in the affairs of the local church? One group thought the questions ought to be restated to read, 'Are the laity accepting enough responsibility?' for it was believed that their place in the church extended far beyond finance and organization, and included a share in the preaching, teaching, and pastoral work. In this, of course, they were going back to the practice, not only of early Methodism, but of Methodism through many years of its history, and, in part, of the Methodism of today. Some spoke of the difficulty of lifting the loyalty of the laity above church membership, attendance at worship and subscriptions, to active service, particularly in the spiritual life of the church, involving the giving of time and thought and energy. In England, five out of seven, and in Australia, two out of three, of the services taken each Sunday are taken by local preachers, without whose splendid work thousands of churches, particularly in rural areas, could scarcely survive. But that service needs to be extended in other directions, and especially in connexion with the leadership of fellowship groups. One of the glories of Methodism has been the voluntary and unstinted service of its laity in the things of the spirit as well as the material concerns of the Church. To let that perish would be an irreparable loss. It is true that the spiritual independence of the minister, and his special pastoral relationship to his people, must be safe-guarded, but these would not be threatened by the laity taking a larger share in some forms of pastoral work.

Lay leaders should, of course, have the benefit of some training, as is now largely done for local preachers and Sunday-school teachers. They should also be trained for other forms of service—youth work, leadership in prayer circles and fellowship classes. There is still a great reservoir of

294

potential service in the laity of the Methodist Church. Probably more such service is given than in any other Church, but it should not be beyond the power of Methodism, with its genius for setting people to work, to release much more.

On another point, whether we are sufficiently aware of our responsibility in local and national politics, there seemed to be some doubt. Few people do more than vote, and many do not do even so much as that, in local or national elections. Party politics have, unhappily—in England, at least—been introduced into municipal affairs. These, as well as the government of the nation as a whole, are left too much in most countries to the professional or semi-professional politician, often on the plea that politics are too dirty a business to be touched by decent people. If they are, that is a sad reflection on Christians. One of their duties in the world is to 'redeem society and reform the nation'—the quotation from the declaration of both Wesley and the Methodist Church of America will be recognized. It is part of our business to influence all the governmental life of the land in which we live.

No one can be half as conscious as I am of the inadequacy of this summary. One or two—but I think only one or two—questions, have not even been touched, but those, I hope, not amongst the most important. I can honestly say that I have scrutinized every word of every report, but, at the end, I feel that the misgiving with which I began has been only too well justified. But the time is past for vain regrets. I can only offer what has been done, in the perhaps too optimistic hope that some of it may be of some little service. If it is, it is entirely due to the work done in the groups. I trust that at least I have not seriously misrepresented them, though so much has necessarily had to be left unsaid.

295

ELEVENTH DAY

Friday 7th September

THE CLOSING devotional session of the Conference was conducted by Bishop Ivan Lee Holt on the morning of Friday 7th September, in Wesley Memorial Church, and the address was given by the Rev. Dr W. F. Howard.

An address given by the REV. DR W. F. HOWARD:

Seventy years ago on this very day the first Methodist Ecumenical Conference met in Wesley's Chapel, City Road, London. We cannot but wonder what those who then came together with pensive memories and tremulous hopes would say if they had been with us during the last ten days. It may be that the veil has been removed and that such a vision has been granted them. If so, I am sure that some swelling doxology must be rising to the throne of the Heavenly Grace. So much has already been achieved. What will have been wrought by the Head of the Church before another seventy years have passed into history?

Before we part, let us call to mind some of the experiences that we have shared. First, it is something that we have met in Oxford. Who can escape its haunting beauty? In months to come some of you will be worshipping with Matthew Arnold in St Mary's Church, or following him with the Scholar-Gipsy and Thyrsis over the Cumnor Hills. But all of us will again and again find ourselves back in the eighteenth century with the Wesleys. Have we not slept and dined at Christ Church where the brothers lived as undergraduates and where Charles was elected Student, or at Lincoln, and seen the room where the young Fellow read and prayed and taught, or at Jesus, where Thomas Coke was Gentleman Commoner? We cannot forget the place which beauty has, or ought to have, in religion, as carry in remembrance these halls and towers which were once built to the glory of God and the service of His Church. Still more have we been reminded of the place of quiet reflection in the life of the soul. Yet as soon as we step out of these homes of learning into the street we are reminded that Oxford is no longer only a University city; it is an industrial centre, and the claims of industry and commerce are forced on our attention. The skill and enterprise, the personal initiative and undaunted courage of one man has laid the foundation of a new monument of national prosperity. Then we think of that man's beneficence in endowing hospitals and medical research, and in widening the facilities for men to enjoy the privileges of University education. At the same time we think of the vast problems raised by the swift development of a new industry. From the study to the street, and back to the study again to think these things out and to relate them to the rule of God in his kingdom on earth. For this Conference has made severe demands upon our thought. The afternoons spent in the Examination Schools as well as the morning sessions in this Church have taught us that in the study of the Bible, in re-examining the foundations of our faith, in relating the Christian message to the world into which we have been born, and in applying it to the social relationships of the present age, there are no easy answers to the questions which are thrust insistently upon us. To sit at the feet of some of our instructors

296

has been a lesson in humility. We cannot with a good conscience take refuge in slick replies and facile solutions. We must read and we must think if we are to be in a position to guide others in the Christian way of life and service.

Perhaps it is at the College tables that we have been brought closest to one another in the personal fellowship which has done so much to break down fences and to bind us in a common loyalty that must never be broken. We in this Conference represent many races and nations. In temperament and tradition we are almost certain to differ widely. No ordinary sympathy is needed to overcome barriers which are not of our own making. But the supreme loyalty that holds us together is that unity in our Lord Jesus Christ which we symbolized in that memorable service of Holy Communion which was celebrated here last Sunday morning. Is there any bond so sacred and so precious in all the world? From time to time it may be that the rashness of politicians or the folly of journalists stirs up feelings which separate nation from nation or class from class. Then more than ever we must hold fast this fellowship as one which nothing can break. It comes to my mind that two of us, living on opposite sides of the North Sea, wrote to each other by what seemed likely to be the last post before war broke out in 1938, declaring that not even war should sunder our oneness in Christ. The clouds were scattered for a time, but when the storm burst a year later I know that we kept our pledge. The last mail from Germany that reached me before that fateful day, 3rd September 1939, brought a card from a young German pastor who had been a student at Handsworth in the year 1933-4. On one side was printed the text: 'Jesus Christ, the same yesterday, today, and for ever.' On the other a verse from the Greek Testament was written in my friend's own hand. Below this, a couplet from one of Charles Wesley's hymns:

'Inseparably joined in one
The friends of Jesus are.'

All through the six years of war that card stood on my study mantelpiece, and whenever some fresh horror roused my fiercest resentment I turned to that card as the messenger of peace. Surely after these bonds of friendship have been drawn so much more tightly than ever before we must resolve that no suspicions must be harboured of one another's good faith or fairness, and every allowance must be made for legitimate differences of opinion. The inevitable tensions of international alliance and of sectional custom and practice in denominational relations can be resolved in the unity of that Spirit who has made all Christians one Body in Christ.

The grace of the Lord Jesus Christ be with us all.

The Conference approved 'A Message to the Methodists of the World', as follows:

The Ecumenical Methodist Conference, assembled in its Eighth Meeting at Oxford, England, sends cordial greetings to all the Methodists through-out the world. Our meeting at Oxford recalls the close association of John and Charles Wesley with its University and Holy Club, and the debt which they owed to its academic life and its place in Christian history.

We met together to look with clear eyes and critical appraisal at the Methodism which we have inherited from our fathers, and its develop-ment through the years. We have considered the life of our Church in all its parts as it exists today. We have sought to make plans for the Church that is to be, so that, under God's guidance, it may fulfil His purposes for it. We have therefore reminded ourselves, in addresses and in discussion, of those teachings which were committed to us from the beginning —the sin of man and his need for salvation which he cannot of himself secure, the invitation to all, of every race and colour, to receive the free grace of God, and find salvation and peace in Christ: the assurance of this salvation given by the Holy Spirit; the following of the way through fellowship and prayer and worship to perfect love of God and man; and the necessity for proclaiming to all men the truth which is in Christ.

Meeting, as we have done, in days so tragic and critical, we have been moved by the Gospel in which we believe to relate it to the present condition of man. At the root of all the world's disorders is sin, and apart from the salvation which is in Christ, there is no hope that these disorders will be cured. We have therefore sought to know God's will for man in all his relationships—in home, school, industry, society, national and international life. In particular, since in Christ all barriers of race and colour are broken down, we declare that race discrimination of every kind must be resisted by the Church, because it is contrary to the mind of Christ.

In all our thought and discussion on these matters, we have rejoiced to recognize the fundamental unity of Methodism in ministry, membership, and life. We are convinced that the more this unity and understanding are acknowledged and developed, the more effective will be the contribution of our Church both to the universal Church and to the life of the world.

To this end certain practical decisions have been taken:

(a) A Constitution has been set up which provides for the representation on the Ecumenical Council of every branch of Methodism in the world.

(b) To maintain the activities of the Council and to facilitate communications between its sections a permanent Secretariat has been set up, to have offices in the United States and Great Britain.

(c) The Council or Conference will meet at intervals of five years, the next meeting to be in 1956.

(d) Permanent committees, in addition to the Executive Committee, to deal with such questions as evangelism, faith and order, women's work, education, the exchange of preachers, youth, and finance.

(e) A special committee has been appointed to further the project, accepted by the Council, of a memorial in Oxford to the Wesleys in the form of an ecumenical Methodist house.

(f) The name of the Council will henceforth be the World Methodist Council.

(g) It has been decided to hold an evangelistic mission simultaneously throughout the world in 1953, the year 1952 to be used as a year of intense spiritual preparation.

We wish to affirm explicitly that, so far from being in rivalry with the World Council of Churches, or wishing to isolate ourselves from the movement toward the reunion of the Churches, our purpose in promoting the closer unity of Methodism is that this may make a stronger contribution to the larger unity of Christ's Church throughout the world.

In full consciousness of the need of man, and the imperfection of our service, we feel urgently moved to recall all the members of our world family to our first works of scriptural holiness, fellowship, and evangelism, and to remind them of the insistent duty of applying the Gospel to all the conditions of human life. We say to every Methodist: 'Let your walk and conversation be such as adorn the Gospel of Christ.'

This is a matter which concerns every minister and member. We hope that it will be given prayerful consideration in every Church.

IVAN LEE HOLT

W. F. HOWARD

Presidents

OSCAR THOMAS OLSON

HAROLD ROBERTS

Secretaries

On the recommendation of the Executive Committee, which met in London on 24th and 25th August, the name of the organization was changed to WORLD METHODIST COUNCIL.

The Conference agreed that certain Standing or Continuation Committees should be formed, as follows: Executive Committee, Finance, on Evangelism, on Women's Work, on Youth and Young Adult Work, on Education, on Exchange of Preachers, on Faith and Order. Members of these committees were nominated by the Committee on Nominations and elected by the Council.

WORLD METHODIST COUNCIL

HONORARY OFFICERS

Honorary President: Dr Wilbert F. Howard, 580 Newmarket Road, Cambridge, England

Honorary Vice-Presidents:

Dr Calvert Barber, Queens College, Carlton, N.3, Victoria, Australia

Mrs Frank G. Brooks, Mount Vernon, Iowa, U.S.A.

Dr R. Newton Flew, Principal's Lodge, Wesley House, Cambridge, England

Bishop Paul N. Garber, The Methodist Building, Richmond, Va., U.S.A.

Bishop S. L. Greene, 1212 Fountain Drive, S.W., Atlanta, Ga., U.S.A.

Bishop Eleazar Guerra, Balderas 47, Mexico, D.F., Mexico

Dr John R. Mott, 528 E. Washington Street, Orlando, Fla., U.S.A.

Professor A. Victor Murray, Cheshunt College, Cambridge, England

Rev. W. J. Noble, 59 Central Avenue, Herne Bay, Kent, England

Bishop G. Bromley Oxnam, 150 Fifth Avenue, New York 11, N.Y., U.S.A.

Mr Joseph J. Perkins, City National Bank Building, Wichita Falls, Texas, U.S.A.

Bishop J. W. Pickett, 12 Boulevard Road, Delhi, India

Dr W. E. Sangster, Central Hall, Westminster, London, S.W.1, England

Bishop W. J. Walls, 4736 South Parkway, Chicago 16, Ill., U.S.A.

Miss Alice Walton, Methodist Missionary Society, 25 Marylebone Road, London, N.W.1, England

Dr J. B. Webb, Methodist Central Hall, 66 Kruis Street, Johannesburg, South Africa

OFFICERS

President: Bishop Ivan Lee Holt, 20 North Kingshighway, St Louis, Mo., U.S.A.

Vice-President: Dr Harold Roberts, 81 Queen's Road, Richmond, Surrey, England

The Secretariat:

Dr Elmer T. Clark, 150 Fifth Avenue, New York 11, N.Y., U.S.A.

Rev. E. Benson Perkins, Central Buildings, Oldham Street, Manchester 1, England

Treasurer: Dr Duncan Coomer, 12 Elgin Road, Bournemouth, England

Associate Treasurer: Mr Edwin L. Jones, 1700 Brandon Road, Charlotte, N.C., U.S.A.

EXECUTIVE COMMITTEE

Bishop Ivan Lee Holt, 20 North Kingshighway, St Louis, Mo., U.S.A.

Dr Harold Roberts, 81 Queen's Road, Richmond, Surrey, England

Dr Eric W. Baker, 2 The Grange Way, London, N.21, England

Dr Elmer T. Clark, 150 Fifth Avenue, New York 11, N.Y., U.S.A.

Bishop Bertram W. Doyle, 1702 Hieman Street, Nashville, Tenn., U.S.A.

Dr Duncan Coomer, 12 Elgin Road, Bournemouth, England

Dr Dorothy Farrar, The College, Ilkley, Yorkshire, England

Professor A. Victor Murray, Cheshunt College, Cambridge, England

Mrs Franklin Reed, Westfield Arms, Westfield, N.J., U.S.A.

Rev. W. J. Noble, 59 Central Avenue, Herne Bay, Kent, England

Dr Oscar Thomas Olson, 1919 East 107 Street, Cleveland, Ohio, U.S.A.

Hon Charles C. Parlin, 20 Exchange Place, New York 5, N.Y., U.S.A.

Rev. E. Benson Perkins, Central Buildings, Oldham Street, Manchester 1, England

Bishop J. W. E. Sommer, Frankfurt a.M., Ginnheim, Ginnheimer Landstrasse 180, Germany

Dr H. Watkin-Jones, Redcliffe, North Grange Road, Headingley, Leeds 6, England

OFFICERS AND EXECUTIVE COMMITTEE, U.S.A.

President: Rev. Dr Oscar Thomas Olson, 1919 East 107 Street, Cleveland, Ohio.

Vice-President: Bishop Paul N. Garber, Methodist Building, Richmond, Va.

Vice-President: Bishop Fred P. Corson, 1701 Arch Street, Philadelphia 3, Pa.

Secretary: Dr Elmer T. Clark, 150 Fifth Avenue, New York 11, N.Y.

Treasurer: Mr Edwin L. Jones, 1700 Brandon Road, Charlotte, N.C.

Bishop Ivan Lee Holt, 20 N. Kingshighway, St Louis, Mo.

Bishop Paul E. Martin, 723 Center Street, Little Rock, Ark.

Mrs Frank G. Brooks, Mount Vernon, Iowa.

Dr M. S. Davage, 810 Broadway, Nashville, Tenn.

Dr Charles B. Ketcham, Mount Union College, Alliance, Ohio.

Hon Charles C. Parlin, 20 Exchange Place, New York 5, N.Y.

FINANCE COMMITTEE, U.S.A.

Edwin L. Jones, 1700 Brandon Road, Charlotte, N.C., Chairman.

Frank E. Baker, Lincoln-Liberty Building, Philadelphia, Pa.

William N. Banks, Grantville, Ga.

M. S. Davage, 810 Broadway, Nashville, Tenn.

Henry Gramling, Gramling, S.C.

Bradshaw Mintener, 600 Pillsbury Building, Minneapolis, Minn.

Charles C. Parlin, 20 Exchange Place, New York, N.Y.

J. J. Perkins, Wichita Falls, Tex.

Andrew H. Phelps, Westinghouse Electric Corp., Pittsburgh, Pa.

STANDING COMMITTEES

Committee on Finance

Chairman: Rev. E. Benson Perkins, Central Buildings, Oldham Street, Manchester 1, England

Rev. Eric Baker, 2 The Grange Way, London, N.21, England

Mr Frank E. Baker, Lincoln-Liberty Building, Philadelphia, Pa., U.S.A.

Mr W. N. Banks, Grantville, Ga., U.S.A.

Mr H. W. Chancellor, Box 2556, Sydney, N.S.W., Australia

Dr Duncan Coomer, 12 Elgin Road, Bournemouth, England

Mr M S Davage, 810 Broadway, Nashville, Tenn., U.S.A.

Ald J. L. Dawson, Fixby House, Fixby, Huddersfield, England

Mr L A Ellwood, Highlands, Warwick's Bench, Guildford, England

Mr Henry Gramling, Gramling, S.C., U.S.A.

Mr W H Green, Fleetwood Labrador, Southport, Queensland, Australia

Mr A H Havelock, O.B.E., 59 Audley Road, Ealing, London, W.5, England

Mr A B Hillis, Chatterton Hey, Edenfield, Ramsbottom, Lancashire, England

Professor A. S. Jackson, 1541 Fourteenth Street, N.W., Washington, D.C., U.S.A.

Mr Edwin L. Jones, 1700 Brandon Road, Charlotte, N.C., U.S.A.

Bishop Raymond L. Jones, Livingston College, Salisbury, N.C., U.S.A.

Ald L. F. Milner, O.B.E., J.P., Cheddleton, 3 Vernon Road, Tetley Rise, Sheffield, England

Mr Bradshaw Mintener, 1955 Kenwood Parkway, Minneapolis, Minn., U.S.A.

Mr Ray H. Nichols, Vernon, Tex., U.S.A.

Hon Charles C. Parlin, 20 Exchange Place, New York 5, N.Y., U.S.A.

Mr H. M. Patrick, M.V.O., J.P., 8 Coraha Street, Auckland, S.E.2, New Zealand

Mr J. J. Perkins, City National Bank Building, Wichita Falls, Tex., U.S.A.

Mr Andrew Phelps, 266 Woodhaven Drive, Pittsburgh 28, Pa., U.S.A.

Mr J. A. Stead, Sutton-cum-Lound, Retford, Nottinghamshire, England

Mr R. Carter Tucker, Scarritt Building, Kansas City, Mo., U.S.A.

Mr W. A. J. Tudor, Bayley Mansions, Bedford Square, London, W.C.1, England

Committee on Evangelism

Chairman: Dr W. E. Sangster, Central Hall, Westminster, London, S.W.1, England
Secretaries:
Dr Harry Denman, 1908 Grand Avenue, Nashville, Tenn., U.S.A.
Rev. Colin A. Roberts, 1 Central Buildings, Westminster, London, S.W.1, England

Bishop A. J. Allen, 2193 East 89 Street, Cleveland, Ohio, U.S.A.
Rev. Albert S. Ashley, 2414 Station Street, Indianapolis, Ind., U.S.A.

Bishop Sante Uberto Barbiere, Rivadavia 4044, Buenos Aires, Argentina

Rev. W. O. Carrington, 694 St Mark Avenue, Brooklyn, N.Y., U.S.A.

Bishop J. H. Clayborn, 1800 Marshall Street, Little Rock, Ark., U.S.A.

Rev. J. W. Curry, 401 North Coit Street, Florence, S.C., U.S.A.
Dr Dorothy Farrar, The College, Ilkley, Yorkshire, England
Dr I. M. Hargiett, 318 West Street, Catherine, Louisville, Ky., U.S.A.
Dr Arthur Hill, F.R.C.S., 4 Park Road, Ipswich, England

Rev. Kelly L. Jackson, 1119 West Lanvale Street, Baltimore, Md., U.S.A.

President D. D. Jones, Bennett College, Greensboro, N.C., U.S.A.

Dr W. H. Jones, 87–9, West Bar, Sheffield 3, England

Rev. A. N. Kemp, Parra Street, Geelong, Victoria, Australia

Dr Alf Lier, Jomfrubratveien 73, Bekkelagshogda, Oslo, Norway

Mrs J. A. B. Lowry, Crewe, Va., U.S.A.

Rev. Arthur Organ, 110 Prospect Street S., Hamilton, Ontario, Canada

Professor H. Cecil Pawson, 58 Dunholme Road, Newcastle-on-Tyne, England

Mr Edwin R. Spann, Perkins School of Theology, Southern Methodist University, Dallas, Tex., U.S.A.

Bishop Charles C. Selecman, 6001 Hillcrest, Dallas, Tex., U.S.A.

Rev. Alan Walker, 1 Grosvenor Street, Bondi Junction, Australia

Bishop A. W. Womack, 1926 N. Capitol Avenue, Indianapolis, Ind., U.S.A.

Dr Friederich Wunderlich, Frankfurt a.M., Ginnheim, Ginnheimer Landstrasse 180, Germany

Committee on Faith and Order

Chairman: Dr R. Newton Flew, Principal's Lodge, Westley House, Cambridge, England

Vice-Chairman: Dr Alf Lier, Jomfrubratveien 73, Bekkelagshogda, Oslo, Norway

Church Relations Section

Chairman: Bishop Ivan Lee Holt, 20 North Kingshighway, St Louis, Mo., U.S.A.

Bishop Willis J. King, Monrovia, Liberia, Africa

Bishop Shot K. Mondol, Methodist Church, Hyderabad, Deccan, India

Rev. W. J. Noble, 59 Central Avenue, Herne Bay, Kent, England

Rev. Dr Oscar Thomas Olson, 1919 East 107 Street, Cleveland 6, Ohio, U.S.A.

Rev. W. R. Shearer, 135 Handsworth Wood Road, Birmingham 20, England

Theological Section

Chairman: Dr Harold Roberts, 81 Queen's Road, Richmond, Surrey, England

Dr G. Calvert Barber, Queen's College, Carlton, N.3., Victoria, Australia

President J. P. Brawley, Clark College, Atlanta, Ga., U.S.A.

Professor W. R. Cannon, Candler Theological Seminary, Emory University, Atlanta, Ga., U.S.A.

Rev. A. Raymond George, Lathbury House, Wesley College, Headingley, Leeds 6, England

Rev. Harald Lindström, Dobelnsgatan 90, Boras, Sweden

Rev. Gerald O. McCulloh, Garrett Biblical Institute, Evanston, Ill., U.S.A.

Professor John Frederick Olson, Syracuse University, Syracuse, N.Y., U.S.A.

Professor A. C. Outler, Southern Methodist University, Dallas, Tex., U.S.A.

Rev. E. Gordon Rupp, 35 Denbigh Gardens, Richmond, Surrey, England

Rev. P. S. Watson, Tranby, Handsworth College, Birmingham 20, England

Committee on Exchange of Preachers

Co-Chairmen: Rev. A. Stanley Leyland, Methodist Church, High Barnet, Herts, England

Dr Karl Quimby, 150 Fifth Avenue, New York 11, N.Y., U.S.A.

Bishop George W. Baber, 110 Boston Boulevard, Detroit, Mich., U.S.A.

Bishop James Chamberlain Baker, 125 East Sunset Boulevard, Los Angeles, Calif., U.S.A.

Dr Earl R. Brown, 150 Fifth Avenue, New York 11, N.Y., U.S.A.

Dr Herbert B. Cockerill, First Methodist Church, Manhattan, Kan., U.S.A.

Dr A. Raymond Grant, 2100 J. Street, Sacramento 16, Calif., U.S.A.

Dr Walter C. Gum, Methodist Building, Richmond 19, Va., U.S.A.

Rev. Charles Harold Jack, 6809 Market Street, Youngstown, Ohio, U.S.A.

Dr Warren Johnston, First Methodist Church, Fort Worth, Tex., U.S.A.

Dr Lester Rumble, 63 Auburn Avenue, N.E., Atlanta, Ga., U.S.A.

Dr W. B. Selah, Galloway Memorial Methodist Church, Jackson, Miss., U.S.A.

Dr H. Watkin-Jones, Radcliffe, North Grange Road, Headingley, Leeds 6, England

Dr Eric W. Baker, 2 The Grange Way, London, N.21, England

Dr Duncan Coomer, 12 Elgin Road, Bournemouth, England

Dr George W. Dorey, Room 511, 299 Queen Street, W., Toronto, Ontario, Canada

Mr L. A. Ellwood, Highlands, Warwick's Bench, Guildford, England

Rev. Edwin Finch, Greyfriars, Lordsbury Field, Wallington, Surrey, England

Rev. J. Allen Fletcher, 25 Milton Road, Harpenden, Herts, England

Professor H. Cecil Pawson, 58 Dunholme Road, Newcastle-on-Tyne, England

Rev. E. Benson Perkins, Central Buildings, Oldham Street, Manchester 1, England

Mr W. A. J. Tudor, Bayley Mansions, Bedford Square, London, W.C.1, England

Committee on the Oxford Memorial

Chairman: Dr Harold Roberts, 81 Queens Road, Richmond, Surrey, England
Secretaries: Rev. Dow Kirkpatrick, Athens, Ga., U.S.A.
   Rev. Reginald Kissack, 21 Lathbury Road, Oxford, England

Bishop C. C. Alleyne, 5561 Haverford Avenue, Philadelphia 15, Pa., U.S.A.
Bishop George W. Baber, 110 Boston Boulevard, Detroit, Mich., U.S.A.
Mr William N. Banks, Grantville, Ga., U.S.A.
Dr Weldon Crossland, 129 Dartmouth Street, Rochester 7, N.Y., U.S.A.
Rev. Rupert E. Davies, 96 Chesterfield Road, St Andrews, Bristol 6, England
President Paul Douglas, American University, Washington, D.C., U.S.A.
Bishop B. W. Doyle, 1702 Hieman Street, Nashville, Tenn., U.S.A.
Dr George Fowler, St James Methodist Church, 46th and Ellis Avenue, Chicago, Ill., U.S.A.
Mr W. H. Green, Fleetwood Labrador, Southport, Queensland, Australia
Dr John O. Gross, 810 Broadway, Nashville, Tenn., U.S.A.
Judge F. A. E. Hamilton, 11-12 Old Law Courts, Winnipeg, Manitoba, Canada
Mr A. H. Havelock, O.B.E., 59 Audley Road, Ealing, London, W.5, England
Rev. L. A. Hewson, Livingstone House, Rhodes University College, Grahamstown, C.P., South Africa
Bishop Paul E. Martin, 723 Center Street, Little Rock, Ark., U.S.A.
Dr N. C. McPherson, St John's Methodist Church, Peabody Avenue, Memphis, Tenn., U.S.A.
Bishop Arthur J. Moore, 63 Auburn Avenue, N.E., Atlanta, Ga., U.S.A.
Professor A. Victor Murray, Cheshunt College, Cambridge, England
Dr C. D. Parker, 19 Staverton Road, Oxford, England
Mr Andrew Phelps, 266 Woodhaven Drive, Pittsburgh 28, Pa., U.S.A.
Mr Ellis Phillips, 107 Bayview Road, Plandome, N.Y., U.S.A.
Bishop F. M. Reid, Allen University, Columbia, S.C., U.S.A.
Rev. E. Gordon Rupp, 35 Denbigh Gardens, Richmond, Surrey, England
Dr Alexander K. Smith, 27 Simpson Road, Ardmore, Pa., U.S.A.
Dr J. Richard Spann, 810 Broadway, Nashville 2, Tenn., U.S.A.
Bishop James Clair Taylor, 333 Boyd Street, Memphis, Tenn., U.S.A.
Mr Abbott Turner, Valdosta, Ga., U.S.A.
Dr Aubrey Walton, First Methodist Church, 723 Center Street, Little Rock, Ark., U.S.A.

President R. L. Woodward, Central College, Fayette, Mo., U.S.A.

Bishop G. W. Washington, 1702 Hieman Street, Nashville, Tenn., U.S.A.

Rev. R. M. Williams, 1914 Eleventh Street, N.W., Washington, D.C., U.S.A.

Rev. B. R. Wyllie, Wesley College, Sydney, New South Wales, Australia

Committee on Women's Work

Co-Chairmen: Mrs H. E. Woolever, 150 Fifth Avenue, New York 11, N.Y., U.S.A.

Dr Dorothy Farrar, The College, Ilkley, Yorkshire, England

Mrs Paul Arrington, 1735 Piedmont, Jackson, Miss., U.S.A.

Sister E. Bemand, St Ann's Bay, Jamaica, British West Indies

Mrs Frank G. Brooks, Mount Vernon, Iowa, U.S.A.

Mrs Stewart Colley, Grantville, Ga., U.S.A.

Miss Henrietta Gibson, 150 Fifth Avenue, New York 11, N.Y., U.S.A.

Miss Elaine Hammerton, 51 Warrington Road, Harrow, Middlesex, England

Mrs Ruth Hughes, 209 Edgecombe, New York, N.Y., U.S.A.

Mrs Abbie Jackson, 2303 Chestnut Street, Louisville, Ky., U.S.A.

Mrs David Lewis, Heatherleigh, Shoal Hill, Cannock, Staffordshire, England

Mrs Franklin Reed, Westfield Arms, Westfield, N.J., U.S.A.

Mrs Ernst Scholz, Berlin-Lichterfelde-West, Paulinenstrasse Nr.30, Germany

Mrs Ferdinand Sigg, 69 Badenerstrasse, Zurich, Switzerland

Mrs Donald Stoate, 22 Woodstock Road, Bristol 6, England

Miss Alice Walton, Methodist Missionary Society, 25 Marylebone Road, London, N.W.1, England

Committee on Youth and Young Adult Work

Co-Chairmen: Rev. Leonard P. Barnett, Ludgate Circus House, London, E.C.4, England

Rev. Harold Ewing, Box 871, Nashville 2, Tenn., U.S.A.

Miss Ruth Aregood, 2201 Avenue A., Kearney, Neb., U.S.A.

Rev. R. C. Bedford, 2 Columbia Terrace, Brock Road, St Peter Port, Guernsey, England

Sister Megan Capon, Kingsway Hall, Kingsway, London, W.C.2, England

Mr M. H. Eddy, M.B.E., Central Hall, 66 Kruis Street, Johannesburg, South Africa

Mr Harold Hayward, 348 Brooksmoor Road, Sheffield 10, England

Mrs M. A. Hakim, c/o E. M. Phillips, Esq., Delhi Gate, Agra, India

Rev. J. C. Hoggard, Little Rock African Methodist Episcopal Zion Church, Charlotte, N.C., U.S.A.

Jameson Jones, Garrett Biblical Institute, Evanston, Ill., U.S.A.
James Matheson, Duke University, 4421 Duke Station, Durham, N.C., U.S.A.
Miss Susan Nichols, 209, Edgecombe, New York, N.Y., U.S.A.
Rev. G. H. Wheen, Methodist Young People's Department, 133 Castlereagh Street, Sydney, Australia

Committee on Education

Chairman: Professor A. Victor Murray, Cheshunt College, Cambridge, England
Vice-Chairman: Dr John O. Gross, 810 Broadway, Nashville 2, Tenn., U.S.A.

President Sarah Chakko, Isabella Thoburn College, Lucknow, India
Rev. R. E. Davies, 96 Chesterfield Road, St Andrews, Bristol 6, England
Dr J. W. Eichelberger, 123 N. 56 Street, Chicago 37, Ill., U.S.A.
Mr W. H. Frederick, Wesley College, Prahran, Melbourne, S.1, Australia
Mr J. M. Gibbs, Sea Roads, The Cliffs, Penarth, Glamorgan, Wales
Miss Elaine Hammerton, 51 Warrington Road, Harrow, Middlesex, England
Mr Donald W. Hughes, Rydal School, Colwyn Bay, Denbighshire, Wales
Miss Susie Kachelhoffer, Central Hall, 66 Kruis Street, Johannesburg, South Africa
President Charles B. Ketcham, Mount Union College, Alliance, Ohio, U.S.A.
Dr John Lewis, Morris Brown College, Atlanta, Ga., U.S.A.
Rev. George R. Osborne, 25 Marylebone Road, London, N.W.1, England
Mr A. B. Sackett, Kingswood School, Bath, England
President M. L. Smith, Millsaps College, Jackson, Miss., U.S.A.
Professor Walter Williams, Iliff School of Theology, Denver 10, Col., U.S.A.
President Lester Welliver, Westminster Theological Seminary, Westminster, Md., U.S.A.

INTERNATIONAL METHODIST HISTORICAL SOCIETY

OFFICERS AND EXECUTIVE COMMITTEE

President: Rev. E. W. Hames, Trinity Theological College, Grafton, Auckland, C.3, New Zealand
*Vice-Presidents: President Umphrey Lee, Southern Methodist University, Dallas, Tex., U.S.A.

* Two Vice Presidents will be nominated from each of the sections of the World Methodist Council.

Dr W. E. Sangster, Central Hall, Westminster, London, S.W.1, England
Bishop Sante Uberto Barbieri, Rivadavia 4044, Buenos Aires, Argentina
Bishop Joseph Gomez, Paul Quinn College, Waco, Tex., U.S.A.

Secretaries: Rev. Frank Baker, 14 Queens Parade, Cleethorpes, Lincs, England
Dr Elmer T. Clark, 150 Fifth Avenue, New York 11, N.Y., U.S.A.
Bishop Fred P. Corson, 1701 Arch Street, Philadelphia 3, Pa., U.S.A.
Bishop Paul N. Garber, Methodist Building, Richmond, Va., U.S.A.
Dr Edgar H. Nease, 1100 Queen's Road, Charlotte, N.C., U.S.A.
Hon. Charles C. Parlin, 20 Exchange Place, New York 5, N.Y., U.S.A.
Dr Jacob S. Payton, Falls Church, Va., U.S.A.
Professor William Warren Sweet, Perkins School of Theology, Southern Methodist University, Dallas, Tex., U.S.A.
Dr Channing H. Tobias, 101 Park Avenue, New York, N.Y., U.S.A.
Dr Duncan Coomer, 12 Elgin Road, Bournemouth, England
Rev. Frank H. Cumbers, 25 City Road, London, E.C.1, England
Dr Maldwyn L. Edwards, 20 Sandon Road, Edgbaston, Birmingham 17, England
Rev. Wesley F. Swift, 9 Ladywood Road, Leeds 8, England

MEMBERS OF THE WORLD METHODIST COUNCIL

Section I—SOUTH AFRICA   7 Members
Dr J. B. Webb, Methodist Central Hall, 66 Kruis Street, Johannesburg, South Africa
Rev. E. W. Grant, Healdtown Missionary Institution, P.O. Healdtown, via Fort Beaufort, C.P.
Mr M. H. Eddy, M.B.E., Central Hall, 66 Kruis Street, Johannesburg, South Africa
Mr W. W. Haley, P.O. Box 2256, Durban, Natal
Rev. L. A. Hewson, M.A., Livingstone House, Rhodes University College, Grahamstown, C.P.
Rev. H. T. P. Young, 237 Musgrave Road, Durban, Natal.
Bishop I. H. Bonner, 28 Walmer Road, Woodstock, Capetown, South Africa

Section II—WEST AFRICA   6 Members
Bishop Willis J. King, Monrovia, Liberia, Africa
Rev. G. R. Acquaah, P.O. Box 161, Lagos, Nigeria, Africa
Rev. M. O. Dada, P.O. Box 403, Accra, Gold Coast, Africa
Rev. R. Kirkpatrick, Uzuakoli, Southern Nigeria, Africa
Rev. Isaac Sackey
Bishop Carey A. Gibbs, African Methodist Episcopal Church, Monrovia, Liberia

308

Section III—CENTRAL AND EAST AFRICA   4 Members

Bishop Newell S. Booth, B.P. 522, Elisabethville, Belgian Congo
Rev. Pierre Schaumba, Katako Kombe, Belgian Congo
Rev. E. G. Nightingale, P.O. Box 79, Lusaka, Northern Rhodesia
Rev. H. Buckley, P.O. Box 163–H, Salisbury, Southern Rhodesia

Section IV—MALAYA, BURMA, PHILIPPINE ISLANDS   6 Members

Bishop L. J. Valencia, 640 Isaac Peral, Ermita, Manila, Philippine
  Islands
Rev. U. Po Tun, The Methodist Church, Mandalay, Burma
Rev. U. On Kin, c/o Rev. Haniel Jones, 256 Creek Street, Ran-
  goon, Burma
Rev. Jose Ferrer, c/o Union Theological Seminary, 726 Taft
  Avenue, Manila, Philippine Islands
Mr Ee Soon Howe, c/o H. V. Lacy, Box 483, Singapore, Malaya
Mr Lik-Kin Ding, 939 N. Broadway, Baltimore 5, Md., U.S.A.

Section V—NORTH INDIA, CEYLON, PAKISTAN   12 Members

Bishop J. Wascom Pickett, 12 Boulevard Road, Delhi, India
Bishop S. K. Mondol, The Methodist Church, Hyderabad,
  Deccan, India
Rev. S. G. Mendis, Clough House, Colpetty, Colombo 3, Ceylon
Rev. C. C. Pande, Rose Ville, Raniganj, West Bengal, North India
Rev. D. T. Niles, 709–13 Mission House, Colombo 10, Ceylon
Rev. S. V. Parekh, North India
Rev. Frank Kline, Co-operative Industrial Association Ltd.,
  Yeotmal, M.P., India
Rev. Clyde B. Stuntz, 60 Nicholson Road, Lahore, W. Punjab,
  Pakistan
Miss Sarah Chakko, Isabella Thoburn College, Lucknow, India
Mr. Y. Theophilus
Rev. James K. Mathews, 150 Fifth Avenue, New York 11, N.Y.,
  U.S.A.
Rev. Mongol Singh

Section VI—EASTERN ASIA   10 Members

Names held in abeyance for the time being.

Section VII—AUSTRALASIA   10 Members

Dr G. Calbert Barber, Queens College, Carlton, N.3., Victoria,
  Australia
Rev. W. Frank Hambly
Rev. R. B. Lew
Dr H. G. Secomb, 430 Little Collins Street, Melbourne, Victoria
Rev. Alan Walker, Waverly Methodist Mission, 1 Grosvenor
  Street, Bondi Junction, Australia
Mr W. H. Green, Fleetwood Labrador, Southport, Queensland

309

Hon. Norman Makin, c/o External Affairs Department, Canberra, Australia
Hon. Mr Justice F. W. Kitto
Mr R. W. Nevile
Mr A. C. Sandow

Section VIII—NEW ZEALAND   5 Members

Rev. E. W. Hames, Trinity Theological College, Grafton, Auckland, C.3, New Zealand
Rev. G. I. Laurenson, P.O. Box 23 W., Auckland, C.1, New Zealand
Rev. J. D. Grocott, P.O. Box 23 W., Auckland, C.1, New Zealand
Mrs G. S. Gapper, 12 Heriot Row, Dunedin, C.2, New Zealand
Sister Rita Snowden, 12 Heriot Row, Dunedin, C.2, New Zealand

Section IX—GREAT BRITAIN   36 Members

Dr Eric W. Baker, 2 The Grange Way, London, N.21
Rev. Frank Baker, 12 Queen's Parade, Cleethorpes, Lincs
Rev. Basil Clutterbuck, 25 Marylebone Road, London, N.W.1
Dr Duncan Coomer, 12 Elgin Road, Bournemouth
Rev. Frank H. Cumbers, 25 City Road, London, E.C.1
Rev. R. E. Davies, 96 Chesterfield Road, St Andrews, Bristol 6
Dr Maldwyn L. Edwards, 20 Sandon Road, Edgbaston, Birmingham 17
Mr L. A. Ellwood, Highlands, Warwick's Bench, Guildford
Dr W. E. Farndale, 10 Mainwaring Road, Lincoln
Dr Dorothy Farrar, The College, Ilkley, Yorkshire
Dr R. Newton Flew, Principal's Lodge, Wesley House, Cambridge
Miss Elaine Hammerton, 51 Warrington Road, Harrow, Middlesex
Mr A. H. Havelock, O.B.E., 59 Audley Road, Ealing, London, W.5
Dr Arthur R. Hill, F.R.C.S., 4 Park Road, Ipswich
Dr W. F. Howard, 580 Newmarket Road, Cambridge
Rev. Reginald Kissack, 21 Lathbury Road, Oxford
Rev. A. Stanley Leyland, Methodist Church, High Barnet, Herts
Mrs David Lewis, Heatherleigh, Shoal Hill, Cannock, Staffordshire
Mr J. F. Mills, 264 Charminster Road, Bournemouth
Professor A. Victor Murray, Cheshunt College, Cambridge
Mr C. T. Nightingale, 8 James Street, Portobello, Midlothian
Rev. W. J. Noble, 59 Central Avenue, Herne Bay, Kent
Rev. J. Hamblin Parsons, 3 Garford Road, Oxford
Professor H. Cecil Pawson, 58 Dunholme Road, Newcastle-on-Tyne
Rev. E. Benson Perkins, Central Buildings, Oldham Street, Manchester 1
Dr Harold Roberts, 81 Queen's Road, Richmond, Surrey
Rev. E. Gordop Rupp, 35 Denbigh Gardens, Richmond, Surrey
Dr W. E. Sangster, Central Hall, London, S.W.1

Rev. W. Russell Shearer, 135 Handsworth Wood Road, Birmingham 20

Mr J. A. Stead, Sutton-cum-Lound, Retford, Nottinghamshire

Mr C. W. Towlson, 5 Carlton Rise, Pudsey, near Leeds

Mr W. A. J. Tudor, Baylay Mansions, Bedford Square, London, W.C.1

Miss Alice Walton, Methodist Missionary Society, 25 Marylebone Road, London, N.W.1

Dr H. Watkin-Jones, Redcliffe, North Grange Road, Headingley, Leeds 6

Mr A. B. Sackett, Kingswood School, Bath

Mr David Foot Nash, Wilmore, Crown Hill, Plymouth

Section X—IRELAND   4 Members

Dr W. L. Northridge, Edgehill, College, Belfast

Rev. J. B. Jameson, 2 Lorelei, Bangor, Co. Down

Mr Norman Robb, 65 Ulsterville Avenue, Belfast

Mr A. E. Anderson, Deanfield, Londonderry

Section XI—WESLEYAN REFORM UNION   2 Members

Dr W. H. Jones, 87–9 West Bar, Sheffield 3

Ald. L. F. Milner, O.B.E., J.P., Cheddleton, 3 Vernon Road, Totley Rise, Sheffield

Section XII—CONTINENTAL EUROPE   12 Members

Bishop J. W. Ernst Sommer, Frankfurt a.M., Ginnheim, Ginnheimer Landstrasse, 180

Dr Friederich Wunderlich, Frankfurt a.M., Ginnheim, Ginnheimer Landstrasse, 180

Dr Paul Huber, Frankfurt a.M., Ginnheim, Ginnheimer Landstrasse, 180

Ernst Scholz, Berlin-Lichterfelde-West, Paulinenstrasse, Nr.30

Dr Ferdinand Sigg, 69 Badenerstrasse, Zurich, Switzerland

Dr William G. Thonger, 5 rue du Champ de Mars, Brussels, Belgium

Bishop Theodor Arvidson, Radmansgatan, 69, Stockholm, Sweden

Rev. Niels Mann, Stockhusgade 2, Copenhagen, Denmark

Rev. Sergei Dubrovin, Apollog, 5, Helsingfors, Finland

Tilsynsman Teol. de Alf Lier, Jomfrubrotv, 73, Bekkelagshoga, Oslo, Norway

Rev. E. Sbaffi, Via Firenze 38, Rome, Italy

One to be selected from Poland

Section XIII—UNITED STATES OF AMERICA   50 Members
Officers and Executive Committee

Dr Oscar Thomas Olson, President, 1919 East 107th Street, Cleveland, Ohio

Bishop Fred Pierce Corson, Vice-President, 1701 Arch Street, Philadelphia 3, Pa.

Bishop Paul N. Garber, Vice-President, The Methodist Building, Richmond Va.

Dr Elmer T. Clark, Secretary, 150 Fifth Avenue, New York 11, N.Y.

Mr Edwin L. Jones, Treasurer, 1700 Brandon Road, Charlotte, N.C.

Mrs Frank G. Brooks, Mount Vernon, Iowa

Dr M. S. Davage, 810 Broadway, Nashville, Tenn.

Bishop Ivan Lee Holt, 20 North Kingshighway, St Louis, Mo.

President Charles B. Ketcham, Mount Union College, Alliance, Ohio

Bishop Paul E. Martin, 723 Center Street, Little Rock, Ark.

Mr Charles C. Parlin, 20 Exchange Place, New York 5, N.Y.

Dr Merrill Abbey, First Methodist Church, Madison, Wis.

Bishop James Chamberlain Baker, 125 East Sunset Boulevard, Los Angeles, Calif.

Mrs J. D. Bragg, 3666 Montana Street, St Louis, Mo.

Bishop Charles W. Brashares, 615 Tenth Street, Des Moines 14, Iowa

Mrs Frank G. Brooks, Mount Vernon, Iowa

Bishop Robert N. Brooks, 631, Baronne Street, New Orleans, La.

Dr Matthew W. Clair, Jr., 213 East 50th Street, Chicago, Ill.

Dr Elmer T. Clark, 150 Fifth Avenue, New York 11, N.Y.

Bishop Fred Pierce Corson, 1701 Arch Street, Philadelphia 3, Pa.

Dr Weldon Crossland, 129 Dartmouth Street, Rochester 7, N.Y.

Dr Stanley Coors, 210 West Ottawa, Lansing, Mich.

Dr George Fowler, St. James Methodist Church, 46th and Ellis Avenue, Chicago, Ill.

Dr Gene Frank, First Methodist Church, Topeka, Kan.

Dr Paul Galloway, Boston Avenue Methodist Church, Tulsa, Okla.

Bishop Paul N. Garber, The Methodist Building, Richmond, Va.

Dr A. Raymond Grant, 2100 J Street, Sacramento 16, Calif.

President Walter K. Greene, Wofford College, Spartansburg, S.C.

Mr J. C. Haley, Brown and Haley, Tacoma, Wash.

Dr Noland B. Harmon, 150 Fifth Avenue, New York 11, N.Y.

Dr Edmund Heinsohn, University Methodist Church, Austin, Tex.

Bishop Costen J. Harell, 2020 Rosewell Avenue, Charlotte, N.C.

President Fred G. Holloway, Drew University, Boston, Mass.

Bishop Ivan Lee Holt, 20 North Kingshighway, St Louis, Mo.

President Charles B. Ketcham, Mount Union College, Alliance, Ohio

Mr Edwin L. Jones, 1700 Brandon Road, Charlotte, N.C.

President Umphrey Lee, Southern Methodist University, Dallas, Tex.

Bishop Paul E. Martin, 723 Center Street, Little Rock, Ark.

Dr E. Burns Martin, First Methodist Church, Hammond Ind.

Chancellor Daniel L. Marsh, Boston University, 266 Bay State Road, Boston 15, Mass.

Mr Bradshaw Mintener, 600 Pillsbury Building, Minneapolis, Minn.

President Joe J. Mickle, Centenary College, Shreveport, La.

Bishop Arthur G. Moore, 63 Auburn Avenue, N.E., Atlanta, Ga.

Mr Ray H. Nichols, Vernon, Tex.

Dr Oscar Thomas Olson, 1919 East 107th Street, Cleveland 6, Ohio

Bishop G. Bromley Oxnam, 150 Fifth Avenue, New York 11, N.Y.

Mr Charles C. Parlin, 20 Exchange Place, New York 5, N.Y.

Mr Joseph J. Perkins, City National Bank Building, Wichita Falls, Tex.

Mr Ernest W. Peterson, *The Portland Journal*, Portland, Ore.

Mr Andrew H. Phelps, 266 Woodhaven Drive, Pittsburgh 28, Penn.

Dr Thomas H. Pryor, First Methodist Church, Kalamazoo, Mich.

Dr Karl Quimby, 150 Fifth Avenue, New York 11, N.Y.

Bishop Richard C. Raines, 305 Underwriters Building, Indianapolis, Ind.

Mrs Franklin Reed, Westfield Arms, Westfield, N.J.

Bishop Roy H. Short, 1856 Challen Avenue, Jacksonville 5, Fla.

President Marion L. Smith, Millsaps College, Jackson, Miss.

Dr Robert J. Smith, First Methodist Church, Enid, Okla.

Dr Ralph W. Sockman, Christ Methodist Church, Park Avenue and Sixtieth Street, New York, N.Y.

Dr Joseph King Vivion, 3950 Woodlawn Drive, Nashville, Tenn.

Mrs H. E. Woolever, 150 Fifth Avenue, New York 11, N.Y.

Section XIV—UNITED CHURCH OF CANADA   8 Members

Mr C. W. Burr, 233 Charles Street, Belleville, Ontario

Dr George Dorey, Room 511, 299 Queen Street, W., Toronto, Ontario

Rev. Victor Fiddes, Orangeville, Ontario

Rev. E. Emslie Hunter

Judge F. A. E. Hamilton, 11–12 Old Law Courts, Winnipeg, Manitoba

Rev. Arthur Organ, 110 Prospect Street, S., Hamilton, Ontario

Dr Gordon A. Sisco, Room 421, 299 Queen Street, W., Toronto, Ontario

Dr S. B. Stokes, 2040 Misener Street, Niagara Falls, Ontario

Section XV—THE AFRICAN METHODIST EPISCOPAL CHURCH, U.S.A.   14 Members

Bishop A. J. Allen, 2913 East 89th Street, Cleveland, Ohio

Bishop G. W. Baber, 110 Boston Boulevard, Detroit, Mich.

Bishop J. H. Clayborn, 1800 Marshall Street, Little Rock, Ark.

Bishop Joseph Gomez, Paul Quinn College, Waco, Tex.

Bishop S. L. Greene, 1212 Fountain Drive, S.W., Atlanta, Ga.

Bishop J. A. Gregg, Edward Waters College, Jacksonville, Fla.

Bishop R. H. Hemmingway, 1620 Sixteenth Street, N.W., Washington, D.C.
Dr A. S. Jackson, 1541 Fourteenth Street, N.W., Washington, D.C.
Dr R. W. Mance, 1429 Pine Street, Columbia, S.C.
Bishop D. Ward Nichols, 209 Edgecomb Avenue, New York, N.Y.
Rev. H. T. Primm, 2321 Thalia Street, New Orleans, La.
Bishop F. M. Reid, Allen University, Columbia, S.C.
Dr Oscar Smith, 716 Walnut Street, Wilmington, Del.
Rev. A. W. Ward, 536 East 34th Street, Chicago, Ill.

Section XVI—A.M.E. ZION CHURCH, U.S.A.   12 Members

Bishop C. C. Alleyne, 5561 Haverford Avenue, Philadelphia 15, Pa.
Dr W. O. Carrington, 694 St Mark Street, Brooklyn, N.Y.
Dr James W. Eichelberger, 123 North 56th Street, Chicago 37, Ill.
Bishop B. F. Gordon, 527 Garnel Street, Charlotte 2, N.C.
Bishop Raymond L. Jones, Livingston College, Salisbury, N.C.
Rev. W. R. Lovell, P.O. Box 1047, Charlotte, N.C.
Bishop J. W. Martin, 4530 South Michigan Avenue, Chicago 15, Ill.
Rev. Dr W. A. Stewart, 1113 23rd Street, N.W., Washington, D.C.
Dr H. B. Shaw, 520 Red Cross Street, Wilmington, N.C.
Bishop J. C. Taylor, 333 Boyd Street, Memphis, Tenn.
Rev. J. S. N. Tross, P.O. Box 1047, Charlotte, N.C.
Bishop W. J. Walls, 4736 South Parkway, Chicago 16, Ill.

Section XVII—COLOURED METHODIST EPISCOPAL CHURCH, U.S.A.   10 Members

Bishop H. P. Porter, 252 N. Middleton Street, Jackson, Tenn.
Bishop R. A. Carter, 4408 Vincennes Avenue, Chicago, Ill.
Bishop W. Y. Bell, Halsey Institute, Cordele, Ga.
Bishop Luther Stewart, 114 Liberty Street, Hopkinsville, Ky.
Rev. B. Julian-Smith, 4043 South Drexel Boulevard, Chicago 15, Ill.
Rev. C. F. Odom, Box 6054, Parkway Station, Jackson, Miss.
Dr C. H. Tobias, 101 Park Avenue, New York, N.Y.
Dr W. R. Banks, Prairie View College, Prairie View, Tex.
Mr Granville Smith, Minden, La.
Major O. Lincoln Reid, 239 West 103rd Street, New York, N.Y.

Section XVIII—FREE METHODIST CHURCH OF NORTH AMERICA   3 Members

Bishop Leslie R. Marston, 311 N. Prairie Street, Greenville, Ill.
Bishop M. D. Ormston, Spring Arbor, Mich.
Bishop C. V. Fairbairn, 1122 South Walnut Street, McPherson, Kan.

Alternates:
Bishop J. Paul Taylor, 843 Wyatt Street, Greenville, Ill.
Professor A. W. Secord, University of Illinois, Urbana, Ill.

314

Section XIX—PRIMITIVE METHODIST CHURCH, U.S.A.
3 Members

Dr Wesley Boyd, 106 South Jardin Street, Shenandoah, Pa.
Rev. William F. Paul, 185 Franklin Street, Plymouth, Pa.
Rev. William B. Sharp, 1683 Lonsdale Avenue, Lincoln, R.I.

Section XX—THE WESLEYAN METHODIST CHURCH OF AMERICA
3 Members

Dr Roy S. Nicholson, 330 East Onondaga Street, Syracuse 2, N.Y.
President Stephen W. Paine, Houghton College, Houghton, N.Y.
Dr William F. McConn, President, Marion College, Marion, Ind.

Section XXI—METHODIST CHURCH IN THE WEST INDIES
5 Members

Rev. K. E. Towers, New Amsterdam, Berbice, British Guiana
Rev. T. S. Cannon, Watsonville, Moneague P.O., Jamaica
Rev. W. H. Armstrong, Governor's Harbour, Eleuthera, Bahamas
Sister E. Bemand, St. Anne's Bay, Jamaica
Miss K. La Trobe, Ulster Spring, P.O., Jamaica

Section XXII—METHODIST CHURCH IN BRAZIL
5 Members

Rev. Almir dos Santos, Rudge Ramos, Sao Paulo, Brazil
Dr Jalmar Bowden, Rudge Ramos, Sao Paulo, Brazil
Bishop Cesar Dacorso, Jr., Rua Jardim Botanico, 648, Rio de Janeiro, Brazil
Dr Rui Ramos, Alegrete, Rio Grande do Sul, Brazil
Exma. Sra. de Hordalia Kuhlmann, 108 Gavea, Rio de Janeiro, Brazil

Section XXIII—METHODIST CHURCH IN MEXICO AND CUBA
5 Members

Dr Milton C. Davis, Centro Evangelico Unido, Apartado 117, Mexico, D.F., Mexico
Professor Gonzalo Baez Camargo, Avenue Republica de Chile, 24-C, Mexico City, Mexico
Bishop Eleazar Guerra, Balderas 47, Mexico, D.F., Mexico
Mr Elias Hernandez, Calles 6a. N. 2208, Chihuahua, Chihi., Mexico
Dr Adrian Acuna Steel, Av. 2, Poniente 314, Puebla, Pue., Mexico

Section XXIV—METHODIST CHURCH IN CENTRAL AND SOUTH AMERICA
6 Members

Bishop Sante Uberto Barbieri, Rivadavia 4044, Buenos Aires, Argentina
Dr B. F. Stockwell, Camacua 282, Buenos Aires, Argentina
Rev. Carlos T. Gattinoni, San Jose 1457, Montevideo, Uruguay
Rev. Legrand Smith, Casilla 175, Cochabamba, Bolivia
Rev. R. C. Rodney
Bishop Enrique C. Balloch, Casilla 67, Santiago, Chile

Total Members—237

REPORT OF THE COMMITTEE ON EVANGELISM

We believe that God has a word for World Methodism. Every session of the Conference has deepened that conviction. Under the guidance of the Holy Spirit, we are being led to a clearer recognition and fuller understanding of the essential and timeless contribution of World Methodism, not only to the Church Universal, but to the millions whom we are commissioned to win for Christ and His Church.

With faith in our historic mission to offer Christ to all men, we believe it would be tragic if this great Conference closed without a clear and definite declaration of the task of World Evangelism.

As directed by the Executive Committee, we considered the possibilities of a world-wide, simultaneous mission during a period to be determined. We believe that a World Methodism, spiritually equipped for such an adventure, might change the currents of contemporary history and write a new chapter in the Acts of the Apostles.

The Committee is not unmindful of the difficulties, including the varying climates and customs and conditions of the many countries represented in the Conference. It does not believe any difficulty to be insuperable, and after prayerful thought and careful consideration, it makes the following recommendations:

That 1952 shall be a year of intensive spiritual preparation, during which the Methodist people in every land shall be called upon to receive for themselves the fullness of the Gospel and to prepare to offer it to others. That 24th May 1952 shall be a day of Dedication in World-wide Methodism.

That 1953 shall be a year of Evangelism, during which we offer Christ to men everywhere. That 26th May 1953 (which is also Whit-Sunday), shall again be a day of Dedication and/or Thanksgiving.

That a Standing Committee be appointed to supervise the distribution of literature and to deal with all other matters related to this great adventure. The Committee recommends that the Rev. Dr W. E. Sangster be Chairman of the Committee, and Dr Harry Denman and the Rev. Colin A. Roberts be Joint Secretaries.

These recommendations are submitted in the faith that the Oxford Conference came for such a time as this, in order to give us clear thinking and warm hearts for the work so dear to the heart of our founder, John Wesley, and which is the Passion of our Living Lord.

REPORT OF THE COMMITTEE ON THE OXFORD MEMORIAL

The Committee on the Oxford Memorial makes the following recommendations, on which it has agreed:

1. To approve the project of establishing in Oxford a World Methodist Centre.
2. The object is to foster mutual understanding and fellowship

between the various branches of our World Church, which delegates at this Conference have found for themselves in living together in Oxford.

3. That the form of this project be the following, or some close modification of it:

(*a*) A House to accommodate about 40 residents (of which some may be married couples), with Chapel, Library, Common Room, Dining Room, Kitchen and quarters for a Warden and the necessary domestic staff.

(*b*) A body of residents, studying at Oxford for longer or shorter periods, having as its nucleus ministerial students, but including also lay students up to the capacity of the House. The House should be open to members of all branches of World Methodism, and the United Churches in which The Methodist Church was a constituent part, who are ready to share sympathetically and fully in the ideals of the Centre.

(*c*) A Warden, who should be a Methodist Minister, charged with the responsibility of guiding the residents in the best use of their time in Oxford, forwarding the ends of World Methodism by gathering into the fellowship of the House representatives of as many branches of World Methodism as possible, and fostering through the common life of the House a mutual thought and insight into the needs of the world.

(*d*) As a more distant objective, an annual lectureship through which Methodist scholarship may make a contribution to the University and to the Universal Church.

4. That the House should be directed by a Board of Management appointed by and responsible to the World Methodist Council. Legal advice should be taken to ascertain how the Council could create a holding corporation.

5. We recommend to the World Methodist Council:

(*a*) That it commend the project to its constituent Churches or Conferences, and request their participation and support.

(*b*) That it appoint a Committee to present the project to the Conferences; and should it find sufficient support, to make the financial arrangements for acquiring a suitable property and endowing the Centre adequately; and when it is agreed that the arrangements, both financial and administrative, have reached a satisfactory state, to take steps to bring the Centre into being.

6. We estimate that the building will cost approximately 50,000 pounds, and that 100,000 pounds should be secured for endowment, this being a total of approximately $420,000.

REPORT OF THE COMMITTEE ON WOMEN'S WORK

We believe that the Christian Church was from the beginning composed of men and women who found that, as with the Jew and

317

Greek, bond and free, there was a new relationship between them in Christ Jesus; and that from the first, the women had recognized work in the Christian community. There is no part of the Church's business which is wholly the concern of men, not wholly the concern of men and women, and this applies especially to any major issue. We believe that only by incorporating the thought, worship and fellowship of women can the mind of Methodism function rightly, and that only so shall we be able to contribute to wider ecumenical thinking.

Constitution

Name: There shall be a Standing Committee of the World Methodist Council on the work of women in The Methodist Church.

Purpose: The purpose of this Standing Committee shall be to strengthen the bonds between Methodist women of all lands, to help women church members to make a full contribution to the life, leadership and evangelism of the Church, and to make known and strengthen the work of the World Methodist Council.

Membership: The Standing Committee shall be composed of the Officers of the Council, *ex-officio*, the Officers of the Committee, *ex-officio*, the women members of the Council, plus one representative to be elected by each section.

Term of office: The term of office of membership of the Standing Committee shall be the period between one meeting of the World Methodist Council and the next. Any vacancies occurring in the interim shall be filled by the appropriate appointing body.

Meetings: The Women's Committee of the World Methodist Council shall meet regularly at the time and place of the meetings of the World Methodist Council, on which occasion officers shall be elected. Additional meetings may be held by vote of the Women's Committee on recommendation of the executive officers of the Committee.

Officers: The Standing Committee shall elect a Chairman, who shall be the presiding officer of the Standing Committee and a member of the Executive Committee of the World Methodist Council. The Standing Committee shall also elect two or more vice-chairmen, a recording secretary, a treasurer, and such other officers as the needs may require.

Duties: The duties of the Standing Committee shall be to:

1. Send regular information by correspondence to the constituent members of the Committee concerning the progress of the Ecumenical Movement.

2. Consult with the Programme Committee of the Ecumenical Conference.

3. Provide for the interchange of ideas and experiences between the Women's Groups of the different countries represented.

4. Arrange for the exchange of official visitors among the national Women's Groups.

5. Publish reports, when necessary, of the development of the Ecumenical Movement as it relates to the place and work of Methodist women in the Church around the world.

Finance: The Women's Committee shall be financed in the same way as the other Standing Committees of the Council. Any money raised by the Women's Committee shall be for the work of the Council as a whole.

REPORT OF THE YOUTH COMMITTEE

I. We desire to register our deep appreciation of the action of the Council in making it possible for a Youth Section to share in the Oxford Conference. The enlarged experience which has come to us here of the fellowship and life of World Methodism has been an enormous enrichment to us all, and we long for vast numbers of young people in our Churches to share this experience.

II. It is our earnest hope that future World Methodist Conferences will likewise include such a Youth Section, to the end that the spirit, vision and concern shared by our senior brethren concerning Methodist ecumenicity may be caught by an increasing number of young Methodists everywhere. We regard this as imperative if the work is to endure and fructify.

III. In future Youth Sections at these Conferences we believe it would be most helpful if those responsible for the nomination of delegates attempt to secure the representation of both young people themselves (from 18–23 or 25) and workers among children and young people. We ask the Council to endorse this suggestion and commend it to the appropriate youth departments of the Churches.

IV. We earnestly believe that the present need is for some means whereby the encounter we have begun here at Oxford may be continued and extended to young people and their leaders throughout the world. To this end, the following suggestions commend themselves to the Committee:

(*a*) The exchange of fraternal youth delegations on as wide a scale as possible on the occasion of national Methodist youth assemblies of various kinds; and that the Youth Committee explore the possibility of holding Ecumenical Methodist Youth Conferences.

(*b*) Interchange of youth workers in summer schools and institutes.

(*c*) Interchange of literature on youth work, giving facts and comment on youth work in the various countries.

(*d*) Initiation of a scheme whereby all kinds of youth groups may be linked with kindred groups in various lands, exchanging news, photos, materials, et cetera.

(*e*) Initiation of a Standing Youth Committee of the World Methodist Council through which such projects as the above may be organized.

V. In all this, we are conscious that any Methodist ecumenical youth movement, as such, must be closely related to, and co-ordinated with, such National Councils of Christian youth as may exist, such as the Youth Department of the British Council of Churches and the Youth Department of the World Council of Churches.

FAITH AND ORDER: FINANCE

The function of the Committee on Faith and Order is to co-operate in an advisory capacity with all Methodist bodies which contemplate union with other groups, to the end that the essential Methodist witness shall be carried into such unions. This Committee has two sections, a Theological Section and a Section on Church Relations.

The Finance Committee recommended an annual budget of $15,000, of which $12,000 should be raised in the United States, $2,000 in Great Britain, and $1,000 in other parts of the world.

THE INTERNATIONAL METHODIST HISTORICAL SOCIETY

A report presented to the World Methodist Council together with the resolutions thereon passed by the Council

THE International Methodist Historical Society was formed by the Ecumenical Methodist Conference meeting at Springfield, Massachusetts in 1947. A President, two Secretaries, and an Executive Committee were appointed, who were commissioned to proceed with whatever activities seemed desirable, and to prepare a constitution for presentation to the Conference at Oxford in 1951.

Frequent correspondence and several meetings of members of the Executive have led to the formulation of the following statement on our Objects and Constitution.

Objects

The objects of the International Methodist Historical Society are:

(*a*) To co-ordinate the work of Methodist Historical Societies throughout the world, and to promote the formation of new ones.

(*b*) To assist in the preservation of books, documents, personal relics, buildings, and sites connected with Methodist history in all lands.

(*c*) To accumulate accurate and up-to-date information about world Methodism.

(*d*) To spread the knowledge of the historical background and present activities of world Methodism by promoting such things as the publication of historical studies, reprints of important original documents, and factual works on modern Methodism; by placing markers on historic sites; by arranging pilgrimages and celebrations of historic events; by organizing a historical lecture in connexion with each world Methodist conference.

320

The purpose of these activities is not mainly antiquarian, but spiritual. The Society desires to preserve in all ways possible a sense of our indebtedness to the past, not in order that we may worship the relics of our forefathers or slavishly imitate their ways, but so that we may keep alive their spirit of informed evangelism, adapted as may be necessary to our changing circumstances.

Constitution

(*a*) The Society shall be affiliated to the World Methodist Council, the President and two Secretaries of each body being *ex officio* members of the other.

(*b*) The Society shall be governed by a Committee consisting of the President and two Secretaries of the World Methodist Council together with the following Officers of the Society:

(*i*) President.

(*ii*) Two Secretaries, one each from the U.S.A. and Great Britain.

(*iii*) Sixteen Vice-Presidents, chosen from each of the major Methodist groupings, viz. Great Britain, continental Europe, Canada, U.S.A., African Methodist Episcopal Church, African Methodist Episcopal Zion Church, Coloured Methodist Episcopal Church, West Indies, Latin America, South Africa, West Africa, Central and East Africa, India and Western Asia, China and Eastern Asia, Australasia and the Pacific, New Zealand.

(*iv*) Other members, not exceeding twelve, representing important interests in the study and promulgation of Methodist history.

(*c*) This Committee shall meet in whole or in part as summoned by either Secretary, though normally the full Committee will not meet except in connexion with the World Methodist Council, when members unable to attend may send substitutes. Necessary business at other times shall be conducted by the Secretaries in consultation with each other and with the affiliated Societies and Sectional Committees.

(*d*) Each Vice-President shall take steps to form a Sectional Committee to serve his area, and to appoint correspondents for each Conference or mission Church within that area.

Activities

The following projects are either in progress or in preparation:

A news bulletin of World Methodism, *World Parish*. (Any suggestions which may render this of great service will be welcomed.)
A factual handbook, *The Methodists of the World*. (Information which will correct, amplify, and keep this up to date is desired.)

A *Who's Who in World Methodism*.
An *Album of Methodist History*.
An *Encyclopaedia of World Methodism*.
An International Index of Methodist Documents.

The following resolution was approved by the Council:

That this World Methodist Council, meeting at Oxford in 1951, commends to the Methodist people everywhere the observance of *Aldersgate Sunday* (the Sunday falling upon or immediately preceding 24th May) as an occasion for remembering the faith of our founders and for rededicating ourselves in universal fellowship to the spreading of Scriptural holiness throughout the world.

Note. The observance of Aldersgate Sunday is supplementary to the projected World Methodist Evangelical Campaign, in which 24th May in 1952 and 1953 are suggested as focal points, although in 1953 these two observances, of Wesley Day and Aldersgate Sunday, will coincide. It is realized that in Churches where the observance of Wesley Day itself has become an established custom it will probably not seem desirable to stress Aldersgate Sunday in addition. Even so, in such places the universal fellowship of Methodism should be emphasized on that day, for Aldersgate Sunday is envisaged not only as an occasion for directing attention to the 'Aldersgate experience' of the Wesleys, but is also intended to bring us together in a 'World Methodism Sunday'.

MEETINGS AND DATES

The Executive Committee recommended that the next meeting of the World Methodist Council should be held in 1956 and in the United States, and this was adopted by the Council. At a later meeting of the Conference, Bishop J. Wascom Pickett invited the body to meet in India, pointing out that 1956 will mark the centennial of Methodism in that country. After discussion, the whole matter of time, place and nature of the 1956 meeting was referred for final determination to the Executive Committee.

The Executive Committee was asked to study the relationship of the World Methodist Council to the World Council of Churches and the International Missionary Council, with particular reference to the matter of dates and programmes. The Committee was also requested to include in the 1956 programme the story of Methodism among the Negro groups in the United States.

RESOLUTIONS AND MESSAGES

At the last session of the Conference the Committee on Courtesies presented a report expressing appreciation for the hospitality of British Methodism and the labours of the Oxford Methodists, which had made the meetings so pleasant and successful.

The Rev. W. J. Noble presented a digest of the findings of the various discussion groups which had met daily, compiled from the statements of the group reporters. Mr Noble also presented the Message of the Conference to the Methodists of the World (see p. 297).

INDEX